THE LAST ANGLO-JEWISH GENTLEMAN

THE MODERN JEWISH EXPERIENCE

Deborah Dash Moore and Marsha L. Rozenblit, editors
Paula Hyman, founding coeditor

THE LAST ANGLO-JEWISH GENTLEMAN

The Life and Times of
Redcliffe Nathan Salaman

Todd M. Endelman

INDIANA UNIVERSITY PRESS

This book is a publication of

Indiana University Press
Office of Scholarly Publishing
Herman B Wells Library 350
1320 East 10th Street
Bloomington, Indiana 47405 USA

iupress.org

© 2022 by Todd M. Endelman

All rights reserved
No part of this book may be reproduced or utilized in any form or by any
means, electronic or mechanical, including photocopying and recording, or by
any information storage and retrieval system, without permission in writing
from the publisher. The paper used in this publication meets the minimum
requirements of the American National Standard for Information Sciences—
Permanence of Paper for Printed Library Materials, ANSI Z39.48-1992.

Manufactured in the United States of America

First printing 2022

Cataloging information is available from the Library of Congress.

ISBN 978-0-253-06174-4 (hardback)
ISBN 978-0-253-06175-1 (paperback)
ISBN 978-0-253-06176-8 (ebook)

For Judy, once again

CONTENTS

Acknowledgments ix

Abbreviations xiii

A Note on Sources xv

Family Tree xvii

Introduction *1*

1 Family Background and Early Years *9*

2 Medicine and Marriage *31*

3 Homestall *57*

4 Race Science *80*

5 Nina and the Hebrew Poets *99*

6 World War I and the Land of Israel *118*

7 The Home Front *147*

8 Communal Work and Personal Loss *165*

9 The Jewish Health Organisation of Great Britain *193*

10 Conflicts at Home and Abroad *222*

viii | *Contents*

11 The Potato Book *251*

12 Communal Gadfly *269*

Afterword *296*

Glossary *303*

Select Bibliography *305*

Index *311*

ACKNOWLEDGMENTS

IT WOULD HAVE BEEN IMPOSSIBLE FOR ME TO write this book without the warm and generous cooperation of the family of Redcliffe Salaman. I first met and interviewed Esther Salaman, his youngest daughter, in March 1999. She welcomed me into her home—and wonderful garden—many times thereafter and introduced me to other relatives whom in time I also interviewed. When I first met Esther, I did not intend to write a biography of her father but rather an article or two on subjects in which his life intersected with larger themes in modern Jewish history. Esther died in 2005 and, to my regret, was unable to see the completion of this project. Nonetheless, she was able to hear me talk about his Lucien Wolf Memorial Lecture of 1953, at which she had been in the audience, at a conference in London in May 2000. *Zikhronah li-vrakhah.*

I am also grateful to Redcliffe's grandchildren, who encouraged me, spent hours talking with me, fed me, and searched their memories for recollections of their grandfather and his siblings. Most wonderfully they shared with me diaries that were still in their possession. Jenny Salaman Manson allowed me to read her grandmother Nina's diary and her father Raphael's boyhood diary. William Salaman provided me with a transcription of his father Arthur's diary and allowed me to explore a suitcase of miscellaneous documents and ephemera that had belonged to his father, which included, among other treasures, a "newspaper" produced by Nina, Redcliffe's wife, and their children after the British conquest of Jerusalem in 1917 and a watercolor of the coat of arms that Redcliffe had commissioned after World War I. Nina Salaman Wedderburn gave me a number of photographs of Redcliffe; her sister Thalia Salaman Polak shared a copy of her mother's privately printed memoir. Peter Salaman Hamburger made available to me his mother Esther's letters. Jane Miller, who has also written about Redcliffe and Nina in her lovely book *Relations*, shared her insights and memories of the family with me on many occasions. Colin Cohen, a grandson of Redcliffe's sister Bessie, shared with me the fruits of his genealogical research and his knowledge of family portraits. Ann Causton allowed me to read her research on Abraham Salaman, her great-grandfather and brother of Redcliffe's father.

ix

x | *Acknowledgments*

Friends in England provided essential support. David Feldman and Naomi Tadmor housed me several times when I was doing research in Redcliffe's papers at Cambridge University. Janet and Mervyn Maze, now Californians, were my hosts in London when I was working in archives there. Tony Kushner helped to make my visits to the University of Southampton a pleasure. Last, I am forever indebted to Bryan Cheyette and Susan Cooklin, who invited me to their son Jacob's bar mitsvah party at the London Zoo in 1999 and who seated me at dinner next to Jenny Salaman Manson, a neighbor of theirs. That fortuitous event led, more than twenty years later, to this biography of Jenny's grandfather.

I also want to acknowledge the gracious hospitality of Geoffrey Wilkerson, the current owner of Homestall, the country house in Barley, Hertfordshire, that was home to Redcliffe for almost a half century. On a memorable day in winter 2014, Geoffrey gave my wife and me a tour of the house and the village, thus enabling me to better imagine life there in the first half of the twentieth century.

Jill Cohen, Flora Margolis, and Michael Endelman helped me to trace articles about Salaman in the pages of the London *Jewish Chronicle*.

I am grateful to librarians and archivists at the following institutions in England and the United States for making available to me materials in their collections: Special Collections, Cambridge University Library; Archives and Manuscripts Section, Hartley Library, University of Southampton; London Metropolitan Archives; the Wiener Library, London; Special Collections, Bodleian Library, Oxford University; and the Center for Jewish History, New York.

Versions of parts of chapters 4, 9, and 12 appeared earlier in the following publications: "Anglo-Jewish Scientists and the Science of Race," *Jewish Social Studies* 11, no. 1 (2004): 52–92; "The Jewish Health Organization of Great Britain in the East End of London," in *An East End Legacy: Essays in Memory of William J. Fishman*, edited by Colin Holmes and Anne J. Kershen (London: Routledge, 2018); "Fighting Antisemitism with Numbers in Early Twentieth-Century Britain," *Patterns of Prejudice* 53, no. 1 (2019): 9–22. I am grateful to their editors for allowing me to reproduce sections of these articles.

During the time I was working on this book, Meri-Jane Rochelson was working on her study of the writer Israel Zangwill, a close friend of Redcliffe and Nina. We shared archival references and together scrutinized the nature of the relationship between Nina and Zangwill. It was a pleasure to correspond and speak with someone who was as deeply engaged in their world as I was. I have also benefited from my conversations with Jean Strouse, who is currently writing a book on the London art dealer Asher Wertheimer, whose family John Singer Sargent immortalized in twelve portraits. (One of Wertheimer's daughters married Redcliffe's brother Euston.) Jean and my friends Vic Lieberman, Anne Kershen, Deborah Dash Moore, and Marsha Rozenblit, as well as my wife Judy, read the entire manuscript with care, offered useful suggestions for improvement, and saved me from a host of errors.

Michael Fried performed miracles with his camera and computer in preparing several photographs for inclusion in the book. I am very grateful to him for his help.

I dedicate this book to my wife, to whom I dedicated my first book forty years ago. This project has engaged her more than my previous ones had, perhaps because there is an intimate, family dimension to it. It is a very different kind of story than I usually tell. Her interest in it convinced me that it was a story worth telling.

ABBREVIATIONS

AJHS CJH	American Jewish Historical Society, Center for Jewish History, New York City
BD	Board of Deputies of British Jews
HL	Herbert Loewe
HL US	Hartley Library, University of Southampton, Southampton, UK
IA	Israel Abrahams
IZ	Israel Zangwill
JHOGB	Jewish Health Organisation of Great Britain
LMA	London Metropolitan Archives
NDS	Nina Davis Salaman
RNS	Redcliffe Nathan Salaman
RNS CUL	Redcliffe Nathan Salaman Papers, Cambridge University Library
RWC	Robert Waley Cohen
SF LMA	Salaman Family Papers, London Metropolitan Archives

A NOTE ON SOURCES

THE BULK OF REDCLIFFE SALAMAN'S PAPERS AND NINA Salaman's papers are at the University Library, Cambridge. His son Raphael deposited them there in December 1975. A second deposit was made in May 1991 and a third in June 1994. These papers are easily accessible, with the exception of his correspondence from 1941 and 1942 on John Rutherford Gardiner, the pedophile rector of Barley. Information about the Gardiner episode is available from other sources, however. In 2009, when I was already at work on the Salaman papers, the late Nina Salaman Wedderburn, Redcliffe's granddaughter, made an additional deposit. The Department of Manuscripts and University Archives had no immediate plans to catalog the newest deposit but kindly gave me access to it. When citing these letters and documents, I refer to them as the Wedderburn deposit. In the early 1950s, Redcliffe wrote several unpublished autobiographical essays. While informative, they do not, when read together, constitute a full-blown memoir or autobiography. I refer to these various autobiographical chapters by the titles that he gave them. Some of the titles are misleading at first glance, especially one he called "Still Births and Abortions," whose subject is not obstetrics. It is difficult to know in what order he wrote these memoirs and, moreover, to determine what the final version of each would have been. He frequently edited them, adding and deleting paragraphs and pages. In at least one instance, he incorporated part of one into a public talk he gave. I do not know whether he intended to publish these memoirs, even privately for family and friends. Like all autobiographical writings, they must be read critically and used with care.

xv

FAMILY TREE

ABBREVIATED SALAMAN FAMILY TREE

Aaron Solomon (Solomon of Leghorn)

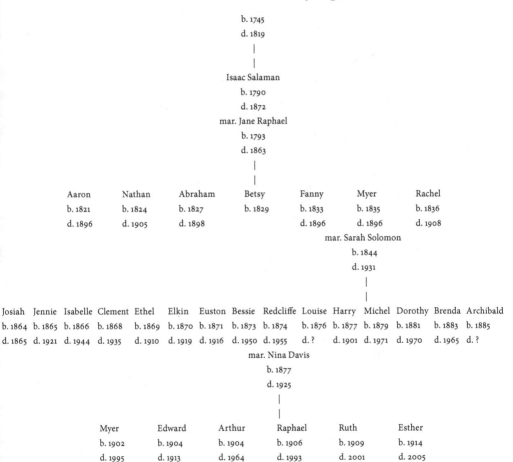

THE LAST ANGLO-JEWISH GENTLEMAN

INTRODUCTION

THE NAME OF REDCLIFFE SALAMAN (1874–1955) IS NOT well known in either Great Britain or the United States. I first came across his name in October 1966 in a class at the newly opened University of Warwick in the United Kingdom, where I was spending my junior year as an exchange student from the University of California–Berkeley. On a list of suggested readings in a seminar on the industrial revolution and its social consequences, the influential Marxist historian Edward Thompson, then at the height of his fame, included Salaman's *History and Social Influence of the Potato*, first published in 1949 and in print to this day. I did not know then that Salaman's book was considered a classic of social history and I did not look at the book, let alone read its almost seven hundred pages, until decades later. But his name stuck, probably because the potato (or any other food staple) was then an uncommon subject for historical research.

I next encountered Salaman in late 1984. I was teaching modern Jewish history at Indiana University and was on sabbatical in Jerusalem doing research for my second book, *Radical Assimilation in English Jewish History* (1990). While working in the papers of the Anglo-Jewish writer Israel Zangwill at the Central Zionist Archives, I repeatedly came across correspondence between Zangwill and Redcliffe Salaman and his wife, Nina (1877–1925). It became clear to me from the correspondence that Salaman, whom I had never thought of in the context of British Jewish history, was an active participant in and perceptive observer of its communal life—its institutional spats and ideological and religious rows. At about the same time, I became aware of a lecture that Salaman delivered in 1953 to the Jewish Historical Society of England on the transformation of Anglo-Jewry over the course of the previous half century. When I read it—the society published it in 1954 after much controversy—I was struck by Salaman's account of the social forces that undermined the rule of the prosperous families who had governed the community during the long nineteenth century. For someone who was not a historian by training—he was a physician with advanced training in pathology—Salaman was remarkably perceptive about the corrosive impact that secularization and integration had on the maintenance of Jewish allegiances. In particular, his understanding of the ties that bound

British Jews—social rather than spiritual ones—was analytically sophisticated and a radical departure from the way in which British Jews usually wrote about themselves. But I made no move to discover anything more about him, although I cited his lecture in *Radical Assimilation*.

A few years later, in 1985, having left Bloomington, Indiana, to teach at the University of Michigan at Ann Arbor, I came across Salaman in an altogether different context. I had purchased a copy of Philip Jones's 1979 guide to archival sources for the history of the British Mandate for Palestine, largely because I was then buying almost everything that was relevant to Anglo-Jewish history. Looking through the guide, I discovered, to my surprise, an entry for Salaman. He appeared there, it turned out, because he had served as a medical officer in the Jewish brigades that took part in the conquest of Palestine in World War I and because he had published a selection of the letters he had written to his wife—*Palestine Reclaimed: Letters from a Jewish Officer in Palestine* (1920). From the entry, I learned that the Cambridge University Library held a collection of his papers. From David Feldman, then living in Cambridge, I obtained a copy of the finding aid for the Salaman collection.

The finding aid was a revelation. It indicated that the Salaman collection was vast—how vast—and how rich—I discovered only when I began working in the collection in the late 1980s. Initially, I was looking for material that was relevant to my *Radical Assimilation*. The longer I spent reading his correspondence and other papers, the more persuaded I became that I had stumbled across a treasure trove whose significance transcended the lives of Salaman and his correspondents. The contours of Anglo-Jewish history became sharper and its course more complex. The concerns and motives of well-known personalities appeared less stereotypical. Issues took shape that previous historians had ignored or marginalized, such as the importance of racial thinking in Anglo-Jewish discourse on Jewish self-definition. I worked in the collection off and on for more than two decades, from the late 1980s through the early 2010s. During that time, I made contact with one of Salaman's two surviving children, the mezzo-soprano and voice teacher Esther Salaman Hamburger (1914–2005), and, through her, with a number of his many grandchildren. They welcomed me into their homes, fed and encouraged me, and shared their memories with me on many occasions. In turn, I was able to tell them about incidents in Salaman's life about which they had never heard. It was a novel experience for me, since previously I had written about persons long dead and events no longer in living memory.

In the course of these conversations, I discovered that diaries and correspondence of Salaman's wife and children survived that were in the hands of descendants and not with the collection at Cambridge. I also discovered that one of his granddaughters had deposited a cache of his papers there that was not yet catalogued. They were (and still are) uncatalogued and do not appear on the finding aid to the collection. In other words, the quantity of primary documents was even more immense than I initially believed. I continued to work my way through the collection, the catalogued and uncatalogued parts at Cambridge, as well as the documents in private hands—without the intention, at least initially, of writing a full-scale biography. Along the way, I wrote two articles about Salaman, one about his work as a Jewish race scientist—a focus of his activity before the ascent of the Nazis in Germany—and the other about his intervention in public debates about *shehitah*, the Jewish method of slaughtering animals for food. In both cases, I addressed dimensions of his life that took me into hitherto opaque but nonetheless critical areas of Anglo-Jewish history.

Around 2000, I decided to write Salaman's biography. The immediate problem I faced in framing what I wanted to write was that he was not a well-known figure. Even fellow Anglo-Jewish historians did not readily recognize his name. This, in itself, was not an obstacle. The problem was that Salaman was difficult to label. He was a man of many parts who played many roles in an age in which specialization was less pervasive than at present. He was an independently wealthy country gentleman who spent almost all his married life on the edge of a small village in Hertfordshire, a dozen or so miles from Cambridge. He was a physician—though he practiced medicine only at the start of his adult life and during World War I—who found an outlet for his scientific interests in pathbreaking work breeding blight-free potato strains, in recognition of which he was elected a fellow of the Royal Society in 1935. He was also, as I mentioned earlier, the historian of the potato and a Jewish race scientist, that is, a Jewish scientist who believed that Jews constituted a physically distinct, though not pure, race. (Salaman's consuming interests in potatoes and Jews were linked by his commitment to neo-Mendelian genetics.) He wrote and lectured widely on both potatoes and Jews in the three decades before World War II. He was also a staunch Zionist, at least from the time of his service in Palestine in 1918–19, which was unusual for someone from the upper ranks of Anglo-Jewish society. While not politically active in the cause, he was in close contact with major figures in the movement in England, including Vladimir

Jabotinsky, Chaim Weizmann, and Lewis Namier. In the interwar period, he founded and led the Jewish Health Organisation of Great Britain, whose program was frequently eugenicist in tone and aim. And, last, he was a communal notable and a gadfly. He devoted countless hours to the Jewish Education Aid Society and Jews' College, the Orthodox rabbinic seminary (although he was not an Orthodox Jew in any conventional sense of the term). After Adolf Hitler seized power in Germany, he worked tirelessly to aid Jewish refugee scientists in Britain.

Because of the diversity of his activities and interests, no one label suffices to describe him. At times, I have thought of him as "the last Anglo-Jewish gentleman," a tag that evokes his Victorian upbringing and the preoccupation of the Anglo-Jewish elite with the ethos and code of gentility. To be precise, he was not the very last of this breed, but he was one of the last representatives of the caste of notables who dominated Anglo-Jewish institutional life from the early nineteenth century to the mid-twentieth century. He was wealthy, educated at elite institutions, genteel in his bearing and manners, at home in the English countryside, intolerant of religious zealotry and fundamentalism, confident in the correctness of his views in matters big and small, and accustomed to being listened to and deferred to. Salaman was keenly aware, moreover, that he represented a type that was rapidly becoming extinct. His lecture to the Jewish Historical Society of England in 1953, "Whither Lucien Wolf's Anglo-Jewish Community?," was in part a eulogy for a system of communal governance and big-tent Judaism that no longer existed but in its time was unique in the Jewish world. The 1964 eruption of the Louis Jacobs Affair, an epoch intracommunal battle between modern Orthodoxy and strict traditionalism that swirled around the future shape of Anglo-Jewry less than a decade after Salaman's death, formally marked the demise of the old, inclusive, latitudinarian Anglo-Judaism that Salaman cherished. Not coincidentally, the only representative of the elite who remained active after Salaman's death—the barrister and judge Ewen Montagu, a grandson of Samuel Montagu, first Lord Swaythling—led the opposition to the less tolerant Judaism of the ecclesiastical establishment (the chief rabbinate and the bet din, or rabbinical court) that seemed to have triumphed at the time. Salaman was no longer alive when the Jacobs Affair erupted, but when an earlier contretemps—the Great Turbot Affair of 1954, a kind of dress rehearsal for the Jacobs Affair that centered on whether turbot was a kosher fish or not—rocked the community, Salaman was an outspoken critic of the new, strict Orthodoxy.

One challenge in writing about Salaman is reconciling seemingly incongruous realms of his activity. For example, while he traveled to London frequently, he lived the life of a country gentleman in the main, overseeing the running of a small estate, mixing socially with the local gentry, and taking the lead in village affairs. Indeed, before World War I, he rode with the local hunt. His was an unusual profile for leadership in the Jewish world (at least outside Britain). Did he sense any dissonance between overseeing the affairs of British Jews, including the management of Jews' College, the Orthodox rabbinical seminary, and living in rural isolation in Hertfordshire, miles from any synagogue or other Jews (outside of his own family)? One might also ask how he reconciled his own agnosticism and, after the death of his first wife, lack of traditional observance with his lifelong identification with and membership in the New West End Synagogue, a pillar of middle-of-the-road Orthodoxy.

I do not know whether Salaman sensed any dissonance. I suspect he did not. I also suspect that the perception of the possibility of dissonance derives from the introduction of anachronistic assumptions into the recounting of the past. Too often readers of history and even, occasionally, those who write it expect men and women in past eras to think and feel in ways that duplicate their own sensibilities and are easily recognizable to them. Such expectations, however, obstruct rather than promote historical understanding. As I used to tell students at the start of every semester, do not think that the only difference between the men and women whom we will be studying and yourselves are the clothes they wore and the material circumstances in which they lived. They inhabited a universe of sentiments and assumptions that were often specific to their time and place. If one assents to this, then the dissonant parts of Salaman's life begin to appear less inharmonious and even his work as a race scientist and eugenicist becomes more comprehensible, however at odds with our own sensibility. In short, Salaman's world had a coherence and a logic of its own. Although he lived until the mid-twentieth century and addressed problems that are still with us, he was very much a late-Victorian Anglo-Jewish gentleman, a product of a milieu that was duplicated nowhere else in the Jewish world of his time or later. The quantity of Salaman's archival legacy makes it possible to reconstruct this milieu in some detail. Doing so, I hope, will leave readers nodding in agreement with the opening line of L. P. Hartley's *The Go-Between* (1953): "The past is a foreign country: they do things differently there."

6 | *The Last Anglo-Jewish Gentleman*

While this is a biography of Salaman, it is more than that. It is also an account of his first wife, Nina, a well-known translator of medieval Hebrew poetry. Like her husband's *History and Social Influence of the Potato*, her landmark translation (1924) of the poetry of Yehudah Ha-Levi, the greatest of the medieval Hebrew poets, remains in print. A feminist as well as a Hebraist—at a time when Hebrew scholarship in Europe and North America was a male preserve—she published historical and critical essays, book reviews, and an anthology of Jewish readings for children, as well as poetry of her own. She kept a kosher home, observed the Sabbath and festivals, and taught her children to read Hebrew before she taught them to read English, all while living in rural Hertfordshire. She was also the first, and only, woman, ever to deliver a sermon in an Orthodox synagogue in Great Britain. Her influence on her husband, especially his Jewish allegiances, was profound. It is difficult to imagine his life taking the course it did had he married someone else.

This is also an account of the Salaman family more broadly. Redcliffe was one of fifteen children, fourteen of whom lived to adulthood. (Large families were common among the Victorian Jewish elite, which was not the case, interestingly, among their counterparts on the Continent). Of the Salaman siblings, Redcliffe was the most accomplished and the only one to devote himself body and soul to Jewish affairs. A few sisters took some interest in their ancestral community; most of his siblings did not, and a few left the Jewish fold completely. It is impossible to explain why the siblings' lives followed such different paths, but it is instructive to see Redcliffe in the context of the choices they made and the ways in which they lived their lives. This perspective illuminates the range of options— occupational, cultural, social, political—that were open to British Jews in the late nineteenth and early twentieth centuries and demonstrates how well-to-do English Jews embraced the enthusiasms of the British elite and found acceptance outside exclusively Jewish circles. It is a reminder as well of how drift and defection thinned the ranks of the Anglo-Jewish upper middle class, a phenomenon of which Salaman was keenly aware and that he highlighted in his 1953 lecture to the Jewish Historical Society of England. Especially fascinating is the rapidity with which defection occurred. In the Victorian period, members of the communal elite tended to contract marriages with families that were part of the same elite. An uncle of Nina's, for example, married a sister of Redcliffe's. The mother-in-law of Herbert Samuel, to whom Redcliffe became linked through marriage,

Introduction | 7

was also Samuel's aunt. This degree of inbreeding was not unusual among well-to-do London Jews before World War I. It became increasingly less common in the interwar years.

I have one further purpose in writing about Salaman. Since graduate school, I have believed strongly that the subject matter of Jewish history has been conceived too narrowly. "Ordinary" Jews rarely merit the same amount of historiographical attention as prominent Jews—rabbis, ideologues, philanthropists, activists, and the like. When I published a collection of essays in 2011, I gave it the title *Broadening Jewish History: Towards a Social History of Ordinary Jews*. Clearly, I do not wish to make the ludicrous claim that Salaman was an ordinary Jew in the sense that Jewish shopkeepers and cabinetmakers—or their wives—were. His wealth, education, and career set him apart from them and, indeed, most Jews everywhere. Nonetheless, few historians, let alone readers of Jewish history, even recognize his name. Out of habit or lacking imagination, they return repeatedly to a small number of personalities and families, letting their views and experiences represent those of Anglo-Jewry (never a social or religious monolith) as a whole. Chief rabbis, Rothschilds, Sassoons, Montefiories, and Montagus, with a Lucien Wolf and a Joseph Jacobs thrown in occasionally, loom large—too large, I would argue—on the stage of Anglo-Jewish history. In sum, reinserting Redcliffe Salaman into the historical record broadens the ways in which we reimagine and remember the past.

Recounting Salaman's life resurrects historical currents and episodes that earlier historians of Anglo-Jewry either marginalized or ignored altogether: the circulation of racial notions of Jewishness in Anglo-Jewry; the eugenicist-inspired interventions of the Jewish Health Organisation of Great Britain in the East End; the proposed transformation of Jewish clergy into English gentlemen; the social and religious fissures beneath the Lucien Wolf Memorial Lecture uproar and the Great Turbot Affair; and the decline and death of the old Anglo-Jewish elite. His biography reveals, often in surprising detail, the dynamics of upper-middle-class Jewish family life from the late Victorian period to the mid-twentieth century and the remarkable degree to which it had absorbed ideals and priorities from its larger environment. Some of the persons with whom Redcliffe and Nina Salaman worked and socialized are well known—Israel Abrahams, Israel Zangwill, Herbert Samuel, Robert Waley Cohen, Herbert Loewe, and Cecil Roth, for example—but the richness of the Salaman archive often shows them in a new, more focused light.

8 | *The Last Anglo-Jewish Gentleman*

One last word of explanation. Throughout this book, I refer to Redcliffe Salaman and other Salamans by their first names. I do this not because I want to suggest the existence of a special tie of intimacy between author and subject. Indeed, much about Redcliffe's inner life remains a closed book. My reason for doing so is prosaic. Scores of Salamans, spanning three or four generations, populate this book. Referring to them by their first names is a way to make clear which Salaman is being discussed. Even so, the problem is compounded by the fact that some first names—Myer, Nina, Esther, and Jenny, for example—were used in more than one generation.

1

FAMILY BACKGROUND AND
EARLY YEARS

1

The ancestors of Redcliffe Salaman were part of the second stream of post-medieval Jewish migration to Britain. The first stream consisted of Jews of Spanish and Portuguese origin (Sephardim), whom Oliver Cromwell "readmitted" in the mid-1650s. The second stream—Ashkenazim from Central Europe (often by way of Amsterdam)—overlapped with the first. It began in the late seventeenth century and continued fitfully until the early nineteenth century. The Ashkenazim who came to Britain in this period were mostly humble traders and, less frequently, artisans seeking to escape the myriad of residential and occupational restrictions that embittered their lives and hampered their ability to earn a living in *ancien régime* states. Redcliffe's forebears were part of this second migratory flow, but neither documentation nor family legend relates where they lived before their arrival. Redcliffe's old friend, the historian of medicine Charles Singer, wrote in a memorial tribute to Redcliffe that the family came to England from Holland in the mid-eighteenth century.[1] Nothing, however, supports that claim. Redcliffe himself never mentioned their origins in anything he wrote. Moreover, even if true, it would not mean that his ancestors were Dutch Jews, since the Ashkenazim of the Netherlands in the mid-eighteenth century were recent arrivals from Central Europe.

We can be sure that, when his ancestors arrived, they were not called Salaman or Solomon. Most Central European Jews acquired family names only in the early nineteenth century. Before then, Jewish men were known by their Hebrew, or synagogal, names—so-and-so the son of so-and-so (e.g., Mosheh ben Yaakov, Yisrael ben Avraham). In the course of time, many Ashkenazi Jews in Britain acquired English family names by assuming their father's name. Mosheh ben Yaakov became Moses Jacobs; Yisrael ben Avraham became Israel Abrahams. At some time in the second half of the eighteenth century, Redcliffe's great-grandfather Aaron (1745–1819), whose father's name was Shlomo (Solomon), became Mr. Solomon. Some branches of the family—most famously that of the Victorian painters Abraham, Rebecca, and Simeon Solomon—retained the spelling.[2]

The earliest documented Salaman in England was this great-grandfather, Aaron Solomon, a straw-hat maker and merchant, who lived in Sandys Street, Bishopsgate. He was often called Solomon of Leghorn (Livorno) because he imported the straw for his hats from Livorno. He had eight children, one of whom, Isaac (1790–1872), began spelling his name Salaman. Family legend has it that the change of spelling was the result of a sign painter's error. Whatever the case, family names and their spelling were often unstable at the time. According to another family tradition, as a young man Isaac was pressed into service in the navy during the Napoleonic wars and was bought out by a distant relative in St. Helena, an important port of call for ships of the East India Company.[3] Isaac, who was still on the island when Napoleon was imprisoned there, returned to London and in 1816 entered the ostrich-feather business, which in time became the foundation of the family fortune.[4] Ostrich feathers are no longer a valuable commodity, but in the nineteenth and early twentieth centuries they most definitely were. In Britain and elsewhere, they adorned the military uniforms of men and the hats, gowns, wraps, and fans of stylish women.

When Isaac entered the business, in the early nineteenth century, it was not yet the booming trade it later became. It was, rather, one of many in London catering to the needs of an expanding, luxury-loving population. He imported feathers from Livorno and cleaned, dyed, and curled them in his home workshop, eventually with the help of his wife and daughters. The economics of his business were much like those of his father and the businesses of countless other small Jewish traders. Isaac lived first in Rathbone Place, near the corner of Oxford Street and Tottenham Court Road, and then migrated to Lamb's Conduit Street, in Bloomsbury, which in the 1830s and 1840s was popular with middle-class Jews. The family lived above the shop, which did business as "Mademoiselle Salaman," a nod to the status of French taste and style. It was visited by fashionable women, dressmakers, and milliners, who at times paid as much as £5 (equivalent to $187 or £135 in 2020) for a single plume.

Isaac's entry into the feather trade was not serendipitous. Livorno, with which his father traded, was the major entrepôt for ostrich feathers in Europe in the first half of the nineteenth century. Three-quarters of the ostrich feathers exported from North Africa (then the major source of the commodity) went there. Spanish and Portuguese Jewish firms had been active in the trade from the late seventeenth century, both in exporting plumes from North Africa and the eastern Mediterranean and in distributing them from Livorno to elsewhere in Europe. I suspect that Aaron's Livorno connections contributed to his son's choice of business.

In 1820, Isaac married Jane Raphael (1793–1863), the daughter of Samuel Raphael, a sign painter. They had three daughters and four sons. The lives of the sons followed radically different paths and for that reason deserve mention. Isaac, whose business was only a modest success and whose resources and horizons were limited, did not give any of his children a secondary education. (His son Myer [1835–96], Redcliffe's father, was a student at the Bayswater Jewish School.) Presumably they (at least the boys) received an elementary Hebrew education, as Isaac was a member of the Western (or Westminster) Synagogue.[5] In 1841, at the time of the first British national census, the business was not prosperous enough that he foresaw his sons joining him in it. Aaron (1821–96) and Abraham (1827–98) were apprenticed to watchmakers, and Nathan (1824–1905) was training as a law stationer, a clerk who made handwritten copies of legal instruments. At that time, Myer was still a young child. About the three daughters' education we know nothing: Betsy (b. 1829), Fanny (1833–96), and Rachel (1836–1908), all of whom in time helped with the business before marrying and leaving home. Isaac's wife Jane also made dresses, work that would have complemented the family's feather business.

At twenty-one, Myer's older brother Abraham sailed to Australia to seek his fortune. He found work as a watchmaker in Sydney, but the long hours strained his eyes and the pay was unrewarding. The discovery of gold in California in 1849—and the quick riches it seemed to promise—stirred his imagination and he sailed for California. He sold liquor and supplies to miners in Monterey, on the coast, and then in Grass Valley, in the western foothills of the Sierra Nevada mountain range. His success led his brother Aaron and a cousin, Henry Sylvester, to join him around 1851. Desiring to marry, Abraham wrote to his parents in London to find him a wife, and in 1854 he sailed from San Francisco to New York, via the hazardous route around the tip of South America, and then on London. He married Bloom Phillips, the daughter of a tailor who lived next door to his parents in Lamb's Conduit Street, and the married couple then sailed to Grass Valley, where they had seven children, six of whom survived, before returning to London in 1869. They bought a house in Maida Vale, a quarter of London popular with newly rich Jewish families, and had two more children. In 1870, Abraham left London once again, this time for New York, where he set up an agency to sell ostrich feathers, presumably with the help of his family in London. The business did not succeed, however, and Abraham, homesick for his wife and children, who had remained in London, returned to them in 1871. Meantime, his brother Aaron in California, who had remained single, took up farming and, at the time of the 1880 US census, was living in Anderson Valley in western Mendocino County, about one hundred miles north of San Francisco, an area well known today for its grapevines and marijuana plants.

Of Isaac's four sons, the youngest, Myer (Redcliffe's father), was the most entrepreneurial and the most successful. He transformed his father's modest business into a thriving, international endeavor. Until 1863, the business was conducted informally as a partnership between Isaac and the four of his children who were living with him in Lamb's Conduit Street—Nathan, Myer, Betsy, and Rachel. (Fanny had married Lewis Nathan in 1855.) That year the business, whose stock, lease on the premises, tools, and materials were valued at £2,000 (equivalent to £216,808, or $292,646, in 2020), was reorganized. The five partners invested £900—Isaac and his youngest son, Myer, invested £300 each and the other three £100 each, Isaac retaining a one-third share. That same year Myer married, and, soon after, his father decided to retire from the business. In early 1864, Isaac's share was divided among the remaining four partners, who, in exchange, agreed to pay him an annuity of £150 a year for life. At the end of 1864, with Betsy and Rachel about to marry, the partnership was dissolved. Each of the sisters received £300 and neither they nor their husbands kept any stake in the business, which now belonged entirely to Myer and Nathan.[6]

Myer, however, was the driving force in the firm. Nathan, eleven years Myer's senior, had become bogged down as a law writer and was supposed to have taken over the clerical side of the business. But, in that he was "entirely devoid of any initiative," he became a silent partner in the business and all of Myer's other enterprises, faithfully doing whatever his younger brother wanted and showing "unswerving devotion to him."

Aaron had been no more successful in California than his brother Abraham had been. In 1882, Myer and his wife visited him in California (the transcontinental railroad had opened in 1869) and persuaded him to return to London, promising to support him. Aaron lived with their sister Rachel and her husband, Abraham Simmons, in Gordon Square, Bloomsbury. He eventually settled in the Caledonian Road near the cattle market because he claimed he could be happy only if he lived near a place reminiscent of his thirty years farming in California. He never married but lived with a woman the last twelve years of his life.[7]

At the same time that the business was reorganized, Myer transferred it to Monkwell House in Falcon Square in the City and dropped the retail side. The reorganization and move predated the ostrich-feather boom that began in the 1880s, but they prepared the firm to profit from it. Ostrich feathers had adorned the dress of well-to-do women from the mid-eighteenth century, but it was the fashion for large, elaborately trimmed hats, from the 1880s until the end of World War I (as well as beplumed fans and boas), that caused the trade to flourish. In addition, the demand for plumes crossed class lines and was no longer confined to the wealthy. Journalists and retailers targeted middle- and lower-middle-class women, who increasingly possessed the means to adorn themselves with ostrich feathers. The demand for plumes was worldwide, but London became the center for their marketing and distribution in Europe and America, replacing Livorno and other southern European ports. Undergirding the shift to London were the burgeoning of South African ostrich-feather farms in the second half of the nineteenth century and the tightening of imperial and commercial links between the Cape of Good Hope and London. As a consequence, most South African plumes were exported to London, to which feather merchants from the rest of Europe and the United States traveled to obtain their stock.[8] The trade thrived, and the number of Jewish feather merchants in London multiplied. The veteran Salaman firm, with decades of experience and expertise and a well-established network of suppliers and customers, was well positioned to take advantage of the ostrich feather boom. By the end of the century, they had offices in London, New York, Paris, and Cape Town.

One sign of Myer's success even before the boom was his decision to marry and his choice of wife. In 1863, he wed Sarah Solomon (1844–1931), the daughter of Josiah Solomon, a partner in a firm of musical instrument makers that later expanded into gramophones. (The maternal Solomons were not related to the paternal Salamans.) His bride's family, like his own, had been in England since the eighteenth century. But her father, unlike Myer's, was a successful businessman and a pillar of the Anglo-Jewish community.

An uncle was married to a daughter of Chief Rabbi Nathan Adler, for example. At the time of her marriage, Sarah was living in Finsbury Circus, then a select upper-middle-class quarter, in the City of London. She had been raised in comfort and educated at Leopold Neumegen's school for Jewish girls in Kew, where she was taught "how to come in and go out of a drawing-room, and the correct manner of entering, sitting in, and leaving a carriage, for which purpose a wheel-less and retired vehicle was propped up on the logs in the school garden."[9] According to Redcliffe, she was one of the best-looking women in her circle. Photographs, portraits, and family stories confirm his impression of her outstanding beauty. According to one story, the earliest Sassoon to settle in London was asked whether he would like to attend the wedding of the most beautiful girl in the Jewish community—that is, Sarah Solomon. (See fig. 1.1.) He attended and presented her with a handsome cashmere shawl, which Redcliffe remembered seeing.[10] The bibliophile Elkan Adler once told one of Redcliffe's daughters that her grandmother used to be called "the beautiful Sarah."[11] In short, Myer's bride was an endorsement of his own worldly rise. As a child and young man, he had lived above the family store. His family was respectable, a good step above the hawkers and old-clothes men who constituted the lowest rung of Anglo-Jewry but still much below the stratum with which he was now allying himself through marriage.

Another sign of Myer's rise in the world was his change of residence. After marrying, he and Sarah moved to 9 Euston Square, close by the railway station. In 1871, at the time of the British census, when they had two children, they employed three servants: a nurse, a cook, and a housemaid, a rough indication of their material status. By 1873, the social status of the square was beginning to decline and its upper-middle-class residents were looking for homes elsewhere. Isaac and Sarah rented a furnished home for six months in Redcliffe Gardens, Kensington, where Redcliffe was born in 1874. (Redcliffe and his older brother Euston [1871-1916] both bore the names of the streets where they were born. This was not an Anglo-Jewish naming practice but a short-lived Salaman quirk. Myer and Sarah gave their other thirteen children conventional names, such as Jenny, Bessy, Brenda, Clement, Archie, and Harry.) They then moved to a large, three-story, double-fronted house, with a shallow drive in front, in Pembridge Crescent, on the western edge of Bayswater, an area much favored by well-to-do London Jews. The structure was much grander than the Euston Square house, one that required a larger staff. At census time in 1881, they employed two

Figure 1.1. Sarah Salaman, Redcliffe Salaman's mother. Courtesy of Jenny Salaman Manson.

nurses, a cook, and a housemaid. Ten years later they employed six female servants: a nurse, a cook, two general servants, and a parlor maid.[12] In 1879, Myer purchased an additional five-acre estate, Wentworth House, in Mill Hill, a rural area at the time. The house was Georgian but had been much altered in the mid-Victorian years. The decision to purchase it was on the spur of the moment. One day, while taking his customary prebreakfast ride, he found himself in Mill Hill, saw a large house for sale, and then and there decided to buy it. His wife was upset and cried, calling the new purchase the Cave of Machpelah (the traditional burial site of the biblical matriarch Sarah). At the time, few English Jews owned country homes. Her social life was focused on London and, in particular, on her mother, sisters, and cousins, with whom she was in daily contact. She had no social interest in the world beyond the Jewish community. For her, living in the country

16 | *The Last Anglo-Jewish Gentleman*

seemed like an act of self-exile. Redcliffe recalled that many in his parents' circle of friends were openly critical of his father's venture. "To spend so much on a house was bad enough, but to forsake the safe and respectable purlieus of Hyde Park and Maida Vale away from the company, not to say shelter, of the close-knit family circle, was, if not madness, something near akin to heresy." While his father's motives are not known, it is clear that social ambition was not one of them. Like his wife, Myer did not seek to cultivate social relations with non-Jewish families of similar wealth. At first, the family divided their time between Bayswater and the country, spending six months at each in turn. Then, between 1890 and 1894, his father built a new house in Mill Hill to replace the old one, purchased an additional two hundred acres, and gave up the Pembridge Crescent house.[13]

Ostrich plumes underwrote Myer's initial rise into the upper middle class, but it was real estate that propelled him into the ranks of the very rich. Myer entered the real-estate market in the late 1850s, at times in partnership with his brother Nathan. In 1877, when he created a trust to provide for his wife and children after his death, he owned seven properties individually in the City and another six, also in the City, jointly with Nathan. In addition, they leased another ten properties in the City.[14] In the next twenty years, they added to their holdings properties in Islington, the Strand, the Haymarket, Bloomsbury, Oxford Street, and Hammersmith. What motivated Myer to invest his money in this way—an unusual strategy in his generation—rather than in stocks, bonds, and other financial instruments, is not known. English Jews became prominent in commercial property development only in the great post–World War II boom. Witness the empires of Jack Cotton, Charles Clore, Harry Hyams, and Harold Samuel, to name only a few.[15] In any case, Myer's strategy was brilliant. When he died in 1896, his estate was probated at £288,674 (worth £38,656,619 or $52,347,634 in 2020) and that of his brother and business partner Nathan at his death in 1905 at £374,299 (worth £45,811,113 or $62,030,538 in 2020).[16] Because probate figures exclude the capital value of land, their wealth was in fact much greater than these numbers suggest. Whatever the value of Myer's property at the time of death, in 1939 its value was £158,552 (worth £10,431,836 or $14,122,515 in 2020). Moreover, the income it generated was impressive: more than £675,000 between 1912 and 1953. The estate was sufficient to allow his fourteen surviving children to live in great comfort without ever having to earn a living. His children also inherited from his brother Nathan, who died unmarried and childless, although, in the case of his estate, other nieces and nephews were beneficiaries as well. In the five decades after his death, Nathan's estate generated almost half a million pounds for his beneficiaries.[17]

2

Redcliffe was born on September 12, 1874, while his parents were living temporarily in Redcliffe Gardens, Kensington. He was the ninth child born to his parents. (The first, Josiah, having died as an infant in 1865, Redcliffe was effectively the eighth child.) Another six children followed Redcliffe, the last being born in 1885, when Sarah was in her early forties. She was thus pregnant, more or less, for the first two decades of her married life. Despite the physical demands of fifteen pregnancies, she retained her youthful beauty through most of her life. Photographs of her in the years before World War I hardly suggest that she had given birth to fifteen children. Household servants no doubt reduced the wear and tear of childrearing.

The household into which Redcliffe was born was organized on recognizably upper-middle-class Victorian lines. He and his siblings saw relatively little of their parents, especially his father, whom they respected but from whom they were emotionally distant. The parents' bedrooms and sitting rooms were on the ground floor and the children's bedrooms and schoolroom on the floor above. The two spaces were separate worlds, and Redcliffe and his siblings did not view their parents' part of the house as theirs. Their nurse, Emily Hewitt, "a most remarkable woman," the daughter of a merchant ship captain, raised them. She began working for the family three years before Redcliffe's birth and remained in their service for forty-three years.[18] As a child, Redcliffe was closer to her than to his parents. Symptomatic was his inability to keep straight his mother's birthday and his nurse's birthday, both of which were in late September.[19] Aside from his nurse, he recalled in old age, he knew little of "the love which comes from the realization of one's own weakness and the sheltering care of one's elders," musing that in a family as large as his "any other relation was well nigh impossible." His nurse remained with the family almost her entire life and received a pension from them when all the children were grown. She wanted to be buried with them at Willesden Cemetery and was willing to convert to Judaism to make that possible, but Chief Rabbi Hermann Adler would not agree to accept a proselyte on those grounds. In any case, although she had been raised a Christian, she rejected Christian theology and never attended church. She did attend synagogue with the family on special occasions and greatly admired the preaching of Simeon Singer, minister of the New West End Synagogue, as well as the singing of its cantor.[20] Redcliffe remembered her as the most consistent upholder of Jewish traditions, within the latitudinarian limits of the family's observance, of anyone in the house.

Conventional upper-middle-class attitudes toward hierarchy and rank suffused the Salaman home. Although his father had struggled as a young man, he was a firm believer in the reality of class differences. He supported the Conservative party and believed in the superiority of the English in every aspect of life—views that Redcliffe shared until his years at Cambridge. Hewitt, too, believed in and transmitted these values. She held herself apart from the other servants, who would not have dreamed of sitting down in her presence (or, for that matter, in the presence of any of the children). The one exception was the undernurse, whom, after a number of years, she treated as an equal. When Hewitt and the undernurse took Redcliffe and his siblings to Kensington Gardens, which they did almost every day, they were free to roam but they were not allowed to talk or play with any but "approved" children, even if middle-class. At the London school where Redcliffe prepared for St. Paul's from 1884 to 1886, class attitudes were uglier and even more pronounced. The masters encouraged the students to think of boys at board schools (locally funded state schools) as inferior creations, while Redcliffe and his classmates themselves referred to them as "cads."[21] Similar prejudices governed his parents' thinking about East European Jews. Redcliffe's older sister Bessie (1873–1950) reminded him during World War II that they were brought up to loathe Polish Jews.[22] In some small ways, Redcliffe never fully shed this bias.

While Redcliffe's parents were at home with middle-class English conventions and customs, they were not well integrated into English social circles. Like most other prosperous Victorian Jews, the Salamans were content to mix socially with other Jewish families of similar rank, especially with families with whom they were related. Despite her good looks and substantial wealth, Redcliffe's mother's interests "began and ended with her family and their affairs." She lived largely within its orbit, and, after her husband's death in 1896, during her long widowhood (she lived until 1931), she rarely visited houses other than those of her own immediate relatives. Redcliffe's father, as well, showed little interest in making his way in non-Jewish society. Both Myer and Sarah remained—contentedly, it would appear—within what Redcliffe called "the clannish structure" of the Anglo-Jewish upper middle class.[23] The same was hardly true of the next generation.

Family Background and Early Years | 19

The religious atmosphere in Redcliffe's childhood home was also typical of the Anglo-Jewish upper middle class. The family's Judaism was nominally Orthodox. They were members of the New West End Synagogue in St. Petersburgh Place, a traditional but architecturally grand synagogue under the authority of the chief rabbinate. (It is now a Grade I listed building, that is, a state-designated and state-protected building of exceptional historical and architectural interest.) It had been established in 1878 to serve the growing number of affluent Jews in Bayswater and was a short walk from the Salaman home in Pembridge Crescent. Redcliffe generally went to the New West End Synagogue on Saturdays and, as he grew older, came to enjoy Simeon Singer's sermons. The family observed the dietary laws, but in their own fashion. The meat they ate was kosher and no pork or shellfish was served, but they did not separate meat and milk. While they observed the Sabbath and the Holy Days, they did not mark the second day of Rosh Ha-Shanah, Sukkot, Passover, or Shavuot, which are traditionally celebrated in the diaspora although not in the Land of Israel. In this, their observance echoed the bibliocentricity of much of native Anglo-Jewry, which often privileged biblically sanctioned religious laws over rabbinically sanctioned laws, even though such practice was in conflict with conventional Orthodox practice elsewhere. One way to characterize this kind of traditional Judaism is to describe it as latitudinarian. It was a Judaism that accommodated a wide range of personal practice, took almost no interest in doctrines and beliefs, valued tradition (viewing its antiquity as its justification), and celebrated the values of communal solidarity and responsibility. Redcliffe later noted that, until he met his future wife Nina, whose Jewish upbringing was different from his own, he did not realize how far his family had traveled unconsciously from the path of Orthodoxy.[24] In any case, the latitudinarian, big-tent Orthodoxy that he absorbed as a child left its impress on him, and he continued to champion it until the mid-twentieth century, by which time it had largely disappeared, having fallen victim to a more demanding, more inward-looking, and more intolerant Orthodoxy.

Redcliffe's Jewish education was as relaxed as his parent's Orthodoxy. From age ten to age thirteen, he had weekly Hebrew and religion lessons from Lydia Aguilar, a first cousin of the novelist and essayist Grace Aguilar. He later described her as "a dear old lady of whom it may be said that she succeeded over a period of some twenty or thirty years in imparting the minimum of knowledge in the maximum number of hours to an entire generation of boys and girls of the leading families of Anglo-Jewry." After his bar mitsvah, he attended Simeon Singer's religion classes at the New West End Synagogue, and, when he was fifteen, he and his sister Bessie studied Hebrew with Singer for about a year.[25] That was the limit of his formal Jewish education. How weak his Hebrew was emerges in his correspondence with his fiancée, the Hebraist Nina Davis, in 1901. She needed to explain to him the meaning of basic terms like *ḥasid* and *tsaddik*, for example. He described himself to her as "an ignoramus who didn't know Hebrew."[26]

Redcliffe was educated at home until age ten, when he was sent to live in a boardinghouse in West Kensington for Jewish boys attending Samuel Brewsher's Preparatory School for St. Paul's, one of Britain's most academically successful public schools (i.e., an elite, fee-paying, secondary boarding school). The boardinghouse was kept by a Polish Jew, Nestor Schnurmann, whom Redcliffe remembered as weak, kindly, and ignorant of English schools.[27] In fact, Schnurmann was a talented linguist who pioneered the teaching of Russian in Britain and later taught at Cambridge and Cheltenham College, a public school where he founded a house for Jewish pupils. Ten-year-old Redcliffe found the experience of living away from home strange and frightening and wrote to Hewitt (rather than to his father or mother), "I am very unhappy and please spread it."[28] In 1886, he entered St. Paul's, then newly installed in Hammersmith Road in Gothic-style buildings designed by the architect Alfred Waterhouse, to which he could walk from Pembridge Crescent. When the family was at Mill Hill, he boarded with relatives in town during the week and returned to Mill Hill for the weekend.

Few Jews entered Britain's public schools before the 1880s, in part because they were not welcome in what were explicitly Christian institutions, and in part because few prosperous Jewish families saw much value—social, cultural, or economic—in a public-school education. The first Jewish boy entered the school only a few years before Redcliffe arrived. Because St. Paul's accepted day students and was convenient to the growing area of Jewish settlement in Bayswater, and because its headmaster from 1877 to 1905, Frederick William Walker, was religiously easygoing, the number of Jewish students there increased at the end of the century.[29] During Redcliffe's years at the school, there were about thirty other Jewish boys. Among them were his older brother Euston (1871–1916), with whom he was not close, his future brother-in-law, the anthropologist Charles Seligman, and the future journalist and publisher Laurie

Magnus. As at other English public schools, Jews were fair game—subject to slights, slurs, and exclusions on account of their origins.[30] The anti-Jewish sentiment Redcliffe encountered there, however, did not leave him emotionally scarred, as it did some Jewish Paulines who were his near contemporaries. Leonard Woolf, for example, who started at St. Paul's in 1894, became aware of his emotional vulnerability as a Jew when he was there. He told Malcolm Muggeridge in 1966 that it was at school that he realized for the first time "that it wasn't merely that my religion was Jewish and somebody else's was Mohammedan."[31] If the novelist and biographer Compton Mackenzie's fictional portrait of Leonard as a schoolboy is accurate (the two overlapped at St. Paul's in the 1890s), Leonard was marked and suffered as a Jew there. Mackenzie wrote: "A Gentile half as attractive as Stern [Woolf] would have won the glances of every ambitious young amorist in the school, but being a Jew he was disregarded." When an older boy befriends him, the former's schoolmates chaff him because the object of his attention is a Jew.[32] In reaction and as a shield, Woolf grew what he called "a carpace" while at St. Paul's—"the façade . . . we must learn to present to the outside and usually hostile world as a protection to the naked, tender, shivering soul."[33]

The difference between the two boys' experience of hostility at St. Paul's is instructive. There is no reason to doubt that the two encountered similar levels of stigmatization. In Leonard Woolf's case, however, the slights and slurs weighed more heavily, probably because he was emotionally predisposed to experience them as personally painful. He came from a family that was less observant and less engaged in communal activities. Often, the more distant Jews were from Jewish institutional life, the more sensitive they were to anti-Jewish slights and slurs, since their self-confidence and happiness depended on Gentile approbation. They were no longer rooted in or consoled by membership in a minority group that drew strength from its own traditions, customs, mores, and values. Redcliffe, on the other hand, even as a fifteen-year-old schoolboy, regarded his Jewishness as a proud distinction that demanded from him, in return, enduring loyalty to his people.[34]

Although Redcliffe suffered little from the antisemitism at the school, he was never really happy there. When his father sent him to St. Paul's, it was with the expectation that he would eventually train as an architect and work in the family's property business. Redcliffe, who had never shown any particular interest in architecture or demonstrated any aptitudes or skills that would be necessary for a career as an architect, was later baffled by his father's choice. The school art master, Robert Harris, whom Redcliffe described as a man "as completely devoid of taste as any man I have ever encountered," also encouraged him in the belief that he should become an architect, largely because he was skilled in constructing perspective drawings from architectural plans. (He even won a school prize for his work.) His father also arranged for him to spend part of his school holidays in the office of William and Frank Brown, who did most of the architectural work for the Salaman estate. Shut up in the firm's stuffy office, he discovered his limitations and realized that he was not cut out to be an architect.[35]

At the same time he was coming to this realization, he developed an interest in biology, largely as a result of the teaching of the junior science master, and began to think of a medical career. Significantly, he later noted, he did not imagine a career in pure science, which would have been unthinkable in a well-to-do, late-Victorian Jewish family such as his. The custom was that sons followed in the commercial or financial footsteps of their father, as his brothers Euston and Elkin (1870–1919) did. Sons who were ill-equipped or unwilling to do so had the options of medicine or law.[36] (His older brother Clement [1868–1935] qualified as a barrister but never practiced.) In any case, Redcliffe was a hard-working but hardly brilliant student. The school reported to his parents at the end of his penultimate year, in July 1892, that he did his best and that he was much improved in science. In Latin, it judged him "moderate"; in French, "very fair"; in English, "fair"; in drawing, "satisfactory"; and in mathematics, "moderate."[37] It was not a record that suggested that a distinguished scientific career lay ahead.

His memories of the school were not fond. Overall, he found the teaching uninspired and the workload oppressive, a detriment to both his health and his intellectual growth. (St. Paul's aimed to win more entrance scholarships to Oxbridge than other schools.) He never looked forward to the start of a new term, even when he was head of the Science Side.[38] His memories echoed those of Leonard Woolf, who thought the school was suffused with philistinism and was, above all, a mill for turning clever boys into classics scholars who performed well on examinations. The masters, he recalled, "despised the intellect and the arts and anything connected with them and so any small boy who showed any unusual intellectual ability or interest." To be bookish, to be a "swot"—a student devoted to his work to the exclusion of all other interests—was "just as despicable in the eyes of the masters as in those of the boys." From the masters, Woolf learned that "one of the most despicable of things was to be too intelligent."[39]

Family Background and Early Years | 23

Outside the classroom, Redcliffe's efforts to make close friends foundered. He took no part in sports (cricket, football, swimming, track, or rowing)—at an institution where athleticism was highly valued. In his last year, he was elected to the Union Society, a debating club for the oldest students, with its own clubroom, library, and newspapers, and in the course of the year spoke at their meetings, defending, for example, the motion that religious disabilities were a disgrace to civilization and opposing motions that endorsed anarchy and condemned the use of Trafalgar Square for public meetings.[40] Whatever satisfaction he derived from membership in the Union Society did not compensate, however, for his difficulty in forging close social ties with schoolmates. In a diary that he kept in 1893, during his last year at St. Paul's, he recorded how he opened his heart to his sister Bessie, his confidante at the time. One Saturday, after prayers in the hall at Mill Hill, the two went out for a walk and he complained to her that he had not yet found "a real sympathetic friend." On another occasion, after noting that he had not felt well (a frequent lament) and that he had slept badly, he wrote, "The want of a real friend disturbs me." It disturbed him so much that he attributed his poor mental and physical health to his loneliness. He wrote in his diary that he felt "thoroughly out of order mentally" and that his state was a result of having "overworked" his brain and "having no friend to talk things out with." In particular, he stewed about his relations with two schoolmates, Pearson and Glover, whom he suspected of not really caring about him. He finally resolved that he would not abase himself to cultivate their friendship and that he would depend only on himself. (Despite his resolution, he and Glover went on a weeklong walking tour of East Anglia in July, after the end of his last term at St. Paul's.) At times, he expressed the need for "an adviser and supporter older and better" than he was, feelings that were no doubt linked to the emotional gap between him and his father.[41]

Some of Redcliffe's unhappiness can be attributed to late-adolescent angst. But there was more at work than that. In his adolescence, he lacked the confidence, bravado, and athletic poise that counted for so much in a late-Victorian public school. Indeed, throughout his life, he was reserved and formal, even stuffy and priggish. He was always appalled, for example, by how much alcohol his fellow officers consumed while serving in the army during World War I. It was his misfortune that his father, who knew little about English schooling, sent him to a public school, where intellectual seriousness, scientific curiosity, and conscientiousness were not highly valued. While he never referred to himself as a swot, his schoolmates probably saw him as one.

Compounding Redcliffe's inner turmoil during this period was his growing religious skepticism. How or why he began to doubt the theology of traditional Judaism is unknown. No single text or experience, as far as I know, led him to deny the existence of God or the efficacy of prayer. Again, he unburdened himself to Bessie, telling her a few days before Rosh Ha-Shanah 1893 of his loss of faith: God and prayer were "remnants of a religion of fear and very human ideas." As for ethics, he thought that they were independent of supernatural belief. One could be just and upright even if one was not a believer. Because his father trusted in an omnipotent God, he decided he would not say anything about his convictions, thereby instigating a breach with him, and that he would attend synagogue as usual. He excused himself from the charge of hypocrisy by reasoning that "one can examine oneself as well there as anywhere." When Yom Kippur came, he fasted and again was in synagogue, but this time he looked at the day differently, "only as an introspection and promise to myself to do better in the future." He never felt, on that Yom Kippur, that he was forgiven by anyone.[42]

Redcliffe's crisis of faith at age eighteen left his other Jewish commitments undisturbed. Having rejected the traditional God of Israel, he nonetheless retained a strong sense of membership in the people of Israel. This sense of belonging and rootedness, along with his commitment to science, provided him with a blueprint for life, orienting his behavior and setting his priorities. He was able to jettison one and cling to the other, to detach the bonds of Jewishness from the supernaturalism of belief, because he was moving toward (or perhaps had arrived at) an essentialist view of Jewishness, a view that would today be described as biological or racial. It is significant that he noted in his diary, several weeks after his conversation with Bessie, that he had just finished reading Benjamin Disraeli's novel *Tancred* (1847), one of Disraeli's most developed expositions of his notion of Jewish racial superiority, and that it had made him "a stronger racial Jew" and even prouder of his Jewishness.[43] While Redcliffe came to think about race in ways very different from Disraeli, they shared the view that race trumped religion, which, in the end, they declared time-bound and epiphenomenal. In embracing this notion, so alien to classical Judaism, Redcliffe was moving in the same direction as Jewish activists and intellectuals in Eastern and Central Europe who were forging new, secular definitions of Jewishness, such as Bundism and Zionism.

Family Background and Early Years | 25

Redcliffe's reference to Disraeli's novel in his diary in 1893 marks the first appearance of the word *race* or *racial* in anything he wrote. Exactly what he meant in describing himself as a "racial Jew" is unclear. Most likely he was invoking the word as a way of declaring that he was a Jew by virtue of birth and collective identity rather than by virtue of doctrine and practice. The contemporary equivalent would be the nonbelieving, nonobservant Jew who describes himself or herself as an ethnic or a cultural Jew. The word *racial*, however, also referred to a *system* of thinking about human differences—in this case, collective differences—that was rooted in biology and that was empowered by Britain's imperial adventures in Africa and Asia. By the end of the nineteenth century, notions of race were ubiquitous in English cultural and political life.[44] They enabled white Britons to distinguish themselves from their imperial subjects and, in some cases, from other European powers and to revel in their superiority. When used (however illogically) in tandem with class and religious differences, it enabled some Britons to distinguish themselves from other Britons. The language and assumptions of racial thinking were inescapable, even for those who were unfamiliar with the work of systematic racial theorists such as the anthropologist John Beddoe. But there is no evidence that in the 1890s the late-adolescent Redcliffe was a racial thinker or a biological determinist, believing in the physical inheritance of mental, cultural, and social characteristics.

As a schoolboy, Redcliffe found some relief from the academic pressures and social disappointments of St. Paul's in the time he spent at the family's country house at Mill Hill. In old age, he recalled that "the words 'Mill Hill' never leave me unmoved; they call me back to a land which was once all my own, a land of infinite promise and, in the enchanted years of childhood, of fulfillment."[45] When he was young, the estate was a vast playground, with its cellars, staircases, orchards, stables, gardens, and meadows. When he was older and his interest in biology kindled, one pastime in particular occupied him: preparing and assembling the skeletons of small animals. These he entered successfully in competition for a Smee Prize at St. Paul's, an award for work of a practical or scientific nature executed out of school hours. The school newspaper reported that he "must have taken great pains in preparing and mounting the skeletons" he showed, that his specimens were of "a good colour," and that he provided both drawings and photographs to point out the various bones to those who were unfamiliar with such matters.[46] In retrospect, he also saw the move to Mill Hill and the building of the new house there as a "great divide" in his life, marking a break between the almost exclusively, inward-looking Jewish life of London and a newer, more interesting life in the country. That the move coincided with the coming of adolescence, with its turmoil and questioning, helped to imbue Mill Hill with an excitement that his Bayswater years lacked.[47]

Looking ahead to university, in January 1891, Redcliffe sat and passed the University of London Matriculation Examination with second-class honors. In all likelihood, he took the examination to hedge his bets, not having yet gained entrance to an Oxbridge college. Whatever the case, his father was elated and purchased £100 of stock in the Natal Land and Colonisation Company in his name to celebrate the event, for he was the first in his family to pass a public examination, his older brothers having tried and failed.[48] In late 1892 he won a science scholarship at Trinity Hall, Cambridge, but his self-doubt and lack of confidence prevented him from fully savoring his triumph. He noted in his diary in January 1893 that he was "heartily sick" of the congratulations friends and family offered him. When they told him how clever he must be to have won a scholarship, he felt like "a humbug." "If they only knew, like myself, how little I know."[49] He capped his career at St. Paul's with a leaving exhibition, a scholarship awarded on the basis of a competitive examination.

3

Redcliffe went up to Cambridge in October 1893, the first in his family to attend university, for it was unusual for British Jews to send their sons to university in the late Victorian period. In fact, there were so few Jews at Cambridge his first year that the Jewish students there were able to assemble a *minyan* only by coercing one or two Jewish tradesmen to join them. Neither Redcliffe nor anyone in his family was familiar with the various Oxbridge colleges, and his choice of Trinity Hall, following the suggestion of the mathematics master, C. H. Bicknell, was "unfortunate." Trinity Hall was not a good fit for a serious, shy Jewish student. The other students were mostly well-born and wealthy, intent on having as good a time as possible, their highest ambition being to "get into the boat" (row for the college, which dominated the sport at Cambridge for many years in the 1890s). In addition, he was the only science student among the seventy-two first-year students in his year at Trinity Hall.[50]

Toward the end of his life, Redcliffe recalled that his life at Trinity Hall was "drab, uninspiring and in many respects distasteful." He remained a rather lone figure, failing to find a sympathetic friend with intellectual interests among the men in his year. His only friend in the college was Walter Pease, a Quaker, the son of Henry Fell Pease, a coal and ironstone mine owner and Liberal member of Parliament for Cleveland. As a Quaker, Pease was, like Redcliffe, something of an outsider. His best friend outside the college was also socially marginal—Frank Bainbridge (who was at Trinity College), the son of a rigid nonconformist chemist in Doncaster, who had "few of the graces and none of the experience of the people I was accustomed to." For that reason, he proved himself unpopular with Redcliffe's family when he spent a weekend at Mill Hill. His only important Jewish friend at Cambridge was Charles S. Myers (who was at Gonville and Caius College), whom he knew from London. Their families were linked in long-standing friendship and shared similar values.[51] Myers was two years his senior but was in residence at Cambridge the entire time Redcliffe was there, often acting as a mentor. Like Redcliffe, Myers studied the natural sciences and trained as a physician, but he eventually devoted his life to experimental psychology and was instrumental in the establishment of many of its pioneering institutions in Britain. His and Redcliffe's friendship deepened over the years, and he was a frequent collaborator with Redcliffe on various communal projects, especially the Jewish Health Organisation of Great Britain.

The ill health that had plagued Redcliffe as a schoolboy also troubled him as an undergraduate. His father frequently peppered him with advice about staying well. Knowing his son's work habits, he wrote him in January 1894, "Don't over do it. I don't want a weedy seedy doctor for a son [but someone] with a healthy mind in a vigorous body that can only be arrived at by the allowance of time for sleep and exercise."[52] Two years later, his father wrote him that he did not care a damn whether Redcliffe earned academic honors. "I want a sound, strong, observant son, not a double first idiot, sickly and nervous."[53] And on the eve of Redcliffe's departure for a holiday in Germany, he warned him to avoid arguments with Germans he would meet, "as you don't fight well."[54] It is hard to imagine that these letters bolstered his son's self-confidence.

If socially Redcliffe's time at Cambridge was disappointing, intellectually it was rewarding and laid the groundwork for his later work on potatoes. Walter Gaskell, whose pioneer research was central to the understanding of cardiac physiology, was a fellow of Trinity Hall. Responsible for the natural science students at Trinity Hall, Gaskell became a hero and father figure to Redcliffe. His brilliance, worldliness, and geniality made a deep impression

28 | *The Last Anglo-Jewish Gentleman*

on Redcliffe, "an undergraduate isolated in an uncongenial mob." Gaskell was, he recalled, "the first outstanding man of genius" he knew. He also learned German at Cambridge, taking lessons from Mathilde Schechter, wife of the Cambridge rabbinics scholar Solomon Schechter.[55] Acquiring German allowed him to later pursue advanced medical training in Germany and gave him access to research on Jewish racial inheritance, which was mostly in German. In May 1896, at the end of his third year, he took the first part of the Natural Science Tripos, a university examination the passing of which is a prerequisite for taking an honors degree. He obtained a first, the highest honors classification. Gaskell urged him to stay on for a fourth year, take the second part of the Tripos, and devote himself to research—which he might have done had his father not died unexpectedly in April. Feeling responsible for his mother, he decided to return to London and live at home to help her, not financially, but in other ways, especially with his younger siblings. He imagined, incorrectly, that she would be unable to cope without him. In fact, she had no special need for his assistance and was unaware of the sacrifice he had made on her behalf. Their relations remained "affectionate" until her death in 1931, and he was always a dutiful son, but the two were never emotionally close. He later realized that he had made a mistake and always regretted forsaking his fourth year at Cambridge.[56]

Later in life, Redcliffe attributed his intellectual independence and willingness to pursue his own path to his experiences at Trinity Hall. He believed that one legacy of his three years there was "the freedom I needed to build my associations where and in such manner as suited my needs and my character." Trinity Hall cured him, he believed, of the flaw of yearning to be part of a crowd. The lesson was not learned immediately, which cost him much "vexation and frustration." There was an additional cost as well. In his own assessment, it fed his arrogance, his firm conviction that his views were unassailable and those of his opponents flawed. On balance, he did not think the costs were too high a price to pay.[57]

Notes

1. "Obituary," *British Medical Journal*, June 18, 1955, 1479.

2. My account of the earliest Salaman generations draws on a typewritten history (2004) and family tree by Ann Causton (a descendant of Redcliffe's granduncle Abraham Salaman); RNS's own unpublished essay, "Boyhood and the Family Background," Add. MS 8171/27, RNS CUL; and the 1841, 1851, and 1861 British census entries for his grandfather Isaac.

Family Background and Early Years | 29

3. On the impressment of Jews into the Royal Navy, see Geoffrey L. Green, *The Royal Navy and Anglo-Jewry, 1740–1820* (London: Naval and Maritime Bookshop, 1989), 50–52.

4. On the commerce in ostrich feathers, see Sarah Abrevaya Stein, *Plumes: Ostrich Feathers, Jews, and a Lost World of Global Commerce* (New Haven, CT: Yale University Press, 2008).

5. Matthias Levy, *The Western Synagogue: Some Materials for Its History* (London: G. Barber, 1897), 67.

6. Business documents, April 2, 1863, January 14, 1864, December 1, 1864, MS 14,744, SF LMA.

7. RNS, "Boyhood and Family Background."

8. Stein, *Plumes.*

9. RNS, "Boyhood and Family Background."

10. RNS, "Boyhood and Family Background."

11. NDS to RNS, June 29, 1918, Add. MS 8171, Wedderburn Deposit, RNS CUL.

12. RNS, "Boyhood and Family Background"; entries for Myer Salaman in British 1871, 1881, and 1891 censuses.

13. RNS, "Boyhood and Family Background."

14. Trust document, September 18, 1877, MS 14,734, SFP LMA.

15. See, for example, Oliver Marriott, *The Property Boom* (London: Hamish Hamilton, 1967).

16. William Rubinstein, "Jewish Top Wealth-Holders in Britain, 1809–1909," *Transactions of the Jewish Historical Society of England* 37 (2002): 151, 158.

17. Stein, *Plumes*, 181n97.

18. RNS, "Boyhood and Family Background."

19. RNS to NDS, September 6, 1901, Add. MS 8171/97, RNS CUL.

20. RNS, "Boyhood and Family Background," and family questionnaire for the BBC program "The Changing Family," February 17, 1932, Add. MS 8171/12, box 2, RNS CUL. The historian of science Charles Singer (1876–1960), a friend of Redcliffe, told a similar story. His nurse, who had been his father's nurse as well and served the family for fifty-three years, "would at one time gladly have become a Jewess, but my father [Simeon Singer] was against this course" (Charles Singer, *The Christian Failure* [London: Victor Gollancz, 1943], 109–10).

21. RNS, "Boyhood and Family Background"; "Life's Residue," Add. MS 8171/10, RNS CUL.

22. Bessie Salaman Cohen to RNS, October 3, 1944, Add. MS 8171/1, RNS CUL.

23. RNS, "Boyhood and Family Background."

24. RNS, "Still Births and Abortions," Add. MS 8171/32b, RNS CUL.

25. RNS, "Still Births and Abortions."

26. NDS to RNS, August 9, 1901, Add. MS 8171/97, RNS CUL; RNS to NDS, September 9, 1901, Add. MS 8171/98, RNS CUL.

27. RNS, "Boyhood and Family Background."

28. RNS, "The Helmsman Takes Charge," LH/X/10, Royal London Hospital Archives.

29. A. Hugh Mead, *A Miraculous Draught of Fishes: A History of St. Paul's School, 1509–1990* (London: James and James, 1990), 97.

30. Andro Linklater, *Compton Mackenzie: A Life* (London: Chatto and Windus, 1987), 38. On antisemitism at other late-Victorian public schools, see Todd M. Endelman, *Radical Assimilation in English Jewish History, 1656–1945* (Bloomington: Indiana University Press, 1990), 98–99. In the interwar years, Jews at St. Paul's were subject to quotas.

30 | *The Last Anglo-Jewish Gentleman*

31. Quoted in Victoria Glendinning, *Leonard Woolf: A Biography* (New York: Free Press, 2006), 35–36.

32. Compton Mackenzie, *The East Wind* (New York: Dodd, Mead, 1937), 6, 11.

33. Leonard Woolf, *Sowing: An Autobiography of the Years 1880–1904*, Harvest Book ed. (New York: Harcourt Brace Jovanovich, 1975), 71.

34. RNS, "Still Births and Abortions." For a view of the Jewishness of Woolf's homelife with a different emphasis, see Fred Leventhal and Peter Stansky, *Leonard Woolf: Bloomsbury Socialist* (Oxford: Oxford University Press, 1919), 6–7. Leventhal and Stansky describe the Woolf home as "observant," a characterization that strikes me as misleading.

35. RNS, "Helmsman Takes Charge."

36. RNS, "Helmsman Takes Charge."

37. Archives, St. Paul's School, London.

38. RNS, "Boyhood and Family Background."

39. Woolf, *Sowing*, 88–89.

40. The school magazine, the *Pauline*, reported the activities of the debating society. A complete run of the magazine is available in the library of St. Paul's School.

41. RNS 1893 diary, entries for January 1 and 9, March 10 and 11, and May 4 and 27, Add. MS 8171/30, RNS CUL [hereafter RNS 1893 diary].

42. RNS 1893 diary, entries for September 8 and 20.

43. RNS 1893 diary, entry for October 14.

44. See, for example, Nancy Stepan, *The Idea of Race in Science: Great Britain, 1800–1960* (Hamden, CT: Archon, 1982); Paul B. Rich, "The Long Victorian Sunset: Anthropology, Eugenics and Race in Britain, 1900–1918, *Patterns of Prejudice* 18, no. 3 (1984): 3–17.

45. RNS, "Boyhood and Family Background."

46. *Pauline*, no. 11 (June 1893), 147.

47. RNS, "Boyhood and Family Background."

48. RNS, "Boyhood and Family Background."

49. RNS 1893 diary, entry for January 7.

50. RNS, "Helmsman Takes Charge."

51. RNS, "Helmsman Takes Charge."

52. Myer Salaman to RNS, September 2, 1895, Add. MS 8171/12, RNS CUL.

53. Myer Salaman to RNS, January 21, 1896, Add. MS 8171/12, RNS CUL. A double first was the highest degree awarded.

54. Myer Salaman to RNS, September 2, 1895, Add. MS 8171/12, RNS CUL.

55. Bessie Salaman to RNS, July 29, 1895, Add. MS 8171/3a, RNS CUL.

56. RNS, "Helmsman Takes Charge."

57. RNS, "Helmsman Takes Charge."

2

MEDICINE AND MARRIAGE

1

Redcliffe left Cambridge, at age twenty-one, a more confident young man than he had been three years earlier when he had matriculated. He spent most of the next eight years in London (1896–1904), studying medicine and then taking the first steps toward what undoubtedly would have been a distinguished career in medical research. (He took time as well to study morbid anatomy and pathology in Germany.) During his London years, he forged strong male friendships, married a learned woman whose Jewish commitments shaped his life and with whom he remained deeply in love until her untimely death in 1925, and took his first steps toward immersion in Anglo-Jewish communal affairs. In retrospect, he remembered this period as one of the happiest in his life.

Although his close Cambridge friend Charles Myers encouraged him to study medicine with him at St. Bart's in the City, Redcliffe chose to train at the London Hospital in Whitechapel—for reasons unconnected to its reputation (then on the rise). Redcliffe, however diligent, was unable to lose himself in his studies and ignore the world around him. In particular, he was eager to learn more about the issue that then dominated the Jewish communal agenda and often agitated the British public as well—the mass settlement of Yiddish-speaking East European immigrants in the East End of London. Their lack of familiarity with English ways, their attachment to Old World customs, their association with the sweatshops and wretched living conditions of immigrant quarters, and their popular image as irreducibly and fundamentally alien made their presence an issue for Jewish families long established in Britain.[1] Above all, the native-born elite feared that the newcomers' pronounced foreignness fueled antisemitism. At the London Hospital, where half the patients were immigrants, Redcliffe believed he could study both medicine and the immigrant community.

32 | *The Last Anglo-Jewish Gentleman*

While he later realized that his decision to train in Whitechapel flowed from his own youthful sense of self-importance, he also saw his choice as an act of homage to his recently deceased father, whose openness to those in need had made a deep impression on him. On several occasions in his unfinished memoirs, he remarked on his father's acts of charity. He recalled that his philosophy of charity was the old-fashioned Jewish "rahmanos" [mercy] variety: he gave alms to whoever asked and "never left the house without cramming his pockets with vouchers for free meals [at charity kitchens]," which he distributed freely as well. His father was also instrumental in providing an annuity to the Hebraist Henry Naphtali Solomon, a cousin, whose boarding school at Edmonton Myer had attended.[2] He supported other relatives who were down on their luck, as well—most notably, his cousin, the dissolute Pre-Raphaelite painter Simeon Solomon, whose alcoholism, homosexuality, and spells in prison and the gutter, put him outside the pale of respectable society. When poorer members of the family died, Myer paid for their burials and tombstones.[3] While his father had never been a companion or a confidant to him, Redcliffe nonetheless wished to emulate him and live up to what he thought were his expectations.

Redcliffe's years at the London Hospital were both taxing and fulfilling. (See fig. 2.1.) As at school and university, he was aware of anti-Jewish incidents and currents at the institution. He thought it would have been a miracle if they were absent because most of the Jewish patients spoke little or no English and were marked as alien by their manners and dress. In this respect, he shared the common belief of the Anglo-Jewish elite that immigrant Jews, by virtue of what they did or did not do, generated anti-semitism. (An alternative explanation would have been that their foreignness activated preexisting, deeply rooted feelings that Jews were different in kind or essence from other people.) In any case, he claimed that he never encountered "the slightest personal anti-Jewish sentiment"—even though his strong Jewish interests were no secret. He recalled, in particular, one incident in which he angrily reprimanded someone making crude remarks about another Jewish medical student. He was having lunch with two other medical students, neither of them Jewish. One, unnamed, was an indifferent student and a difficult person but a protégé of a famous surgeon on the staff of the hospital, and the other was an Oxford man named Payne, with whom Redcliffe later became friends. A shy, somewhat gauche Jewish student entered the lunchroom and the unnamed student turned to Payne and remarked that that bloody, disgusting Jew was a disgrace to the hospital.

Medicine and Marriage | 33

Figure 2.1. Redcliffe Salaman as a medical student at the London Hospital. Collection of the author.

Payne continued to eat his lunch without saying a word. Redcliffe exploded. He asked the offender by what right he, a worthless waster, could speak as he had. Shocked to be confronted in this way, he mumbled some excuse. Payne later told Redcliffe that he was ashamed that he had remained silent.[4] My sense is that Redcliffe's fiery response, while not out of character for him, was not typical of the Jewish haute bourgeoisie, which preferred quieter means of opposing antisemitism.

As a medical student, Redcliffe's record was excellent. It would have allowed him to rise to the higher ranks of the profession. But rather than taking the path to becoming a consultant or a surgeon, he chose to specialize in pathology, a nonclinical and less lucrative area. He found a powerful

34 | *The Last Anglo-Jewish Gentleman*

patron in the neurologist Henry Head, registrar and then assistant physician at the London Hospital. Head took Redcliffe to work with him, between his medical and surgical examinations, in Frederick W. Mott's laboratory at the Claybury Asylum at Woodford Bridge, Essex (now in the London borough of Redbridge), a newly created London County Council psychiatric hospital. Mott was a pioneer biochemist known for his work on neuropathology and endocrine glands in relation to mental illness. Redcliffe spent an inspiring six months there, during which time he studied pathologic histology (the structure, function, and composition of diseased tissues), learned much about post-mortems, and wrote and published his first scientific paper— "Report on a Case of Tabes, with Especial Reference to the Changes in the Posterior Root Ganglia," *Neurological Archives* 1 (1899).[5] From Claybury he returned to the London Hospital, finished his career as a student, and then received several successive hospital appointments.

In 1901, the London Hospital offered him a post as assistant director of a pathological institute it intended to open. Redcliffe did not think much of the state of pathology in Britain at the time, when physicians with no specialized training performed post-mortems. He considered post-mortems "dreadful performances"—"more suggestive of a terrier worrying a rat than anything that could be dignified by the term of a scientific investigation."[6] And so, before assuming the post, he wanted to do advanced work in pathology in Germany, where medical research and training were more highly developed. The hospital allowed him to go, and he spent fourteen months in Germany training with two noted pathologists, Max Borst in Würzburg (for two months, beginning in June 1901) and Carl Benda in Berlin (for twelve months, beginning in August 1901).[7] Before turning to his experiences there, however, more needs to be said about his time at the London Hospital as a student and fledgling physician.

As I noted earlier, the London Hospital was located in the Whitechapel Road in the East End, an area that was home to both recent arrivals from Eastern Europe and local inhabitants whose wretched squalor and hopeless poverty were long-standing. The patient intake at the hospital reflected the makeup of the area. Medical students from respectable homes who trained there, like Redcliffe, were exposed to living conditions and social and cultural attitudes that were largely foreign to them. In his memoirs, Redcliffe wrote at length about the revulsion he experienced when making maternity visits to women in their homes. He recalled once attending a woman in a barely furnished garret, which he reached by climbing a ladder. "There was a broken down bed with a single blanket, a chair without a back, a tin basin without a towel, and the poor mother herself practically naked. Of food or drink there was none." One incident, in particular, struck him with horror. When he pulled back the sheets covering the woman he was attending, he discovered "a shriveled up child of about 15 months old lying at the food of the bed, covered by the [bed] clothes." The child was alive but "more like a dried up monkey than a human child." He soon learned that the mother had had many children and that she was starving the child to death, having insured its life, in order to collect the insurance money. This practice, he subsequently learned, was not uncommon in London slums. By contrast, the East End Jewish homes he visited seemed to him to be in better condition, even if equally poor. Present were clean linen, hot water, and a few women from the neighborhood to assist the doctor and comfort the mother.[8]

Exposure to the extreme poverty of the East End loosened Redcliffe's attachment to the Conservative Party, an attachment that he had inherited from his father. British Jews tended to vote Liberal at midcentury—largely because Liberals championed Jewish emancipation—but, by the last decades of the century, well-to-do Jews were just as likely to vote Conservative, that is, to vote their class interest. Accelerating the shift was William E. Gladstone's resort to anti-Jewish rhetoric in the Bulgarian Agitation in the late 1870s and other Liberal attacks on Benjamin Disraeli that targeted his Jewish background. In his youth, everyone in Redcliffe's family and their circle of friends was Conservative. At the general election of 1895, shortly after Redcliffe turned twenty-one, their family doctor in Mill Hill "just gathered me up, swept me to the poll and told me how to vote—Conservative, of course." Afterward, he felt ashamed at his passivity. The seven years he spent in the East End changed his politics forever: "the overcrowding, the mean, shabbily and heavily exploited homes, the economic insecurity of the masses and, above all, the ravages of drink" made him realize the inadequacy of a laissez-faire system. He compared the scene on Whitechapel Road and in the receiving room of the London Hospital on a Saturday night to a battlefield that only a William Hogarth or Thomas Rowlandson could have captured.[9] He abandoned the Conservatives after the first election in which he voted and remained active in the Liberal interest until 1929, at which point he thought the party no longer had a future. That year he resigned as president of the Royston and District Liberal Association, which he had headed since 1907, a few years after moving to the country, and urged the Liberals of

North Hertfordshire to approach Labour to try to find a candidate who was acceptable to both of them.[10]

During his years in the East End, veteran communal leaders recruited Redcliffe, though still in his twenties, for communal service. In 1897, the learned bullion broker and philanthropist Frederick David Mocatta asked him to become active in the work of the Home and Hospital for Jewish Incurables, then in Victoria Park Road, to which Redcliffe devoted himself most of his life.[11] That same year he was elected a member of the Maccabaeans, a dining club of Jewish professional men and intellectuals with a strong cultural and philanthropic interest in matters Jewish. Established in 1891—his future father-in-law, Arthur Davis (1846–1906), was a founding member—its membership included the leading intellectual lights of the native-born Jewish community: Israel Abrahams, Herbert Bentwich, Joseph Jacobs, Claude Goldsmid Montefiore, Lucien Wolf, and Israel Zangwill. Redcliffe's brother Clement (1865–1935) was also a member, having been elected in 1893. Although Redcliffe was not a regular at the Maccabaean dinners, he attended from time to time, as did his brother-in-law, the biochemist Samuel Schryver, and his friends, the anthropologist Charles Seligman and the historian of medicine Charles Singer.[12]

During Redcliffe's London Hospital years, Simeon Singer of the New West End Synagogue (and Charles's father), enlisted him to study and report on Christian missions to the Jews in the East End. While the number of Jews who became Christians as a result of missionary labors was always insignificant, their work had provoked communal leaders since the early nineteenth century, when the first such missions were established. What most angered them were the material inducements that the missions used to attract impoverished and often troubled Jews to their doors, including food, clothing, housing, schooling, apprenticeships, and medical care. As the number of immigrants in the East End multiplied, so too did the number of missions, since immigrants were the most vulnerable segment of the Anglo-Jewish population—indeed, the only segment to whom the missionaries had unimpeded access.[13] Redcliffe's report has not survived; the impression the missions made on him remained with him. He was scathing about their value: "Their only contribution to society was to further corrupt a handful of weak-kneed Jews ready to adopt any creed at a price." His was the view of most Anglo-Jewish notables, but it missed the heart of the matter. The missions attracted immigrant Jews, most of whom were uninterested in changing their religion, because they catered to immigrant needs (illness, unemployment, hunger, for example) that neither the state nor the community's charities were able to meet fully. Indirectly, Redcliffe hinted at this when he described the scene at a medical mission in the East End: "poor women with their squalling children in their arms, sitting on bare benches, dumbly suffering but studiously deaf" to the missionary's half-hour sermon, "an essential prerequisite of treatment." Ten years later, he and the Hebrew scholar Herbert Loewe reviewed the work of the East End missions and, in one case, they were able to convince a sponsor, the Presbyterian Church, of the abuses that the missions fostered. The church carried out its own investigation and shut them down for several years. In the long term, however, the thought of so many Jewish souls left untended convinced the church to reopen them.[14]

Around 1900, Leopold de Rothschild (1845–1917) wrote Redcliffe "a charming letter" suggesting that he join the Board of Deputies of British Jews, the long-standing representative body that safeguarded Jewish interests in the political world. At the board, the politics of rotten boroughs and patronage was still in full sway, and a large number of its members represented provincial communities to which they had no connection. Rothschild would arrange Redcliffe's election as the representative of a small provincial congregation, which, otherwise, would have found prohibitive the cost of sending one of its own members to the board meetings in London. The arrangement was the usual mode of recruitment to self-perpetuating communal institutions. It ensured that their governance remained in the hands of a limited number of well-to-do, often related families, the so-called Anglo-Jewish notability. A seat on certain boards and committees was a coveted distinction that bestowed honor and status within the Jewish community, although it also consumed time and energy. "Accession to the more important communal positions needed an apprenticeship; young men who were not too pressed by professional studies or financial stringency would devote several evenings a week to such work."[15] Redcliffe declined the offer.

While at the London Hospital, he also entered the fray of communal debate for the first time, initiating a half-century of immersion in religious and political issues. On November 21, 1902, the London *Jewish Chronicle* published a letter from the pseudonymous "Mary Magdalena Moses" proposing that Jews should acknowledge the teachings of Jesus and discard their ancient ceremonies and promoting the radical, denationalized Judaism of Claude Goldsmid Montefiore and the just-established Jewish

38 | *The Last Anglo-Jewish Gentleman*

Religious Union, which eventually transformed into what is known in Britain as Liberal Judaism. Redcliffe responded the following week. What most rankled him about the proposal was its assumption that Jews were like everyone else. For him, the Jews were "a peculiar people" who had lived in religious and historical isolation for almost four thousand years. As a result, they were "so markedly differentiated in body and mind from the other nations" that they constituted in effect "a separate biological variety of the human species."[16] His letter was, in one sense, one more contribution to an ongoing debate, initiated by the decline of the *ancien régime* and the first proposals for Jewish integration into state and society a century earlier, about the nature of the Jews and their assimilability. Were they a religious, national, or biological group? The rise of political antisemitism in the late nineteenth century, with its goal of reversing Jewish emancipation and integration, raised the temperature of the debate everywhere in Europe. Jewish self-definition weighed as heavily on Jewish thinkers as it had ever done.

Redcliffe's response had another dimension as well. As a schoolboy, Redcliffe had called himself, in the diary he kept at the time, a "racial Jew." Invoking this term around the same time that he abandoned the God of traditional Judaism implied that his Jewishness was not rooted in theology. His response to "Mary Magdalena Moses" was an elaboration of this idea, one to which he held, with some modification, for half a century. At this time, however, he lacked the vocabulary of race science. In all likelihood, he was not yet familiar with the extensive literature on the racial character of the Jews. But it is clear that he had already imbibed or arrived at a biological definition of the bonds of Jewishness. When he began to think more systematically about the biological history of the Jews in the 1910s, he was not breaking with the liberal, emancipationist position that Jews differed from their neighbors only by virtue of their religious beliefs and practices. He was, rather, elaborating a view that he had held since his school days. His letter to the *Jewish Chronicle* in 1902 marked the first time that he spoke publicly about it.

2

As odd as it might seem, Redcliffe's appearance as a controversialist in 1902 owed much to his decision to marry, or, to be more specific, to his having fallen in love with and become engaged to Nina Davis. In his memoir, he recorded the exact circumstances that led to his engagement. At a Sabbath morning service at the New West End Synagogue in late May 1901,[17] his eyes wandered to the women's gallery facing him.

> There I saw a young woman directly opposite who stood out from all others by reason of her stately figure and her truly queenly beauty. The curious thing was that I had on rare occasions seen her before, knew who she was and how she was already distinguished as a serious scholar and writer. Perhaps it was on that account I had completely dismissed her from my mind. I could only mutter to myself "Idiot. You have been thinking of this one, flirting with the other, all but proposing to a third, whilst all the time the one woman in the world for you, you have never troubled even to talk to."[18]

He lost no time, since he was leaving for Germany in two weeks. He asked his sister Isabelle (1866–1944), who was married to Nina's uncle Edward Davis, to invite Nina for a weekend at their home, Ivy Tower, in rural Hendon, where he too would "happen" to be present. To her surprise, he asked her to marry him and, on Sunday, June 1, 1901, they announced their engagement. Two days later, she described him in a letter to a friend in the United States as "very fair" (he was a redhead), with "very strong regular features & a fine head." She declared that he had "the broadest, most open & sympathetic character" she had ever known, noting that he was interested in art, literature, religion, and music. Most important, in her view, he felt his Judaism was "the most precious possession" he had.[19]

Nina Davis was not a complete stranger to Redcliffe. Had he wished, he could have come to know her earlier. Their parents were acquainted with each other, but they did not move in the same social circles. Both families attended the New West End Synagogue; both lived in Bayswater before the Salamans moved full-time to Mill Hill in the early 1890s, the Salamans in Pembridge Crescent and the Davises in Gloucester Terrace, a twenty-minute walk apart. In her early teens, Nina attended a New Year's Eve party at the Salamans, complete with conjuring, dancing, and late-night dining.[20] Presumably it was not the only time she was invited there. There were, however, differences in their backgrounds as well. Redcliffe's parents were seriously wealthy; Nina's were merely prosperous—upper-middle-class, to be sure, but not wealthy by Salaman standards. In addition, the Salamans were casually Orthodox; the Davises were seriously Orthodox (with one particular twist).

Nina's family background was unusual. Her father, Arthur Davis, was a distinguished Hebrew scholar—by avocation rather than vocation—whose family was neither observant nor learned. Her father was a third-generation

Englishman; his father, John Davis (1810–72), the son of a Bavarian immigrant, was born in Thame in 1810 and settled permanently in Derby in 1843, where there were few Jews and no congregation. (The number of Jews increased little over the century; in the mid-1880s, there were only six Jewish families in the city.) The Davis family were precision instrument makers (telescopes, opera glasses, thermometers, barometers, mining equipment, and the like).[21] Arthur's father was a scholarly man, a friend of Herbert Spencer, who also grew up in Derby, but he was not a Hebraist and not an observant Jew. Religious observance, let alone knowledge of Hebrew, was absent from the Davis home, and, over the generations, most of the Davises drifted away from Judaism. When a Davis from Derby approached Redcliffe's and Nina's son Raphael (1906–93), himself an engineer, for help in writing a history of the family engineering firm, which was still in existence, he did not want the family's Jewish origins to be mentioned. Nina's niece Cathy Davis described a Davis cousin who remained in Derby in the mid-twentieth century as "anti-Jewish." This cousin's mother and his wife were both Christian and he did not let his children know that the family was of Jewish origin, about which they only learned—to their shock—when Cathy told them.[22]

Arthur Davis followed a very different path. At an early age, he evinced a passion for Hebrew and religious observance, which surprised and inconvenienced his family, and, through independent study, he acquired a high level of proficiency in Hebrew. Six weeks after Nina was born, Arthur, his wife, Louisa (ca. 1851–1923), and their two daughters, Elsie (1876–1933) and Nina, moved to London. The family lived in Maida Vale and Kilburn before moving to Gloucester Terrace sometime in the 1890s. While living in Kilburn, Davis was in close touch with a circle of Jewish intellectuals and professionals in Kilburn and St. John's Wood who met in each other's homes to discuss questions of Judaism.[23] An informal group, they were known as the Wanderers, a reference to their wandering from home to home, to their license to wander from the subject under discussion, and, of course, to the folkloric Wandering Jew. The dominant figure in the group was the Romanian-born Solomon Schechter, then lecturer in Talmud at Jews' College and later reader in rabbinics at Cambridge (1890–1901) and president of the Jewish Theological Seminary in New York (1902–15), as well as the architect of the Conservative Jewish movement in the United States. The inner circle of the Wanderers included the writer Israel Zangwill, the historian and folklorist Joseph Jacobs, the journalist and historian Lucien Wolf, the amateur theologian and communal worker Oswald Simon, the Judaica scholar Israel Abrahams, the barrister Herbert Bentwich, the painter Solomon J. Solomon, and Asher Myers, editor of the *Jewish Chronicle*. (Zangwill, Abrahams, Solomon, and Herbert's son Norman became fixtures in the lives of Nina and Redcliffe.) The shared belief that underwrote their ongoing conversation was the conviction that the Judaism of the major communal institutions—the United Synagogue and its member congregations (with their begowned, gaiter-wearing "Reverends"), the chief rabbinate, and Jews' College—was cold, lifeless, and philistine. Schechter referred to it as "flunky Judaism" because of its deference to the wealthy notables who headed the community. They sought to breathe a new, livelier spirit into Anglo-Judaism and to foster Jewish letters and scholarship in a community where they were largely absent and complacency reigned after the removal of Jewish disabilities.

Once settled in London, Arthur devoted most of his leisure time and then all his retirement time to Hebrew studies, working both at home and in the British Museum. He labored, in particular, on two projects. The first was a study of the *neginot* (cantillation marks) in the Masoretic text of the Hebrew Bible, the authoritative text for rabbinic Judaism, which scholar-scribes in the Land of Israel and Babylonia redacted, copied, and diffused from the seventh to the tenth centuries CE.[24] The second was a more ambitious project: to publish a new English translation of the *mahzor*, the synagogue liturgy for the festivals. Believing that existing translations inadequately expressed "the full force and beauty of the Jewish liturgy in its ancient form,"[25] he recruited friends and family to help him. He and Herbert Adler, a barrister, educationist, and nephew of Chief Rabbi Hermann Adler, translated the prose sections of the liturgy, and the two Davis daughters and Israel Zangwill translated the poetry. The full work appeared in six volumes between 1904 and 1909 and remained the most widely used festival prayer book in Britain and the Commonwealth until the translation of Chief Rabbi Jonathan Sacks replaced parts of it early in the twenty-first century.

Aside from the usual problems besetting any translation work, issues rooted in the politics of Anglo-Jewish Orthodoxy also arose, and it is worth considering them for the light they shed on the religious climate of the time. Because Arthur Davis wanted the approbation of the chief rabbi, he had to agree to the latter as the final authority on both the translation of the text and the selection of the texts, especially the *piyyutim* (medieval liturgical poems, written in linguistically complex Hebrew and Aramaic), whose content frequently offended acculturated Jews. The chief rabbi was not a Hebraist of distinction, and so he delegated the role to the Dutch-born Samuel Hirsch, a tutor at Jews' College. Hirsch did not impede their work, but Herbert Adler was "not much impressed with his utility," as he wrote Nina after her father's death.[26] A more serious problem was the treatment of the *piyyutim*. In the nineteenth century, Reform-minded congregations in Western and Central Europe and North America, including some otherwise Orthodox bodies, dropped many of the *piyyutim* from congregational worship. They did so both to reduce the length of the service and to excise ideas and language that were offensive. In London, synagogues had petitioned Chief Rabbi Nathan Adler since the 1840s to eliminate them, and some had done so. In 1880, however, Adler ruled that the synagogues could not choose which ones they wanted to recite, that all of them must be included or none. Davis and the others wanted to print those they had translated but not the entire corpus. Nathan Adler's successor, Chief Rabbi Hermann Adler, forbade them, since it would give the impression that they were changing the ritual, which he was loathe to do, probably because he was unsure of his own expertise in Jewish law and feared attacks from staunch traditionalists.[27]

An example of how Hermann Adler's timidity impeded their work arose in connection with the *eleh ezkerah* [these I will remember], a martyrology in the *musaf* (additional) service on Yom Kippur. The *eleh ezkerah* recalls the deaths of ten rabbis who were executed for teaching Torah during the Hadrianic persecution (early second century CE). It elaborates on their virtues and their fortitude in the face of horrific deaths. The lurid details it recounts are unhistorical, as is the poetic license it takes in weaving their stories into one narrative, with their executions taking place on the same day. Davis and Adler, who wished to omit the martyrology, even asked various synagogues whether it was still said, but the chief rabbi ruled that they could not omit it because it was old and because the ten rabbis were really martyred. As a solution, Adler thought that Nina might translate it into verse—"very freely and without dwelling on anything that is repugnant." This, he felt, would solve a difficult problem—how to include the martyrology without affronting English-speaking Jews—for, by casting it in verse, "one could make the thing appear like a vision in the mind of the writer, who ruminates on his people's sufferings and who sees the martyrdom of the ten rabbis kaleidoscopically."[28]

Nina solved the problem by avoiding a literal translation of the Hebrew text, replacing it with a loose verse translation that aesthetically heightened the force of the martyrology. Thus, she turned its opening lines into a concise statement of the lachrymose view of Jewish history:

> These things I do remember; O I pour
> My soul out for them. All the ages long
> Hatred pursueth us; through all the years
> Ignorance like a monster hath devoured
> Our martyrs as in one long day of blood.[29]

When she came to the tortures that the martyrs endured, she tended to omit or tone down gruesome details. For example, in the case of Rabbi Ishmael, whose skin was stripped from his face while he was still conscious (according to the traditional text), Nina offered these lines:

> Terror makes me dumb
> To tell the tortures that mine eyes beheld;

And then there was the problem of Israel Zangwill, who was responsible for translating some of the verse. Zangwill was not an observant Jew, and, moreover, in November 1903 he had married Edith Ayrton, who was not Jewish (although her stepmother, the physicist Hertha Marks Ayrton, was). Yet the *mahzor* translation was an Orthodox project in the sense that the chief rabbi endorsed it and it was intended for use in the synagogues under his authority. For Arthur Davis and his daughters and for Herbert Adler, that was not a problem. They were comfortable with the "big tent" traditionalism of Anglo-Jewry, but, for the chief rabbi, Zangwill's mixed marriage was a problem. And so, when the work began to appear, it was agreed not to include the names of the translators of the poetic texts (Nina and Elsie Davis and Israel Zangwill) on the title page, thus protecting the orthodoxy of the project, and to list only the names of the two editors, Herbert Adler and Arthur Davis. The names of Zangwill and the Davis sisters appeared only in an appendix at the end of the set.[30]

Arthur Davis's pragmatic toleration was symptomatic of mainstream Anglo-Jewish traditionalism. While he attended synagogue regularly and observed the Sabbath and dietary laws conscientiously—Redcliffe thought him extremely observant—his practice of Judaism reflected the eclectic Orthodoxy of upper-middle-class Victorian Jewry rather than the Orthodoxy of British Jewry a century later. For example, when the family vacationed at the seaside, in Deal, Kent, they received precooked kosher meat from Dover and poultry from London but apparently did not worry about the *kashrut* of the dishes, pots, pans, and utensils in the house they rented.[31] In the absence of a synagogue in Deal, they marked the arrival of the Sabbath by chanting the Torah portion of the week, normally done in the synagogue on Saturday mornings, and occasionally the *haftarah*.[32] Yet when Arthur Davis was serving on a jury in London and was not released in time to reach his home before the start of the Sabbath, he stayed overnight in a hotel near the Inns of Court. Despite his own strong sense of the correctness of his way, he did not try to impose his views on others, avoided controversy, and consequently got on well with his son-in-law. In 1903, when Redcliffe and Nina invited her parents to attend the Passover *seder* at their home, he was sensitive to the fact that he was more observant than his son-in-law and gave him the opportunity to withdraw the invitation and observe the holiday in his own fashion.[33] Theologically, he was certainly no fundamentalist. In responding to a question that Redcliffe posed about the authenticity and authority of the Torah, he rejected the doctrine that God revealed the Law *in toto*, written and oral, to Moses on Mt. Sinai, explaining that neither Moses nor his followers made this claim.[34] The bibliocentrism of Anglo-Jewish traditionalism also inflected and tempered his observance of Orthodox Judaism.[35] Thus, the Davis family did not fast on the Ninth of Av, which commemorates the destruction of the First and Second Temples, since the day is not mentioned in the Bible and was ordained by the rabbis.

Arthur Davis was also imbued with the spirit of communal service that was characteristic of the upper ranks of Anglo-Jewry. His most important contribution, aside from his work on the *mahzor*, was the establishment, with Herbert Bentwich, of the Educational Aid Society in 1896. The society provided financial loans to Jewish artists, musicians, and university students from impoverished (usually immigrant) homes. At first, Davis and Bentwich personally funded it, each contributing £100, and ran it without outside assistance. When Davis retired from the society's work in 1904, Redcliffe took his father-in-law's place and remained active for decades. Among those whom the society helped were the sculptor Jacob Epstein and the painters Mark Gertler, David Bomberg, and Bernard Meninsky. Redcliffe always took pride in having brought Epstein's case to the society in 1905. The painter Solomon J. Solomon had told Redcliffe about Epstein's promise and George Bernard Shaw and the painter William Rothenstein had also vouched for him. Redcliffe offered £20 a year for two years for Epstein's support and Rothenstein £5. Two years later, the society renewed the loan. Redcliffe later recalled that Epstein, certainly the most successful of the artists whom the society assisted, never repaid the society.[36]

Arthur Davis conveyed his enthusiasm for the "force and beauty" of ancient Hebrew texts to Elsie and Nina. With no sons, he gave his daughters a rigorous Hebrew education, teaching them himself every day of the year once they reached the age of four. When they grew older, the lessons lasted from seven to eight each morning. Nothing was allowed to interfere with them. Nina's lessons continued until she reached the age of eighteen, by which time she was an accomplished Hebraist. She published her first translation of a medieval Hebrew poem, "The Song of Chess," in the London *Jewish Chronicle* in 1894, when she was seventeen.[37] The poem, often attributed to the twelfth-century philosopher and biblical commentator Abraham ibn Ezra, is one of the oldest extant descriptions of the rules of chess. That same year, she published a translation of a Talmudic passage (B. Taanit 16 a and b) and a poem of her own that it inspired, "The Ideal Minister of the Talmud," in the *Jewish Quarterly Review*, the scholarly journal edited by Claude Montefiore and Israel Abrahams. The *mishnah* on which the *gemara* comments concerns the order of the liturgy for fast days. The *amoraim* play on a phrase in the *mishnah*—"they stood in prayer"—to ask who is qualified to be appointed to a leadership role. Nina built on this phrase to describe, in verse, the ideal minister, the Anglo-Jewish term for its religious officiants, most of whom lacked rabbinical ordination and whose public duties included reading the Torah and delivering sermons. Most of what she wrote was conventional. Two themes, however, reflect matters about which she cared passionately throughout her life. The first was the centrality of the reading of the Torah in the synagogue and the power of the Hebrew language:

> The sacred words sink deep in every heart,
> And leave an impress of authority,
> Holding them there with true and mighty force.

The second was the hope for national redemption. When the ideal minister reads from the Torah, "telling of glory which hath passed away," he echoes God's voice and inspires his listeners "with hope that yet once more/The glory will return which hath been theirs." The theme was, of course, a traditional one, but one that preoccupied her and inspired or meshed with her interest in the medieval poet Yehudah Ha-Levi, and, later, with her support for Zionism.[38]

Between 1894 and 1900, Nina published two dozen translations of medieval Hebrew poems in the *Jewish Quarterly Review*, ten of them by Yehudah Ha-Levi, whose poetry was the focus of her later work. Her translation activity in this period culminated in the 1901 publication of *Songs of Exile by Hebrew Poets* by the Jewish Publication Society of America. Israel Zangwill, whose novel *The Children of the Ghetto* the society published in 1892, had introduced Mayer Sulzberger, chair of its publication committee, to her work in 1898.[39] Her honorarium was £50, in exchange for which she assigned the rights to the publisher.[40] The title she chose for the collection was significant, but I will reserve an account of her scholarly work for later; for now, it is sufficient to say that, before her marriage to Redcliffe, she was already known as a poet and a translator, at least in the English-speaking Jewish world.

There is no question that Nina's immersion in classical Judaica, her traditional upbringing, her inbred antiassimilationism, and her commitment to the renewal of Jewish culture had a decisive impact on Redcliffe's thinking and what he did with his life. To be sure, there is evidence that, even before their engagement, questions about the fate and future of the Jews already occupied him. Still, it is not far-fetched to imagine his life taking a very different course had he married someone else. One only has to contrast his life with that of his brothers and sisters. A few of them—Jennie (1865–1921), Clement (1868–1935), Isabelle, and Bessie, in particular—took an interest in Jewish matters, but none did so with the time-and-energy-consuming devotion that he did, giving over days and nights to his many committees and campaigns. Several other of his siblings, moreover, simply had little to do with the organized Jewish community, while others intermarried and drifted away. His brother Elkin (1870–1919) had his children baptized.

3

In the four months after their engagement, while he was in Berlin and she in London, they wrote frequently and lengthily, with great seriousness, about Jewish matters. To some extent, they were getting to know each other, discovering the other's thoughts about what a Jewish marriage and home were, what they would observe and not observe, and what they expected of each other. They had not, after all, known each other well before their engagement, and this was their first extended opportunity to become familiar. In

Redcliffe's case, this was also in all likelihood the first time that he articulated his views about the nature of Jewishness and the obligations it imposed. The correspondence ushered in a degree of self-reflection and self-definition that was probably new to him. In any case, it offers us a rich view of their thinking at the time.

From their letters, it emerges that both Redcliffe and Nina were alert to the drift and defection that were increasingly characteristic of well-acculturated, upper-middle-class Jews in England and elsewhere in Western Europe.[41] They wrote with scorn and anger, as well as regret and sadness, about those who did not want to be Jews and chose to hide or flee their Jewishness. Redcliffe's chief example was the Jewish family from whom he rented a room in Berlin, the Meyers. The couple had had their teenage son, Hans, baptized—as "a commercial speculation"—on the advice of an uncle. Redcliffe thought his parents, who were unobservant but had only Jewish friends, had miscalculated since the *getaufter Knabe* [baptized lad] (as he called him) was a "Jew in face" and could never pass as a Christian.[42] He also learned from Frau Meyer that among Berlin Jewish families the question of whether to raise the children as Christians or Jews was openly and frequently discussed.[43] In general, the Berlin Jews whom Redcliffe encountered did not impress him. One incident, in particular, troubled him. While accompanying the Meyers to a beer garden, the behavior of "some very common showy Jewish girls" at a nearby table upset him. His comments about them to Frau Meyer were sufficiently pejorative that Herr Meyer jokingly accused him of being an antisemite. In telling Nina about the incident, he explained that he was unable to restrain himself: "I detest so to see Jews making real fools of themselves and *masquerading* [my emphasis] that I can't help being bitter. And because they are Jews, I cannot excuse them. Of course, I know that I am far too critical about others. . . . I sometimes feel I can see the skeleton of perpetual grief behind the money, wrapping, and jewels of these people."[44] His reaction was similar when he attended synagogue on Yom Kippur in Berlin. The congregants grated on him. "I seem to see 'No Dignity' written on all their faces and in synagogue[.] I too often got appalled by the total lack of dignity of the people—no respect, either for men, much less their God."[45]

For her part, Nina wrote frequently about women from her circle of friends and acquaintances who were intermarrying. Olga d'Avigdor, for example, met Frank Fletcher, a teacher in one of the London Board Schools

48 | *The Last Anglo-Jewish Gentleman*

with a largely Jewish student body, at a club in the Whitechapel Road for social and charity workers in the East End. D'Avigdor came from a family deeply involved in communal life and, before her marriage, she was known for her work with educational charities.[46] May Marion Hartog, the daughter of the zoologist Marcus Hartog, was engaged to William Cramp, a lecturer in electrical engineering at the Central Technical College in South Kensington. She had met her future husband at the home of the electrical engineer William Ayrton, whose second wife, the pioneering woman electrical engineer Hertha Marks, was her cousin. Nina's father consequently told her and Elsie that they might not invite May to their house. Nina let Redcliffe know that she would have liked to invite May to their own wedding, but that it was impossible now.[47] She also wrote him of the intermarriage of her cousin Marcus Davis. The tragedy, she noted correctly, was that the descendants of mixed marriage were always lost to Judaism.[48] In the case of May Hartog, Redcliffe thought it a pity that "such a brilliant family as the Hartogs should be lost to the Jews." But he also acknowledged that Nina was correct in noting that she was "nothing before and won't be much more now."[49] What was to be done? Both she and Redcliffe agreed that the right kind of Jewish education was the best way to prevent intermarriage— by which he meant, an education that allowed Jewish youth to themselves recognize "the advantages of a united front." Yet he was not sure that social ostracism was the best course. He, for one, wanted to invite May to their wedding, and thought that the "dodging around waiting to see whether people are received or not" was "childish." With what Nina had told him about May's upbringing, he thought there was far more reason not to receive May's *parents*. At the same time, Nina's news about May aroused his intellectual curiosity. Anticipating his later work on race science, he asked whether it would it be possible to study whether "the monotheistic spirit of Judaism" survived uncontaminated over several generations of intermarriage. If it did, then ostracism made no sense, since, in his view, the ethical dimension of Judaism trumped its other aspects.[50]

Intermarriage also became an immediate family issue. While Redcliffe was in Berlin, his brother Clement became engaged to an actress and former child performer, Dora Tulloch, who was not Jewish. Nina kept him informed of the drama that unfolded at Mill Hill after the announcement of their engagement. Neither Redcliffe's mother nor Dora's mother was happy about the match. His mother did not happily receive congratulations, and Nina, not wanting to upset her future mother-in-law, wondered whether she should even write to Clement to offer her congratulations. It was then decided that Morris Joseph, rabbi of the Reform synagogue, would convert Dora after a few weeks of instruction. (No Orthodox rabbi would have converted her under the circumstances.) But Sarah Salaman still confided to Nina how terribly disappointed she was with Clement's choice. "Of course, she sees how much worse it might be," she wrote to Redcliffe. The synagogue wedding was quiet and unconventional. No formal invitations were sent out and there was no celebration after the ceremony.[51] Dora retired from the stage after marrying, but her conversion failed to placate Sarah Salaman. Her conversion led Nina to write Redcliffe that she had never been able to understand the objections of Jews to voluntary converts. She then immediately proposed an explanation: "Perhaps it is that lately the conversion has become a farce—the man only caring to get through the form & go back to no religion at all, & the wife, finding none & perhaps going back to the old one & bringing up the children as Christians since she knows nothing of Judaism."[52] Nina's account of conversions of convenience was accurate in Dora's case. None of her and Clement's children remained within the Jewish community and she was buried in the churchyard near their home in Treborough, Somerset. In another letter, she suggested that Jewish objections to intermarriage, even with the conversion of the non-Jewish partner, were due to "an instinct of self-preservation."[53]

Redcliffe and Nina both deplored radical assimilation, but they clashed and wrangled at length over the role of ritual observance in Jewish life. Indeed, this issue more than any other took center stage in their correspondence. Neither of them accepted the doctrine, the bedrock of strict Orthodoxy, that Jews must observe the *mitsvot* because God commanded them to do so at Sinai (whether or not they served some other purpose). Nina, having grown up in a traditional home, accepted observance in an almost matter-of-fact way. She told Redcliffe that she was more interested in the beauty of a custom and the feelings it evoked than in its "why & wherefore, even if it is a little custom which only reminds us of our Eastern origin," such as men covering their heads at prayer. For her, the ideas undergirding the *mitsvot* were not the most important reason for observing them. Yet she also assigned a positive value to the keeping of the *mitsvot*. Restrictions— she was referring primarily to the laws prohibiting work on the Sabbath and the Festivals—were for people who would otherwise never reflect on the spirit of Judaism. Once "the spirit of the thing" permeated an individual's life, the regulations became unnecessary—or unnoticeable, since they had become an intrinsic part of his or her life.[54] She believed that the thoughtless, wholesale discarding of traditions, which she called a turning away from "reasonable" Orthodoxy, came from "people blaming the thing itself instead of blaming the wrong employment of it."[55] When they fetishized (my term, not hers) ritual, it became an end in itself. Her example was fasting on Yom Kippur, which many Jews viewed as essential in itself, the end-all and be-all—to the extent that that they marginalized fasting's spiritual goals.[56] The "enlightened" Orthodox, with whom she grouped herself, must not move too fast and discard traditions if they wanted the "ignorant" Orthodox to follow their example. Forms were necessary for the regeneration of Judaism because they were reminders of deeper spiritual matters. For herself, she liked "the knowledge that we do these things because we are Jews & that they are continual symbols & reminders of our distinctive part in the world." But, she assured Redcliffe, she did not feel it was "<u>wrong</u> to do this or not to do that"; together, once they were married, they would be able "to judge & blend & and do what we decide is the best."[57]

Nina's position was closer to orthopraxis than orthodoxy. She had made her position clear in an article in the *Jewish Quarterly Review* in 1901, which appeared before her engagement, in which she rejected the notion that Judaism had "dogmas." In the article, she emphasized its pluralism, its admission of many interpretations: "there are probably nearly as many aspects of Judaism as there are variously poised Jewish minds."[58] Thus, her Judaism was individualistic, voluntaristic, and selective; it allowed her to pick and choose. In this sense, it was a quintessentially modern religion. It was also bibliocentric, like her father's Judaism. As she wrote in the 1901 article, the Bible was "the source of Judaism." Her Judaism stressed "a whole-hearted reverence and loyal allegiance, a whole-hearted recognition and thankfulness that by means of a book we have been enabled to learn, if we will, all that man can know of righteousness and of God."[59] Her position was in tension with rabbinic tradition, which was at the heart of most varieties of Orthodoxy then and now. Rabbinic Judaism, from its inception, emphasized the dual nature of the Law (written and oral, biblical and rabbinic) and their inseparability and harmony. She owed the bibliocentricity of her Judaism to her father and he, in turn, to a long-standing, peculiarly Anglo-Jewish religious current.

For all of its flexibility and modernity, Nina's defense of tradition made Redcliffe testy. He was not an observant Jew and had never felt less Jewish by not observing. He wrote to her soon after leaving for Berlin that too "excessive" a regard for keeping customs led not only to irreligion but to replacing it. Whatever obligations being a Jew entailed (he was not sure of what they were) they were too serious to be "a mere dependent on the bylaws of a kitchen and the regulations of a boarding school." While he insisted that religion should not be "a burden that only galls and never comforts," he also recognized that "what to others is a burden is to you a pleasure." As for him, he had told her earlier, in July, "I shall not pay much attention to customs."[60] That was not what she wanted to hear. At the end of the month, he reassured her that, while he was not trying to combat Orthodoxy, he would not observe the second day of the Festivals. The question of second days was "so extravagant that there should be no need for a second thought."[61] And in early September he again told her that he would not observe the second day when they were married, noting that the only reason she had given him for observing it was "a ludicrous complaint that they hadn't a telegraphic system in Palestine."[62] (In antiquity an extra day was added to each of the Festivals outside the Land of Israel—except Yom Kippur—because of uncertainty of the day on which the Sanhedrin announced the New Moon, on which the calculation of the Festival day depended.)

The sharp tone of Redcliffe's remarks about Jewish observance continued through most of September. On September 17, he wrote her that he could never be consistently Orthodox or even see things from that perspective, telling her that he had such a horror of restrictions that he got "absurdly excited." He also told her that he could not live as her father did—"I should die." To not travel freely on the Sabbath and the Festivals was a travesty. "To be hourly dependent on the presence of a kosher butcher or a railway line to bring indifferent food from a neighbouring town surely is not the meaning of the Mosaic law."[63] Two days later, he wrote that he could never agree to "the hemming in of all one's senses" and "the blind followings."[64] Redcliffe's unrelenting attacks on Jewish observance troubled Nina, who repeatedly told him that she feared that their attitudes were incompatible. Sensing the strength of his feeling, she also felt it necessary to reassure him that, once they were together, they would be able to work things out. In the spirit of selectivity, she wrote that once married they would make their own life and their own religion together, living as they saw fit. They would have one religion, not two, and both be true to themselves and loyal to the Jewish people.[65] At last he became aware of how offensive his remarks were to her and, on September 21, the eve of Yom Kippur, apologized, asking what he could do to make up for hurting her.[66]

Their disagreement was not an academic exercise. On both sides, it touched on matters of self-definition and self-concept. There was also an immediate, emotional dimension to the conflict. During the four months that Redcliffe was in Berlin, they wrote to each other at least once a day, often twice a day. It was a passionate correspondence in every way. They knew exactly the times when mail was picked up and when it was delivered and waited eagerly for each other's letters. Because Nina did not write on the Sabbath or on the Festivals, however, there were days when Redcliffe received no letters from her. In the newness of their relationship and the intensity of his feelings for her, the gap was intolerable to him. The Sabbaths and Festivals, he argued more generally, were not intended to separate people and inflict suffering. They should be times of joy. He objected, he told her, to any proscription that harmed one's mind or body on what was supposed to be a day of rest and peace.[67] On August 31 she wrote for the first time in her life on the Sabbath while home sick in bed.[68]

In some ways, Redcliffe's position was close to that of Reform Judaism. Interiority and ethics seemed to take precedence over the laws of the Torah. "The truest religion is that which a man feels inside him."[69] And the Jews whom other Jews looked up to were those who had done something for others, not those who were strictly observant.[70] It would nevertheless be an error to label him a Reform Jew. In fact, he was very hostile to Reform Judaism, at least the form it took in Germany and the United States. In part, his hostility was due to its strong assimilationist stance and its rejection of the national character of the Jewish people. And, in part, it was due to the extreme way Reform labored to remake Judaism, often in order to diminish Jewish distinctiveness. While in Berlin, he attended a Sunday service (a replacement for the traditional Saturday morning service) at the radical Reform congregation there. He was struck by the fact that the men were hatless and that the entire service was in German. Reform, he thought, had "entirely overshot the mark" by trying to make Jews "identical with the heathens." Rather, the goal should be to render "the garments of Judaism more up-to-date so that their incongruity should not so attract the eye that the figure inside is lost sight of."[71]

Running throughout their correspondence and intertwined with the issues of both observance and continuity was an overriding concern with the nature of the ties that bound Jews together. This was, of course, the central theme in the public debate on the Jewish Question. By this time, Redcliffe was utterly convinced of the racial character of the Jews. Race, not religion and not nationality, held them together. In an extraordinary declaration for an upper-middle-class English Jew, he wrote to her that the Polish Jew was a brother to him, however much they differed over religion. The "scientific" (that is, secular) Jew felt himself a brother to all Jews.[72] He was even thinking of undertaking a study "to show how and why the 'Jewish' mind and the actions that follow therefrom are different to other minds."[73] As for the love of Zion, it was "a gift or a cult" but hardly "an inherited quality." He felt "no duty or service" to the Land of Israel as he did to England and thus harbored no "Zionist patriotism"—feelings that changed during World War I.

Nina was less sure than Redcliffe about the respective strength of the ties of race, religion, and nationhood. She would have liked "a feeling of religious brotherhood" to be the strongest bond, but with the great majority of Jews such was clearly not true. She also felt that the extent to which each exerted influence varied from person to person. Yet, like Redcliffe, she felt more akin to a foreign Jew than to an English Christian, a bond that she defined as partly racial and partly national—by which she meant "a patriotic feeling that 'far away and long ago' we had a country of our own." In this sense, Nina was a Zionist in embryo. But, having declared her nationalist sentiments, she then retreated in the very same letter. Since religion was the meaning of Jewish existence, the combination of religion and nationalism in one country would be "much too strong" and would imperil the Jewish religion. In any case, she concluded that it was better for the Jews to have the whole world as their Zion.

Their correspondence concluded at the end of September when Redcliffe returned from Berlin to London. On October 23 they were married at the New West End Synagogue. The wedding was impressive and formal. Chief Rabbi Hermann Adler officiated, the service was fully choral, and the sanctuary was bedecked with flowers and palm trees. Nina wore a gown of white satin and chiffon, decorated with real orange blossoms. A flat wreath of orange blossoms rested on her head. Young Clement Davis, a son of Nina's uncle Edward and Redcliffe's sister Isabelle, wearing a white satin suit and a white felt cavalier hat, held the train. Foreshadowing their later intense attachment to the idea of the return to Zion, the glass that Redcliffe shattered with his foot at the end of the ceremony was not an ordinary water glass but a specially made glass, with a twisted stem, engraved in Hebrew with the words "If I set not Jerusalem above my memory of the sanctuary which is desolate." Along with their many kin, the congregation included the Wanderers (and their families), members of the Anglo-Jewish

54 | *The Last Anglo-Jewish Gentleman*

notability (Montagus, Samuels, Franklins, and Mocattas), the extended Adler clan, and Israel Zangwill and his brother Louis, along with the Zangwills' mother and sisters.[74] After a reception at the Davis home in Gloucester Terrace, Redcliffe and Nina left for the Continent. They honeymooned in Brussels, Cologne, Worms, Heidelberg, Lucerne, Venice, the Austrian Tyrol, and Munich and then settled into an apartment in Berlin. Redcliffe continued his work in pathology there until September 1902, when they returned to London and Redcliffe took over the de facto directorship of the Pathological Institute of the London Hospital.[75]

Notes

1. Eugene C. Black, *The Social Politics of Anglo-Jewry, 1880–1914* (Oxford: Basil Blackwell, 1988); Geoffrey Alderman, *Modern British Jewry* (Oxford: Clarendon Press, 1992), ch. 3; David Feldman, *Englishmen and Jews: Social Relations and Political Culture, 1840–1914* (New Haven, CT: Yale University Press, 1994), part 3.

2. RNS to Cecil Roth, October 4, 1937, Add. MS 8171/12/G6, RNS CUL.

3. RNS, "Boyhood and Family Background"; RNS to Wilfred Samuel, October 4, 1951, Add. MS 8171/12/H1, RNS CUL.

4. RNS, "The Helmsman Takes Charge," LH/X/101, Royal London Hospital Archives.

5. A list of his scientific publications is appended to Kenneth M. Smith, "Redcliffe Nathan Salaman, 1874–1955," *Biographical Memoirs of Fellows of the Royal Society* 1 (1955): 238–45.

6. RNS to David Nabarro, July 18, 1946, Add. MS 8171/27, RNS CUL.

7. RNS, "Application of Redcliffe N. Salaman, Candidate for the Post of Assistant Director to the Pathological Institute of the London Hospital, January 1902," and "Biographical Notes Prepared for the Royal Society," July 1947, Add. MS 8171/27, RNS CUL.

8. RNS, "Helmsman Takes Charge." See also Lara V. Marks, *Model Mothers: Jewish Mothers and Maternity Provision in East London, 1870–1939* (Oxford: Clarendon Press, 1994).

9. RNS, "Life's Residue," Add. MS 8171/27, RNS CUL.

10. RNS to J. C. Dellar, October 11, 1929, and RNS to treasurer, North Hertfordshire Liberal Association, October 11, 1929, Add. MS 8171/1/1, RNS CUL.

11. RNS to Saemy Japhet, September 14, 1944, Add. MS 8171/1/5, RNS CUL.

12. "The Maccabaeans: List of Members, 1897/5658," MS 126/1/1; dinner book, 1911–26, Maccabaeans Papers, MS 126/1/5, HL US.

13. Todd M. Endelman, *Leaving the Jewish Fold: Conversion and Radical Assimilation in Modern Jewish History* (Princeton, NJ: Princeton University Press, 2015), 247–50.

14. RNS, "Helmsman Takes Charge."

15. RNS, *Whither Lucien Wolf's Anglo-Jewish Community?*, Lucien Wolf Memorial Lecture 1953 (London: Jewish Historical Society of England, 1954), 20–21.

16. *Jewish Chronicle*, November 28, 1902.

17. In the memoir, he writes that it was in July 1901, but that date would have been impossible, since by late June he was already engaged and writing to Nina from Berlin. On

the basis of a datebook of Nina's that has survived, it would have had to have been in May. NDS, datebook for 1901, entries for May 31 to June 6, Add. MS 8171/30, RNS CUL.

18. RNS, "Chance at the Helm," lecture, 1950, Add. MS 8171/27, RNS CUL.

19. NDS to Ray Frank, June 4, 1901, Ray Frank Litman Papers, AJHS CJH.

20. NDS, diary, 1890–91, entry for December 31, 1890, Add. MS 8171/59, RNS CUL.

21. David J. Hind, "Davis Derby—a History of Engineering," *Mining History* 14, no. 2 (Winter 1999): 1–8.

22. Esther Salaman Hamburger, Nina Salaman Wedderburn, and Miriam Polianowsky Salaman, interview by the author, London, May 22, 2000; Cathie Davis to Myer Salaman, September 9, 1955, Add. MS 8171/12, RNS CUL.

23. Norman Bentwich, "The Wanderers and Other Jewish Scholars of My Youth," *Transactions of the Jewish Historical Society of England* 20 (1964): 51–62.

24. Arthur Davis, *La-menatseah bi-neginot maskil: The Hebrew Accents of the Twenty-One Books of the Bible* (London: D. Nutt, 1892). A second edition, with a new introduction, appeared in 1900.

25. NDS, "Notes on Arthur Davis by His Daughter Nina," Add. MS 8171/12c and d, RNS CUL.

26. Herbert Adler to NDS, January 21, 1909, Add. MS 8171/59, RNS CUL.

27. Herbert Adler to NDS, November 19, 1908, Add. MS. 8171/59, RNS CUL.

28. Herbert Adler to NDS, June 5, 1908, Add. MS. 8171/59, RNS CUL.

29. Arthur Davis and Herbert Adler, eds., *Service of the Synagogue: A New Edition of the Festival Prayers with an English Translation; Day of Atonement*, 2nd ed., pt. 2 (London: George Routledge and Sons, 1905), 178.

30. NDS to RNS, June 25, 1904, Wedderburn Deposit, RNS CUL.

31. NDS to RNS, July 28 and August 8, 1901, Add. MS 8171/98, RNS CUL.

32. NDS to RNS, August 2, 1901, Add. MS 8171/98, RNS CUL.

33. RNS to Norman Bentwich, November 22, 1940, Add. MS 8171/1/4, RNS CUL; Arthur Davis to NDS, February 24, 1902, and April 8, 1903, Wedderburn Deposit, RNS CUL.

34. Arthur Davis to RNS, May 6, 1902, Wedderburn Deposit, RNS CUL.

35. On bibliocentricity in Anglo-Judaism, see Steven Singer, "Orthodox Judaism in Early Victorian England," PhD diss. (Yeshiva University, 1981); Feldman, *Englishmen and Jews*, ch. 2.

36. RNS to Norman Bentwich, November 22, 1940, Add. MS 8171/1/4, RNS CUL. See also Papers of the Educational Aid Society, Hartley Library, University of Southampton, Southampton.

37. *Jewish Chronicle*, June 22, 1894. She included it in her collection of translations, *Songs of Exile by Hebrew Poets*, trans. Nina Davis (Philadelphia: Jewish Publication Society, 1901), 126–31. The New York–based *Jewish Encyclopedia* (1901–6) reprinted her translation in full in its article "Chess."

38. NDS, "The Ideal Minister of the Talmud," *Jewish Quarterly Review* 7, no. 1 (October 1894): 141–44.

39. Israel Zangwill to NDS, September 30, 1898, Wedderburn Deposit, RNS CUL.

40. Henrietta Szold to Israel Zangwill, February 7, 1899, Wedderburn Deposit, RNS CUL.

41. Todd M. Endelman, *Radical Assimilation in Anglo-Jewish History, 1656–1945* (Bloomington: Indiana University Press, 1990), ch. 3; Endelman, *Leaving the Jewish Fold*, ch. 3.

42. RNS to NDS, August 15 and 18, 1901, Add. MS 8171/97, RNS CUL.

43. RNS to NDS, August 25, 1901, Add. MS 8171/97, RNS CUL.

44. RNS to NDS, August 16, 1901, Add. MS 8171/97, RNS CUL.

56 | *The Last Anglo-Jewish Gentleman*

45. RNS to NDS, September 23, 1901, Add. MS 8171/98, RNS CUL.

46. NDS to RNS, August 16 and 17, 1901, Add. MS 8171/98, RNS CUL.

47. NDS to RNS, September 10, 1901, Add. MS. 8171/98, RNS CUL.

48. NDS to RNS, September 22, 1901, Add. MS. 8171/98, RNS CUL.

49. RNS to NDS, September 10, 1901, Add. MS. 8171/97, RNS CUL.

50. RNS to NDS, September 20, 1901, Add. MS 8171/97, RNS CUL.

51. NDS to RNS, July 4, 6, 13, 14, and 15, August 21, 1901, Add. MS 8171/98, RNS CUL.

52. NDS to RNS, July 16, 1901, Add. MS 8171/98, RNS CUL.

53. NDS to RNS, August 21, 1901, Add. MS 8171/98, RNS CUL.

54. NDS to RNS, September 10, 1901, Add. MS 8171/98, RNS CUL.

55. NDS to RNS, September 17, 1901, Add. MS 8171/98, RNS CUL.

56. NDS to RNS, September 21, 1901, Add. MS 8171/98, RNS CUL. Redcliffe had already told her that he objected to the fetishization of fasting, but, as he often did, he had put the matter more sharply: it made him sick to hear Jews—even educated Orthodox Jews—ask "Did you fast well?" It was "disgusting" (RNS to NDS, September 5, 1901, Add. MS 8171/97, RNS CUL).

57. NDS to RNS, September 19, 1901, Add. MS 8171/98, RNS CUL.

58. Nina Davis, "An Aspect of Judaism in 1901," *Jewish Quarterly Review* 13, no. 2 (January 1901), 243.

59. Ibid., 246.

60. RNS to NDS, July 5, 1901, Add. MS 8171/97, RNS CUL.

61. RNS to NDS, July 26, 1901, Add. MS 8171/97, RNS CUL.

62. RNS to NDS, September 8, 1901, Add. MS 8171/97, RNS CUL.

63. RNS to NDS, September 17, 1901, Add. MS 8171/97, RNS CUL.

64. RNS to NDS, September 19, 1901, Add. MS CUULS to NDS, September 19, 1901, RNS 8171/97, RNS CUL.

65. RNS to NDS, September 17, 1901, Add. MS 8171/97, RNS CUL.

66. RNS to NDS, September 21, 1901, Add. MS 8171/97, RNS CUL.

67. RNS to NDS, September 9, 1901, Add. MS 8171/97, RNS CUL.

68. NDS to RNS, August 31, 1901, Add. MS 8171/98, RNS CUL.

69. RNS to NDS, August 22, 1901, Add. MS 8171/97, RNS CUL.

70. RNS to NDS, September 21, 1901, Add. MS 8171/97, RNS CUL.

71. RNS to NDS, September 24, 1901, Add. MS 8171/97, RNS CUL.

72. RNS to NDS, July 16, 1901, Add. MS 8171/97.

73. RNS to NDS, August 12, 1901, Add. MS 8171/97, RNS CUL.

74. *Jewish Chronicle*, October 25, 1901.

75. RNS to David Nabarro, July 18, 1946, Add. MS 8171/27; NDS, date book, 1901, Wedderburn Deposit, RNS CUL.

3

HOMESTALL

1

When Redcliffe and Nina returned to London in 1902, their life together unfolded uneventfully at first. They lived with his mother at Mill Hill while looking for a house for themselves—and for their first child, Myer Head Salaman (1902–95), who had been born in Berlin on August 2. (He was named after Redcliffe's father and after his mentor at the London Hospital, the neurologist Henry Head.) The house they found, Frognal End, which had been built for the recently deceased man-of-letters Walter Besant, was in Frognal Gardens in the old part of Hampstead, not far from the Heath. They did some work on the house and in December moved in. On March 4, 1904, Nina gave birth to twin boys, Arthur Gabriel (1904–64) and Edward Michael (1904–13).

Redcliffe, who had taken up his post at the London Hospital immediately on his return, was soon consumed by his work as teacher, administrator, and researcher. Traveling to the East End of London from Hampstead each weekday, he launched the Pathological Institute, supervising the opening and equipping of its new building, hired a fellow Cambridge man, Geoffrey Slade, to assist him, lectured twice a week to students, and continued his own research. A major problem for him was the dreadful state of the post-mortems the hospital's physicians were then conducting, as I mentioned earlier. Symptomatic of their backwardness, he told a clinical pathologist in 1946, was their failure to dissect the posterior ganglia and to expose and examine the thoracic duct, now standard procedures. Gradually he persuaded the physicians to relinquish their rights. He himself performed about 1,300 post-mortems during his first year. Because the nominal director of the institute, the bacteriologist William Bulloch, never set foot in the building, the burden of administration fell entirely on his shoulders.[1]

58 | *The Last Anglo-Jewish Gentleman*

Then misfortune struck and his life took an unexpected course. One morning, in November 1904, without warning, he began to spit blood. He had become infected with a tubercular bacillus,[2] probably from his work at the institute. He was not the only member of the hospital staff whom tuberculosis struck at the time. In the two years since his return, four young doctors at the London Hospital had died and many more had fallen ill but recovered. His own assistant, Slade, died about six months after his own collapse from the infection. Overwork and exhaustion contributed to weakening his resistance and that of the others who fell ill. His own, self-imposed, work habits were punishing, in addition to which the hospital, which was short of staff at all levels, was a hard taskmaster and exploited its junior members. In reference to the sweatshops of the East End, Redcliffe described the hospital's treatment of them as "super-sweating."[3] On November 21, he informed the hospital's governing board that he would be leaving the Pathological Institute for at least six months to recover in Egypt.[4] He chose Egypt because his friend Charles Myers, who had suffered a similar health breakdown, had gone there to recuperate. But his doctor told him that doing so was a mistake because, instead of resting, Redcliffe would rush around looking at pyramids and mummies. And thus Switzerland replaced Egypt, much to Nina's disappointment. Gustave Schorstein, a house physician at the London Hospital with a particular interest in tuberculosis (he was also the brother-in-law of Claude Goldsmid Montefiore), told him of a small, out-of-the-way village, at an altitude of more than five thousand feet, where he might regain his health—Montana sur Sierre, in the heart of the French-speaking Alps, in the canton of Valais.[5]

Having decided on Switzerland, Redcliffe moved to a residential hotel, The Knowle, in the coastal resort of Sidmouth, South Devon, on the Channel. He rested there while Nina remained at home in Hampstead, weaning the twins. They then rented out their house, left the three boys and their nanny at Redcliffe's mother's in Mill Hill, his doctor having told him not to take the children with them, and departed for Switzerland. After reaching Vevey, on Lake Geneva, they took a sled to the village. The small hotel where they stayed was a wooden, chalet-like building, with no more than twenty visitors at a time. Their room, with large French windows, opened onto a spacious, south-facing verandah, with the whole range of the Bernese Alps facing them. For three months, from breakfast to dinner, he lay on a chaise lounge on the verandah, reading, watching the play of light on the mountain opposite, and dozing. In March 1905, in order to escape the thaw in Montana, they moved to the Grand Hôtel du Righi Vaudois in Glion, overlooking Lake Geneva, not far from Montreux. By this time, Redcliffe was on the road to recovery, having gained twenty-five pounds since he first fell ill. They returned to London at the beginning of June 1905.[6]

Although his health was much improved, Redcliffe realized that he could not continue to live and work as he had and that he needed to reorient his life. Free of the need to earn a living because of his inheritance, he and Nina decided to live in the country, since it would be good for his health and they would not need to go abroad in the winter and separate from the children. In October, while driving in the country, they came across Homestall, a house on the edge of the village of Barley, in northern Hertfordshire, about fourteen miles from Cambridge, on the road from Royston to Saffron Walden. (See fig. 3.1.) They quickly decided to buy the house and moved there in November.[7] Homestall was originally a Tudor farmhouse, but, in the nineteenth century, much enlarged, it became the country home of families whose wealth had been made elsewhere. In the late nineteenth century, Charles Mavor, a stockbroker, had added a large wing on the east end, including a master bedroom suite and a billiard room (which became Redcliffe's study). While not a grand country house, Homestall was a substantial residence. In 1913, Redcliffe added an arts-and-crafts nursery wing on the west end (fig. 3.2), designed by the architect and urban designer Richard Barry Parker, who is best known for his work on Letchworth Garden City. A granddaughter described the house, with its many additions, as "a curious hotchpotch and not conventionally beautiful."[8] The most prominent features of the addition were, in Nicholas Pevsner's words, "the very large brick chimney of clustered shafts, and the water-cum-viewing tower with overhanging top storey and concave pagoda-like roof with cupola."[9] The conspicuous tower was intended to be Nina's study, but it turned out to be too drafty for her to use it. Redcliffe and Nina embossed their initials and the date—RNS 1913 NDS—on the lead gutters and mounted a weather vane with the Hebrew letter *shin* on the tower, a reference to the Hebrew spelling of the family name (fig. 3.3). When the 1913 addition was completed, Homestall included eight bedrooms, a large hall, a dining room, a library, a nursery, and Nina's tower retreat.

Homestall, Redcliffe's home until his death in 1955, came to play an outsize role in his life. Barley was a small village—its population in 1901 was 505—and Homestall was the most notable house in the village. Redcliffe, by virtue of his occupation of the house and the wealth that allowed him

Figure 3.1. Homestall, Barley. Collection of the author.

Figure 3.2. The arts-and-crafts nursery wing of Homestall (1913). Collection of the author.

Figure 3.3. The weather vane at Homestall, topped by the Hebrew letter *shin*, a reference to the Hebrew root (*shalom*) of the family name. Collection of the author.

to live there, became the most prominent personage in the village and the neighborhood. The authority he came to wield was not rooted in law but in the social conventions of the English countryside, where deference to the wealthy was still alive, even in the early twentieth century. He became, in effect, the village squire. As such, for example, he hosted balls in his barn for the servants from area homes. While not groomed for that role by birth—what Jew was?—he seemed to experience little difficulty in assuming it. His privileged upbringing and his education, at St. Paul's and Cambridge, bestowed on him the bearing and the manners to play the role. Gentility, the amorphous quality that distinguished gentle folk from the mass of Britons, was integral to his outlook, behavior, self-perception, and public persona. In the eyes of the villagers, Redcliffe was undoubtedly a gentleman. Moreover, the fact that he did not soil his hands in commerce but was independently wealthy, living off the accumulated profits of ostrich feathers and London real estate, also enhanced his status. (This also gave him the time to immerse himself in local affairs.) He was also accustomed to country life and recreations having spent so much of his youth at Mill Hill. He strode country lanes, rode, and hunted foxes with confidence.

Redcliffe even took up farming briefly. A few years after settling in Barley, still under the influence of a youthful romanticism that glorified the landowner and the cultivator, he decided that buying some agricultural land and farming would add enormously to living in the country. At the time, there were no farms on the market in the neighborhood, which was dominated by large landowners. And so, he put the idea aside and largely forgot it. Then, by chance, one of the biggest landowners in the area decided to sell a 150-acre farm, opposite Homestall, that he had previously put out to lease. But the venture was not profitable, and Redcliffe gave up farming at the end of World War I. To celebrate the termination of what had become a financial drain, he purchased a portrait by Thomas Benjamin Kennington of an Arab chief who had fought with T. E. Lawrence.[10] (This was after his return from Egypt and Palestine, when he was under the influence of a different kind of romanticism.)

Redcliffe was hardly the first English Jew to root himself in the countryside. Since the Georgian period, Jews who had made their fortunes in London had purchased country homes, imitating the behavior of upwardly mobile Britons of whatever origins.[11] For them, the acquisition of a country property was not necessarily a strategic step toward full social integration—that is, it was not a conscious assimilatory move (whatever its long-term consequences) but a widely accepted marker of material success. In most cases, they did not reside full-time in the country but continued to live and work most of the year in London. Redcliffe was unusual in that Homestall was his only home. When he and his family went to London by train (Barley was three miles from Royston, on the Cambridge-King's Cross line), they stayed with his mother or with one of his siblings.

As a Jew, however, an additional layer of complexity attached itself, at least potentially, to Redcliffe's transformation into a country gentleman and village squire. From the early Victorian period until the mid-twentieth century, English society, at least the property-owning part of it, was preoccupied with defining who was and who was not a gentleman.[12] The question obsessed novelists, journalists, critics, and moralists. The continual expansion of the upper middle class forced the traditional, land-based elite to clarify repeatedly the meaning of gentility, since the possession of wealth alone was not a sufficient criterion. Wealth continued to count, of course, but so did birth and how wealth was acquired. As Anthony Trollope, a frequent critic of nouveau-riche Jews, observed in *The Prime Minister* (1876), "It is certainly of service to a man to know who were his grandfathers and who were his grandmothers if he entertain an ambition to move in the upper circles of society."[13] Observers invoked less tangible markers of gentility as well, especially from the mid-nineteenth century. They included, in no particular order, morality, honor, selflessness, generosity, loyalty, trustworthiness, courage, self-control, responsibility, independence, manliness, sociability, sound principles, good taste, and a fondness for country recreations. Gentility was a measure of socioeconomic status and a standard of conduct. In the end, the final arbiters of who was and who was not a gentleman were those whose approval and acceptance aspirants to gentility were seeking. One could not merely declare oneself a gentleman. One had to be acknowledged as such—by visible signs of acceptance, such as invitations to country house weekends, balls and dinners, and membership in clubs and societies.

If gentility was problematic for the Victorian newly wealthy in general, then how much the more so was it for Jews. Often they were self-made men of foreign birth or of recent foreign descent. Their wealth was new, rather than inherited, and derived from commerce and finance, rather than from agricultural land. They were also, frequently, uncanny objects of suspicion and distrust. Even those who possessed great fortunes, wide culture, and social polish found themselves the targets of snide comments and whispered asides rooted in centuries-old beliefs about Jewish deviousness, untrustworthiness, and covetousness.

Redcliffe did not suffer from the alleged defects of being a foreigner or a self-made man. He was polished, well-spoken, educated, beautifully but not flashily dressed, and accustomed to living well from birth. Moreover, neither he nor Nina, like their parents before them, was a social climber, like so many of the Jews who populated Victorian fiction. They were too serious minded, too critical minded, and too immersed in Jewish life to worship at the altar of ancient titles and long pedigrees. In that sense, Victorian and Edwardian fiction is not a good reflection of their experience in Hertfordshire. Redcliffe was accepted as the most prominent personage in the neighborhood. To be sure, he and Nina belonged to a different stratum of society than the other inhabitants of the village, and so they did not mix socially

64 | *The Last Anglo-Jewish Gentleman*

with them, other than at customary times and in customary settings, such as the village flower show. Those who were invited to dine at Homestall were professionals, scientists, and men of letters who lived in the area or in Cambridge. Or they were visitors from London—an endless stream of family, friends, and coworkers on communal projects. But, from the start, Redcliffe and Nina did receive the visible marks of recognition and acceptance that were their due as the occupants of Homestall. Soon after Redcliffe's arrival, he was appointed secretary of the Barley debating society. (The topics that year included gardening, beekeeping, small holdings, and women's suffrage, in favor of which the majority of members voted.)[14] In 1907, he was appointed to the Royston magistrate's bench, on which he served until he was obliged to retire at the age of seventy-five, his last twenty-three years as its chairman. He frequently attended the Hertford and St. Alban's Quarter Sessions appeal committee and for decades headed the parish council.[15] He also served as president of the Royston Liberal Association from 1907 to 1929. Especially important to Redcliffe was his membership in the Duodecimo Society, to which he was elected in 1913. Founded in 1891, it was "a small select company of liberal-minded souls [in the area] who from time to time met in each other's houses" for talks and discussions. He served as president in 1922 and 1929 and delivered a regular stream of papers, beginning in 1912 with one on nature versus nurture.[16]

Redcliffe's acceptance was not universal, however. While he never portrayed himself as a victim of anti-Jewish hostility, he was sensitive to the exclusions and slights that beset English Jews in countless ways, and he was active in the campaign against the more virulent antisemitism of the 1930s. On occasion, even in the benign surroundings of the English countryside, his Jewishness was thrown in his face. In March 1910, when he was an unsuccessful Liberal candidate for the Hertfordshire County Council, his opponent, Edward T. Morris, characterized him as a foreigner, telling voters at an election meeting at the Royston town hall that they did not need "a man from Jerusalem to look after their roads." Redcliffe responded that he was born in England, that his family had been there for two hundred years, and that he had spent the first thirty years of his life living on his father's estate, which was separated from Hertfordshire only by a ditch. He told the audience that if Benjamin Disraeli, a Jew, had looked after the empire, he, Redcliffe Salaman, could be trusted to look after their footpaths. He also reminded Morris that his reference to "a man from Jerusalem" should have called to mind "the man from Jerusalem" whom Morris publicly professed to worship and imitate.[17]

Decades later, during World War II, when Redcliffe and the Anglican historian of Jewish-Christian relations James Parkes, a resident of Barley since 1935, supported the prosecution of the local, child-molesting rector, John Rutherford Gardiner, much of the village turned against him, at least temporarily. Gardiner, who had come to Barley in 1928, had been abusing boys in the parish for some time, but he crowned his iniquities, as Parkes put it, when he turned his attention to boys who had been evacuated there from London. In spring 1941, Redcliffe notified the chief constable, who sent detectives to the village to investigate. Gardiner confessed to them and to the bishop, who told him to resign. This he ostensibly did, but meanwhile he begged Redcliffe and Parkes to plead with the chief constable on his behalf. They agreed, for they were content simply to see him leave Barley, but then they discovered that he had not sent a letter of resignation to the bishop but a letter negotiating for a pension. He was tried and sentenced to nine months in a mental institution. Many of the villagers rallied around Gardiner, viewing him as an innocent, persecuted saint, "done in by spite," and were up in arms against Redcliffe and Parkes, both of whom could be cast as outsiders. "None seemed to have inquired as to whether the matter was true or whether they approved of their children being 'debauched,'" Redcliffe wrote to his daughter Esther. The rancor lasted for several years. In 1942, the two men were absurdly accused of climbing into the Barley church roof to steal wooden beams for cottages that Redcliffe owned in the village. And in 1945, at the first election after the end of the war, when Labour ousted the Tories, the villagers declined to reelect Salaman and Parkes as the chairman and vice chairman of the parish council. In their place, ironically, they elected Redcliffe's gardener and Parkes's manservant.[18]

One flagrant example of exclusion, which Redcliffe rarely mentioned, was the failure of his old college, Trinity Hall, to elect him to a fellowship. Redcliffe was associated with the university from 1926 to 1939, as the founding head of the Potato Virus Research Institute. He was a distinguished scientist whose achievements the Royal Society recognized when it elected him as a fellow in 1935, and he was also eminently clubbable. The college's failure to recognize his eminence in this conventional way suggests that other considerations might have been operative. Only in 1955, just before his death, did Trinity Hall elect him to an honorary fellowship. Their failure to act earlier had long rankled him; it was a deeply felt grievance, he told his daughter Esther in February 1955. One obituary writer noted that his

66 | *The Last Anglo-Jewish Gentleman*

election gave him much pleasure but then slyly added that it was a pity it had not come earlier when he might have enjoyed it.[19]

2

In his first year at Barley, with his health fully restored, Redcliffe was content to live the life of a country gentleman, a life of ease and leisure and occasional public service. But he soon tired of this way of living, fearing that he was unconsciously drifting into the role of a Jane Austen character. As he wrote in the preface to his *History and Social Influence of the Potato* (1949), "I discovered, as I believe her men would also have done, had not their careers invariably terminated with their energetic capture and mental sterilization at the altar, that 'respectability,' even with a corresponding income, is not enough. . . . Whilst in the winter months I was sufficiently occupied with hunting, in the summer, having no liking for golf, tennis, or cricket, I was at a loose end."[20] Because pursuing his interest in pathology was impossible, he cast about for scientific work that he could take up while living in the country without any institutional affiliation. He landed on the study of heredity, which at the time was attracting more attention and resources and taking new directions. His choice was not surprising, in light of his belief in the racial foundation of Jewish cohesion and his interest, already expressed while living in Berlin, in the inheritability of Jewish traits.

At nearby Cambridge, the biologist William Bateson, a fellow of St. John's from 1885 and professor of biology from 1908 to 1910, headed an informal school of genetic research that reinforced and extended the work of the Austrian monk Gregor Mendel, often described as "the father of modern genetics." Between 1856 and 1863, Mendel had researched the transmission of hereditary traits in plant hybrids—peas, specifically—in the garden of the monastery at Brno, where he taught. At that time, the common belief was that the hereditary traits of the offspring of any species were a diluted blend of the traits of their parents. Mendel had found, on the contrary, that there were dominant and recessive traits that were transmitted randomly from parents to offspring and that traits passed from parents to offspring independently of one another. Although he had experimented with pea plants, he hypothesized that traits in all living things were transmitted in the same way. In 1865, Mendel had delivered two public lectures on his results and, the following year, a local science society in Brno had published his papers in its journal, but at his death in 1884 his work was largely unknown. It was not until the end of the century that botanists and biologists studying heredity discovered and realized the importance of what became known as Mendel's laws.

Bateson, who was ignorant of Mendel's work at first, studied the transmission of traits in several animal species and concluded that when all of the individuals of a species bred together freely, their offspring did not regress to one mean form but exhibited variety. Hoping to establish definitively the true nature of the mechanisms of biological heredity, he urged scientists to carry out long-term systematic breeding experiments. His circle at Cambridge, which consisted largely of women associated with Newnham College, including his wife and her sister, carried out a series of breeding experiments. In 1900, he came across one of Mendel's articles, which he translated into English, and with the aid of one of the Newnham circle replicated Mendel's work on peas. It was Bateson who first suggested the use of the word *genetics*—in a letter in 1905—to describe the study of inheritance and the science of variation, and it was he who first used the term publicly— at an international conference on plant hybridization in London in 1906.

When Redcliffe visited Bateson in Cambridge in 1906, the latter suggested that he join the small group of amateurs and professionals whose work he was guiding. With material from Bateson, Redcliffe carried out breeding experiments at Homestall on, successively, butterflies, rhinoceros-skin mice, guinea pigs, and Breda combless poultry. All were, in his words, "more or less complete failures."[21] He then began work on hair samples of native Papuans and children of mixed Papuan-European descent, which his friend, the anthropologist Charles Seligman, who had married Redcliffe's sister Brenda (1883–1965) in 1905, had gathered on the Cooke Daniels expedition to New Guinea in 1904. While he concluded that the study of hair shapes might be promising, he found that Seligman's samples were insufficient to allow serious investigation. He next moved on to rabbit hair. Charles Chamberlain Hurst (known as "Bateson's bulldog"), one of the earliest English Mendelians, lent him his collection of rabbit pelts, which he had used to study the inheritance of coat color but which Redcliffe employed to investigate the inheritance of hair shape. In the course of his work, he discovered that in rabbits that were hybridized for coat color distribution, there was a clear segregation of characteristics in the coats of the hybrid animals, a phenomenon he named somatic segregation. He presented the results to Bateson, who was skeptical and wanted more evidence. And so, he put the work aside and did not publish it until 1919.[22]

68 | *The Last Anglo-Jewish Gentleman*

Growing increasingly frustrated, he decided to try his luck with common kitchen-variety vegetables from his own garden. He discussed the matter with his gardener, Evan Jones, who suggested potatoes, immodestly claiming to know more about the potato than any living person. He asked Jones to obtain two varieties, one with white tubers and the other with red tubers. Gesturing toward the kitchen garden, Jones declared that everything was at hand and brought him examples of two varieties—both of which, it turned out, he misidentified. With these two, he embarked in 1906 on a forty-year genetic study of the potato, at first privately in his garden at Barley. He wrote, "Whether it was mere luck, or whether the potato and I were destined for a life partnership, I do not know, but from that moment my course was set, and I became ever more involved in problems associated with a plant with which I then had no particular affinity, gustatory or romantic."[23]

Redcliffe set out to experiment with potatoes as Mendel had done with peas, crossbreeding varieties over several generations to discover which characteristics were dominant and which recessive. Soon after starting his experiments, having decided he wanted to grow some wild potato species as well, he wrote to the Royal Botanical Gardens at Kew asking them to send him a few tubers of *Solanum maglia*, a native of Argentina and the only wild species he knew by name. These tubers were supposed to have deep purple skins, but those that Kew sent had white skins. Apparently, Redcliffe subsequently learned, Kew's stock of *S. maglia* had died out and another variety of wild potato accidently received its label. Redcliffe planted the Kew tubers, later determined to be *S. edinense*, and discovered, to his surprise, that this variety of wild potato was naturally resistant to blight (*Phytophthora infestans*). In his words,

> I obtained self-fertilized seed from the parent *S. edinense* plants, which in 1909 gave rise to a family of forty plants. Blight was particularly bad that year and the next, and killed off all the neighbouring potato plants, whether established varieties or new seedlings derived from them. Thirty-three of the *S. edinense* seedlings were also killed, but seven were untouched. The seven resistant seedlings were grown in subsequent years and retained their resistance. One which was allowed to remain in the kitchen garden at Barley for seventeen consecutive seasons never showed the least sign of infection by blight.[24]

Redcliffe's research now took a new direction. Having previously bred potatoes as a convenient medium for genetic research and knowing very little about plant diseases, he now concentrated on the genetic resistance of some varieties to disease. Convinced that resistance to blight could be found only in nondomesticated potatoes, he obtained several other varieties, including a wild potato from Mexico, *S. demissum*. By 1910, he had planted seedlings of this species in his garden. They turned out to be resistant to blight. The following year, he began to hybridize the immune seedlings with domestic stocks and by 1914 had produced a series of hybrid families that were both blight-resistant and commercially viable.[25] This was "the first decisive stage" in the fight against a disease that was costing the United Kingdom about £5 million per annum between 1845 and 1939.[26]

At the time that Redcliffe was commencing his work at Barley, another agricultural threat, the potato wart disease (*Synchytrium endobioticum*)—a fungus that first appeared in Britain in 1876—was also making inroads. Its advance led the Board of Agriculture to assign special inspectors in 1907 to investigate its spread. The following year, one of the inspectors, G. C. Gaugh, made a discovery that intersected with Redcliffe's work. When visiting potato fields struck by the wart disease, he noticed that a few varieties remained immune and began working to determine which ones they were. The Board of Agriculture immediately set up wart testing stations on highly infected soils, but it soon encountered a major stumbling block: widespread confusion about the names of potatoes. The same variety might be known in the potato trade under a score or more of different names. For example, there were more than two hundred names for the variety "Up-to-Date" and more than seventy names each for "Abundance" and "British Queen." The testing for resistant varieties could not proceed until the muddle was cleared up. Thus, the Royal Horticultural Society created the Potato Synonym Committee and Redcliffe was made a member, becoming chairman in 1919 after the death of its first chairman. The work of the committee, by clearing up the confusion of potato variety names, put an end to the common commercial practice of marketing old varieties under new names at inflated prices. As a member, he also carried out the first major study of the morphology (form and structure) of potato varieties. The fruit of his work was his textbook *Potato Varieties*, which Cambridge University Press published in 1926.[27] Meanwhile, in 1910, he began publishing the results of his work in genetic and agricultural journals. A steady stream of articles followed—over fifty in all—which lasted until the start of World War II, when he turned his attention from the breeding of the potato to its history and social impact.[28]

3

Living a Jewish life at Barley in the early twentieth century required effort. The village was physically distant from London, while nearby Cambridge was not a lively hub of Jewish life. From the mid-nineteenth century until 1937, a tiny congregation—university students, in the main, with a sprinkling of full-time residents—met for Sabbath and Festival services in various rented rooms. Student attendance was irregular, and only from 1904, when Israel Hersch established a boardinghouse in Cambridge to serve Jewish boys attending the Perse School, where he taught mathematics and science, was there a regular Saturday *minyan*. Nina traveled frequently to Cambridge to use its library and to meet with Israel Abrahams, reader in Talmudic and Rabbinic literature from 1902 until his death in 1925. She and Redcliffe took an interest in the Jewish undergraduates, who numbered between twenty and thirty at any time before the war. They invited the students to garden parties at Homestall, and Redcliffe occasionally addressed Jewish student societies. As for kosher provisions, they came to Barley by train from London, as did the weekly *Jewish Chronicle* and a steady stream of visitors. But in the neighborhood of Barley, there were no other Jews.

The "Jewish" country house closest to Homestall was Newton Hall, home to the independently wealthy New York–born archaeologist and classical art scholar Sir Charles Waldstein [Walston from 1918], a fellow of King's College. The distance between Barley and Newton was only seven and a half miles, but the Salamans and the Waldsteins did not socialize regularly. The Waldsteins were indifferent to or alienated from matters Jewish and moved largely in non-Jewish social circles.[29] They also lived much more grandly. Newton Hall was a large, imposing, neo-Georgian red-brick house. The following anecdote, recorded by Nina in her diary, captures the difference between the two households: when their daughter Ruth (1908–2001), then five years old, went to tea at Lady Waldstein's (her husband was knighted in 1912), she mistook the liveried footman, with his blue coat bestrewn with shiny gold buttons, for the "night," whom she had been told lived there.[30]

There was also an eclectic quality to the Jewish life that Redcliffe and Nina fashioned at Barley—in part of necessity, owing to their rural surroundings. But it was also the result of their effort to create a Jewish home that met both their needs. In this they were fortunate: Nina's sense of what Judaism required was more elastic than her father's, while Redcliffe, recognizing that his wife was more Jewishly learned than he, was open to

Figure 3.4. Nina Salaman in the garden, Homestall, before World War I. Courtesy of Jenny Salaman Manson.

the observance of rituals and customs that were not overly burdensome to him. His openness derived, I think, both from his commitment to Jewish solidarity and from his love for his wife. In any case, she took the lead in setting the Jewish tone and character of their home. What emerged was a level of observance that fell somewhere between the relaxed Orthodoxy of Redcliffe's upbringing and the much stricter (but very Anglo-Jewish) Orthodoxy of hers. They observed the Sabbath, beginning with a festive meal on Friday night and the blessings over the candles, wine, and *halah*. Redcliffe recited the *eshet hayil* (woman of valor), Proverbs 31: 10–31, in

72 | *The Last Anglo-Jewish Gentleman*

praise of Jewish womanhood and his wife's virtues, and they concluded the meal with *birkat ha-mazon*, or grace. On Saturday, they remained at home, reading an abbreviated Sabbath service in the morning, as well as the weekly Torah portion, irrespective of the presence of a *minyan*. There were no lessons for the children that day. In the fall, they usually attended High Holiday services at the New West End Synagogue in London, staying with one of Redcliffe's siblings. In 1919, when they were vacationing at East Preston on the Sussex coast for the month of September and putting up in London would have been difficult, they celebrated Rosh Ha-Shanah with Israel Zangwill, who lived in East Preston, gathering in his study for the service.[31] The other festivals they usually observed at Barley, erecting, for example, their wickerwork *sukkah*, decorated by the children, for the eight days of the fall Sukkot festival. Woven into their observance was a playful or imaginative element, intended to instruct, as well as hold the attention of, the children. For example, at Passover in 1918, Myer disappeared from the *seder* table at one point and returned dressed as a wayfarer. Israel Abrahams, who was celebrating with them, asked Myer where he was going and he responded "To Jerusalem." Abrahams, who had arranged the intervention, then said, "Next year in Jerusalem—this year come and keep the Passover with us."[32]

The most remarkable feature of the Jewish home they created was the Hebrew education that Nina gave to her children. (See fig. 3.5.) Eager to transmit both her love for and expertise in Hebrew, she taught them herself, starting when they were very young. Myer began to have daily lessons of one-quarter hour when he was four years and two months old. The twins, Arthur and Edward, were a few months older when she began to teach them. Raphael Arthur (1906–93), who was born at Barley on April 24, 1906, was five. The Hebrew she taught them was not the modern language that was then taking root in the new Jewish towns and villages in the Land of Israel, but the classical language of the Hebrew Bible and prayer book. She focused on the comprehension of written texts rather than on conversation, although did not ignore the latter altogether. She began with frequently recited prayers, like the *shema*, and then went on to biblical texts, especially the narratives in Genesis, which easily capture the imagination of children. Unlike most Hebrew instruction in Britain at the time, which was in the hands of overworked and underpaid East European–born *melammedim*, her approach to the language was systematic and included matters of both syntax and grammar. In a diary in which she recorded details of the

Figure 3.5. The Salaman family at Homestall, c. 1911. From left to right: Arthur, Raphael (standing), Ruth (in Nina's arms), Nina, Sarah (Redcliffe's mother), Redcliffe, Myer, and Edward. Esther was born later, in 1914. Courtesy of Jenny Salaman Manson.

children's education and development, she frequently noted their progress in Hebrew. For example, in February 1909, she wrote of Myer:

> He reads from Genesis in Hebrew, a sentence or two, translating the words he knows and sometimes writing down a few words. Then I read to him a small piece from another part of the Bible in English—it is 2 Samuel just now—which interests him very much. I do not gloss over the imperfections of the heroes, but read the accounts as history, only omitting parts which he could not understand. The whole thing takes about 35 minutes before his rest in the morning. The twins still read a few words at each lesson and they sometimes play a Hebrew game, something like Loto.[33]

The Hebrew lessons occupied several hours of her day when she was teaching all four of the boys. In November 1912, she recorded that she taught Raphael at 9 in the morning before he went off to kindergarten, Myer from 11:15 to 12, and the twins from 12 to 12:45.[34] (By the time her daughters, Ruth and Esther, were old enough to begin Hebrew lessons, Nina was too sick to teach them regularly.)

For Nina, Hebrew lessons were not supplemental to the secular lessons the children received: they were a central part of their education. She did not begin to teach her eldest son to read English until more than two years after she had started his Hebrew lessons. When he easily completed the first lessons in the English textbook that she gave him, she decided "not to be in a hurry to encourage him to read English," especially since his Hebrew was progressing so well.[35] Her motive for teaching her children Hebrew at an early age was straightforward: it was the national language of the Jews, in which they had expressed their national genius. When the women at a London dinner party seemed surprised on learning that she was teaching her children Hebrew, and one of them said it would be as much use to them as learning Greek, she replied that "they ought to know their own literature first," a notion that had never occurred to the women before.[36] In 1915, when her eldest son had outgrown home schooling, she sent him daily to Cambridge, where, among other subjects, he studied Aramaic, Talmud, and the *Shulhan Arukh* with Israel Abrahams.

Nina was heavily invested—emotionally and culturally—in teaching her children Hebrew. Pedagogically, it was a mixed blessing. While it made her an enthusiastic instructor, it made her an exacting and often impatient one as well. The eldest son, Myer, mastered the language and rarely disappointed her. At one time, he considered studying for the rabbinate and, when he entered Cambridge, he won the John Stewart of Rannoch Scholarship in Hebrew, even though by then he was no longer enthusiastic about becoming a rabbi. But even he could make her cross on occasion. She once complained to Redcliffe, "He is sometimes so slow at thinking and makes the same mistake so many times."[37] The other boys fell afoul of her more frequently. While preparing Raphael for his bar mitzvah, she described him to Redcliffe as "backward compared to the others" and thought that he might not be capable of doing the *haftarah* for his portion. "He seems unable to remember the meaning of words and I don't know how to remedy that."[38] When he was twelve, Raphael recorded in his diary (a short-lived project) how his Hebrew lessons usually reduced him to tears:

> I am going to try to get over the habit of always crying when Mama scolds me at a Hebrew lesson. I don't cry when Mama scolds me otherwise. But when I was younger I used to cry at every Hebrew lesson, so it has grown more a habit now. Hebrew has always had a queer effect on me. I always feel frightened before a lesson. I always used to keep a good store of handkerchiefs in my pocket before a Hebrew lesson.[39]

It was Arthur, however, who suffered most from Nina's temper and impatience. In 1928, three years after her death, in a moment of despondence and self-pity, he remembered her in a diary he was keeping at the time. The shockingly frank passages warrant quoting at length:

> She was the worst mother conceivable. I was continually in mortal dread of her and spent most of the early days doing anything to keep out of her sight. As a teacher she had no patience & hit us about in a most disgraceful way. Hebrew lessons meant nothing but fear & trembling at all of us. That's what made me the nervous wreck that I am. I never once in twenty years remember her calling me "dear" or anything of the sort. In fact, I can remember practically nothing but scolding. It destroyed my self-confidence & made me feel I was less than nobody, which now in truth it has caused me to become.
>
> One of the greatest surprises of my life was when on first going to school I found that the masters did not come & thrash you over the face & curse you for everything. No wonder we liked school. I still feel the terror of her presence. Why did she do it? In other respects, she was wise enough & always charming to those outside the home circle. Very likely she thought it best for us, I don't know. Anyway she whispered to me she was sorry, when she was dying, but I couldn't answer.[40]

Arthur's memory of his mother, like all childhood memories of parents, was inherently subjective. Still, it suggests, at a minimum, that Nina was not temperamentally suited to teaching her own children. Indeed, she recognized this shortcoming in herself. She wrote to Redcliffe in 1917 that teaching the children often made her impatient, admitting that she did not think she was made to be a teacher. It was not so much the teaching that she found trying as the children's inability to remember what she had taught them.[41] More generally, as a parent, she was aloof and "rather grand . . . and formidable," her daughter Ruth recalled; she was not "very cuddly or easy to talk to."[42] Solomon J. Solomon's 1918 portrait of her (fig. 3.6), now at the Jewish Museum, London, confirms her daughter's impressions. It shows a handsome, intelligent, determined woman, serious and self-assured, with little time or toleration for nonsense. Of course, her recourse to the use of physical force was not uncommon in early-twentieth-century childrearing—she even smacked three-year-old Raphael on at least one occasion[43]—but it was not a useful teaching aid, to say the least. Moreover, it left an emotional scar on at least one of her children, although it is doubtful that Arthur's lack of self-esteem was due only to her impatience and lack of sympathy. It was also at one with the structured formality of parent-child relations at Homestall, which was typical of upper-middle-class homes. The

Figure 3.6. Solomon J. Solomon, oil portrait of Nina Salaman (1918), on loan to the Jewish Museum, London. Courtesy of Peter Hamburger.

children lived in a separate wing of the house, tended and taught (except for Hebrew) by various nurses, governesses, and tutors. When they were young, they spent time with their parents only after tea, when they would be "fussily dressed up" and taken downstairs to their parents' part of the house for half an hour or so—to perform or to be read to.[44]

Nina's instruction of her children included more than language lessons. She also strove to teach them about Judaism and Jewish history, using both formal and informal methods. For example, she read to Myer excerpts from Lady Magnus's *Outlines of Jewish History* (1886), beginning when he was seven and simplifying the language as she went along.[45] She also took the opportunity to instruct the children in more informal settings. When taking Edward for a walk one June morning—he was six at the time—the topic of the difference between Christians and Jews arose, and she asked him if he knew what the difference was. He answered, "Well, if you saw people having dinner and saw one eat a rabbit you'd know he was a Christian." His answer led her to think it was time to offer him a more substantial explanation.[46] When the Beilis ritual murder trial in Russia was in the news in 1913, she explained to Myer the details of the blood accusation. His response was that even if the accusation were true, the Jews would not choose a Christian to sacrifice because Moses would not have allowed it.[47]

During Nina's lifetime, the Salaman children grew up in what is best described as a protected, hothouse Jewish environment. To be sure, they were physically isolated from other Jews and saw other Jewish children only when family and friends came to visit or when they traveled to London. But at home Nina and Redcliffe (to the extent that he was involved) created a secure zone in which the family's Jewishness was an integral or natural part of home life, inseparable from the routines of day-to-day living, rather than supplemental to them. Living in the country also shielded the children both from immediate contact with anti-Jewish sentiment and from less Jewishly observant and Jewishly committed Jews in Britain. When they met Jewish children from dissimilar backgrounds, they were often surprised—at their ignorance, lack of observance, and indifference or hostility to Jewish tradition. For example, when Redcliffe's brother Elkin (1870–1919) and his family were visiting Homestall, his son Edmund noticed the Passover *haggadot* and asked Myer what they were, telling him that they did not have any in his home.[48] (Three years later, in 1913, Edmund and his three siblings were baptized; in 1925, Edmund changed his name from Salaman to Fox, his mother's maiden name.)[49] When Myer went away to boarding school (Clifton and then Bedales), he was shocked and upset when he discovered that the other Jewish boys were often irreverent about Jewish rituals and laws. The unpleasantness he experienced and the anguish it caused Nina belong to a later chapter, however. It bears mention here because it was an unintended consequence of the home life Nina created at Barley.

Notes

1. RNS to David Nabarro, July 18, 1946, Add. MS, 8171/27, RNS CUL.

2. Redcliffe's granddaughter, Nina Salaman Wedderburn, a cancer researcher, told me that it might not have been tuberculosis but something similar. In any case, Redcliffe and his doctors treated it as tuberculosis, which is what matters.

3. RNS, "The Helmsman Takes Charge," LH/X/101, Royal London Hospital Archives.

78 | *The Last Anglo-Jewish Gentleman*

4. RNS to London Hospital House Committee, November 21, 1904, Minutes, January 19, 1903, to August 14, 1905, LH/A/5/49, Royal London Hospital Archives.

5. RNS, "Helmsman Takes Charge."

6. NDS to Ray Frank, March 16 and December 9, 1905, Ray Frank Litman Papers, AJHS CJH. Excerpts from Nina's letters to Ray Frank were included in Simon Litman, *Ray Frank Litman: A Memoir* (New York: American Jewish Historical Society, 1957), 115–34.

7. NDS to Ray Frank, December 9, 1905, Ray Frank Litman Papers, AJHS CJH.

8. Jane Miller, *Relations* (London: Jonathan Cape, 2003), 33.

9. Nikolaus Pevsner and Bridget Cherry, *The Buildings of England: Hertfordshire*, rev. ed. (London: Penguin, 1977), 8. Pevsner, a German-born Jew who converted to Christianity while a university student, denied his Jewish origins and initially sympathized with Nazism. He did not comment on the unusual weathervane.

10. RNS, "Chance at the Helm."

11. Todd M. Endelman, *Radical Assimilation in English Jewish History, 1656–1945* (Bloomington: Indiana University Press, 1990), 11–19, 36–40.

12. The literature on gentility in English society and culture is enormous. See, for example, G. Kitson Clark, *The Making of Victorian England* (New York: Atheneum, 1967), 251–74; Robin Gilmour, *The Idea of the Gentleman in the Victorian Novel* (London: George Allen and Unwin, 1981); Philip Mason, *The English Gentleman: The Rise and Fall of an Ideal* (New York: William Morrow, 1982); David Castronovo, *The English Gentleman: Images and Ideals in Literature and Society* (New York: Ungar, 1987); and, in a more popular vein, Hugh David, *Heroes, Mavericks and Bounders: The English Gentleman from Lord Curzon to James Bond* (London: Michael Joseph, 1991).

13. Anthony Trollope, *The Prime Minister*, The World's Classics ed. (Oxford: Oxford University Press, 1990), 1.

14. Jack Wilkerson, *Two Ears of Barley: Chronicle of an English Village* (Royston: Priory, 1969), 82.

15. RNS, "Chance at the Helm."

16. Thomas Darling, "Passing of Dr. R. N. Salaman," *Herts and Cambs Reporter*, June 17, 1955. The society issued a special pamphlet in 1943 to commemorate its four hundredth meeting. I used the copy in the possession of Redcliffe's grandson William Salaman in Cambridge.

17. *Herts and Cambs Reporter*, March 11, 1910.

18. Colin Richmond, *Campaigner against Antisemitism: The Reverend James Parkes, 1896–1981* (London: Vallentine Mitchell, 2005), 144, 147–49; Haim Chertok, *He Also Spoke as a Jew: The Life of the Reverend James Parkes* (London: Vallentine Mitchell, 2006), 340. Both Richmond and Chertok discuss the willingness of church officials to tolerate Gardiner and their generosity to him after his release. The materials about the case in the Salaman Papers at the Cambridge University Library are closed to researchers. Quote is from RNS to Esther Salaman, June 21, 1941, Esther Salaman Papers, in possession of Peter Hamburger, Tibberton, Gloucestershire.

19. RNS to Esther Salaman, February 21, 1955, Esther Salaman Papers; Kenneth M. Smith, "Redcliffe Nathan Salaman, 1874–1955," *Biographical Memoirs of Fellows of the Royal Society* 1 (1955), 243.

20. RNS, *The History and Social Influence of the Potato*, rev. ed. (Cambridge: Cambridge University Press, 1970), xxix.

21. RNS, *History and Social Influence*, xxx.

22. RNS, "Chance at the Helm."

23. Ibid.

24. RNS, *History and Social Influence*, 177.

25. Ibid.

26. Ibid., 178.

27. Israel Reichert, "Redcliffe N. Salaman (on His 75th Birthday)," *Palestine Journal of Botany*, Rehovot vol. 7, no. 2 (1949): 187–88.

28. A list of his most important scientific papers is appended to Smith, "Redcliffe Nathan Salaman," 243–45.

29. Except on one occasion. In 1894, alarmed at the increase in antisemitism in England, Waldstein published *The Jewish Question and the Mission of the Jews* (New York: Harper and Brothers, 1894), a refutation of antisemitism and a call for radical assimilation. See also Todd M. Endelman, *Leaving the Jewish Fold: Conversion and Radical Assimilation in Modern Jewish History* (Princeton, NJ: Princeton University Press, 2015), 295–97.

30. NDS, diaries, November 1914, in possession of Jenny Salaman Manson, London.

31. NDS, diaries, September 1919.

32. NDS to RNS, March 29, 1918, Add. MS 8171, Wedderburn Deposit, RNS CUL.

33. NDS, diaries, February 1909.

34. Ibid., November 1912.

35. Ibid., January 1909.

36. NDS to RNS, May 19, 1911, Add. MS 8171, Wedderburn Deposit, RNS CUL.

37. NDS to RNS, September 23, 1913, Add. MS 8171, Wedderburn Deposit, RNS CUL.

38. NDS to RNS, January 5, 1919, Add. MS 8171, Wedderburn Deposit, RNS CUL.

39. Raphael Salaman, diary, January 9, 1919, in possession of Jenny Salaman Manson, London.

40. Arthur Salaman, diaries, January 8, 1928, in possession of William Salaman, Cambridge.

41. NDS to RNS, November 5, 1917, Add. MS 8171, Wedderburn Deposit, RNS CUL.

42. Quoted in Miller, *Relations*, 7.

43. NDS to RNS, September 3, 1909, Add. MS 8171, Wedderburn Deposit, RNS CUL.

44. Miller, *Relations*, 27.

45. NDS, diaries, March 10, 1910.

46. Ibid., June 7, 1910.

47. Ibid., October 1913.

48. Ibid., July 24, 1910.

49. *London Gazette*, April 7, 1925, 2442.

4

RACE SCIENCE

1

The idea that the world's population is divided into distinct races—permanent categories of humans akin to species, and that the physical and cultural differences among them are rooted in biology—lost scientific credibility in the aftermath of World War II and the Holocaust. There were challenges to the idea of race before the war, but the destruction that the idea underwrote between 1933 and 1945 was so overpowering that racial thinking was largely discredited in the world of science.[1] The lack of credibility in the notion of race, combined with the continual excoriation of racism in contemporary political life (except on its fringes), creates barriers for readers in the twenty-first century against understanding the ubiquity and respectability of racial thinking in the nineteenth and early twentieth centuries. The language of race was pervasive in scientific, cultural, and political discourse. It was so pervasive that Jews were unable to escape or ignore its influence. Jewish writers, preachers, and publicists, most of whom were not biological determinists, repeatedly referred to Jews as a race. Their use of the term was imprecise, which is not surprising, in light of the fluidity and inconsistency of racial thinking. In some cases, it functioned as a synonym of Jewish peoplehood, signifying the collective nature of Jewish life and fate.

For Jewish scientists in Britain and elsewhere, however, race thinking was both an intellectual and an existential challenge. It was not the idea of race itself that was troublesome but rather the subsidiary idea that accompanied it—the belief that races were ranked hierarchically and that Jews were an inferior race, marked by a distinctive mental and physical pathology. Those who faced the challenge pursued various strategies. Some disputed the stability and permanence of racial traits and the existence of pure races, arguing rather for the influence of environment on racial development. Others accepted the idea of racial difference but then turned conventional stereotypes on their head, thus subverting them. Others, like Redcliffe, fused elements of both approaches in their thinking.

Redcliffe was what historians now call a race scientist. That is, he not only acknowledged the legitimacy of racial categories but he also worked to understand the history of the Jews in biological terms and to disseminate his conclusions in popular and scientific forums. In the teens, twenties, and thirties, he was the most prominent Anglo-Jewish scientist to address notions of racial difference, lecturing widely and writing frequently on racial themes. It would be convenient to dismiss his work as eccentric or misguided or perhaps even embarrassing. But to do so would be a mistake, for it would obscure the historical climate in which he worked while simultaneously invoking ahistorical, presentist criteria to judge his behavior and thinking. It is more fruitful to ask how and why he understood the history of the Jews in biological terms and what this tells us about the pressures and currents with which he and other British Jews had to contend.

2

Redcliffe's belief in the racial character of the Jews predated his work as a race scientist. Recall that in 1893 he noted in his diary that reading Disraeli's novel *Tancred* had made him "a stronger racial Jew." (See chapter 1.) By the time of his marriage, in 1901, he was convinced that religious practice and belief were not the foundations of his or other Jews' sense of Jewishness. He wrote to Nina from Germany that summer, "Personally I have never felt less a Jew by not observing." Being a Jew for him was a status too great "to be a mere dependence on the bylaws of a kitchen and the regulations of a boarding school." If asked what bound Jews together, he had no hesitation in saying that it was race primarily and religion secondarily. The fact seemed to him almost self-evident, in view of the low level of "religious feeling amongst a large majority of the Jews" in Britain. For "scientific" Jews like himself, racial feeling was "a very important [factor], if not the most, in union." "When I am among Christians & the question at all arises of defending one's position as a Jew it is always the racial element that at once appeals—and in that way I feel that the Polish Jew is a brother though we may differ considerably in religion." Like other Jews who were no longer able to believe in the religious tenets of his ancestors, "blood logic"—the phrase is the historian Susan Glenn's—was a way to describe the common

82 | *The Last Anglo-Jewish Gentleman*

destiny of and sense of community among Jews.[2] He also made clear to Nina that nationalism (Herzlian Zionism was in its infancy at the time) did not underwrite his feelings of solidarity, telling her that he felt no duty or service to Zion in the way that he did to England. "The love of country—i.e., Zion—seems to be a gift or cult. It can hardly be an inherited feeling."[3]

Sentiments like these underwrote Redcliffe's turn to race science, but they did not precipitate it. It was, rather, his work at Barley in breeding blight-free strains of potatoes that was decisive, for it was that work that focused his mind on questions about the transmission of physical character-istics from one generation to the next. The inheritance of resistance to blight was at the heart of his potato research. He later recalled a Proustian moment when he made the leap from the heredity of the potato to the heredity of the Jews. One morning in 1910, while sitting at the breakfast table at Barley, he opened a letter from his brother Clement reminding him of a business meet-ing in a few days. The letter conjured up an image of his brother, his non-Jewish Scottish wife, and their five children. In his own words: "I seemed to see them sitting around the table and became suddenly conscious of the fact that there was not a trace of what is commonly recognized as being 'Jewish' in their appearances. My brother himself was never taken as a Jew—and might very well have been selected as a prize Nordic. Turning to my wife, I asked her what her impressions would be and she confirmed my own."[4]

The realization prompted Redcliffe to undertake research on the inher-itance of Jewish "racial" characteristics. He immersed himself in the litera-ture of Jewish race science, most of which was the work of German Jewish physicians and social scientists, and eventually corresponded with leading figures in the field in the United States and on the Continent, including Maurice Fishberg, Ignaz Zollschan, and Samuel Weissenberg. Redcliffe's research method was unsophisticated. He gathered and analyzed photo-graphs and genealogies of Jewish families into which non-Jews had married and traced the physical consequences of their mixing from generation to generation, as manifested in their facial features. In the 1910s, with the help of family and friends, he amassed a large body of multigenerational visual data.[5] A family friend, for example, wrote him in 1910, "Yesterday I saw a little girl whose mother is Jewish and her father is a Christian. As the child looks most Christian, I thought you might like to know it!"[6] Among those who supplied him with photographs and genealogies were the Judaica col-lector Israel Solomons and the Hebrew scholar Herbert Loewe, who mailed him charts and photographs from India. He also gathered photographs of monuments, statues, stelae, and bas-reliefs from the ancient Near East and of illuminated manuscripts from medieval Europe in order to trace continuities in facial and bodily appearance over the centuries. Later, while serving as medical officer to the Jewish regiment in Palestine in World War I, he photographed Jewish recruits from the Middle East, Eastern Europe, and North America and added these to his collection.

Writing to her American friend Ray Frank Littman, Nina described how Redcliffe's work on the inheritance of characteristics, hitherto limited to potatoes, expanded to Jews:

> He has lately taken up a very absorbing point in heredity—the inheritance of Jewish characteristics in appearance. The idea of this investigation occurred to him through observing that the children of mixed marriages (Jew & Gentile) are practically always Gentile looking. This led him to think of "Jewishness" as a "Mendelian character," & so far he finds that it follows the laws of heredity just as certain "characters" in plants & animals are found to do so. He finds that "Jewishness" is a recessive & therefore a pure character & that in intermarriage with western races the Jew is lost to sight & absorbed.

She then added that Redcliffe had some questions for her: were the children of mixed marriages in the United States Jewish-looking? did she know of marriages between hybrids (the children of mixed marriages), and, if so, what did their offspring look like? Redcliffe had not yet found a case of that kind.[7]

One obstacle he encountered in collecting evidence was the refusal of some descendants of Jews to contribute materials, not because they opposed race research, but because they feared making public their Jewish antecedents. Morris Rosenbaum, minister of the Borough Synagogue in south London, explained to Redcliffe in 1911 that there were families who refused to lend photographs even when they were told that their names would not be used: "Last week I called on a lady whose family for three generations offers illustrations of marriages involving all possible permutations and combinations of J. and G., which possibly would afford good material for judging of the dominant and recessive physical characteristics resulting from mixed marriages. Although she spoke quite frankly of her family connections, she became quite angry when I introduced the subject of borrowing photographs."[8] Refusals like this did not derail his project. The large number of photographs and family trees that survive in his papers at Cambridge suggest that he had no shortage of materials to analyze. Working with Jews was not the same, however, as working with potatoes. The presence or absence of potato blight was not difficult to detect. The presence or absence of physical traits that were conventionally coded as Jewish was a different matter, more subjective and open to challenge. In his work on Jewish heredity, Redcliffe downplayed the significance of the most commonly cited markers of racial difference—head shape, eye color, nose shape, stature, and hair color. Instead, he concentrated on the genetic history of a far more elusive physical marker—what he called a millennia-old Jewish facial expression. In this he followed the example of the pioneer Anglo-Jewish social scientist Joseph Jacobs, at whose behest the eugenicist Francis Galton made his well-known composite photographs of London Jewish schoolchildren in 1883.[9] Like Jacobs, Redcliffe acknowledged that this expression was "elusive of description" but maintained nevertheless that it was "so characteristic" that Jews or those who knew them well infallibly recognized it when they saw it. When he turned to the constitutive elements of the expression, he admitted the difficulty of being precise. Still, he made a few stabs at describing it. In his first publication on the topic, in the newly launched *Journal of Genetics* in 1911, he wrote,

> The nose is often peculiar, not because of its length or even its convexity, which may be often outdone in non-Jews, but by the heavy development of the nostrils. . . . The eyes are generally elongated, and a fairly characteristic feature is the length of the upper eyelid. The face which exhibits the expression of Jewishness is never of the angular type with square jaw, a type which is extremely rare amongst Jews. Far more usual is to find rounded features, long sloping jaw, fairly developed chin which is rounded and not square, a good-sized forehead devoid of that angularity in the region of the temples which is not uncommon amongst Teutonic people.[10]

A year later, in a similar article in the *Eugenics Review*, he associated the Jewish face—"when seen at its best"—with "the long and heavy nose, eyes somewhat close together with long upper eyelids, rounded angles to the jaw, prominent and rounded chin, and rounded and spacious forehead." Its main characteristic was "the general traction . . . of all the features downward towards the chin and at the same time the absence of angularity." He also stressed that this cast of features was inherited from antiquity and not acquired in centuries of persecution and suffering.[11]

The novelty of Redcliffe's work on race science was the introduction of Mendelian methods, with which he was familiar from his potato-breeding experiments. Unlike other Jewish race scientists, as Dan Stone notes, "he was committed not to biometrics or social statistics but to genetics."[12] His initial research, which took less than a year to complete, focused on the facial features of 362 children who were the issue of 136 mixed marriages (50 in which the father was non-Jewish and 86 in which the father was Jewish). He discovered that 93 percent of the children of these mixed marriages resembled one parent only and thus concluded that "the Jewish facial type, whether it be considered to rest on a gross anatomical basis, or whether it be regarded as the reflection in the facial musculature of a peculiar psychic state, is a character which is subject to the Mendelian law of Heredity."[13] For example, he found that Jewish features were recessive to North European features while dominant to what he called the Pseudo-Gentile type (non-Jewish-looking Jews, like his brother Clement), whose origins he explained in a later publication. This approach was at odds with contemporary ethnographic research, which stressed the blending of inherited characteristics in the offspring of hybrid marriages.

Redcliffe did not hesitate to popularize his ideas in nonscientific circles. As the newly elected president of the Union of Jewish Literary Societies, he devoted his inaugural lecture on October 28, 1910, at Jews' College to the topic of Jewish heredity. In addition to setting out the principles of Mendelianism and his own findings, he took up a theme that was central to racial antisemitism: the relationship between physical and mental characteristics. To assert that Jews looked different from other peoples was not especially controversial. More troubling was the assertion that Jewish thinking and behavior also were rooted in biology and were thus inheritable, unchanging, and impervious to external influence. Although he later modified his position, at this point Redcliffe was confident—and presumably comfortable asserting—that the mental followed the physical and that character accompanied race.[14] The *Jewish Chronicle* reported his talk at length and then the following week used his work to drive home a message of its own: "If the intellectual ability of the Jew disappears along with his facial distinctiveness" and "the child of intermarriage is merged, mentally and physically, in the dominant mass of Christianity," then "Jewish faith and practice" stand no chance of survival. For the Jews, intermarriage means "'the end of all things,' religious and racial."[15] The newspaper also printed an interview with Redcliffe after the publication of his article in the *Journal of Genetics*.[16]

The *Jewish Chronicle*'s extensive coverage of Redcliffe's first work on race is indicative of the place that the Jewish Question, as it was called, occupied on the Anglo-Jewish agenda. The fate and future of the Jews, the nature of their collective identity, and their integration into state and society were

86 | The Last Anglo-Jewish Gentleman

questions that were still very much alive, even decades after the removal of civil disabilities. More generally, the language of race and considerations of racial identity permeated more than at any time previously the making of public policy and the shaping of cultural life. Redcliffe was not the only Anglo-Jewish scientist to bring the matter of Jewish racial identity to Anglo-Jewish readers. In its first two volumes (1910–12), the short-lived London journal the *Jewish Review* published four race articles. Solomon Herbert, an early Manchester psychoanalyst, contributed "The Making of a Nation: A Jewish Problem," in which he asserted the hereditary element was the most important factor in the makeup of an individual and that the Jewish problem was first and foremost a biological one. Redcliffe's friend Charles Myers asked, "Is There a Jewish Race?," and, while providing a less definitive answer than Redcliffe did, was not reticent about listing inherited traits of Jews: their power of organization, their dislike for manual labor, their ability in science and philosophy, their love for music and drama, their sobriety, and their devotion to their offspring. The Manchester Zionist Harry Sacher reviewed Maurice Fishberg's *The Jews: A Study of Race and Environment* (1911), damning Fishberg as "a crusader of assimilation" and "a Jew who has dropped his Judaism" and devoted five hundred pages "to persuad[ing] other Jews to do the same." According to Sacher, Fishberg argued that Jewish distinctiveness was a myth that melted away in the light of science. The destiny of the Jews, who everywhere resembled their neighbors, was to disappear. And the Austrian anthropologist and radiologist Ignaz Zollschan contributed "The Jewish Race Problem," in which he asserted "the particular race value of the Jews" while attacking the notion of the permanence of racial traits and affirming the influence of the external environment.

As these articles suggest, Redcliffe's ventures into race science in 1910 and 1911 were not eccentric or singular in the Anglo-Jewish context. Interest within the Jewish community was also stimulated by the preparation for and the aftermath of the Universal Races Congress, which met in London in late July 1911.[17] The gathering was not the brainchild of race scientists but of Felix Adler, the founder of the Ethical Culture movement, and other humanitarians and progressives who wished to promote interracial harmony and believed that the races of the world could learn from each other's experiences. Prior to the congress, its organizers met on May 11 at the home of the Liberal member of Parliament Stuart Samuel, elder brother of Herbert Samuel, with a group of Jews who wished to be represented at the event.[18] Redcliffe's friend Charles Myers made the case for the scientific, ethical, and historical importance of exploring the racial dimensions of the Jewish experience and for Jewish representation at the congress. He was supported, among others, by Redcliffe's brother-in-law Charles Seligman and by one of the editors of the *Jewish Review*, Joseph Hochman, Simeon Singer's successor at the New West End Synagogue. The journalist Lucien Wolf, while he supported Jewish participation, took the opportunity to register his doubt whether there was such a thing as a Jewish race. Moreover, he added, even if there were, it would not be wise to accentuate the fact in the face of the claims of antisemites about the Jewish race.

Redcliffe participated neither in this preliminary meeting nor in the congress itself, where Israel Zangwill delivered the chief Jewish address. He was invited to the meeting at Samuel's house and he was slated to be asked to speak at the congress.[19] But he was traveling in the United States and Canada at the time of the preliminary meeting, attending to business matters and meeting on racial topics with US researchers—Maurice Fishberg, Franz Boas, and the pioneer Anglo-Jewish social scientist Joseph Jacobs, who had left London for New York in 1900 to join the staff of the *Jewish Encyclopedia*.

Redcliffe sailed from Liverpool for New York on the RMS *Baltic* on April 22 and landed on April 30. He was accompanied by his youngest sibling, Archie (1885–1962) and Cecil Morris Cohen.[20] The first thing he did after settling into his room at the Waldorf was to telephone Fishberg, who, it turned out, was familiar with his work. They made plans to meet that evening. He then met his brother Euston, who lived in Manhattan and headed the family's ostrich feather office on East Eleventh Street. After dinner, Fishberg showed Redcliffe and Euston around the Lower East Side—"the Ghetto," as Redcliffe called it. It struck him as very much like Whitechapel, where he had trained, only more crowded and dirtier. They finished the evening at a café "frequented by the cream of the intellectuals and socialists."[21] At the time, Fishberg was the better known of the two researchers, but Redcliffe was not impressed—he described him to Nina as learned but not original. Indeed, he claimed that Fishberg thought that his (Redcliffe's) work "was the biggest thing anyone had done about the Jews" and that he had thought about holding up the publication of his own book until he could learn more about Redcliffe's work but that it was too late.[22]

The next day he visited Joseph Jacobs, and the two of them "talked heredity." He was unable to reach Franz Boas, who taught at Columbia University, and left for Chicago on May 3 without speaking with him. In

Chicago he took a special interest in the stockyards and the slaughter-houses, observing both kosher and nonkosher slaughtering of animals, pronouncing the former the better of the two. In light of his later involvement in *shehitah* controversies in Britain, it seems that he meant the Jewish method of slaughter was quicker and less painful. From Chicago, he took the train to St. Paul and then continued on to Calgary.[23] There he, Archie, and Cecil Cohen completed the purchase of a 2,400-acre horse-breeding farm, which his brother and Cohen had initiated when they were there in November 1910. The price was $100,000, an enormous amount for the time. (A large house in Calgary could be purchased for $2,000.) I can only speculate why Redcliffe invested in the farm. Perhaps, because he was a country gentleman who enjoyed country pursuits, especially hunting, ranching in the wilds of Canada appealed to him. (Before World War I, he hunted regularly at Barley and on visits to his brother Michel [1879–1971], who lived at Porlock, Somerset, in southwestern England, and who served as master of the Exmoor hunt from 1906 to 1911.) Breeding, it goes without saying, also may have attracted him.

The Calgary property was extensive and already well developed when they bought it. The sale included a large house with modern conveniences, cattle, and purebred Belgian horses, which were in demand for pulling wagons, carriages, and farm implements. Previous owners of the ranch had included a polo-playing Englishman, an Irish nobleman, who lived at the ranch only during the summer months, and two Belgians, who began breeding prizewinning purebred Belgian horses there in 1903. Redcliffe never took an active role in the management of the farm, leaving that to Cohen, who remained in Canada, and Archie, who returned to England permanently only during World War I. The three men apparently owned the ranch for several years and leased the land to tenants after they no longer actively managed it.[24]

Having finished his business in Calgary, Redcliffe returned to the United States and spent time in Chicago, Washington, DC, and New York before sailing for Liverpool, where he landed on July 2. In Chicago and Washington, he had attended services at large Reform synagogues and was bothered by the absence of traditions. While he was not a spiritual person, a pious Jew, or an Orthodox believer, his reaction to the services shows how religious traditions (that is, those he had grown up with) resonated with him emotionally and culturally. He disliked praying without covering his head, the recitation of prayers in a German-accented, churchy, sing-song

English, and the elimination of traditional Hebrew-language melodies. As he told Nina, he entered the synagogue "to get a bath in my bloody own tunes" and instead "had some frozen soda water sprayed over me." When he met the rabbi of the Washington congregation after the service, the latter asked him how he had liked the service. Redcliffe told him that, if his eyes had been shut, he would have thought that he was in a church, that he had come to refresh himself "in the grand old music" and had been bitterly disappointed. He was not opposed to making adjustments here and there in synagogue practice, but he could not understand why Jews would "suffer this tawdry stuff to replace proud old velvets." In New York, before sailing, he saw Fishberg once more, this time dismissing him in a letter to Nina as a journalist and not a true scientist.[25]

While Redcliffe was in North America, he and Nina wrote to each other frequently. Among the events she told him about was a disturbing encounter with Israel Zangwill, which, to her discomfort, was to be repeated on further occasions when she and Redcliffe were apart. Nina and the children were spending six weeks in the seaside town of Worthing, Sussex. Zangwill, his wife, and their children lived at East Preston, six miles away. The two families visited each other frequently. Zangwill, who was more than a dozen years older than she, had known her since she was a girl, having been a friend of her father, and had encouraged her literary and scholarly ambitions. After a country walk with him, she confessed to Redcliffe that she was afraid of him. "When alone with you he stares at you so and you feel he could touch you if you gave him the slightest chance. He has a wonderful mind, but that sort of feeling in a married man with children repels one." Later, at the train station, Zangwill told her that being married and having children had not changed her, that she remained the same poetic personality she was earlier in her life, and that he felt the same way toward her that he had before she married. She tried to defuse the situation by saying that she felt even more complete now that she was married. His response was that she had "an individuality strong enough to stand above all these things." Knowing that she was going to have a car in the days ahead, he said he would go for some drives with her if she would like. She then said that she hoped his wife would be able to come with them as well. In any case, she told Redcliffe that to prevent being alone with him she would take along their son Myer.[26] The encounters did not wreck future contact between the two families, which became even more frequent and close, but it certainly complicated matters.

3

When Redcliffe returned to Britain, he found his views on race under attack and he threw himself into defending and further propagating them. Even before the Universal Races Congress met, his neighbor, the Cambridge classicist and archaeologist Charles Waldstein, protested the classification of Jews as a separate race at the congress. In a letter to the London *Times*, Waldstein, an advocate of radical assimilation, asserted that Jews were as much Europeans as persons of Celtic, Saxon, Norman, Flemish, Teutonic, Slavic, or Latin origin. As proof, he cited the (dubious) fact that most American and European Jews traced their descent to ancestors who were continuously settled in their countries of residence "as far into the past as those of any other European race."[27] Redcliffe opened his second publication on race science, in *The Eugenics Review*, with an attack on Waldstein and others who denied the racial identity of the Jews. He again insisted that Jews were a racial entity, but this time, by tracing their biological history from the biblical period to the present, he addressed what was a critical question for race scientists at the time—were the Jews a pure race or a mixed race? Fishberg and those who denied the racial character of the Jews maintained that during their long sojourn in the Diaspora they had received a constant admixture of blood from surrounding peoples. To them, this explained why, for example, the cephalic measurements of Jews were similar to those of the peoples among whom they lived.

Salaman conceded that in the ancient Near East the Jews did intermarry freely with Assyrians, Babylonians, Hittites, Canaanites, and even Philistines. As he correctly noted, it would have been impossible for any people living at the crossroads of that world, as the Jews had, to maintain a biological purity as understood in the animal and plant world. Thus, he did not regard the Jews as a pure line descended from the family of Abraham. Then, at some point (which he later identified with Ezra's ban on intermarriage in the fifth century BCE), the Jews ceased to intermarry. The European communities that descended from the Jews who were exiled by Rome were inbred and free from European admixture—at least until they started intermarrying in the age of emancipation. The question—whether the Jews were a "pure" race (however understood)—was central to the debate on the racial origins of the Jews. It was critical to determining the biological difference or similarity of contemporary Jews with other groups. Redcliffe's answer was that the Jews were an admixture originally, but that early in their history they ceased to be. Ezra's ban on intermarriage froze their biological makeup, which underwent no further development. Still, as Dan Stone comments, whatever answer Jewish race scientists gave, their participation in the debate about Jewish racial origins "helped to perpetuate a way of thinking that was ultimately inimical to Jewish interests."[28] Even those who denied that Jews were a race helped to strengthen the legitimacy of biological discourse about Jews.

More formidable critics than Waldstein responded to Redcliffe's early publications. They attacked the most vulnerable aspect of his analysis—his notion of the Jewish face and his treatment of it as a Mendelian trait—but not for its racial underpinnings but for its conceptual and methodological arbitrariness. The future political theorist and Labour Party strategist Harold Laski, then a seventeen-year-old research assistant at Karl Pearson's eugenics laboratory at University College, London, dismissed Redcliffe's methodology as "scientifically ludicrous" in *Biometrika*, the journal of the anti-Mendelian biometric school of eugenics, following the publication of Redcliffe's second article. Laski mockingly asked whether each feature in the Jewish facial expression was a separate Mendelian unit and whether each unit was then recessive to the corresponding unit in the gentile face so that the whole Jewish face was recessive to the gentile face. If so, he failed to see that "the shape of a Gentile nose should be dominant to the shape of a Jewish nose in precisely the same way as a Jewish chin should be recessive to a Gentile one." Moreover, he charged, Salaman's method was hopelessly flawed because the identification of the Jewish face depended on what the observer "felt." Laski believed that if Salaman had shown his photographs to gentiles, the results would have been different.[29]

Redcliffe wrote to Laski after his article appeared, but no copy of his letter survives in his papers. But Laski's reply does: "I thank you for your interesting if somewhat dogmatic letter. It seems to me that we differ fundamentally in our conception not only of scientific method but also of what are to be called scientific 'facts' and agreement is hardly possible." Privately, Redcliffe dismissed Laski as "a clever but extremely young and inexperienced man."[30] He never publicly responded, however, to Laski's criticism.

Samuel Herbert, who was also comfortable with classifying Jews as a race, raised similar objections to Redcliffe in a letter to the *Jewish Chronicle* in February 1912. The "Jewish face" was too nondescript a feature to be made the basis of scientific research. While it was "comparatively easy for everyday purposes to distinguish by the mere look a Jew from a non-Jew,"

92 | *The Last Anglo-Jewish Gentleman*

it was impossible in doubtful cases to draw definite lines of demarcation that would stand up to rigorous scientific scrutiny. When Herbert tried to replicate Redcliffe's experiment, his results did not support Redcliffe's conclusions. Anyone who took the trouble to collect instances of the children of mixed marriages would discover, as he had, that the Jewish type was not always recessive in the children of the first generation. Apart from this, the more basic problem was that the "Jewish face" was "too indefinite and complex a feature to serve as a biological unit in the study of Mendelian inheritance."[31] Redcliffe responded lamely the following week in the *Jewish Chronicle*, writing that, while not resenting criticism, he was a busy man and could only answer criticism of his scientific work that appeared in scientific publications.[32]

Herbert continued to press his case. The next volume of the *Eugenics Review* included more or less the same letter,[33] to which this time Redcliffe responded in the following volume of the journal. He began by stating that it was always difficult to "answer a critic whose first weapon is abuse"— surely an oversensitive response to Herbert's measured words. Aside from asserting that he had anticipated several smaller objections of Herbert in his two articles, he made two major points. The first was that Mendelian inheritance studies were in their infancy and that no one could say with authority what was and what was not a Mendelian character or whether something was too simple or too complex to be controlled by a unit character. The second was that he had collected 136 cases of the offspring of intermarriages, while Herbert had worked with only 12 cases. He added, moreover, that since the publication of his article he had received information of many more cases, whose results matched those in his article.[34] Herbert followed up with a further letter to the *Journal of Eugenics*, very briefly restating his case.[35]

Redcliffe unwittingly confirmed the validity of the criticism that his method was arbitrary in his home one evening in January 1912. Zangwill and his non-Jewish wife, Edith, were staying at Barley, and Redcliffe conducted an impromptu experiment to test the ability of his wife and guests to identify persons as Jews from photographs. He asked them to view two groups of photographs of mostly undergraduate males. In the first group of 63 photographs, there were 9 Jews and 54 gentiles. Israel Zangwill fared poorly. He mistakenly identified 18 gentiles as Jews. Nina did much better; her only error was misclassifying one Jew as a gentile. In the second group of 38 photographs, the number of Jews and gentiles was equal. Israel

Zangwill again inflated the number of Jews by identifying 11 gentiles as Jews. Edith, who did not participate in the first round, also did poorly. She transformed 4 gentiles into Jews and 6 Jews into gentiles.[36] The results of this impromptu test, however, had no discernible impact on Redcliffe's view that the Jewish face was easily recognizable. While he recorded the results, he never discussed them publicly.

Until the mid-1930s, Redcliffe continued to publish and lecture about the racial nature of Jewishness. Having arrived at what he considered a solution to the question "Who are the Jews?" he broke no new ground in lectures and essays that were published after his initial formulations in 1911. Rather, he elaborated on what he had written, offering more detail and filling in gaps. His most important restatement of his views was his presidential address to the Jewish Historical Society of England on December 14, 1920—"Racial Origins of Jewish Types." At the start, he admitted that his choice of topic was not the usual fare of those who lectured to the society and that it fell outside the scope of Anglo-Jewish history, although he noted in mitigation that the chief sources on which he drew—representations of ancient Near Eastern peoples—came from English museums. In his lecture, he offered a more precise biological history of the Jews in antiquity, tracing the history of the peoples who contributed to the genetic makeup of the Jews and describing the distinctive physical characteristics of each. The Jews, he told his audience, were the biological product of intermarriage between their biblical ancestors, who were nomadic Semites, and three of their neighbors—Amorites, Hittites, and Philistines—before the destruction of the First Temple in 586 BCE. Each contributed genetically to what would eventually become the Jewish race. The Amorites were the source of the fair complexion and red hair that was a common feature among Jews, including the Salaman family. The Hittites brought to the mix those features, such as nostrility, that contemporary Europeans most commonly associated with Jews, while the Philistines (rather than Teutonic peoples) contributed what Salaman called the Pseudo-Gentile type among Jews. This kind of amalgamation, however, came to an end with Ezra's ban on intermarriage in the fifth century BCE and later with the advent of Christianity. The physical differences among the Jews of his day reflected the complexity of their origins before their return from Babylonia. The contributions of the different groups, he stressed, were never lost.[37]

While Redcliffe was undoubtedly correct that the ancestors of the Jews were a mixed lot—the biblical narrative says as much—his conclusions

94 | *The Last Anglo-Jewish Gentleman*

about what Jews inherited from each group depended on knowledge of the appearance of each group. For example, how did he know that the Hittites were "a white people with black hair and eyes and the aquiline, strongly Jewish nose"? His assertions, as his illustrations to the published version of his lecture make clear, derived from his impressions of how these peoples were represented in ancient monuments, primarily sculptures, that he had seen in the British Museum or in photographs in scholarly publications. For example, the reliefs at the Karnak temple complex at Thebes depicting the victories of the pharaohs from 1500 BCE to 800 BCE provided numerous representations of Amorites and Hittites. He expanded on the physical inheritance of the Philistines five years later in the *Palestine Exploration Quarterly*, asking "What Has Become of the Philistines?"[38] Here he explained that the Philistines had not disappeared but had been gradually absorbed into the ancient Israelites. Their persistence was manifest in the Pseudo-Gentile type among contemporary Jews: "The same delicate features, the same subangular character of the features, the same Grecian brow leading in one straight line to the straight short nose are there in the Pseudo-Gentile Jew of to-day."[39] In this article, he also estimated the percentage of Jews belonging to each group: 50 percent were Hittite, 15 percent Semitic, 20 percent Pseudo-Gentile, and 15 percent not readily classifiable.[40]

Although unnoticed at the time, Redcliffe's account of the genetic history of the Jews targeted two assumptions of contemporary racial antisemitism. First, it complicated the idea that the Jews were a Semitic people pure and simple by tracing their origins to several peoples who intermarried in antiquity, two of whom were not Semitic—that is, did not speak a Semitic language. The Philistines were from Crete; the Hittites from Asia Minor. Moreover, it was the non-Semitic Hittites who stamped their physical type "indelibly" on the majority of Jews.[41] This meant that Jews who looked "Jewish" did not look "Semitic" but "Hittitish." Second, his account undercut "Aryan" claims to exclusive ownership of Nordic physical features by linking the presence of blue eyes, fair hair, and light complexion among Jews to intermarriage with Philistines in the biblical period rather than to liaisons with Europeans in the medieval and early modern period.

4

In retrospect, the most dangerous theme in racial thinking was the idea that behavioral traits, not just physical traits, were racially determined. On this point, Redcliffe was hesitant. He never elaborated in any systematic way how traits that were commonly associated with Jews (immunity to alcoholism, for example) were linked to hereditary makeup. He talked about connections but never constructed a full-blown system of racial determinism in which emotional traits and aptitudes were the outcome of biological descent. In his 1911 article in the *Eugenics Review*, he was agnostic: "At present one is in entire darkness as to whether the physical features that one recognizes as Jewish are allied with any peculiar psychical qualities, although such would not be at all surprising were it indeed the fact." Here he mentioned three "Jewish" traits—a talent for music, mathematics, and chess—that might show "that there is perhaps a psychical group of features parallel with the physical."[42] He was similarly noncommittal in a lecture two years later to the University of London Zionist Society. He first told his audience that he could not answer with any confidence whether there was a typical Jewish mental or ethical outlook. But then he added that, if the face were an index to the mind and if there were a characteristic Jewish face (which he obviously believed there was), there was then a corresponding mental makeup that it reflected. He noted, for example, that schoolteachers told him that the non-Jewish-looking offspring of mixed marriages were unmistakably less Jewish in their ways, thoughts, and mental activities than their purely Jewish schoolmates. He was elusive, however, about what exactly this mental makeup was, calling it a substratum impossible to define. As for those traits that antisemites routinely attributed to Jewish heredity—materialism, love of money, lack of honor—they were characteristics that Jews acquired when they were ghettoized and then lost when they entered the wider world.[43]

Redcliffe continued to think about the possible correlation between mental and physical traits in the 1920s. In his 1925 article on the Philistines, he took a different tack and asked whether the three Jewish facial types (Hittite, Semitic, and Pseudo-Gentile) were each linked to different sensibilities. While admitting that there was no statistical way to solve this "elusive" problem, he recorded two observations about possible links. First, on examining a large number of portraits of Anglo-Jewish notables (presumably from the photographs he had collected), he was struck by the fact that almost all the outstanding philanthropists were of "an outspoken Hittite type of countenance." He then linked the Hittite facial type with the quality of *rakhmones* (compassion). Second, observing young native-born Jewish men from the agricultural villages of Palestine during World War

96 | *The Last Anglo-Jewish Gentleman*

I, he noticed the prevalence of the Pseudo-Gentile type among them. This type he correlated with physical prowess, muscularity, and the spirit of adventure.[44]

Other Anglo-Jewish scientists speculated about the inheritance of nonphysical traits in similar ways. Redcliffe's critic Solomon Herbert wrote of a number of Jewish racial inheritances—a tenacity for life, intellectual ability, the absence of alcoholism, and a tendency to mental and nervous disorders.[45] Charles Myers, as we saw earlier, maintained that all Jews displayed the same prominent characteristics: their power of organization, dislike of manual labor, ability in science and philosophy, love for music and drama, sobriety, and devotion to their offspring. (Yet Myers also stressed the importance of external forces in shaping Jews—English Jews thus differed from French, Italian, and Russian Jews.)[46] In a private memorandum from 1927, Redcliffe's brother-in-law Charles Seligman hypothesized that there were two distinct strains among Jews. One he called "the desert strain," by which he meant "a strain of thought and action more or less akin to that of the Arab as one knows him in fact and history." The other strain he associated with "Armenoid blood" (what Redcliffe called the Hittite type). Its characteristic was "the showy efflorescent style that one certainly finds among some Jews." In the same memorandum, he also speculated about the psychological differences between Jews and Christians. Among the latter, he singled out a sadomasochistic tendency that reveled in contemplating the details of the Passion of Jesus—a tendency that he thought was entirely absent among Jews. He also compared Jewish and Christian attitudes toward alcohol. To the Jewish mind, he noted, being a teetotaler and seeing any virtue in it were beyond comprehension.[47] In short, Redcliffe's musings about the inheritability of nonphysical racial traits were not unusual among Jewish scientists in the 1910s and 1920s.

That said, neither Redcliffe nor any other Anglo-Jewish scientist developed a full-blown system of hereditarian determinism, the most pernicious part of the racial thinking of the period. In its most extreme form, that belief denied altogether the transformative power of environmental circumstances and the ability of individuals to transcend their inheritance. At its most dangerous, as the ideological foundation of Nazi racism, it condemned to death all Jews everywhere by virtue of their origins. I do not think it is a coincidence that Redcliffe never followed such a path and that what he did write about the mental and emotional traits of Jews was fleeting and vague. Nor do I think it a coincidence that no other Anglo-Jewish scientist took that route. They tended to refer in the most general terms to the musical and mathematical abilities of the Jews, their immunity from alcoholism, their proneness to mental disorders, their excessive concern for their children, and so forth, and either left it at that or attributed such traits to historical and sociological conditions. Like Salaman, they too avoided, even if unconsciously, the slippery slope of full-blown biological determinism. The reason for this, I suspect, is not that they could foresee the harm that antisemites might wreak under the banner of biological determinism, but that this kind of determinism collided with their own allegiance to liberal ideas about the ability of human beings to shape their own destiny.

Notes

1. Elazar Barkan, *The Retreat of Scientific Racism: Changing Concepts of Race in Britain and the United States between the World Wars* (Cambridge: Cambridge University Press, 1992); Gavin Schaffer, *Racial Science and British Society, 1930–62* (Houndmills, UK: Palgrave Macmillan, 2008). Barkan emphasizes the challenges to race thinking that predated World War II, while Schaffer explores the persistence of the idea of racial categories after the war. The two accounts complement, rather than contradict, each other.

2. Susan A. Glenn, "In the Blood? Consent, Descent, and the Ironies of Jewish Destiny," *Jewish Social Studies*, n.s., 8, nos. 2–3 (Winter–Spring 2002): 139–61.

3. RNS to NDS, July 5, 9, and 16, 1901, Add. MS 8171/97, RNS CUL.

4. RNS, "Chance at the Helm."

5. These materials are at Cambridge, Add. MS 8171/19, RNS CUL.

6. Jesse Lewis to RNS, September 16, 1910, Add. MS 8171/19, RNS CUL.

7. NDS to Ray Frank Littman, March 6, 1911, Ray Frank Littman Collection, American Jewish Historical Society, Center for Jewish History.

8. Morris Rosenbaum to RNS, July 12, 1911, Add. MS 8171/19, RNS CUL.

9. On Jacobs's importance to the development of "Jewish" race science, see John M. Efron, *Defenders of the Race: Jewish Doctors and Race Science in Fin-de-Siècle Europe* (New Haven, CT: Yale University Press, 1994), ch. 4.

10. RNS, "Heredity and the Jew," *Journal of Genetics* 1, no. 3 (1911): 279–80.

11. RNS, "Heredity and the Jew," *Eugenics Review* 3 (1911–12): 190–91.

12. Dan Stone, "Of Peas, Potatoes, and Jews: Redcliffe N. Salaman and the British Debate over Jewish Racial Origins," *Simon Dubnow Institute Yearbook* 3 (2004): 221–40.

13. RNS, "Heredity and the Jew," *Journal of Genetics*, 285.

14. *Jewish Chronicle*, November 4, 1910.

15. *Jewish Chronicle*, November 11, 1910.

16. *Jewish Chronicle*, October 20, 1911.

17. Michael D. Biddiss, "The Universal Races Congress of 1911," *Race* 13, no. 1 (1971): 37–46; Paul Rich, "'The Baptism of a New Era': The 1911 Universal Races Congress and the Liberal Ideology of Race," *Ethnic and Racial Studies* 7, no. 4 (October 1984): 534–50; and Susan D.

98 | *The Last Anglo-Jewish Gentleman*

Pennybaker, "The Universal Races Congress, London Political Culture, and Imperial Dissent, 1900–1939," *Radical History Review* no. 92 (Spring 2005): 103–17.

18. *Jewish Chronicle*, May 12, 1911.

19. NDS to RNS, April 29, 1911, Add. MS 8171/101, RNS CUL.

20. Little is known about Cohen. He does not appear to have been related to Salaman. He remained in Canada until his death. According to the 1916 Canadian census, he was a rancher, a Canadian citizen, and a Jew, while his English-born wife and daughter, also Canadian citizens, were Anglicans, whose "race" was English.

21. RNS to NDS, May 1, 1911, Add. MS 8171/102, RNS CUL.

22. Ibid.

23. RNS to NDS, May 2, 3, 4, and 5, 1911, Add. MSS 8171/102, RNS CUL.

24. Jack Switzer, "British Jews Buy the Belgian Horse Ranch—1911," *Discovery* 17, no. 3 (October 2007): 6–7.

25. RNS to NDS, June 9, 1911, Add. MS 8171/102, RNS CUL.

26. NDS to RNS, May 19, 1911, Add. MS 8171, Wedderburn Deposit, RNS CUL.

27. *The* [London] *Times*, April 5, 1911.

28. Stone, "Of Peas, Potatoes, and Jews," 224.

29. Harold J. Laski, "A Mendelian View of Racial Heredity," *Biometrika* 8 (1911–12): 424–30.

30. RNS to unknown recipient, December 15, 1914, Add. MS 8171/4h, RNS CUL.

31. *Jewish Chronicle*, February 9, 1912.

32. *Jewish Chronicle*, February 16, 1912.

33. *Eugenics Review* 3 (1911–12): 349–51.

34. *Eugenics Review* 4 (1912–13): 91–93.

35. *Eugenics Review* 4 (1912–13): 203.

36. RNS, photographic test notes, January 23, 1912, Add. MS 8171/19, RNS CUL.

37. RNS, "Racial Origins of Jewish Types," *TJHSE* 9 (1920): 163–85.

38. RNS, "What Has Become of the Philistines? A Biologist's Point of View," *Palestine Exploration Quarterly* 57, no. 2 (1925): 68–79.

39. Ibid., 77–78.

40. Ibid., 41.

41. RNS, "Racial Origins of Jewish Types," 184.

42. RNS, "Heredity and the Jew," *Eugenics Review*, 199.

43. RNS, "The Jew and Assimilation," lecture, University of London Zionist Society, March 9, 1913, Add. MS 8171/19, RNS CUL.

44. RNS, "What Has Become of the Philistines?," 79.

45. Solomon Herbert, "The Making of a Nation: A Jewish Problem," *Jewish Record* 1 (1910–11): 450–53.

46. Charles S. Myers, "Is There a Jewish Race?," *Jewish Record* 2 (1911–12): 122, 124.

47. Charles Seligman, comments on a letter of G. Pitt Rivers, August 4, 1927, MS 262/4, Charles Seligman Papers, Royal Anthropological Institute, London.

5

NINA AND THE HEBREW POETS

1

In Barley, in addition to giving her children Hebrew lessons, Nina continued to translate medieval Hebrew poetry and to publish essays on Jewish themes in both popular and scholarly periodicals. She was not an original or subtle thinker, but her observations about Jewish practice and belief were discerning and expressed in a way that was accessible to a wide audience. It is significant to note that her thinking is not easily categorized as either traditional/Orthodox or as progressive/Reform, at least as those terms are usually understood. It was, however, very much in the tradition of Anglo-Jewish bibliocentricity, an approach to Judaism that privileged the Bible as a source of religious inspiration without abandoning the weight of rabbinic tradition. In addition to her writing, she took an active role in promoting Hebrew scholarship in Britain, in fostering the Hebrew education of Jewish girls, and in campaigning to improve the position of women, both within the Jewish community and on the national scene. If she was not a public figure like her contemporary Lily Montagu, one of the founders of Liberal Judaism in Britain (a radical, denationalized variety of Reform Judaism), she was at least well known within the Jewish community. Redcliffe supported and encouraged her scholarly work and took immense pleasure in the recognition she received.

2

The best guide to Nina's approach to Jewish thought and practice is an article—"An Aspect of Judaism"—she published in the learned journal the *Jewish Quarterly Review* in 1901, the year she and Redcliffe married.[1] She began by explicitly rejecting the Reform notion that Judaism developed over time, primarily because it implied that later-day expressions of Judaism were higher, nobler, and more spiritual than earlier expressions. For her, the highest expression of Jewish ethics and morality was the Bible. It expressed the "essence of the highest and holiest ideals." "No words have since been uttered by man in communion with God of a nature so sublime as those found in the Hebrew psalms." She knew, of course, that the practices of Judaism had changed over the millennia—the sacrificial cult gave way to the synagogue service, for example, with the destruction of the Second Temple in 70 CE—but the changes were, in her view, a matter of "adaptability," not "development." The unstated implication of her assertion was that rabbinic (postbiblical) Judaism, the Judaism of the Talmud and its codes and commentaries, was a later variation of the Bible's teachings. This, of course, was at variance with the traditional rabbinic teaching that God revealed both the Written Law (the Bible) and the Oral Law (the Talmud) simultaneously to Moses at Mount Sinai and that it was the task of the rabbis to demonstrate the seamless compatibility of the two by means of exegesis.

The bibliocentricity of Nina's Judaism belonged to an Anglo-Jewish current of thinking that dated to the early Victorian period and was not found elsewhere in Europe. The belief in the primacy of biblical texts over rabbinic texts owed much to the pervasive bibliocentricity of English culture more generally and to the evangelical critique of rabbinism as legalistic, ethically cramped, and unspiritual. Its rhetorical advantage was that it made Hebrew scripture, sacred to Christians as well, the bedrock of Judaism and put the Jews at the starting point and the center of the history of revelation. Those English Jews who absorbed this outlook emphasized the Bible as the primary source of divine wisdom and law and held that all its commandments were binding, unlike commandments rooted in rabbinic interpretations, which in their view were not fully incumbent on modern Jews. They tended not to reject explicitly the oral law but rather downplayed its priority, usually asserting that, while the rabbis of antiquity were wise, holy men, their enactments were not eternally binding and some might have to be changed to meet altered circumstances.

In her article of 1901, Nina devoted relatively little space to the question of law (*halakhah*). Her view was that the commandments (*mitsvot*) existed to sustain, govern, and regulate religious enthusiasm. Quoting the maxim from *Pirkei Avot* that, were it not for government, men would swallow each other alive, she assigned the *mitsvot* the function of government—"our indispensable discipline." Without them, "the undirected flame [of religious enthusiasm] would be likely to go astray and consume the soul wherein

Nina and the Hebrew Poets | 101

it was kindled." The law was thus both a stimulus to religion and a discipline for holding Jews within bounds, "a sort of spiritual ballast, holding us steadily between heaven and earth."[2] As her own practice showed, she adhered to Jewish law but not in a way that would have been acceptable to many Orthodox Jews at the time or later.

While Nina privileged the Bible among the sacred texts of Judaism, she was no biblical fundamentalist. She was well aware that critical biblical scholarship had undermined its literal narrative. To her, this was unimportant and beside the point. What mattered was not the literal meaning of the text but the grains of truth and beauty embodied in it. A biblical story—or, for that matter, a rabbinic tale—was true because of the idea it was intended to convey, "the truth it sets before the eyes of man." She clung to the narrative for the sake of what it encased. It was, moreover, a narrative that shone with the patina of history. It was the form that Jews had loved throughout the centuries, "for whose sake we have lived and suffered and survived."[3]

While Nina's emphasis on the biblical text established a link between Judaism and Christianity, it was not her intention to narrow or bridge the theological gap between Jews and Christians, as the founders of Liberal Judaism in Britain were doing. Indeed, the whole tenor of her religious thinking was unapologetically particularistic. Drawing on the eighteenth-century notion that every nation has a peculiar "genius"—its own ways of thinking, acting, and communicating—Nina wrote frequently of the Jewish genius for religion, by which she meant the ability to understand human nature and human needs through life and history. The Jews—and no other people in antiquity—received God's revelation and "rose to a special knowledge, a peculiar understanding," especially the insight that religion gains "a hold over the mind and heart" when it binds together the greatest thoughts of religion with the details of life. At one point, she referred to the genius of Judaism as "that glorious identification of life and religion, whereby man, in the familiar presence of holiness, can laugh in his own soul and lose nothing of reverence."[4]

The genius of Judaism, she believed, obliged the Jews, "a people scattered among the nations and endowed with imperishable life," to play a special role in the world. They were "a kingdom of priests and a holy nation" (Exodus 19:6), "a holy power by which all the nations of the earth shall be entirely blessed," the "custodians and teachers of an ideal of holiness for the world's attainment."[5] Their task was not only to embody holiness but to play a crucial role in the future development of religion—in

102 | *The Last Anglo-Jewish Gentleman*

particular, in the emergence of the "fullest and purest final religion." She did not explain how the emergence would happen but, in her mind, there was a strong redemptive or millennial dimension to the role. In the remote future, "beyond our sight," Judaism would enable the creation of a spiritual center for the world, to which "all nations shall flow . . . and it shall be called Zion, the holy one of the Lord."[6] However vague Nina's vision of the end of history, it was a vision that assigned the Jewish people a (the?) central role in its realization and prophesied the nations of the world acknowledging their spiritual precocity and preeminence. In its triumphalism, it echoed both traditional themes in Jewish thought and progressive reworkings of those themes, as found in varieties of Reform Judaism in Germany and the United States at the time.

There was, then, a spiritual quality to Nina's thinking about Jews that was absent in Redcliffe's thinking. Her thought was imbued with faith in the working of God in history and of God's selection of the Jews to play a particular role in its unfolding. They shared a collective view of the Jews, but he expressed it in biological terms and she in traditional religious categories. When she wrote her essay in 1901, her invocation of Zion was not a reference to the Zionist movement, then in its infancy in Britain. Rather, she used *Zion* as a synonym for Jerusalem, as was customary in classical Hebrew texts. In this case, she drew specifically on the prophecy of Isaiah concerning the end of days:

> In the days to come,
> The Mount of the LORD's house
> Shall stand firm above the mountains
> And tower above the hills;
> And all the nations
> Shall gaze on it with joy.
> And many peoples shall go and shall say:
> "Come,
> Let us go up to the Mount of the LORD,
> To the House of the God of Jacob;
> That He may instruct us in His ways,
> And that we may walk in His paths."
> For instruction shall come forth from Zion,
> The word of the Lord from Jerusalem. (Is. 2:2–3)

If Nina was not a political Zionist at the turn of the century, she was certainly a cultural and spiritual nationalist. Her thinking is permeated with assumptions, not always fully articulated, about the collective character of the Jews and their collective destiny. What sets Jews apart and makes them a cohesive unit in her mind is their selection, their genius, and their destiny. She returned repeatedly to this theme throughout her life, in public and private, and in her poetry and prose. In a sermon she delivered in the Cambridge synagogue in 1919, she declared that it was the strength and genius of Judaism that it annually reminded the Jewish people (when the earliest weekly portions of the Torah were read in the synagogue in the fall) that the patriarchs "were sent out into the world with a conscious purpose." That purpose, in support of which she cited Genesis 22:18 ("In your seed shall all the nations of the earth be blessed"), was to remain "a family apart," chosen "to fight against false theories as to what is divine, and to combat the false ideas of men as to the nature of the life they should lead."[7] Abstract speculation—about the nature of God, transcendence and immanence, reward and punishment, and the afterlife—played no role in her approach to Judaism, nor did theology contribute a vocabulary for Jewish collective self-definition. In her 1901 article, she wrote explicitly that Judaism put little stress on "belief" and that it was not a collection of dogmas but "an inspiration and a discipline." The existence and unity of God were "instinctive knowledge . . . a part of man, inseparable from his life, admitting of no question." No dogmas or articles of faith commanded belief in the idea of the unity of God.

Also prominent in her 1901 article was her concern with educating Jews to read and understand Hebrew. In her view, the only way to perceive "the spirit of our religion," to grasp its "true and full meaning," was to know it in its original language. In particular, she became concerned with providing Jewish girls, who rarely received any instruction in Hebrew, with a solid education in the national language. If Judaism was to survive and flourish in Britain, then Jewish girls must acquire "a fundamental understanding of the form and spirit of the Hebrew language." Girls were central to this project because when they became mothers they alone, not their husbands, would be in a position to impart to their children a knowledge of the Hebrew language and a feeling for Judaism. Fathers were too busy supporting their families and taking part in public life. Mothers, on the other hand, spent the greater part of their time with their children. Her analysis and solution drew from the Victorian assumption that women were, by nature, better suited than men to cultivate the spiritual development of their children.

In 1921, when she published an anthology of Jewish readings for children of ages ten to fifteen (*Apples and Honey*—it was published simultaneously in the United States and Great Britain), she included an article on Jewish girls and Judaism that she had published earlier in *The Sinaist*, then edited by Leo Jung. As in 1901, she assigned women the heavy task of ushering in redemption: "Jewish girls, then, hold in their hands the destiny of our people as a power for good in a world which we are hoping in our days to see reborn."[8] And as before, she placed responsibility for raising children with a knowledge of Hebrew and Judaism on women—because they spent the greater part of their time with their children. As a response to the problem of widespread ignorance in Anglo-Jewry (among both men and women), hers was a naive and unrealizable solution. Few Jewish women knew enough, even if they were willing, to instruct their children as she was doing at Barley. But her insight that intensive immersion in Hebrew from an early age was an effective way to combat the hegemonic influence of English-language schooling was correct. She sensed, even if she did not articulate it, that the relative toleration that liberal societies extended to Jews could also weaken Jewish loyalties.

The texts that she chose to include in *Apples and Honey* reflect a sensitivity to—and discomfort with—the marginalization of women in traditional Jewish life. Although she nowhere recorded her selection criteria, the prominence of women writers and translators, some of them her contemporaries, suggests she was thinking about their usual absence in public presentations of Judaism. Among those whose work she included were writers whom Jewish literary scholars rediscovered in the late twentieth century: the novelist, poet, and historian Grace Aguilar; the historian and children's author Katie Magnus, whose husband Philip, the Victorian educational pioneer, was an acquaintance of Redcliffe's; and the American poet Emma Lazarus. She also included the work of women writers and translators whose work remains largely unknown, despite the recent boom in women's studies. Among them were the Yiddish and Hebrew translator Helena Frank, a granddaughter of Hugh Grosvenor, first Duke of Westminster. Raised a Christian—her German Jewish grandfather, Myer Frank, had settled in Manchester early in the eighteenth century and there converted to Christianity and married a Christian—she was an active Zionist, visiting the Land of Israel several times. Nina also chose work by the Lithuanian-born Yiddish translator and English novelist Hannah Berman—both she and Frank were supporters of the Jewish Free Reading

Room in the Whitechapel Road—and the American sketch writer and novelist Martha Wolfenstein. Among the other Anglo-Jewish writers included were Sophie Marcousé and Regina M. Bloch, both of whom were active, like Nina, in the Federation of Women Zionists (a union of local societies that was established in 1918). Indeed, it was Marcousé who first suggested the idea of compiling the anthology at a meeting of the federation's literary committee, which Nina chaired. Two of the other female contributors who shared Nina's commitment to Jewish nationalism settled eventually in Mandatory Palestine: London-born Hannah Trager—who spearheaded the establishment of the Jewish Free Reading Room in 1917, pioneered the writing of English-language children's literature about the Land of Israel, and campaigned for women's suffrage during the Mandate—and New York–born poet and educator Jesse E. Sampter, who was raised in the Ethical Culture movement and became a Unitarian as a young adult but then left for the Land of Israel, where she became part of Henrietta Szold's inner circle of women friends in the 1920s and 1930s.

Nina's feminism was not only literary. She took an interest in the votes for women campaign that agitated Britain in the years before World War I and served as a vice president of the Jewish League for Woman Suffrage, an organization of West End Jewish women, founded in 1912, which also worked to improve the status of women within the Jewish community. (Redcliffe also served as a vice president, and both of them made modest donations to the organization.)[9] At least once, in 1912, she accompanied Israel Zangwill when he spoke to a suffrage meeting and sat on the platform with the other notables there.[10] And she did not hesitate to challenge Jewish women who opposed the cause. Once, in the drawing room of one of the Franklin clan, when Mrs. Franklin was expressing her disapproval of the league and of ministers who sermonized about the suffrage issue, she interjected that "it was in accordance with Judaism to preach about anything that affected one's life." To this, Mrs. Franklin responded that, even so, it was not "English" to do so.[11] Nina also actively supported the league's communal goals and joined a small delegation from the league to the chief rabbi in 1913 asking him to support their demand that female seat holders (subscribing members in their own right, usually widows and single women) be allowed to vote in synagogue elections. He agreed, but in 1914 the council of the United Synagogue rejected the request. (Earlier and independently, three synagogues had approved the change, and an additional five did so in 1914 as a result of the league's agitation.)[12]

Figure 5.1. Nina Salaman, frontispiece, *The Voices of the Rivers* (1910). Collection of the author.

Nina's was not, however, a militant suffragette, like Edith Zangwill, Israel's wife, for example, whom she told that she would not value the vote if it were given grudgingly.[13] She certainly did not share the views of those Jewish women from backgrounds similar to hers who disrupted synagogue services to protest the imprisonment and forced feeding of suffragettes. The most famous such instance occurred on Yom Kippur in 1913 at the New West End Synagogue, where Nina and Redcliffe attended services when they were in London. Three suffragettes stood in the women's balcony and loudly prayed, "May God forgive Herbert Samuel [the postmaster general in Asquith's government], Sir Rufus Isaacs [the attorney general] for denying freedom to women. May God forgive them for consenting to the torture of women."[14]

Figure 5.2. Nina and Ruth Salaman (1910). Courtesy of Jenny Salaman Manson.

Nor would she have condoned the behavior of the even more militant Hugh Franklin, Herbert Samuel's nephew, who horsewhipped Home Secretary Winston Churchill in 1910, smashed his windows in Ecclestone Square in 1912, and set fire to an empty railway carriage in Harrow in 1913.[15] Nor was she as active in the Jewish League as some members of Redcliffe's family. His sister Jennie Cohen (1865–1921) served as the organization's treasurer until World War I, hosted meetings at her home, and embroidered the league's banner. Another sister, Isabelle Davis (1866–1944), wrote a twopenny pamphlet for the group, "Some Reasons Why the Jew Should Desire Woman Suffrage." It is interesting to note that Redcliffe's second wife, Gertrude Lowy (1887–1982), was a militant suffragette in her twenties. She was sentenced to two months of hard labor in 1912 for taking part in a windowsmashing episode, but her radical days were long behind her when she and Redcliffe married in 1926.[16]

108 | *The Last Anglo-Jewish Gentleman*

While supportive of the suffrage movement, Nina was even more de-voted to enhancing the role of Jewish women in communal life. As a long-time advocate of providing Jewish girls with a solid Hebrew education, she was an enthusiastic supporter of the Talmud Torah for Girls that met in a school in Redman's Road, Stepney, and at one time a member of the committee that managed it. The school, which used the *ivrit be-ivrit* method (teaching spoken Hebrew in Hebrew) to teach the language as a living language, was founded in 1912 by the Russian-born Hebrew educator Aaron Selig Doniach and the English-born civil servant Leon Simon.[17] Both men belonged to a small circle of Hebrew-speaking intellectuals in London. Doniach later taught modern Hebrew at the London School of Oriental Studies and Simon, while rising in the ranks of the General Post Office, promoted the thought of the father of cultural Zionism Ahad Ha-Am, whose work he translated and whose life he wrote. At its peak, the Talmud Torah enrolled two hundred students. Nina supported the school financially, split-ting the income from her books and articles between it and the Federation of Women Zionists.

3

In addition to her family, the focus of Nina's life at Barley was her transla-tion work. Although earlier she had translated liturgical poetry (*piyyutim*) for her father's *mahzor* project, she now concerned herself largely with the Hebrew poets of medieval Spain (1000–1200). The choice was not seren-dipitous. Since the late eighteenth century, medieval Spanish Jewry had occupied a place of honor in the imagination of western Jewish scholars and publicists. Acculturated Western Jews, longing for inclusion in state and society and wishing to distance themselves from the mass of Yiddish-speaking Ashkenazi Jews in the East, whom they saw as benighted and insular and as a threat to their own acceptance, created a mythic, highly romanticized image of Spanish Jewry.[18] What appealed to those who con-structed the myth of Sephardi superiority was the fact that Sephardic Jews had absorbed the style of the dominant culture while remaining learned, passionate Jews. Their vernacular had been the language of the land in which they had lived, and their dress, demeanor, and cultural habits had been the same as their neighbors'. They had consciously synthesized Jew-ish religious and cultural traditions with the dominant Arabic culture. Moreover, its outstanding representatives had distinguished themselves as poets, philosophers, grammarians, courtiers, and even, in a few instances, military commanders. For Jews whose hopes for full acceptance had been frustrated, especially in Germany, they were Jews worthy of adulation, role models for their own age. By the late nineteenth century, when Nina began to publish her translations, the myth of Sephardi superiority was well established almost everywhere in the West. In the case of England, the Sephardim themselves promoted and disseminated the idealized image. Its most militant proponent was the baptized Jew Benjamin Disraeli, who used it to enhance his own status when faced with aristocratic disdain for his Jewishness.[19] For Disraeli, Jews from the Iberian peninsula were different in kind from other Jews; they were superior by virtue of their culture, learning, wealth, descent, manners, and even blood.

I do not want to suggest that Disraeli's exaggerated articulation of the mythic image of Iberian Jewry was the source of Nina's fascination with the medieval Hebrew poets. Both, however, drew on well-established, widely circulated themes. For Nina, these poets embodied a sensibility that had been absent in Ashkenazi Jewry for centuries, a sensibility that modern Jewish scholars in the West much admired. They were devout but erudite seekers of the beautiful, open to the foreign and the new. They offered a model of robust, almost sensual Jewishness that was a stark alternative to the *halakhah*-centric *Frömmigkeit* of the *yeshivah* world of East European Jewry. Neither she nor Redcliffe ever romanticized the latter. Despite its intellectual vitality and its reverence for tradition, the culture of East European Jewry never served them as a model. It was too foreign, too far removed from their upbringing, their life in the Hertfordshire countryside, and their deeply embedded, genteel Englishness.

The Iberian poets whom Nina translated pioneered the writing of secular Hebrew poetry. Until the mid-tenth century, most Hebrew poetry was liturgical; it was incorporated into the synagogue service and was intended to be recited communally. Its language was esoteric, allusive, and often obscure, suffused with learned references to rabbinic literature and rabbinic interpretations of scripture. In Muslim Spain, the Jewish encounter with the high culture of the Arab world revolutionized the writing of Hebrew poetry.[20] Speaking a distinctive form of Arabic and using Arabic (written in Hebrew characters) for prose works, Jewish literary figures continued to use the Hebrew language when they wrote verse. They recast its style, its form, and its thematic content, however, merging biblical Hebrew diction, imagery, and tropes with Arabic prosody, form, and style. They embraced genres from courtly Arabic culture that were hitherto unknown in Jewish culture: love songs, wine poems, friendship poems, satirical poems, epithalamia (poems in celebration of a marriage), panegyrics to and eulogies of allies and patrons, meditations on national longing, and introspective addresses to the soul.

Iberian Hebrew poetry presents formidable challenges to the translator. As a rule, the translation of poetry is more difficult than the translation of prose, whatever the source language, for obvious reasons. Some might even argue that the translator of poetry must be a poet himself or herself to effectively render its nuanced, complex tones. Whatever the case, medieval Hebrew poetry from Spain poses challenges that are distinctly its own. One obstacle is the referential style of the poets. So fully immersed in the Hebrew Bible were they that they constantly cited or echoed it—without, however, any indication that they were doing so, since they knew that their readers would recognize the references and allusions and appreciate their use of them. Thus, the translator of this body of work must have an intimate familiarity with the biblical texts with which the poets were working. In addition, he or she must be familiar with the midrashic context in which the rabbis played with a biblical text, adding to it an associative meaning. As the scholar of medieval Hebrew poetry Raphael Loewe explained, "This last associative aspect is of particular importance, as it may sometimes contribute a level of meaning that has accrued to a text independently of, or even in defiance of, its original context or meaning, in virtue of the use that has been made of it, *obiter dictum*, in the Talmud."[21] The translator must know when the poet is building on both well-known and obscure rabbinic references to biblical texts that transform their initial meaning. A further challenge is that the poets were writing in a language that they did not speak but knew (however intimately) from prayer and study alone. They thus wrote in a stylized, artificial manner, a manner that is difficult to capture and can seem unnatural, contrived, or archaic. The translator must also cope with rhyme schemes that are easy to achieve in Hebrew but are much more difficult in English, which does not have the rhyming potential of a Semitic language. Nina preferred rendering her translations in free verse, although in some instances she also offered alternative metered and rhymed versions.

Adina Tanenbaum's learned assessment of translators of medieval Hebrew poetry speaks well of Nina's translations. While noting that they now have "a certain antiquarian charm"—which is not surprising from someone with her late-Victorian upbringing—and that they can "seem less than immediately appealing or accessible," she concludes that they reveal "great erudition" and "tremendous sympathy for her subject, whose stylistic mastery and lyric grace she admiringly acknowledges."[22] Less generously, in surveying common strategies for rendering Iberian Hebrew poetry into English, the poet and translator Peter Cole wrote that she, like Israel Zangwill, adopted "an ersatz Victorian poetic idiom."[23] If her tone and diction were undoubtedly Victorian, they were hardly "ersatz"—she was, by birth, a Victorian.

To her contemporaries, her translations, of course, did not have an antiquarian tone, and they praised them extravagantly. Israel Abrahams, reader in rabbinic literature at Cambridge from 1902 to 1925 and the most important scholar of Judaism in Britain at the time, highly prized her translation skills. For years the two met weekly on Tuesdays in room 12 of the Cambridge University Library, and after she was no longer able to travel because of her illness, he traveled to Barley.[24] After one session in Cambridge, she wrote to Redcliffe, then serving in the military, that Abrahams had told her that she was able to "make out the difficult passages better than he." When she showed him some obscure lines and read them aloud in Hebrew, he called out, "Translate, translate! I can't take it in like you can!"[25] Expressive of his admiration for her work is that on occasion he would take charge of her older boys, shepherding them around the museums of Cambridge, to allow her to work uninterruptedly in the library. Later, when the boys were away at school, he would turn up around eleven in the morning in room 12 and spend the whole day with her. As she wrote to Redcliffe, "I don't know that I *do* very much, but he talks and sees what I have done sometimes and it is always useful."[26]

One poet in particular became the focus of her work—Yehudah Ha-Levi (ca. 1075–1141), the most widely revered of the medieval poets. She included twelve of his poems in the small book of translations that the Jewish Publication Society of America (JPSA) published in 1901, *Songs of Exile*, when she was still Nina Davis. When JPSA launched plans to publish the Schiff Library of Jewish Classics (funded by an endowment from the banker and philanthropist Jacob Schiff) in 1916, it invited her to do the Yehudah Ha-Levi volume. She submitted her manuscript in 1922 but it sat untouched for months, the heads of the JPSA distracted by the organization's financial problems. By this point, Nina was seriously ill. Eager to see the volume appear while his wife was still alive, Redcliffe intervened, asking the JPSA to do all it could to hurry the publication of what was her *magnum opus*.

112 | *The Last Anglo-Jewish Gentleman*

Disagreements between Nina and the editors—about the spelling of the poet's name and the titles Nina gave to some of the poems—delayed matters further, but, in the end, copies reached Barley in early January 1925, seven weeks before her death.[27]

Although Yehudah Ha-Levi was universally acknowledged as the most accomplished of the Spanish Jewish poets, I want to point to two other reasons for which Nina may have devoted herself to his work. The first is the strong devotional nature of many of his poems. While the poet wrote about love, friendship, brides and grooms, and other secular themes, he also wrote about divine omnipotence and righteousness, the human hunger to draw close to and find favor with God, and the consolations of faith. They were themes that spoke to Nina's religious sensibility. It is not surprising that the largest section in the JPSA volume consists of devotional poems (37). By contrast, she included only four friendship poems and only fifteen love and bridal poems. The remaining section, which she titled "The Journey to Zion," included twenty-two of the poet's Zionides, that is, poems on the tribulations of exile, the yearning for redemption in the Land of Israel, and the hazards of the voyage to Zion. Nina gave that group of poems a place of honor at the front of the volume. Yehudah Ha-Levi's religious nationalism—his stress on the spiritual poverty and emotional affliction of exile and the redemptive role of the Land of Israel—stirred her imagination. Which, I believe, was the second reason that she embraced him with such enthusiasm. In her introduction to the volume, she declared his songs to Zion "his most beautiful" poems. In them, she wrote, he spoke without recourse to the poet's "ordinary artifices." His soul became "the instrument" with which he communicated and "on his heartstrings" he "played the song of Israel's hope." The overlap between the poet's yearnings and the translator's dreams was close. This is not to say that the encounter with his poetry transformed her into a Jewish nationalist, a believer in the collective destiny of the Jewish people and the redemptive place of the Land of Israel, for she was already, by virtue of her upbringing, an inchoate nationalist. His poetry, rather, confirmed and heightened sentiments that were already her own.[28]

This kind of sentimental, apolitical Jewish nationalism was more widespread in Anglo-Jewry than most historical accounts acknowledge. Drawing on traditional religious ideas about the holiness of the Land of Israel and long-standing engagement with philanthropic projects there, it preceded and then coexisted with Herzlian Zionism. Nina's participation in the Palestine Exhibition and Bazaar, in May 1912, to provide aid to the Bezalel School of Art and Craft, and the Evelina de Rothschild School, the first school for girls in Jerusalem, is a good example. Held in the Portman Rooms, Baker Street, the two-day event included a bazaar, a café, musical performances and dramatic presentations, and exhibitions about Jewish life in Palestine, such as a model of Zikhron Yaakov (one of the first modern Jewish settlements in the Land of Israel, founded by Edmund de Rothschid in 1882) and an exhibition of Jewish handicrafts. Alfred de Rothschild's private orchestra played on both days. Nina, along with her sister-in-law Isabelle Davis and Alide Gollancz, wife of the English literature scholar Israel Gollancz, ran a bookstall in the bazaar, which was intended to re-semble a Jerusalem street. Her son Myer, wearing a red fez, ladies' boots, and an embroidered coat, helped out, taking books around on a little tray. Those who visited the bazaar and exhibition, as well as those who staffed its booths or performed on its stage, were not necessarily Zionists, as the mix of children who acted in a Hebrew-language children's play, *Joseph and His Brethren*, shows. They came from families with strong Zionist al-legiances, like the Gasters and the Bentwiches, and from families who were indifferent or hostile to the movement, like the Montagus and the Frank-lins. Ivor Montagu, for example, son of the second Lord Swaythling, a fu-ture film producer, table-tennis promoter, and Soviet agent, played a buyer of corn.[29] The *Jewish Chronicle*, commenting on the success of the event and the press of visitors, asked what it signified. In answering, it summed up the appeal of this sentimental nationalism: "It means partly that the practical work of Palestinian regeneration appealed to the practical mind of Anglicized Jewry. But it also meant more—that in spite of all assimila-tive influences, the old Jewish sentiment could still tug pretty effectively at the heart-strings of the people. East End and West End were united on the common ground of the old Jewish ideal—the old love of Palestine."[30]

4

In the years before World War I, Nina continued to supervise the education of the children, of whom there were eventually six: Myer, who had been born in Berlin in 1902; the twins Arthur and Edward, who had been born in London in 1904 before the move to Barley; Raphael, who was born in Barley in 1906 and the two girls, Ruth and Esther, who were born in Barley as well, in 1908 and 1914 respectively. At first, as we have seen, Redcliffe

114 | *The Last Anglo-Jewish Gentleman*

and Nina educated the children at home, but, as the boys grew older, they began to look elsewhere. Had they been more conventional parents, that is, more socially ambitious and less intensely Jewish, they would have sent the boys to boarding school at age eight or so to prepare them for public school when they were older. But the Hebrew education of the children was critical to Nina. In addition, she was attracted to the principles and methods of the Parents' National Education Union (PNEU), which supported home schooling, and devoted much time to instructing the various nursery governesses in its principles. The PNEU program drew on the ideas of the pioneering educational reformer Charlotte Mason and was known for emphasizing the individuality of children and their needs and for rejecting the most severe, unthinking practices of English education. Its chief promoter and propagandist in Britain was Henrietta Franklin, daughter of Lord Swaythling and sister of Lily Montagu and the Liberal politician Edwin Montagu. It is likely that Nina was introduced to the PNEU program through her connections with the Franklin and Montagu families.[31] In fall 1911, she and Redcliffe decided that the three oldest boys needed something else, and they began sending them to "the little dog-school" in nearby Royston in the mornings.[32] In the afternoons, Nina continued to give them Hebrew lessons. With the older boys away, she taught Raphael before they returned home. The Royston school was not rigorous, however, and Nina came to think it a waste of time.[33] The following fall, when Myer was ten and the twins eight, they hired a male tutor, who came to the house daily. The tutor, Daniel Hopkin, the son of a Welsh agricultural laborer and a recent law graduate of St. Catherine's College, Cambridge, lodged in the village. He was a great success: he expanded the boys' world and they flourished under his supervision. He gave the three older boys lessons from 9:30 to 12:45, while Nina took Myer and then the twins for Hebrew for forty-five minutes each before lunch. Raphael was sent to the small kindergarten (four children in all) at the rectory in the morning. In the afternoon, after the boys rested, Hopkin played football or cricket with them, took them for runs, or taught them boxing; they came indoors about 4 p.m., read and practiced their musical instruments until tea time, after which Hopkin left.[34] (Hopkin later qualified as a barrister, became a Labor member of Parliament, and served as a stipendiary magistrate in London.)

The Salamans' near-idyllic situation came crashing down in December 1913. On Friday afternoon, December 19, the boys celebrated the end of the term with sport activities, in which the village boys joined. "It was a very cold foggy day; the field was wet and muddy." Nina noted in her diary. The three older boys caught chills, even though they changed their clothes after coming inside. The following day, Arthur developed croup, which then turned into pneumonia, but by Tuesday he was on the road to recovery. Myer had a sore throat and some hoarseness, but remained otherwise healthy. Edward showed no sign of illness until Monday and then rapidly declined. He died of pneumonia on December 24, at the age of nine and a half. On Thursday, his body was taken to Willesden Jewish Cemetery in London for burial in the Salaman family plot the following day. Nina, who was six months pregnant with Esther, did not attend but remained at home with Charles Myers's wife Edith, who came to Barley to comfort her.[35]

The death of Edward scarred all of them—in the case of his twin Arthur, for life. In 1951, as an adult, Arthur confided to his diary his memories of the evening Edward died. The twins were in the night nursery at Barley, both feverish and delirious, but Edward worse than Arthur was. They came to their senses every now and then and, at one such moment, Edward called to Arthur, using a name from their own private language. He did so several times. Arthur knew that he wanted him to answer his name in their private language but felt ashamed to use "the rather silly name" he had for Edward because there was an undernurse in the room and, fearful of her ridicule, he "hadn't the courage to do it in her hearing." He pretended to be asleep; Edward kept on calling but he never answered, "so he stopped & died later that night." In Arthur's mind, if he had answered him, Edward would have lived. The events of that night when he was nine years old, he wrote in 1951, "come back every now & again & put me in a state of horror & misery." They have "made it impossible for me to refuse a request, or say no to anyone. I can't bear to hear a child cry, & indeed am often afraid to be with children in case one of them might cry. I can still hear the secret language when that happens, & I know it's no bloody good answering now."[36] After Edward's death, Arthur developed a nervous tic.[37] Nina's diaries from the period tell us little about what she experienced, although it is not difficult to imagine. She does record that they delayed telling four-year-old Ruth about Edward's death, even after she began asking about him.[38]

Notes

1. Nina Davis, "An Aspect of Judaism in 1901," *Jewish Quarterly Review* 13, no. 2 (1901): 241–57.

2. Ibid., 246.

3. Ibid.

4. Ibid., 242, 248.

5. Ibid., 251.

6. Ibid., 257.

7. NDS, *Jacob and Israel*, Cambridge Jewish Publications no. 5 (Cambridge: Cambridge University Press, 1920), 1.

8. NDS, "Women and Judaism," *Sinaist* 1, no. 3 (June 1917). This essay was reprinted with a slight change in title in her anthology, *Apples and Honey: A Gift-Book for Jewish Boys and Girls* (London: William Heinemann, 1921), 39–42.

9. *First Annual Report of the Jewish League for Woman Suffrage, 1913–1914* (London: Jewish League for Woman Suffrage, 1914).

10. NDS to RNS, May 16, 1912, Add. MS 8171, Wedderburn Deposit, RNS CUL.

11. NDS to RNS, April 16, 1913, Add. MS 8171, Wedderburn Deposit, RNS CUL.

12. Anne Summers, *Christian and Jewish Women in Britain, 1880–1949: Living with Difference* (London: Macmillan Palgrave, 2017), 73.

13. Edith Zangwill to NDS, February 27, 1913, Add. MS 8171/5, RNS CUL.

14. Linda Gordon Kuzmack, *Woman's Cause: The Jewish Woman's Movement in England and the United States, 1881–1933* (Columbus: Ohio State University Press, 1990), 134.

15. Todd M. Endelman, *Radical Assimilation in English Jewish History, 1656–1945* (Bloomington: Indiana University Press, 1990), 110–11.

16. On the participation of Jewish women in the suffrage movement, see Kuzmack, *Woman's Cause*; Anne Summers, "Gender, Religion and an Immigrant Minority: Jewish Women and the Suffrage Movement in Britain, c. 1900–1920," *Women's History Review* 21, no. 3 (2012): 399–418; and individual entries in Elizabeth Crawford, *The Woman's Suffrage Movement: A Reference Guide, 1866–1928* (London: University College, London Press, 1999).

17. *Jewish Chronicle*, April 19, 1912, March 24, 1922; NDS to RNS, November 23, 1917, Add. MS 8171, Wedderburn Deposit, RNS CUL.

18. Ivan Marcus, "Beyond the Sephardi Mystique," *Orim* 1, no. 1 (1985): 35–53; Ismar Schorsch, "The Myth of Sephardi Supremacy," *Leo Baeck Institute Year Book* 34 (1989): 47–66; John M. Efron, *German Jewry and the Allure of the Sephardic* (Princeton, NJ: Princeton University Press, 2015).

19. Todd M. Endelman, *Broadening Jewish History: Towards a Social History of Ordinary Jews* (Oxford, UK: Littman Library of Jewish Civilization, 2011), ch. 10.

20. Ross Brann, *The Compunctious Poet: Cultural Ambiguity and Hebrew Poetry in Muslim Spain* (Baltimore, MD: Johns Hopkins University Press, 1991); Raymond P. Scheindlin, *Wine, Women, and Death: Medieval Hebrew Poems on the Good Life* (New York: Oxford University Press, 1999); Peter Cole, *The Dream of the Poem: Hebrew Poems from Muslim and Christian Spain, 950–1492* (Princeton, NJ: Princeton University Press, 2007).

21. Raphael J. Loewe, "The Bible in Medieval Hebrew Poetry," in *Interpreting the Hebrew Bible: Essays in Honour of E. I. J. Rosenthal*, ed. John A. Emerton and Stefan C. Reif (Cambridge: Cambridge University Press, 1982), 138.

22. Adena Tanenbaum, "On Translating Medieval Hebrew Poetry," in *Hebrew Scholarship and the Medieval World*, ed. Nicholas de Lange (Cambridge: Cambridge University Press, 2001), 172.

23. Cole, Introduction to *Dream of the Poem*, 17.

24. Herbert Loewe, "Nina Salaman, 1877–1925," *Transactions of the Jewish Historical Society of England* 11 (1929): 231.

25. NDS to RNS, March 17, 1917, Add. MS 8171/104, RNS CUL.

26. NDS to RNS, January 31, 1919, Add. MS 8171, Wedderburn Deposit, RNS CUL.

27. Jonathan D. Sarna, *JPS: The Americanization of Jewish Culture, 1888–1988* (Philadelphia: Jewish Publication Society, 1989), 153.

28. *Selected Poems of Jehudah Halevi*, ed. Heinrich Brody, trans. Nina Salaman (Philadelphia: JPSA, 1924), xxv–xxvi. Two other Anglo-Jewish women also published translations of Yehudah Ha-Levi's poetry, Alice Lucas and Amy Levy, although the latter, largely ignorant of Hebrew, translated from the German of Abraham Geiger. For a comparison of their translations, see Cynthia Scheinberg, "'And We Are Not What They Have Been': Anglo-Jewish Women Poets, 1839–1923," in *Jewish Women Writers in Britain*, ed. Nadia Valman (Detroit: Wayne State University Press, 2014), 53–60.

29. Miscellaneous printed materials on the Palestine Exhibition and Bazaar, May 13 and 14, 1912, are in Add. MS 8171/5, RNS CUL; NDS, diaries, May 1912.

30. *JC*, May 17, 1912.

31. RNS, "The Helmsman Takes Charge," LH/X/101, Royal London Hospital Archives; Monk Gibbon, *Netta* (London: Routledge and Kegan Paul, 1960).

32. NDS, diaries, October 1912.

33. NDS, diaries, July 1912.

34. NDS, diaries, November 1912; RNS, "Helmsman Takes Charge."

35. NDS, diaries, December 1913.

36. Arthur Gabriel Salaman, diaries, February 18, 1951, in possession of William Salaman, Cambridge. Arthur prefaced his entry with these words: "For thirty-eight years I have been wondering whether or not to write down what I am writing now. During this time I expected to meet someone who I could tell it to, to get the thing out of my system, but I haven't met such a person, & if I had it would still be in my system just the same. If it does good to tell your things to someone else, perhaps it does good to write these things down."

37. Jane Miller, interview by the author, June 1, 2011, London.

38. NDS, diaries, December 1913.

6

WORLD WAR I AND
THE LAND OF ISRAEL

1

Redcliffe, Nina, the children, and Redcliffe's mother were vacationing in the North Sea coastal town of Filey, Yorkshire, when they heard of the assassination of Archduke Franz Ferdinand, heir to the Habsburg imperial throne, on June 28, 1914, in Sarajevo, Bosnia. Many years later, Redcliffe recalled the shock he felt when he first heard the news. "I have never felt so profoundly moved by any political announcement before or since." He had the vivid impression of "a great gulf suddenly opening beneath my feet." He told Nina and his mother that he expected the assassination to spark a Europe-wide war. They thought he was daft.[1] He was not. He was prescient.

The impact of the war on Redcliffe and Nina was transformative—in ways that they might not have foreseen. The demise of the Ottoman Empire and the issuance of the Balfour Declaration sent Redcliffe to Egypt and Palestine and gave his and Nina's hitherto vague Jewish nationalism a political edge. By the end of the war, they had become strong supporters of Zionism, viewing the return to Zion as crucial to the well-being of the Jewish people. The shift was not merely ideological. Their embrace of Zionism changed the texture and the arc of their lives, adding a new dimension to the ways in which they expressed their Jewishness. It also gave a focus to Redcliffe's life that he felt, correctly or not, it had previously lacked; it lifted his sprits and relieved the depression he suffered from intermittently throughout his life. At the same time, his absence from Barley during the war—in military hospitals in England and then on active duty in Egypt and Palestine—forced Nina to assume greater responsibility for the upbringing and education of their children and for the management of Homestall. She emerged from

World War I and the Land of Israel | 119

World War I a stronger personality—more worldly, less risk averse, more independent.

2

Redcliffe was forty years old when Britain went to war, just over the age for active service. Caught up in the patriotic wave that swept the country—and especially the families of the Anglo-Jewish notability—he immediately volunteered to serve as medical officer to the recruiting office in nearby Royston and to lead the local special constabulary, a volunteer force that drilled sometimes at Homestall. When the boys' tutor, Daniel Hopkin, joined the army as a second lieutenant in September, he also took over the task of giving them their lessons. None of these activities, however, satisfied him. He felt uncomfortable urging young men to join up and fight while he remained in safety, living comfortably at Homestall.[2] He wrote to Hopkin in late November, complaining that he had nothing to do (which was not entirely true). His work as a justice of the peace had slowed down since the usual offenders were now serving with the army. The potatoes were dug. "What then is an active man to do?" he asked. Watch for zeppelins? Speculate incessantly about who might be a German spy? His friend Charles Myers was serving at the duchess of Westminster's hospital in the French coastal resort Le Tourquet and wanted Redcliffe to join him there, where a vacancy had opened up. As he told Hopkin, "I very much wished to see this great struggle at closer quarters and also thought I should be of some use out there." His physician examined him and thought he would not come to any harm because of his earlier chest problem but urged him to finish a project at the Royston hospital before joining. By the time he had finished, the vacancy was filled, to his great disappointment.[3]

Something else was weighing on his mind as well. Emotionally, avoiding service was associated in his mind with weakness and a lack of masculinity. He was haunted, in particular, by his failure as a young man to serve in the British army in the Boer War (1899–1902), although he had made an effort to do so at the time. A few months after the start of the war, in January 1900, having learned that he had passed his final medical examination, he had gone to the War Office and put his name down for the Royal Army Medical Corps—without consulting anyone in his family. He later recalled that he had been "fired up more by the desire for adventure than by a sense of duty."[4] But he was never called and never served. It is worth noting that his failure to serve in the Boer War followed a period of late adolescence when he had been plagued by ill health, some of which probably was psychosomatic or psychogenetic in origin. Recall that his father had repeatedly reminded him that he was weak and sickly, even telling him, before departing for a trip to Germany, to avoid arguments while traveling since "you don't fight well."[5]

Toward the end of 1914, he no longer was able to tolerate his status as a civilian. Teaching the boys was not fulfilling, and in January 1915 a new tutor, L. M. Westall, arrived. Restive and unhappy, Redcliffe was determined to enlist. "Once more the old passion resurged; it was still not too late." Nina, who initially opposed his serving in the war, relented after several weeks. He enlisted as a medical officer in the medical corps but first spent six weeks at the London Hospital familiarizing himself with recent developments in medical care, for he had not practiced medicine for a decade. He hoped to serve in a hospital in France but instead spent three and a half uneventful years at military hospitals in England,[6] from April 1915 to September 1916, at Purfleet, Essex, and from September 1916 to September 1917, at Colchester, also in Essex.

His wartime work in military hospitals did not cure him of his restlessness and unhappiness. What disturbed him most about the military was the excessive consumption of alcohol by the other medical officers. Whether he was a prig or whether, by virtue of his upbringing, he was unaccustomed to heavy drinking. That so many of his fellow doctors were alcoholics disgusted him, for he had "never imagined that men who had studied and practiced medicine could sink so low."[7] After receiving one of Redcliffe's accounts of the drunkenness, Nina responded, "What beasts these drinking officers are!" She added that Jews could feel their superiority on this score. It seemed proof to her that they were "somehow and somewhere made different." When he wrote Nina two years later that Jewish officers were among the heavy drinkers, she naively responded, "I don't believe one would find it with any who have kept up any remains of Judaism."[8]

In letters to Nina, he also expressed discontent about the direction his life had taken, what he had—or had not—accomplished. He complained about a lack of focus in his life so far and the sense of futility that it had engendered. He wondered whether it had been quixotic to give up clinical practice and retire to the country. He also expressed regret that he had not accompanied his friends Charles Myers and Charles Seligman on the Cambridge anthropological expedition to the Torres Straits Islands (between

World War I and the Land of Israel | 121

Australia and Papua New Guinea) in 1898, a formative event in the history of British social anthropology.[9] Clearly, he was depressed—and probably not for the first time. Nina reminded him that he was never fully contented with any work he undertook. "You never think anything is useful enough. Why not make up your mind what work here [Barley] you would really like and make a shot for it?"[10] She often tried to bolster his confidence and cheer him up, telling him, for example, that his discovery of the Jewish racial type was an important accomplishment and that devoting himself to his fellow Jews was "a good thing to do and big and difficult." She even suggested that fate might be preparing him for "some Jewish ideal," although it is difficult to know what she had in mind.[11]

Redcliffe was also worried about the future of the family businesses—ostrich feathers and real estate—whose dividends allowed him to live as a country gentleman. His older brother Euston, whom he once characterized as "a man of great enterprise," had headed the ostrich-feather firm since the death of their father in 1896, spending much of his time in New York at the firm's office there, but Euston died of typhoid fever in February 1916 while serving with the British army. His older brother Elkin, with whom Redcliffe had quarreled, was also active in the firm, but he died in May 1919 in the influenza pandemic. Redcliffe never intended to take an active role in either business (and certainly had no qualification to do so, other than his self-discipline and intelligence), but the death of first one and then the other of his two older brothers raised the possibility. The question was whether his two other brothers, Clement and Michel (1879–1971), could or would shoulder more responsibility. (One other brother, Harry [1877–1901], had committed suicide in 1901, and the other living brother, Archie (1885–?), was mentally disabled. Needless to say, it did not occur to anyone at the time that one of the sisters might assume a role.) Nina thought it would be a waste of his talent—"a sin"—for him to go into the business, devoting his powers to ostrich feathers while Clement and Michel were "at large." In Nina's eyes—and probably in Redcliffe's as well—Clement and Michel lived lives devoid of larger purpose. They were clever "in their way," she believed, and "quite capable of some work after all these years of play."[12]

Clement, a qualified barrister, lived in the country in Somerset with his wife and five children. One of Redcliffe's children characterized him as "idle and vain."[13] Michel was a more endearing figure. He had studied painting at the Slade in the mid-1890s, along with his sister Louise (1876–?), and, while he did not continue to paint seriously, he became a patron of painters, Augustus John in particular. At the Slade, he met and married another student, Chattie Wake, and they moved to the country, where he lived in a succession of impressive country houses as a gracious host, entertaining painters and writers, family and friends. Michel was particularly devoted to the chase and was master of the Exmoor hunt from 1906 to 1911. Before World War I, Redcliffe visited him frequently and joined in the hunting. To Nina, the manner in which Michel and Chattie lived seemed extravagant and irresponsible. They were always buying things, such as dinner services and glassware, carriages and horses, and never seemed to do without anything they fancied, thinking only of their comfort and pleasure. Chattie did not keep track of household expenses, leaving the task to the nurse, and Nina wondered how Michel managed to pay his bills. After one visit in September 1906, Nina remarked on the irregularity of their household routine. Chattie did not come downstairs until about 2:30 in the afternoon and was regularly late for meals. But Michel never complained about her behavior, she noted, as long as she appeared every evening in a different dress with some new wonderful accessory.[14]

Other visitors found Michel and Chattie's hospitality irresistible. The poet and critic Humbert Wolfe and his wife Jessie stayed at their magnificent home in Porelock, Somerset, in 1911. She thought it the most beautifully furnished home she had ever seen and Michel and Chattie perfect hosts, "whose delight was to entertain their friends, rich or poor, and to do so perfectly by giving them the freedom to entertain themselves and treat the house as their own."[15] The actor Alec Guinness, struggling at the time, who married Michel's daughter Merula in 1938, remembered how intimidated he was when Merula first took him home (then a house in Ockley, Surrey). With its "horsy and huntin' talk," he found the atmosphere "alarmingly hearty." He also recalled that Humbert Wolfe once said to him of his father-in-law, "You can't be an artist, a country gentleman, *and* a Jew," but that he thought that "Michel appeared to succeed well enough on all three levels."[16]

With the deaths of Euston and Elkin, Michel, who had served in France and the Middle East in the war, took over the management of the family's business interests. He never moved to London but spent several days a week there, returning to the country whenever he could. In 1919, he was at the family office two days a week, Nina wrote to Redcliffe, who was still in Palestine.[17] Michel was not a success as a businessman. In part, the reason was that the ostrich-feather business crashed in 1914 from oversupply and shifting fashions in women's dress in Britain, France, and the United States.

World War I and the Land of Israel | 123

Even the savviest businessman could not have prevented the decline of I. Salaman and Company, once the largest wholesale ostrich-feather firm in the world. While the much-diminished firm, shorn of its overseas affiliates, still employed about eight hundred people in 1922, by the end of the decade the number was down to about fifty. By then, its business was reduced to selling off the vast stock of plumes in its warehouses to manufacturers of feather dusters in Germany, France, and the United States.[18] The family's property holdings, M. and N. Salaman Estates, on the other hand, was a potential goldmine. But Michel lacked the experience, knowledge, drive, and acumen to exploit its potential. The East European Jewish developers who powered the London commercial property boom after 1945—Harry Hyams, Jack Cotton, Charles Clore, Harold Samuel, Max Joseph, and the like—fared better, but then they were not country gentlemen who hunted. One of Redcliffe's granddaughters told me that in the family it was said of Michel that he ran and ruined Salaman Estates.[19]

3

In summer 1917 Redcliffe was rescued from the doldrums into which he had fallen by the government's decision to form what became known popularly as the Jewish Legion. Here some background is necessary. Early in the war, it became clear to both the British government and the World Zionist Organization that one likely outcome of the war would be the dismemberment of the Ottoman Empire—which would work to both their advantages.[20] The World Zionist Organization could not, however, actively promote the dismemberment. It was officially neutral, as it did not want to antagonize the Turks and endanger the existing Jewish settlements in the Land of Israel. But some Zionists in London—the Russian-born journalist Zev Jabotinsky, in particular—reasoned that Jewish participation in Britain's Middle East campaign would advance Zionist claims in negotiations at the end of the war. Soon after the start of the war, Jabotinsky, on his own initiative but with the support of Chaim Weizmann, then researching synthetic dyestuffs at the University of Manchester, began lobbying the government to create a Jewish fighting unit in the British army. He enjoyed the active support of a few British military and political figures who looked favorably on the Zionist movement. Among them were the Anglo-Irish big-game hunter and adventurer Lt. Col. J. H. Patterson, who had commanded the Zion Mule Corps at Gallipoli from April to December 1915; David Lloyd George, prime minister in the wartime coalition government from 1916 to 1922; the Conservative member of Parliament Leopold Amery, who, unbeknownst to his contemporaries, was the son of a baptized Hungarian Jewish mother; and C. P. Scott, editor of the *Manchester Guardian*. The War Office was not sympathetic, however.

In December 1916, when Lloyd George became prime minister, he was receptive to the idea of forming a Jewish fighting unit. The war on the western front had stalled in the trenches and the slaughter was mounting. Desperate for a breakthrough victory, he was resolved to open a second front—in the Middle East. In spring 1917 Egyptian-based British troops actively engaged the Turkish army in the Sinai peninsula and in Gaza and in April 1917 successfully repelled a German army attack on the Suez Canal. That same month the war cabinet committed Britain to conquering the Holy Land.

Meanwhile, on the domestic political scene, events conspired to advance the cause of a Jewish fighting unit.[21] At the start of the war, the government had relied on voluntary recruitment to fill the ranks of the army. As the war dragged on, however, relying on volunteers ceased to provide sufficient manpower, and in January and May 1916 the government introduced universal male conscription in stages. While prosperous, native-born Jews had flocked to enlist at the start of the war, East European–born Jews, many of whom were not British citizens, did not. They were unsympathetic to Britain's ally, tsarist Russia, whose anti-Jewish measures had embittered their lives before emigration. Moreover, not having been raised and educated in Britain, they did not share the overheated patriotism that stirred the native-born community, which, in turn, saw the immigrants' failure to respond to the call to enlist as an embarrassment and a scandal. The well-to-do viewed this lack of enthusiasm for the war as a threat to their own security and standing, fearing it would feed long-standing prejudices about the imperfect identification of Jews with British life. In July 1916, the government ordered Russian male immigrants of military age who did not hold British citizenship (perhaps as many as thirty thousand men) to choose between enlistment and deportation to Russia, where they would face conscription into the Russian army. The notion of enlisting Russian Jews in Britain in an all-Jewish unit to do battle with the Turks now took on added luster, for, it was argued, the prospect of fighting Turks in the Holy Land was a more attractive enticement to enlist than the prospect of fighting Germans in the trenches in France. In April 1917 the war cabinet approved the creation of the unit, having been convinced that it would attract Jewish immigrants in Britain—and elsewhere in English-speaking lands—who would otherwise be disinclined to fight. Like other Russian Jews who joined the British army, they were promised naturalization, at no cost, after completing three months of satisfactory service.

The idea of a Jewish battalion came to Redcliffe's notice early in the war. In December 1914, long before Jabotinsky began his campaign in London, the psychoanalyst David Eder, a cousin and close friend of Zangwill, wrote to Redcliffe to cultivate the latter's support for it. The idea of a Jewish battalion in the British army, Eder later remembered, first surfaced in a conversation between Zangwill, Leopold Greenberg, editor of the *Jewish Chronicle* and a follower of Herzl since 1896, Joseph Cowen, a long-time Zionist activist (also a cousin of Zangwill), and himself at an ABC tea shop in the Strand in London in the first weeks of the war.[22] A lively debate about the proposal filled the correspondence columns of the *Jewish Chronicle* from mid-October 1914 to early January 1915. Redcliffe, who was not a Zionist at the time, was fascinated by the idea but on reflection thought it undesirable, fearing the "horrible possibility" that a Jewish battalion would fight a Jewish battalion in the enemy army or even a regiment in which there was a large number of Jews. (This was a recurrent theme in modern Jewish discourse on military service.)[23] Within a matter of days, however, he moderated his view and told Eder that he had no objection to forming Jewish companies or smaller units within existing battalions but thought that finding Jewish officers to staff them would be a problem since they would want to remain with the units in which they were already serving. He added that, whether a success or not, the experiment would be "instructive." Still, he feared it would be a failure.[24] In any case, nothing came of the initiative.

After the war cabinet decided to create a Jewish fighting unit, Redcliffe became less pessimistic about the project's possible success. Colonel Patterson, whom the government appointed on July 27, 1917, to form the Jewish Regiment, as it was then called, convened a meeting of Jewish notables at the War Office on August 8 to rally support within the Jewish community, which was divided over the wisdom of its creation because of the Zionist complexion of the proposal. Redcliffe was among the non-Zionists who were invited.[25] When it became clear to him that the War Office was resolved to have the unit, he told the meeting that the Zionists had presented them with a fait accompli and that there was nothing to discuss. "There is only one thing left for us—try to make the Regiment a success and a credit

Figure 6.1. The badge of the Jewish Legion, with the Hebrew word *kadimah* (Forward!) at the base.

to the Jewish people."[26] Soon afterward, he joined the provisional executive committee to promote the regiment, and on September 5 he took part in the deputation that called on Lord Derby at the War Office to counter assimilationist efforts to reverse the government's decision. The assimilationists failed to block the formation of the unit, but they did succeed in convincing Derby to omit the word *Jewish* in its official name, a symbolic victory that rankled both Redcliffe and Nina. Despite Derby's decision, however, the legion's soldiers wore distinctive uniforms that made clear their Jewish character. Their left sleeve bore a *Magen David*, and later their cap badge bore a menorah (a symbol of the Temple) and the word *kadimah* ("forward" or "eastward") in Hebrew characters (see fig. 6.1).

On August 23 the formation of the Jewish Legion was announced in the *London Gazette*, and on September 2 Redcliffe left the Colchester military hospital where he had been stationed in preparation for transferring to the new unit. On September 12, Army Council Instruction 1415, "Formation of

Battalions for the Reception of Friendly Alien Jews," named, for the first time, the regiment to which the battalions would be attached—the Royal Fusiliers. The first battalion would be the Thirty-Eighth (the next available service battalion number of that regiment). When the Thirty-Eighth left for Palestine, another would be formed—the Thirty-Ninth. Eventually, there would be four Jewish battalions—the Thirty-Eighth, the Thirty-Ninth— which included volunteers from the United States, Canada, Argentina, and Palestine—the Fortieth, and the Forty-Second, which never left England for service overseas. The choice of the Royal Fusiliers was probably because they were the local infantry regiment for the East End of London.[27]

Redcliffe joined the Judeans, the unofficial name of the unit, as medical officer to the Thirty-Eighth battalion at Crown Hill, Plymouth, on October 1, 1917. Thus began what Nina called his "great adventure".[28] The fog of discontent weighing so heavily on him lifted. He felt exhilarated. His life seemed purposeful. In a talk to the Anglo-Jewish Association in 1950, he later recalled this period in his life as profoundly meaningful: "The insistence of a tradition which had suddenly acquired flesh and blood, the glamour of prophetic inspiration, the startling beauty of a country in which the fertile valleys are set like jewels in a framework of barren crags and mountains were themselves enough to weaken even the most complacent and assimilated Anglo-Jew."[29] The letters that he wrote home to Nina, which he edited and published as *Palestine Reclaimed* in 1920, testify to the exhilaration that he experienced during his service with the Jewish Legion.[30]

In contrast to Redcliffe's enthusiasm, most of the established Jewish community remained hostile to the Jewish battalions even after their establishment. Michael Adler, the minister of London's Central Synagogue and the senior Jewish chaplain in France, urged Jews who were already serving not to transfer to the unit.[31] Although Adler was the son of a Spitalfields tailor, his manner and outlook were those of the well-to-do Jews to whom he ministered in London. Emblematic of his aspiration was his habit of always wearing his sword even when other officers did not.[32] Nina thought the hostility of the communal notables was "disgusting" and that they would recognize the "stupidity" of their opposition if they would consider "what a failure these men [native Yiddish-speakers born in tsarist Russia] would be in other regiments."[33] Israel Abrahams repeatedly reminded Nina of his opposition, even remarking that it was a great mistake to sing the Zionist anthem *Ha-Tikvah* during religious services at the Judeans' camp. "He is as strong as ever against our being a nation and against our fighting for Palestine," she reported to Redcliffe, "and says his party [the anti-Zionist camp] is organizing against it."[34] As Nina's remarks reveal, those who fought the creation of the Judeans were in essence expressing their enmity to Zionism and its insistence on the national character of the Jews. The chronological overlap between the struggle for the Jewish Legion and the negotiations that led to the Balfour Declaration (November 2, 1917) reinforced the link between the two. Jewish officers in conventional units—who were drawn from native-born, upper-middle-class families—showed little enthusiasm for transferring to the Jewish units. One exception was Fred Samuel, the husband of Redcliffe's sister Dorothy (1881–1970), a battle-hardened officer who had served in the Boer War and in the trenches in France. At Redcliffe's urging, he transferred to the Judeans and took command eventually of the Fortieth battalion. A nephew of the petroleum magnate Marcus Samuel, the first Lord Bearsted, neither he nor any of his extended family were Zionists. (There was no connection between the petroleum Samuels and the banking Montagus-Samuels.) None of Redcliffe's brothers serving in the British army—Euston, Elkin, or Michel—followed his example. Daniel Hopkin, however, the Salaman boys' former tutor, transferred to serve with Redcliffe. He was not Jewish, as many of the officers leading the Jewish battalions were not, but he shared Redcliffe's enthusiasms. Later, his marriage to an Egyptian Jewish woman cemented his identification with the Jewish national cause.[35]

Except for the veterans of the Zion Mule Corps, the recruits with whom Redcliffe dealt at Plymouth were ill prepared to take on soldiering. Many were involuntary draftees, lacking British patriotism or Zionist zeal. Nor were they in the best physical shape, having lived all their lives in the East End and its provincial counterparts and, in most cases, having worked in trades that were notorious for their insalubrious conditions.[36] The chaplain to the Jewish Legion, Leib Aisack Falk, described them as "pale and sunken-chested *schneiders*" (tailors), who before their arrival in Plymouth, sat bent over their machines for long hours. Under "the glorious sunshine of Devon with its fogless atmosphere," he saw them transformed into "robust-looking fellows with expanded chests and hardened muscles," standing erect and responding with military precision to the commands of their officers.[37] Their transformation was not, perhaps, as miraculously thoroughgoing as Falk remembered it in his memoir. Redcliffe took a dimmer view. He complained about their hygiene and expressed despair that they were such bad material. He compared the task of whipping them into shape to that of Moses managing the ever-complaining Hebrews in their journey through the desert.[38] And, once in Palestine, before they came under enemy fire, while marching toward Jericho, he groused to Nina that many of them lacked any serious commitments: they "don't care a damn about anything Jewish, English, military, or, indeed, their own comfort."[39] The men, in turn, saw his insistence on personal hygiene and military order as intrusive and demanding and some referred to him as the *meshugeneh* (crazy one).[40] The term suggests the enormity of the class divide between Redcliffe, whose dress was immaculate, and the men in his battalion. Nina, on the other hand, attributed their shortcomings as soldiers to having lived under tsarist oppression. For her, this was another argument for Zionism.[41] When she visited Redcliffe in Plymouth in December 1917, she was impressed with what she saw. Watching nine hundred men marching to synagogue on Shabbat was "a fine sight." When a rabbi from Jerusalem lectured them at length in "impassioned" Yiddish, she told Israel Zangwill, "they drank it all in with delight."[42]

The Thirty-Eighth battalion left Plymouth in the first week of February 1918. Half the men proceeded directly to Southampton, the port from which they would embark, while the other half was given the honor of marching through Whitechapel and the City.[43] Nina and Myer traveled to London to say goodbye to Redcliffe. On the morning of February 4, half the battalion (426 men and 12 officers), accompanied by the band of the Coldstream Guards, marched with fixed bayonets from the Tower of London, where it had spent the night, to Mansion House, where the Lord Mayor, accompanied by his wife and the City sheriffs, took the salute from the balcony. The troops then continued to Whitechapel and Mile End, where the mayor of Stepney, Zionist officials, and a flock of local politicians received them at the Pavilion Theatre. The sight of the all-Jewish battalion, flying the Union Jack and the flag of the Zionist movement (later to become the flag of the State of Israel), moved the spectators who crowded the streets of the East End. Colonel Patterson, Major Hopkin, and Redcliffe were on horseback, and Nina and Myer caught sight of them several times. There was a luncheon afterward for the men and officers at Camperdown House, headquarters of the Jewish Lads' Brigade (opposite Aldgate East station); later that afternoon, the battalion marched to Waterloo Station and boarded a train for Southampton. The next morning, the War Office replaced Redcliffe with another medical officer and ordered him to disembark. The order was a bureaucratic blunder, and he returned to Plymouth furious and terribly upset. The next month, he and the Thirty-Ninth battalion, commanded by

130 | *The Last Anglo-Jewish Gentleman*

Colonel Eliazar Margolin, sailed from Southampton.[44] Unlike the soldiers who served under him, Margolin was a seasoned military man. Born in Russia and brought to Ottoman Palestine by his parents, he grew up in Rehovot and was an outstanding horseman. As a young man, he went to Australia, seeking adventure, and became a successful businessman. He served with the Australian army in Egypt and France before transferring to the Jewish Legion, largely at Jabotinsky's urging.[45]

4

The Thirty-Ninth battalion landed in Alexandria, Egypt, in late April 1918 and joined the Thirty-Eighth at the British camp at Helmieh, outside Cairo. There it remained until August 5, when it left for the front. In his free time there, Redcliffe took advantage of the camp's proximity to Cairo to visit the city's museum of antiquities and explore its crowded Jewish quarters, hospital, and schools. While there, he also traveled with Margolin to Jerusalem, under British control since December 1917, to attend the ceremony on Mt. Scopus on July 25, at which the foundation stone was laid for the Hebrew University. It was Redcliffe's first trip to Jerusalem. Unlike other Western visitors in the nineteenth and early twentieth centuries, he was not dismayed or overwhelmed by the squalor and filth of the Jewish Quarter of the Old City (his hotel was just inside the Jaffa Gate). Rather, his first impression was of the city's topographical grandeur. As he wrote to Nina after returning to camp, "If Jerusalem were nothing more than a collection of mud hovels, it would still be the Queen of Cities and worthy of one's heart's desire, for it is enthroned on the hills with a dignity that nothing can impair." He wrote even more rapturously about the future home of the university: "No University in all the world has such a site, and none can ever have such a soul-inspiring stimulus which nature and tradition seem to have marked out as a turning-point in the world's history."[46] He then quoted Isaiah 2:3 and Micah 4:2, which he knew from the Sabbath liturgy, when it is chanted at the opening of the ark. "For the law [Torah] will go forth from Zion, and the word of the Lord from Jerusalem." This is the same religious note that Nina hit when talking about the destiny of the Jewish people. When he returned to his hotel that night, after several receptions, he was exhausted but elated, "full of the strong hope that Judaism and Jews had still something to do and something to say for the peace of mankind."[47]

The Thirty-Ninth battalion left Helmieh on August 5, marched to Kantara on the Suez Canal and, after crossing it, continued northward to Sarafand on the coastal plain (three miles northwest of Ramla), site of the largest British military base in the Middle East.[48] Although only fifteen miles from the front, occasionally within earshot of guns, Redcliffe's medical duties were still not burdensome. He had time to visit the Rothschild wine cellars at Rishon Le-Zion, whose cellar master knew Nina's work, and to ride with Margolin and several others to the Jewish agricultural village at Rehovot, which he pronounced "most picturesque." On August 13, the Thirty-Ninth moved eastward toward the Jordan Valley. Now Redcliffe's medical work became more time-consuming. The march over rugged terrain took a toll on the feet of the soldiers and he was repeatedly called on to tend and dress their injured feet. He also lectured the troops on malaria, which they had not yet encountered but would when they entered the Jordan Valley.[49] By mid-September, they were at the front.

By this time, the battle for Palestine was nearly complete. General Edmund Allenby's plan for the final campaign was to mount a full-scale attack from the south through the coastal plain, where he concentrated his troops. To deceive the Turks into thinking that the major British attack would come in the Jordan Valley, he mounted an elaborate deception. The Thirty-Eighth and Thirty-Ninth battalions, as well as other British forces, were deployed above and in the Jordan Valley to keep the Turks from discovering the massing of units along the coast. The brigades undertook patrols for reconnaissance and intelligence, probed and harassed the enemy line, and marched back and forth behind the front line, sending clouds of dust into the air to deceive the Turkish defenders about their numbers. Allenby's elaborate deception worked, and he was able to push northward, completing the conquest of Palestine.

The climate and geography of the terrain where the Jewish battalions fought were extreme. In the Jordan Valley, temperatures over 100 degrees Fahrenheit in summer were common; elevated humidity levels made it more unbearable. The British military handbook on Palestine noted that "nothing is known of the climate in summer time [in the Jordan Valley], since no civilized human being has yet been found to spend summer there."[50] The sulfurous dust was thick and fine, and clouds of it rose to choke and blind the marching men, while their feet were sucked down at each step. Even worse, the marshlands of the valley were breeding grounds for mosquitoes, the carriers of malaria. In Redcliffe's battalion, 60 percent of the men were infected during their time there, including Hopkin and half the officers, although many of them did not fall ill until after they had left the valley. Caring for the sick consumed all his time. With the end of the fighting in the valley, the Thirty-Ninth battalion was ordered to garrison Es Salt, a trading and communications center on the road between Amman and Jerusalem, clustered on three hills overlooking the valley. The march there was an arduous climb, twenty-eight miles, rising from 1,300 feet below sea level to 2,385 feet above. After twenty-one hours, the battalion entered Es-Salt on September 24, the Turks having fled. Redcliffe's medical cart had bogged down along the way, and there were no medical facilities there or transportation to take the sick to hospitals. In addition, dead camels and horses littered the center of the town and the roads from the town and choked and polluted the river that ran near it. It fell to Redcliffe to organize the burial of the decaying animals. The battalion was then ordered, on October 1, to take 1,500 German and Turkish prisoners of war to Jerusalem. On the march from Es Salt to Jerusalem, the men "fell out in heaps," stricken with malaria—about forty a day between Jericho and Jerusalem. The hospitals in Jerusalem were overflowing, and Redcliffe set up a makeshift hospital, housing 150 men in tents, in the unit's own camp. In mid-October, the battalions, including the sick, were transferred to Sarafand. More men fell sick, including his two medical orderlies and all but one of his sixteen stretcher bearers. The disease reduced the Thirty-Ninth to a quarter of its strength.[51] Redcliffe attributed the spread of malaria entirely to "lack of knowledge and foresight on the part of the senior administrative medical officers." When the number of wounded in battle was fewer than expected, they had ordered the surplus of beds to be returned to Cairo. In addition, they had failed to take into account that autumn was the season for malaria and that the incubation period for the disease was ten days.[52]

Redcliffe's war ended more or less with the transfer of the battalions to Sarafand in October 1918, although he remained with his unit until March 1919. His service in the war was neither distinguished nor undistinguished, largely because, of the two Jewish battalions that fought in the Jordan Valley, his, the Thirty-Ninth, was assigned a less challenging set of duties than the Thirty-Eighth. The latter spent a significant amount of time in front-line combat. It faced the Turks from June 27, 1918; the Thirty-Ninth, Redcliffe's unit, did not join them until September 15 and only took over the Thirty-Eighth's defensive positions on September 22. Two days later, it marched to Es-Salt for mopping-up operations. One measure of the contrast in the battlefield experiences of the two battalions is that the men and officers of the Thirty-Eighth won thirteen medals and eight mentions in dispatches, while those of the Thirty-Ninth won none. It seems that the British command sent the Thirty-Eighth into battle earlier because it had the larger number of seasoned veterans—Jews who had seen combat in the Zion Mule Corps at Gallipoli or in British units at the western front.[53]

In the months before his discharge, Redcliffe found himself fighting a battle of a different sort. He and other Jewish officers tried, unsuccessfully, to counter the British military's policy of stripping the Jewish battalions of any role in the establishment of British rule and the rebuilding of the Land of Israel. But to understand that campaign, it is first necessary to examine the transformative impact of his service with the Jewish Legion, a transformation that owed little to his military duties or exposure to combat.

5

At the start of the war, Redcliffe was not a Zionist, although he was not an assimilationist either, since, as a racial thinker, he rejected the cornerstone of assimilationist faith that Jews were bound together solely by the ties of religion. Colonel Albert E. Goldsmid, an early Jewish advocate of the return to Zion, had enrolled him in Hibbat Tsiyyon [Love of Zion], a precursor of Herzlian Zionism, in 1894, when he was a student at Cambridge, but Hibbat Tsiyyon in Britain was largely a nonideological philanthropic project, a way of helping persecuted Russian Jews. He later recalled that his support for it had been "too academic and impersonal to be of use either to me or Zion."[54] As he wrote Chaim Weizmann in 1949, Zionism did not mean very much to him then. He and Nina were familiar with the movement, but they were not supporters of the state idea. Nina wrote him in March 1917 that Palestine was not necessary for "Jews who feel they can develop better on their own lines on their own soil" and that even as an asylum for the persecuted it would not succeed because it could not absorb all of Russia's Jews.[55] Recall that when Patterson convened a group of communal leaders at the War Office on August 8, 1917, Redcliffe attended as a non-Zionist.

The announcement of the Balfour Declaration in November 1917 and the British conquest of Jerusalem the following month began to recast the inchoate nationalism of Redcliffe and Nina. What had seemed an unobtainable and fanciful goal was less chimerical now. Balfour's letter to Lord Rothschild seemed to suggest that Britain would work to create "a national home for the Jewish people" in the Land of Israel. Notwithstanding the ambiguity of the declaration's commitment, these two related events were turning points in modern Jewish history. They stirred Redcliffe and Nina deeply. For Nina, they looked "extraordinarily like a fulfillment of the prophecies—the nations bringing us back."[56] Redcliffe recalled that the declaration "at a stroke revealed to her the immanence of a spiritual Zionism she had always cherished. Once more the *Shekhinah* would hover over Jerusalem and out of Zion would go forth the Law." To mark the event, they planted a new orchard in the meadow of Homestall and called it the Jerusalem Orchard.[57] When news of the conquest of Jerusalem reached Barley, the children—Myer, Arthur, Raphael, and Ruth—handwrote and illustrated a commemorative booklet, "The Homestall Magazine," "to celebrate the taking of Jerusalem, and the rising hopes of the Jews throughout the world." The introduction explained the symbolism of the frontispiece: "The knight is the Jewish nation, and is spurring on to his vision, the temple. He does not shrink from the shafts of death. He is attended by good Spirits." Myer contributed two pages of Greek and Hebrew maxims—in Greek and Hebrew characters.[58] On December 2, the English Zionist Federation organized a celebration to thank the government at the London Opera House, presided over by Lord Rothschild. Nina traveled to London to attend but left the boys at Barley, fearing German air raids. Her sister-in-law, Dorothy Samuel (her husband Fred Samuel was serving with Redcliffe in Palestine), accompanied her. Zangwill, one of the speakers, arranged for her to sit on the platform with other leading figures, and she gave her spare ticket to another of Redcliffe's sisters, Bessie Cohen.[59] Along with Lord Rothschild and Herbert Samuel, who also spoke, Nina was one of the few representatives of the native-born Anglo-Jewish elite who attended. Jews from the East End of London filled most of the seats. The recognized lay leaders of Anglo-Jewry, with the exception of Rothschild, stayed away.[60]

If the Balfour Declaration contributed to Redcliffe's new attachment to Zionism, it was his service in the Jewish Legion, more than anything else, that cemented it. It was not, however, the experience of combat or the male bonding of wartime that was decisive. The military contribution of the Jewish battalions to the Palestine campaign was minimal. They spent more time garrisoning towns and guarding prisoners than fighting Turks and Germans, and Redcliffe's most challenging task was the struggle against malaria. Rather, it was his encounter with the young Zionists working the land that left an indelible impression—"an experience the life of which I had never dreamed of." In his eyes, the young men and women of the New Yishuv were the very embodiment of virility, athleticism, physical beauty, courage, and straightforwardness. They heralded the transformation of the Jewish people that settlement in the Land of Israel would effect. Here is a typical passage from the letters he wrote to Nina: "The colonists, boys and girls, are a fine lot, and it stirs one's heart to think that these are the same blood and bone as the cringing, shuffling Halukah type [recipients of charity] which swarm in the old city. They are straight and healthy, clean in mind and body, look you boldly in the face and smell of the earth. Somehow, good looks seem to abound among them."[61]

When seven hundred volunteers from Palestine (some of whom had taken refuge in Egypt) joined the battalion at Helmieh in July 1918, the difference between the Jaffa contingent, drawn from the New Yishuv, and the Jerusalem contingent, drawn from the Old Yishuv, struck him forcefully. The former were, almost to a man, "athletic, beautifully built, bold-looking fellows." The latter were a mixed lot that included bearded, pious Ashkenazim with sidelocks and undersized Yemenites, whom Redcliffe thought should not have been recruited in the first place. The Jaffa contingent outclassed the Jerusalem contingent in the way that "a shire stallion would a worn-out coster's pony."[62]

Redcliffe's descriptions of the young men and women whom he met highlighted two characteristics in particular: their lack of artifice and their physical magnificence. "No one who has seen much of the colonists can fail to be impressed by the naturalness and ease of the people. One sees neither that straining after effect nor the restlessness so often characteristic of the European Jew."[63] A forty-five-year-old "Jewish peasant woman" he met in Rishon Le-Zion behaved "in that simple, natural, homely way that knew no embarrassment, asserted no equality nor recognized any inferiority." Her daughter was "the same fine, well-developed natural girl one sees here, cultivated and educated, but contented and full of grace and maturity."[64] When soldiers from his battalion and colonists celebrated the New Year for the Trees together, they fraternized "in the most natural and unaffected manner," their encounter absent all "hooliganism . . . flirtations or nonsense." They were straightforward "healthy men and women, boys and girls mixing, chatting, laughing together without restraint."[65] In another letter, Redcliffe made more explicit what is implicit in these descriptions—the deleterious impact of modern urban conditions on the Jewish character, a common trope in Zionist discourse. In the Land of Israel, Jews who were "hucksters" in Europe acquire "the best attributes of an aristocrat." In the future, the regeneration of the Jews would take place there and Anglo-Jewry would "have to invent some more real hall-mark than a top hat and a subscription to the Board of Guardians if it wishes to retain its prestige."[66]

Redcliffe was also besotted with the physical beauty of the young Jews, both male and female, whom he met. One young man from Smyrna—"short and sturdy, with a handsome open face, lovely teeth, and a broad smile"—so impressed him that he "felt a David and Jonathan feeling toward this youth and could have kissed him."[67] The New Yishuv was producing "splendid specimens of humanity" and, in twenty years, he predicted, Palestine would be famous for "its handsome Jews."[68]

During his military service in Palestine, Redcliffe came to believe that the resettlement of the Land of Israel was essential for the revitalization of the Jewish people. What he saw convinced him that living on and cultivating the Land was transformative. Young people whose parents were ordinary Jews were "transmuted into real men and women full of courage and self-respect" by rooting themselves in the landscape.[69] Romantic faith in the redemptive power of agricultural labor was, of course, common to most streams of Zionism, but in Redcliffe's case, it is interesting to note, he acquired it experientially, as a result of his time in Palestine, rather than culturally and ideologically, as in the case of so many Central European Jewish intellectuals. His belief in the transformative power of the return to Zion also drew on a sociological insight. He reasoned that when Jews ceased to be a stigmatized minority they would shed the nervousness, oversensitivity, and feelings of inferiority that characterized their behavior in the Diaspora. As he wrote to Nina, "Here a man has not to think of what others more or less unsympathetic may think of him, his acts, beliefs, or opinions: he is 'at home.'"[70] Or, as he told several Jewish audiences in London in 1926, Jews in the Land of Israel no longer cared much about *mah yomru ha-goyyim* (what will the gentiles think). For him, this was a turning point in Jewish history: Jews were reclaiming their dignity, fearlessness, and idealism.[71]

One indication of Redcliffe's intoxication with the Land of Israel was his fantasy that he and his family would settle there after the war. In August 1918, he wrote to Nina that if they were beginning their married life they would "unquestionably" want to make their life there. "As it is," he continued, "I suspend all judgment till you have come yourself."[72] Nina was less enthusiastic, not having experienced Redcliffe's intoxication. She told him that the idea of giving up everything they had in England was unsettling and questioned whether there was anything there for the children. "Perhaps it is selfish but one feels one wants to 'wait and see' a little how things settle down."[73] In any case, it became a moot issue when she was diagnosed with cancer soon after his return.

Another indication of his new enthusiasm for Zionism is that he attempted to learn Hebrew. Early in his marriage, he had flirted with the idea and asked his father-in-law to recommend a tutor, which he did—Solomon Ulisianer, headmaster of the Talmud Torah in Great Garden Street in the East End.[74] Redcliffe seems not to have followed through at the time. He began learning to speak Hebrew once he joined the Jewish Legion in Plymouth and continued the lessons after arriving in Egypt. Nina peppered him with questions about the Sephardi pronunciation he was learning, expressed regret that he was learning to write cursive Hebrew script rather than the square characters that she and Israel Abrahams used, and envied him that he had seven hundred Hebrew speakers with whom to practice.[75] He seems to have made little progress—for reasons that are not clear. Perhaps the idea of speaking Hebrew was more attractive than was the hard work of learning to do so. In any case, once the battalion went into battle, his study of Hebrew came to a complete standstill and later resumed only sporadically.[76]

6

Redcliffe's wartime service gave focus and direction to a life that hitherto had seemed to him unproductive and helped him to overcome feelings of inadequacy that went back at least to his adolescence. Other Jewish officers from well-established families who served in Palestine tended not to see their experience in this therapeutic or transformative light. The experience of his brother-in-law Fred Samuel, who commanded the Fortieth battalion, is instructive in this regard. As was the case with Redcliffe, his wartime correspondence with his wife, Dorothy, has survived. After the war, he entered his family's merchant bank, and, while he served as treasurer for the Board of Guardians for nine years, he was neither a tireless communal worker nor a Jewish nationalist in the way that his brother-in-law was. Yet even he, who did not share Redcliffe's Jewish enthusiasms, experienced some feelings of heightened Jewishness at this time. In the weeks after the Balfour Declaration and before his transfer to the Jewish Legion, he wrote to his wife that he felt "very sensitive to Jewish sentiment just now," although he did not know why, and expressed a wish that he had heard the speeches at the Zionist celebration at the London Opera House.[77] After a Rosh Ha-Shanah service in the Egyptian desert at Tel-el-Kebir, he told Dorothy that, for the first time, he felt touched by his surroundings. "Am I a prince in Israel? I feel patriarchal, like Abraham, but Sarah was not by my side."[78] He was also favorably impressed with the Jewish farmers he met: they were "awfully nice, plain people" and real workers, with culture to boot; their homes were clean and their children delightful. Despite his claim that he was no sentimentalist, he admitted that hearing Hebrew spoken everywhere stirred him immensely.

Sentiments like these, however, were not representative of Samuel's outlook more generally. While he described his battalion (which included American and Palestinian recruits, among them Zionist activists like David Ben-Gurion and Yitzhak Ben-Zvi) as "a jolly crowd" and "splendid fellows," he soon grew tired of their ideological fervor, their insistence on speaking Hebrew, and their passion for speechmaking. They were too emotional, too political, too argumentative, too self-promoting, and too left-wing. He feared that "all their fine ideals" were only "skin deep" and that those with "deeper feelings" were "very narrow-minded." While still in Egypt, he wrote his wife that he was not at all keen on going on to Palestine, except to see Redcliffe and other friends, and that he was at heart a snob and "a League of British Jews" Jew, referring to the anti-Zionist organization that was formed after the Balfour Declaration. One indication of his distance from Redcliffe's nationalist views is that Col. Patterson wrote to Redcliffe in December 1920 to tell him that he would say nothing unkind about his brother-in-law in his own book about the Jewish Legion, even though he had told Samuel when he saw him in Cairo that he "would show him up to all Israel as he well deserved!"[79] (The antagonism was mutual. In his letters to his wife, Samuel criticized Patterson for his romantic attachment to Zionism, his lack of judgment, his propensity to see antisemitism everywhere, and his pursuit of methods that antagonized both the British and the Arabs.)[80] Daniel Hopkin, who liked Samuel personally, also saw that he was out of touch with the Zionist sympathies of the men he commanded. He wrote Redcliffe that his brother-in-law had "not one scrap of imagination" and that his strained relationship with Patterson was harmful to "a body of men who could have been a great credit to the movement."[81]

The conflict in which Redcliffe found himself enmeshed at the end of the fighting was not new and had been brewing since the government first considered the idea of a Jewish fighting unit.[82] From the start, the War

Department was not enthusiastic about the Jewish Legion, whose creation was a political rather than a military initiative. There were two reasons. First, the highest ranks of the army were drawn from the upper class and shared the prejudices of that class, including a snobbish dislike of Jews. Second, many officers (not all, of course) were hostile to Zionism because they feared it would anger the local Arab population, whom they were prone to romanticize (à la Lawrence of Arabia), and complicate British imperial interests. The first major manifestation of their hostility was to refuse to give the unit a Jewish name, thus minimizing its Jewish visibility. Once the battalions were in Egypt and Palestine, they came under the command of the Egyptian Expeditionary Force (EEF), whose staff officers were unenthusiastic about assigning them a critical role. The time that the Thirty-Eighth and Thirty-Ninth spent in combat came to less than two weeks. Afterward, Allenby and his staff made no public announcement of the participation of the Jewish Legion in the conquest of Palestine, although they lauded the Arab contribution to the advances on Amman and Damascus. Aggrieved and cut down by malaria, some men of the Thirty-Eighth and Thirty-Ninth even blamed the EEF for deliberately assigning them to fight in the Jordan Valley in the hope of reducing their numbers.

Redcliffe fully shared their sense of outrage. In his view, the problem was twofold. First, the Jewish battalions were not attached to any brigade or specific division and were thus "orphans—not wanted, much less cherished, by any of the people amongst whom we have been." One consequence was that the battalions had difficulties in obtaining supplies. In Jerusalem, after the march from Es-Salt, for example, they were given no hospital accommodations and had to struggle to be evacuated to Sarafand. And at Sarafand they spent a week without tents and had "to beg and fight" for them although the other troops there were fully supplied. More fundamentally, he felt that both the government and the military saw them as "an odd lot" that they did not understand and that they had not yet made up their minds about—an observation that is equally true about British attitudes toward Jews more generally at any time in the modern period.[83]

After the armistice, the British military authorities made little use of the Jewish battalions. They did not want to take any steps that Arab nationalists might see as preparation for handing over control to the Jews. Thus, they assigned the battalions the most marginal of tasks, "purposely hiding" them so as to avoid antagonizing the Arabs, instead of using them everywhere, as Redcliffe desired, "to show the Arabs that the Jews are to be respected."[84] The Fortieth battalion was kept in Egypt and not allowed to enter Palestine, while the Thirty-Eighth and Thirty-Ninth were kept in Sarafand. To ensure peace, Redcliffe believed, the military administration (the Occupied Enemy Territory Administration, or OETA) "truckled to the noisy pan-Arabic party," disarming the voluntary police in the Jewish settlements while allowing "the wholesale pilfering of arms and ammunition by the Arabs." It received every Arab nationalist demonstration "with courtesy" but cold-shouldered and obstructed Jewish industrial expansion, hygienic work, and agricultural development.[85] Its policy mystified and estranged the New Yishuv, as well as Redcliffe. It also enraged many in the battalions who had enlisted in the legion in the belief that they would form the basis of a Jewish army to defend the Yishuv.

In December Redcliffe tried to transfer to the Zionist Commission, a Jewish mission backed by the British government and headed by Chaim Weizmann (but run, in effect, by David Eder). Its task was to organize relief work, repair damage to the agricultural settlements, and advise the military authorities in their relations with the Yishuv. The commission left England in March 1918 and remained in Palestine for three and a half years, during which time it functioned as a kind of Jewish government in embryo. Redcliffe thought that his medical training and experience with treating malaria would be useful in its work, but the military authorities refused his request for a transfer. And so he remained with the battalion at Sarafand, doing little, while "real constructive work of utmost importance" went undone. He was especially disappointed because he had thought that doing "real Palestinian work" would help him decide whether he should remain there permanently.[86] Eder tried several times to get Redcliffe transferred, but he too had no success. The problem was, as Redcliffe recognized, that OETA was "unfriendly to Jewish interests." Meanwhile, the Palestinians in the Jewish Legion were angry that their units were not being reconstituted as the nucleus of a national militia and not being given a role in holding the country. Redcliffe was sympathetic to their long-term goal, but he thought that they were being unrealistic. They were too excitable, too intellectual, and too impatient, "forever expecting a short cut to their goal." By March, he was even more disgusted with and hostile to OETA. He complained that all the provincial military governors were recruited from the Egyptian service and thus unaccustomed to dealing with Jews. He thought that OETA might have inspired confidence if it had appointed one governor in the area of the farming settlements or Jerusalem who was known to be sympathetic to Jewish interests. (OETA also refused to station Jewish troops in any of the historically Jewish cities—Jerusalem, Safed, Tiberias, and Hebron. It also banned Jewish soldiers from entering the Old City of Jerusalem during Passover 1919.) Redcliffe also well understood why OETA officially was neutral but, in reality, was pro-Arab "if not anti-Jewish"—it was "the easiest policy to pursue." The Jews would not give the British any real trouble but the Arabs might.[87]

Redcliffe's frustration and disappointment at the failure of the British to move forcefully and quickly on the commitments of the Balfour Declaration was tempered, to some extent, by his awareness of Arab opposition. Contrary to popular myth, he and other Zionists who knew the Land of Israel at first hand were not blind to the Arab presence or deaf to their grievances. It must be remembered, however, that the Arab population of Palestine—largely rural, impoverished, and illiterate—lacked modern political experience and institutions. Arab nationalism was in its infancy. Few foresaw its later emergence as an obstacle to the realization of Jewish sovereignty in the Land of Israel. Moreover, the notion of a specifically Palestinian nation (as opposed to an Arab nation embracing all the Arabs of the former Ottoman empire) was decades in the future, not gaining force until long after the establishment of the State of Israel in 1948.

The flaw in Redcliffe's understanding of the Arabs was that he viewed them through a Eurocentric, imperial, upper-middle-class lens and was unable to see them sympathetically. For him, the Arab of Palestine was a "degraded representative of his race"—"an expert thief" whose God was *baksheesh* and who was unprepared to take his place in modern civilization. He noted repeatedly how little the Arabs had accomplished in comparison with the Jews, who alone, he thought, could make the land fruitful, turn sandy deserts into fertile plantations, and bring back "the milk and honey tradition"—for him, no mere figure of speech.[88] In an article in the *Contemporary Review* in 1920, soon after his return to England, he once more compared Arabs and Jews, this time in terms of the condition of their children. The Jewish children of the agricultural settlements were handsome, well-mannered, and friendly. On the other hand, the Arab children of the villages were "totally uneducated, are as dirty as children who are never compelled to wash can become, the greater number are dressed in rags . . . and [competed] with the hawks and crows for the refuse of the [British military] camps. Poor little mites spend whole days hanging round the destructor in camp sorting out the refuse for some unconsidered trifle."[89]

Like most Europeans, he was convinced that the Arabs of Palestine would benefit from the influx of Jewish capital, intellect, and knowledge of European science and industry and would be content with that. As evidence, he noted that the only flourishing Arab villages were those near Jewish agricultural settlements, on which "the dirty and ignorant" *fellahin* earned money as laborers and from which they learned "the decencies of life."[90] He did not believe that hostility between Arabs and Jews was deeply rooted or innate and that they "would get on perfectly well if the politicians [Arab and British] would but leave them alone." In the end, he thought, there was land enough for both of them.[91]

Redcliffe's comments about the Arabs of Palestine are offensive by later standards but were entirely typical for the time. English soldiers and imperial officials, like most residents of the British isles, believed that their civilization, their way of life, was superior to those of other European nations, let alone those of non-Western peoples over whom they ruled. They were not value-free multiculturalists and to damn them for not being so is wildly ahistorical. They harbored a raft of prejudices about people who were different from them and such prejudices underwrote their understanding of how the world should be organized. When Redcliffe sent the manuscript of *Palestine Reclaimed* to the diplomat and Conservative member of Parliament William Ormsby-Gore prior to publication, Ormsby-Gore suggested that he tone down his remarks about the Arabs because well-to-do, educated Muslims would use them to make propaganda among the *fellahin*. Still, Ormsby-Gore's suggestion was strategic, not moral. He, like Redcliffe, thought that the task of the Jews was to raise "the Arab from the present low moral and material condition into which he has sunk." Indeed, he used even more incendiary language than Redcliffe did: "A slum is a cancer in the heart of a city and the whole city suffers from it. Unless the Jews raise the Arabs, the Arabs will lower the Jews." Redcliffe took Ormsby-Gore's advice and rewrote one passage, not wanting to stoke the antagonism between the two "races."[92] Later he became more sensitive to the language he had used. When the Association of Jewish Ex-Servicemen republished *Palestine Reclaimed* in installments in 1934 and 1935, he insisted that they remove passages that were hostile to the local Arab population.[93]

At the end of March 1919, Redcliffe left the Land of Israel. He traveled to Egypt and then went on to England. Angry about the way in which the Jewish battalions were treated, he took pride, nonetheless, in their performance. He returned to Barley newly energized, full of hope for the future of the Jewish people, his own commitments sharpened and strengthened. He was delighted to be with Nina once again and to resume his potato research.

Notes

1. RNS, "The Helmsman Takes Charge."
2. RNS, "Helmsman Takes Charge."
3. RNS to Daniel Hopkin, November 27, 1914, pasted into NDS, diaries, November 1914.
4. RNS, "Helmsman Takes Charge."
5. Myer Salaman to RNS, September 2, 1895, Add. MS 8171/12, RNS CUL.
6. "Helmsman Takes Charge."
7. Ibid.
8. NDS to RNS, March 30, 1916, January 1, 1918, Add. MS 8171, Wedderburn Deposit, RNS CUL.
9. NDS to RNS, September 19, 1916, Add. MS 8171/103, RNS CUL.
10. NDS to RNS, November 11, 1916, Add. MS 8171/103, RNS CUL.
11. NDS to RNS, September 13 and 19, 1916, Add. MS 8171/103, RNS CUL.
12. NDS to RNS, January 24, 1916, Add. MS 8171, Wedderburn Deposit, RNS CUL.
13. Esther Salaman Hamburger, interview by the author, March 25, 1999, London.
14. NDS to RNS, September 14, 15, 16, and 17, 1906, Add. MS 8171, Wedderburn Deposit, RNS CUL.
15. Philip Bagguley, *Harlequin in Whitehall: A Life of Humbert Wolfe, Poet and Civil Servant, 1885–1940* (London: Nyala, 1997), 105–7.
16. Alec Guinness, *Blessings in Disguise* (London: Hamish Hamilton, 1985), 220. Guiness, unfortunately, does not devote much space to his father-in-law in his memoir.
17. NDS to RNS, March 21, 1919, Add. MS 8171, Wedderburn Deposit, RNS CUL.
18. Stein, *Plumes*, 80–81.
19. Jane Miller, interview by the author, June 1, 2011, London.
20. Accounts of the temporary convergence of British and Zionist interests during World War I are numerous and often contentious, especially in the context of the subsequent history of the British Mandate and the State of Israel. The following are a sample: Isaiah Friedman, *The Question of Palestine, 1914–1918: British-Jewish-Arab Relations* (London: Routledge and Kegan Paul, 1973); Mark Levene, *War, Jews, and the New Europe: The Diplomacy of Lucien Wolf, 1914–1919* (Oxford: Oxford University Press, 1992), pt. 2; Bernard Wasserstein, *Herbert Samuel: A Political Life* (Oxford: Clarendon Press, 1992), ch. 8; Jehuda Reinharz, *Chaim Weizmann: The Making of a Statesman* (New York: Oxford University Press, 1993); Tom Segev, *One Palestine Complete: Jews and Arabs under the British Mandate*, trans. Haim Watzman (New York: Metropolitan, 2000), ch. 2.
21. Martin Watts, *The Jewish Legion and the First World War* (Houndmills, UK: Palgrave Macmillan, 2004), chs. 3–4.
22. David Eder, *New Judea*, September 17, 1926, quoted in Leonard Stein, "Eder as Zionist," in David Eder, *Memoirs of a Modern Pioneer*, ed. J. B. Hobman (London: Victor Gollancz, 1945), 135.
23. Derek J. Penlsar, *Jews and the Military: A History* (Princeton, NJ: Princeton University Press, 2013), ch. 4.

144 | *The Last Anglo-Jewish Gentleman*

24. RNS to David Eder, December 4 and 15, 1914, Add. MS. 8171/3b, RNS CUL.

25. Watts, *Jewish Legion*, 104–5.

26. Quoted in Vladimir Jabotinsky, *The Story of the Jewish Legion* (New York: Ackerman, 1945), 96.

27. Watts, *Jewish Legion*, 114.

28. NDS, diaries, September and October 1917.

29. RNS, "The Jews—Race, Nation, Religion," typescript, address to the Anglo-Jewish Association, December 19, 1950, Add. MS 8170/10c, RNS CUL.

30. RNS, *Palestine Reclaimed: Letters from a Jewish Officer in Palestine* (London: George F. Routedge and Sons, 1920).

31. Roman Freulich, *Soldiers in Judea: Stories and Vignettes of the Jewish Legion* (New York: Herzl, 1964), 25.

32. NDS to RNS, October 6, 1915, Add. MS 8170, Wedderburn Deposit, RNS CUL.

33. NDS to RNS, November 7, 1917, Add. MS 8170, Wedderburn Deposit, RNS CUL.

34. NDS to RNS, November 1, 1917, Add. MS 8170/104, RNS CUL.

35. RNS, "Helmsman Takes Charge."

36. For the background and motives of the men who enlisted in the three Jewish battalions, see Michael Keren and Shlomit Keren, *We Are Coming, Unafraid: The Jewish Legions and the Promised Land in the First World War* (Lanham, MD: Rowman and Littlefield, 2010). Drawing on diaries, memoirs, and letters, the authors provide a social history of the Jewish Legion, working from the bottom up.

37. Quoted in Keren and Keren, *We Are Coming*, 114.

38. NDS to IZ, November 27, 1917, A120/200, IZ Papers, Central Zionist Archives, Jerusalem.

39. RNS, *Palestine Reclaimed*, 55.

40. Keren and Keren, *We Are Coming*, 35.

41. NDS to RNS, February 21, 1919, Add. MS 8170, Wedderburn Deposit, RNS CUL.

42. NDS to IZ, December 9, 1917, A120/200, IZ Papers, Central Zionist Archives, Jerusalem.

43. Martin Sugarman, https://www.jewishvirtuallibrary.org/the march-of-the-38th-royal -fusiliers.

44. NDS, diaries, February and March 1919.

45. Suzanne Welborne, "Margolin, Eliezer (1875–1944)," *Australian Dictionary of Biography*, vol. 10 (Melbourne: Melbourne University Press, 1986).

46. RNS, *Palestine Reclaimed*, 34–35.

47. Ibid., 36.

48. On British military activity on the Suez Peninsula and in the Land of Israel, see Anthony Bruce, *The Last Crusade: The Palestine Campaign in the First World War* (London: Thistle, 2013).

49. Ibid., 50.

50. Quoted in Watts, *Jewish Legion*, 188.

51. Ibid., 76–78, 93. See also Baruch Hurwich, *"Kol ha-am hazit"—ha-sherut ha-refui be-erets yisrael* (Tel Aviv: Ministry of Defense, 1997), 32–36.

52. Watts, *Jewish Legion*, 94.

53. Julian Thiesfeldt Saltman, "'Odds and Sods': Minorities in the British Empire's Campaign for Palestine, 1916–1919," PhD diss., University of California–Berkeley, 2013, 109.

54. RNS, "Life's Residue," March 1951, Add. MS 8171/6, RNS CUL. On the history of Zionism in Britain, see Elhanan Oren, *Hibbat Tsiyyon be-Britanyah, 1878–1898* (Tel Aviv: Ha-kibbuts Ha-meuhad, 1974); Stuart A. Cohen, *English Zionists and British Jews: The Communal Politics of Anglo-Jewry, 1895–1920* (Princeton, NJ: Princeton University Press, 1982); David Cesarani, "The Transformation of Communal Authority in Anglo-Jewry, 1914–1940," in *The Making of Anglo-Jewry*, ed. David Cesarani (Oxford: Basil Blackwell, 1990), 115–40; Stephan Wendehorst, *British Jewry, Zionism, and the Jewish State, 1936–1956* (Oxford: Oxford University Press, 2012).

55. NDS to RNS, March 20, 1917, Add. MS 8171/103, RNS CUL.

56. NDS to RNS, November 10, 1917, Add. MS 8171, Wedderburn Deposit, RNS CUL.

57. RNS, "Life's Residue."

58. A copy is in the possession of Arthur's son, William Salaman, Cambridge.

59. NDS, diaries, December 1917; NDS to RNS, December 2, 1917, Add. MS 8171, Wedderburn Deposit, RNS CUL.

60. Leonard Stein, *The Balfour Declaration* (New York: Simon and Schuster, 1961), 564–565.

61. RNS, *Palestine Reclaimed*, 37.

62. Ibid., 25, 28–29. The Israeli historian Etan Bloom claims that Redcliffe's negative view of Yemenite Jews shaped Arthur Ruppin's view of their biological and mental inferiority, but he provides no evidence of his claim. It is true that Redcliffe declared that Yemenite Jews were not "racially" Jews but were "black, long-headed, hybrid Arabs," but he expressed that view only in 1920, in his *Palestine Reclaimed*, long after Ruppin's racial views had crystallized. Redcliffe would certainly not have encountered Yemenite Jews in pre–World War I Britain. Indeed, Bloom undermines his own claim when he notes that Ruppin expressed views similar to those in Redcliffe's 1920 book "as far back as 1905" (Etan Bloom, *Arthur Ruppin and the Production of Pre-Israeli Culture* [Leiden, Neth.: Brill, 2011], 227–28).

63. RNS, *Palestine Reclaimed*, 194.

64. Ibid., 42.

65. Ibid., 163.

66. Ibid., 158.

67. Ibid., 199–200.

68. Ibid., 110–11.

69. Ibid., 37.

70. Ibid., 194.

71. RNS, "Anglo-Jewry and Its Attitude towards Zionism," typescript, 1926, Add. MS 8171/50, RNS CUL.

72. RNS, *Palestine Reclaimed*, 47–48.

73. NDS to RNS, January 20, 1919, Add. MS 8171, Wedderburn Deposit, RNS CUL.

74. Arthur Davis to RNS, April 28, 1903, Add. MS 8171, Wedderburn Deposit, RNS CUL.

75. NDS to RNS, July 25 and August 4, 1918, Add. MS 8171, Wedderburn Deposit, RNS CUL.

76. RNS, *Palestine Reclaimed*, 69.

77. Fred Samuel to Dorothy Samuel, December 7, 1917, MS A2097/9/3, Frederick Dudley Samuel Papers, HL US [hereafter, Samuel Papers].

78. Fred Samuel to Dorothy Samuel, September 13, 1918, MS A2097/11, Samuel Papers.

79. J. H. Patterson to RNS, December 8, 1920, Add. MS 8171/52, RNS CUL.

80. Fred Samuel to Dorothy Samuel, October 14 and 21 and December 30, 1918, MS A2097/11, Samuel Papers.

81. Daniel Hopkin to RNS, January 4, 1921, Add. MS 8171/52, RNS CUL.

82. Watts, *Jewish Legion*, 204–38.

83. RNS, *Palestine Reclaimed*, 99.

84. Ibid., 121.

85. RNS, "The Prospects of Jewish Colonisation in Palestine," *Contemporary Review*, January 1, 1920, 671.

86. Ibid., 147–48.

87. Ibid., 158, 196–97.

88. Ibid., 119.

89. RNS, "Prospects of Jewish Colonisation," 669.

90. RNS, *Palestine Reclaimed*, 115.

91. RNS, "Prospects of Jewish Colonisation," 671.

92. William Ormsby-Gore to RNS, December 3, 1919, and RNS to William Ormsby-Gore, December 4, 1919, Add. MS 8171/52, RNS CUL.

93. RNS to A. Gordon, October 5, 1934, Add. MS 8171/1, RNS CUL.

7

THE HOME FRONT

1

Redcliffe's four-year absence from Barley weighed heavily on Nina. She missed him acutely, even regretting at times that she had not moved to be closer to him while he was still stationed in England. His absence also left her with new responsibilities. She was now in charge of the day-to-day management of Homestall—hiring and firing staff, overseeing accounts, sorting out breakdowns in electricity and water supply, overcoming shortages of food and fuel, making repairs, and the like. She worried as well about the cost of running the house and paying for the boys' education, even though Redcliffe's mother took care of Raphael's school fees. Their bank account was frequently overdrawn—the Salaman ostrich-feather business had stopped paying dividends—and she had to watch their expenses closely.[1] Arthur and Raphael, for example, wore the same bar mitzvah suit, retailored to fit them, that Nina had purchased originally for Myer.[2] Redcliffe's absence also made her more than ever responsible for the education of their children, which, with its emphasis on Hebrew, became more challenging as they grew older. In particular, as the boys entered their teenage years, it became difficult to continue educating them at home. She then faced the task of finding a school that welcomed Jews and that would allow the boys to continue their Hebrew lessons. Moreover, it also had to be an intellectually challenging school that was free of the worst excesses of English public-school life (bullying, predatory sexual activity, and philistinism). At the same time, Redcliffe's absence bestowed on her more independence than she had enjoyed previously.[3] She continued to pursue her work on medieval Hebrew poetry and to champion Hebraist causes and Zionism from 1917. Her increasing cultural stature allowed her to mix more in male company,

148 | *The Last Anglo-Jewish Gentleman*

and her closeness to two men in particular—Israel Zangwill and Israel Abrahams—discomfited Redcliffe at one point.

2

The most challenging task confronting Nina was finding the right school for the boys. (Educating the girls at home was not a problem—at the start of the war, Ruth was five years old and Esther only a few months old.) Choosing a boys' school was a routine undertaking in most upper-middle-class homes, but, in her case, it was more complicated. She had to find a setting that would nurture their social and intellectual development and, at the same time, that would welcome them as Jews and accommodate their observance of Judaism. It was a challenge because there were limits to the acceptance of Jewish difference in British culture and society. Schooling was not a multicultural enterprise, sensitive to validating religious, ethnic, and cultural particularisms. Nina's goal of transmitting to her children what she had received from her father did not mesh with the monocultural character of English public schools and the behavioral norms of adolescent schoolboys. Her travails illuminate the larger problem that challenges minorities in the modern world who wish to maintain a collective identity—how to embrace particularism and universalism, separatism and inclusion, simultaneously.

When Daniel Hopkin, the boys' tutor, left Barley to join the army in September 1914, Redcliffe took charge of the boys' lessons, but the arrangement did not last long. In January 1915, Redcliffe and Nina engaged a new tutor, L. M. Westall.[4] This too did not work out. The new tutor was not a success with the boys, and, as Myer complained to his father, did not compare favorably to Hopkin: "Mr. Westall doesn't take any real interest in any other person except himself. He doesn't find out things for you and make secrets with you about things that interest you like Mr. Hopkin did. Besides he doesn't help Mamma at all."[5] By spring 1915, Myer received only intermittent instruction from Westall. Instead, once a week, he accompanied Nina when she went to Cambridge and took lessons there—in cello, voice production, music theory, drawing, French, and Talmud (with Israel Abrahams).[6] Meanwhile, Nina pursued the possibility of sending him to a public school in London. St. Paul's, his father's school, was out of the question because the current headmaster was antisemitic. Westminster declined to admit him, probably because he would have been thirteen (an advanced age) when he started in the fall. In the end, she decided it was better to give up the idea of sending Myer, who had never been away to school, to a large, impersonal institution in metropolitan London. She also met with the headmaster of the Leys School in nearby Cambridge, a public school established by Methodists in 1875, but quickly realized that he was reluctant to accommodate Jewish boys. He would not accept day boys—Myer would have had to board there—and he would have had to attend chapel. The headmaster explained to Nina that he had accepted Jewish boys in the past and that they had attended chapel, preferring to fit in with everyone else (not unusual for Jewish boys at public schools).[7] The interview made her realize the need for a good Jewish public school. "What fools we are," she wrote Redcliffe, "to go begging Xtian clergymen to take our boys and expect them to alter their rules for them."[8] She also considered sending him to live and study with Herbert Loewe, lecturer in Hebrew at Oxford since 1913, but Israel Abrahams's wife Freda warned her off. Although the Loewes were "delightful people," Freda thought that they would "sicken" Myer with their orthodoxy. Nina was not so sure, noting that their orthodoxy had not sickened the Loewe boys, Raphael and Michael.[9]

After much agonizing, Nina decided that the only solution was to send Myer, then thirteen, and Arthur, then eleven, to the Perse School in Cambridge, starting in September 1915. (Edward had died of pneumonia in 1913.) The Perse School was an undistinguished public school, dating from 1615. But for Nina, in addition to its proximity to Barley, it possessed another advantage. Perse was one of several public schools at the time with a Jewish boardinghouse. At the Perse School, the founder of the house (in 1904) and long-term master was the Cambridge-educated Israel Hersch, who also taught mathematics and science at the school. The boys in his house were served kosher food, received Hebrew lessons, and trooped off to the Cambridge synagogue on Saturdays, ensuring a *minyan* during term time.

On the face of it, the Perse School seemed a good fit for Myer and Arthur. Myer, however, did not have an easy time there. The other boys in the Jewish house made fun of his flawless Hebrew pronunciation, for example. One of Moses Gaster's sons, who was at the school, told him that his pronunciation was correct and that that was how it was done at the Gaster home, but that it was "no good doing it at school as it puts them out."[10] Myer's distress was symptomatic of a larger problem. He and his brothers were not accustomed to the society of schoolboys. In particular, they were not prepared for the cruelty of other schoolboys, eager to mock those whose ways were different from their own. They were also not accustomed to mixing with Jewish boys who came from homes where Jewish consciousness was less pronounced and Jewish observance more relaxed. The centrality of Judaism and Jewishness in their upbringing, it bears repeating, was not typical of the Jewish upper middle class. In addition, both boys were frequently sick—incessant coughs and colds—during their first term at the school. In one instance, Myer's respiratory infection developed into pneumonia. No doubt frightened that the tragedy of Edward's death might repeat itself, Nina did not send the boys back to Perse for the next term.[11] In the meantime, they continued to be educated at home.

The following fall Myer was sent to Clifton College in Bristol, whose Jewish house, established in 1878, was the first at an English public school. Clifton was a more highly regarded school than Perse and many well-to-do Jewish families sent their sons to the Jewish house there (called Polack's House, after the family who founded it and provided it with masters for three generations). But Myer's experience there was not much better than at the Perse School. He complained of antisemitic comments from masters. One, for example, claimed that the hostile tone in the Book of Esther underwrote the whole of Jewish life, citing the case of Russia, where, he alleged, the Jews lived as if they were in an alien land and exploited the native inhabitants, creating animosity.[12] He also complained, once again, of the other Jewish boys' attitude toward Judaism. The Jewish atmosphere that Nina cultivated at Barley was nowhere in evidence. The other boys in the house laughed at Jewish rites and mocked them as hypocritical, attitudes that they seemed to share with their parents. He accused them of hating Jews, whom they stigmatized as moneylenders, and of thinking only of winning the favor of Christians by abandoning Jewish observance. He thought the sole reason their parents sent them to the Jewish house is that they would not be treated well in the other houses. And he complained about widespread cheating, swearing, and indifferent teaching.[13]

Equally upsetting to Nina were his worries about homoerotic activity in Polack's House. Myer was fourteen years old when he started Clifton and, by virtue of his upbringing, naive and unworldly. He was not prepared for the homoerotic atmosphere that was common in English public schools. Shocked and dismayed, he did not hesitate to tell his mother about the sexual carryings-on, although he used euphemisms to describe them, perhaps because he lacked the vocabulary to do otherwise and certainly because he did not want to shock or offend his prudish mother. According to Myer, morality at Clifton was worse than at other public schools. (How he knew that is a mystery.) The very worst thing that boys in the house did he called "breaking the law" (mutual masturbation? fellatio? anal intercourse?) when writing or speaking to his mother. One boy who corrupted little boys and had "broken the law" four times was sent home to Singapore. Nina also was unprepared for the dangers of public schools. She told Redcliffe that she had not had "any conception of what I know now!" Once alerted to them, she read Alec Waugh's public-school novel *The Loom of Youth* (1917), which further enlightened her.[14] The subject of violent controversy, Waugh's novel described, in the author's own words, "the inevitable emotional consequences of a monastic herding together for eight months of the year of thirteen year old children and eighteen year old adolescents."[15] Myer having confirmed to her the truth of the book's revelations, she sent a copy to Redcliffe in Palestine. As Redcliffe had been a day boy at St. Paul's, she assumed he was ignorant of life at a boarding school. If he had known, she guessed, he would not have allowed Myer to go to Clifton.

Myer remained at Clifton for two unhappy years. Meanwhile, in May 1918, Nina enrolled Arthur and Raphael at Bedales, a progressive, coeducational boarding school, in rural Hampshire, founded in 1892 as an alternative to the traditional, semi-authoritarian public school. The school turned out to be a much better fit for all three boys. Nina first visited Bedales in February 1918, probably having heard of the school from the painter Solomon J. Solomon, who was painting her portrait at the time and who had sent his son and daughter there, or from Edith and Israel Zangwill, whose eldest child Ayrton was there. She was impressed from the start—with the school's setting, the buildings, the classrooms, the dormitories—all looked "clean and bright," as did the boys and girls, who had "such a different look from ordinary school boys—so bright and fresh with nothing of that worn and driven look one sees at Clifton." In line with its progressive orientation, the students had to make their own beds, chop wood for the fires, and work in the school's dairy and farm. The school was nondenominational and easily accommodated Jewish boys and girls. They were released from Saturday classes and allowed to have their own services. In hall, they were not served pork and, while removing pork made for a lack of variety in their diet, Nina thought they had enough to eat.[16] Of course, this does not mean that they never experienced antisemitism there. In his diary of 1918–19, Raphael cites many examples of antisemitic comments he heard.

When Nina visited Arthur and Raphael at Bedales in early July 1918, their happiness brought home to her how miserable Myer was at Clifton

152 | *The Last Anglo-Jewish Gentleman*

and she decided to transfer him. But Bedales had no room for him. She did not know what to do. No ordinary public school would accept a boy who was already sixteen. She wondered whether University College School in Hampstead might be a possibility. To her relief, Bedales relented in mid-August and agreed to take Myer.

The boys were happier there, but they still encountered the problem of being among Jewish boys and girls whose Jewish upbringing, such as it was, differed from their own. They encountered, for example, children from mixed marriages who denied or mocked their Jewish descent. Among them was Ayrton Zangwill. Edith and Israel Zangwill did not raise Ayrton and his sister Peggy and brother Oliver as Jews or give them religious upbringing of any kind. At Bedales, Ayrton mouthed the boarding-school antisemitism of the other students, possibly because it was a way of fitting in. Ayrton's behavior was not pleasant for Myer and his brothers, since the two families had often spent time together. When Edith Zangwill heard about "anti-Semitic talk" at Bedales, she asked Nina what she had heard of Ayrton's reaction. Nina told her what her boys had said: that he spoke slightingly of Jews like the others and denied that he was Jewish, although he admitted his father was. She said she would speak to him about it and that her husband was worried as well and would write to Ayrton.[17] In August 1918, Nina told Redcliffe that she was not going to take the children with her when she visited the Zangwills at their home in East Preston, Sussex, because she did not think Ayrton and Peggy were good influences on them. "Edie's plan of no religion" was a failure; it was a pity that Israel left the children's upbringing entirely to her.[18]

The painter William Rothenstein's son John, later an art historian and museum administrator of note, was also at Bedales at the time. Nina and Redcliffe had known Rothenstein from the time he first came to public attention and owned several of his pictures, including a portrait of Redcliffe that he had painted around 1906. Rothenstein's wife, Alice Knewstub, was not Jewish, and he was not active in Jewish communal life, but he had served with Redcliffe before the war on the committee of the Educational Aid Society, which gave financial aid to students from immigrant homes. John Rothenstein was also known at Bedales for Jew-baiting comments. Once, after saying derogatory things about Michael Franklin, the son of Ernest and Henrietta (Netta) Franklin and a frequent butt of anti-Jewish remarks, Rothenstein turned to another Jewish student at the table and said, "He and you are both of the same old tribe." Arthur then added, "So am I for that matter." Then one of the girls present, turning to Rothenstein, threw in "So are you." Rothenstein was indignant: "I can prove to you that I'm not one[,] as one of my ancestors [presumably on his mother's side] was a Protestant bishop!" Arthur was confused, partly because Rothenstein seemed so proud of saying he was not a Jew and was the first to persecute Jews newly arrived at the school. He asked Nina whether in fact Rothenstein was a Jew, adding that even at Bedales there was "a good deal of 'Jewering.'" After telling Arthur how to respond, she explained to him that Rothenstein's behavior was one example of the dangers of intermarriage. She blamed his "foolish, ignorant mother" for his antisemitism and told Redcliffe, "One feels Will ought to know."[19]

<h2 style="text-align:center">3</h2>

While not free of antisemitism—what institution at the time was?—Bedales was a welcome alternative to the conventional public school. The school allowed its Jewish students to conduct their own services and, at the time that the Salaman boys were there, two separate groups formed—one Liberal and the other Orthodox. The former coalesced around the Franklin and Waley boys and the latter around the Salaman boys. Both groups were minuscule and both were champions of their respective religious outlooks—as were their parents. Netta Franklin, the mother of the Franklin boys, was a sister of Lily Montagu, one of the leading lights of Liberal Judaism in Britain. When Nina had discussed Bedales with Solomon J. Solomon, he had expressed delight in the possibility that she would send Arthur and Raphael there, for then his daughter Iris, who was tired of the Liberal service, could join them.[20] So invested were the parents in the form of Jewish worship available to their children that Nina and Netta Franklin corresponded, angrily and at length, in 1918 about the merits and demerits of the two services.[21] (Liberal Judaism, like classical Reform Judaism in the United States, denationalized Jewish belief and practice and emphasized spiritual ideals and ethical behavior rather than observance of *halakhah*. Its services were largely in English and shorter in length than those of traditional synagogues. Liturgically, it was to the left of not only of the mainline Orthodoxy of the United Synagogue but of British Reform Judaism as well.)

Bedales also allowed the boys to continue their Hebrew education. In September 1918, Nina arranged for the Hebraist Aaron Doniach, whom she knew from her work for the Talmud Torah for Girls, to give the boys

Hebrew lessons. He visited the school on occasional Sundays and sent them lessons by mail the rest of the time. Before the correspondence course began, she observed Doniach teaching the boys at her mother's house in London, writing excitedly to Redcliffe of his teaching style and skill. He was "full of fire—and humour too." The way he taught nine verses about Abraham (Genesis 24: 1–9) was "masterly" (her emphasis). Tellingly, in describing Doniach, an East European Jew, to Redcliffe, she noted that he was also "clean," which was "a great thing if he is to go down sometimes to Bedales." She also commented on his facial features. His face was "queer and full of Judenschmerz," but it rather grew on her.[22] In fact, she was sufficiently impressed that she began modern Hebrew lessons with him in January 1919, meeting every fortnight for Hebrew conversation at the newly established School of Oriental Studies, where he was studying at the time. He convinced her to change her and the children's pronunciation of Hebrew from the Ashkenazi to that in use in the New Yishuv, which she characterized as "more correct and prettier."[23]

Nina also took responsibility for preparing Myer, Arthur, and Raphael for their bar mitsvahs at the New West End Synagogue in London. She would have done so, of course, whether Redcliffe was away or not. The preparation included having the boys fitted for suits and top hats, which were customary in upper-middle-class British synagogues. Myer's was on July 24, 1915, and, it is no surprise, he did beautifully (according to his mother, whose standards were high). After the service, the family lunched at the house of one of Redcliffe's sisters, Jennie Cohen. The gifts he received from close relatives say something about his seriousness. Jennie and her husband Herbert gave him a *Sefer Torah*; his parents, the ornaments for the *Sefer Torah*; Redcliffe's mother, a cello; and Herbert Loewe, a scroll with the *haftarot*.[24] Arthur's bar mitsvah was in May 1917; Nina's mother hosted a luncheon for twenty-eight (all family members except Israel Abrahams) at her home following the service. Raphael's was on June 13, 1919. Redcliffe had returned that April from Palestine. Zangwill was at the service and, at the luncheon that followed, proposed Raphael's health and made a speech in his honor. Lavish evening parties not being the custom at the time, Redcliffe and Nina went off with Zangwill that night to see *Romeo and Juliet*.[25]

Although Myer's boarding-school experiences were difficult, he retained his keenness for Hebrew and Judaism. Having decided at the age of nine that he wanted to become a rabbi[26]—a decision no doubt encouraged by his mother—his years at Clifton did not weaken his resolve. In January 1919, while Redcliffe was still abroad, Myer's aunt Jennie, the wealthiest of the Salaman siblings thanks to her marriage, offered to help support Myer financially if he chose a rabbinic career.[27] The motive for her offer was to allow him to remain financially and thus professionally independent of the Anglo-Jewish system of synagogue employment that made rabbis and readers subservient, poorly paid employees, subject to the authority of the chief rabbi and the lay leaders of their congregations. One consequence of this system was that the men who staffed British synagogues were overwhelmingly from humble rather than genteel homes. They were not drawn from the ranks of the commercial, financial, or professional middle class. Rather, they were often born abroad or the children of immigrants and hence had not acquired the social and cultural patina that an "Oxbridge" education bestowed. They were not, in any sense, gentlemen. Myer, on the other hand, was, and thus his decision and his parents' support for his career choice were remarkable.

When Myer left Bedales in 1920, he lacked the training in classical languages that he needed for Cambridge, and so he spent six months in Oxford, living in the home of Herbert Loewe. Loewe found a classics tutor for Myer while himself continuing his Hebrew studies. By this time, Myer was less certain about his decision to become a rabbi. He had expressed some uncertainty as early as 1918.[28] This—and his inability to think of a preferable alternative—continued to worry him, and he unburdened himself to Loewe. Loewe's advice was to take matters slowly—that it was not necessary to enter university having mapped out his future and that he would be better off marking time and keeping the rabbinate "somewhat in the background" until he was sure of himself.[29] In time, Myer's interests shifted and he followed in his father's footsteps, studying the natural sciences and later obtaining a medical degree. While he took an active role in the Cambridge Hebrew Congregation at university, often leading services, delivering *divrei Torah*, and serving as its president, once he left Cambridge, he no longer pursued the study of Hebrew or took an active role in Jewish affairs.

4

As with Redcliffe, the Balfour Declaration and the British conquest of Palestine deepened Nina's Jewish nationalism. Electrified by the events, she declared them "extraordinarily like a fulfillment of the prophecies—the nations bringing us back."[30] In February 1918, she wrote "Marching Song of the Judeans," which the composer and pianist Cécile Hartog set to music. (It was not a success with the troops.)[31] It is notable that the song is not martial in the least. Its theme, rather, is the age-old link between Zion—"our Mother"—and her sons, who "are coming to thine aid," that is, to liberate her from foreign domination, which has left her "lying waste." The Judeans are coming to save her, for only they, "thy children, precious in thy sight," can "bring the blessing to thy soil."[32] In the song, it is not Zion who redeems her children, but rather the Jewish battalions who redeem Zion by coming to her aid. Hers is a twist on the conventional Labor Zionist idea that those who rebuilt the Land of Israel would, in the process, rebuild and remake themselves.

Ideas about the collective character and destiny of the Jews permeated Nina's earlier work, but the poems she wrote from 1917 were overtly messianic in tone, clear evidence of how moved she was. In "The Daybreak" (1917), Zion is rising from "the vale of tears." The "golden light" that is breaking in the east portends redemption not for the Jews alone but for the entire world. She urges Jews to work with heart and soul for the rebuilding of Zion so that she can stand as "a beacon to the world" (or *la-goyyim*, a light unto the nations):

> Help now Zion, that, through her, the sorrow
>   Of a hapless wounded world be healed,
> That, through you, the dawn of Zion's morrow
>   Be a light to all the earth revealed.[33]

In "The Requital," which she wrote in the same period, Nina made the Jews and rebuilt Zion the fulcrum for the salvation of the world, which she described as "falling," "suffering," and "stricken." Addressing the Jewish people, she wrote,

> Long have you walked the world,
> Patient to serve the world,
>   Done as she bade you,
>   Been what she made you,
>   Under the rod of her,
>   Making a god of her—
>   Now you can stand
> Upright and save the world,
>   Free on your land.[34]

Nina also became increasingly angry with those British Jews who opposed the idea of a Jewish state because they thought it endangered their status as citizens. The most vocal champion of anti-Zionism at this time was the League of British Jews, which Lionel de Rothschild, Philip Magnus, and the second Lord Swaythling founded one week after the Balfour Declaration was issued. Its ideological heft came from Claude Goldsmid Montefiore and Lucien Wolf. The efforts of the league to reverse or temper the government's commitment to the Balfour Declaration appalled Nina. Horrified by material she had received from the league, she wrote to Redcliffe that foisting "this cowardly rubbish" on the community at the time, "when every Xtian one meets is elated with the glorious results of Jewish hopes," was "an incredible disgrace." That the league quoted from G. K. Chesterton's Jew-baiting journal the *New Witness* especially outraged her.[35] She frequently argued with Israel Abrahams, who was close to Claude Goldsmid Montefiore and Lily Montagu and was outspoken in his opposition to political Zionism. In letters to Redcliffe, she complained about his persistent advocacy of the league's position. After arguing with Abrahams at lunch one day in Cambridge, she reported to Redcliffe that he went on in "the same old way about our *not* being a nation and the fearful danger of possessing a national home."[36] For the sake of her relationship with Abrahams, she tried to stay off the subject, but, in her view, he was obsessed with it. As she wrote Redcliffe in January 1918, "You have to be awfully careful of what you say now, as he blazes out at the least thing. He thinks the whole position of the Govt. is an antisemitic plot to make us all aliens." At a café in Cambridge, Abrahams let go with a blast, saying "all sorts of awful things about 'You Zionists.'" But he stopped when someone they knew entered the café and he changed the subject. After this incident, they agreed not to discuss Zionism to avoid quarreling.[37]

5

Redcliffe's absence during the war posed another challenge to Nina: it allowed Israel Zangwill to continue his flirtation with her. To deny him opportunities for acting in inappropriate ways when they met (what Redcliffe called acting "silly" and "sentimental"), she tried to avoid being alone with him.[38] After visiting the Zangwills at their home at East Preston, Sussex, in summer 1916, she reported to her husband that Zangwill had been "very affectionate" but that she had been able to cope with it.[39] Redcliffe, while willing to concede much to "the poetic temperament," nonetheless urged her to let him know how uncomfortable he made her. (He attributed Zangwill's behavior to what he thought was an unsatisfactory marriage.) In early summer 1917, she confronted Zangwill directly. She came away with the impression that he was not unhappy that she had raised the matter. He told her that he hoped their relationship would always be "a great friendship" and that he was fond of Redcliffe and hoped he was fond of him in return. But Nina warned him that he must not do anything to endanger the friendship and he promised he would not.[40] Despite these unpleasant moments, they remained close friends to the end.

During the war, Nina's growing stature and Redcliffe's absence allowed her to mix freely with male scholars and writers, not just Zangwill, but others as well. In 1918, for example, she joined the all-male council of the Jewish Historical Society of England, to which she had lectured previously. (The first woman to serve on the council, she was slated to be its president in 1922 but was unable to accept the office because of her illness.) The time she spent alone with other men occasionally troubled Redcliffe. After receiving a now-lost accusatory letter from him in November 1916, she responded angrily. She justified her behavior by explaining that there were no women "who know anything about what I do" and that she would be "in a real fix" if she were not friendly with Zangwill and Abrahams. She told him that, when she was with Abrahams, she thought of nothing but the subject of her work and that to imagine otherwise was "ludicrous." Of course, she wrote, she was not happy that they had to live apart—indeed, she was miserable and depressed—but his distrust and suspicion made their separation worse. She ended the letter angrily: "I am quite ready to say I don't altogether know you—but hope to perhaps in another 15 years."[41] By the time the subject of Zangwill's behavior again arose eight months later, the tension between them had dissipated. She reassured him of her love: "It is such a joy that you know all my love for you and give me all yours, my greatest treasure." She praised him as well for not harboring petty jealousies.[42]

Like other women in Britain whose husbands were away from home, Nina expressed her new sense of independence in various ways. She took up bicycling, for example, which was then associated with feminism, suffragism, and the New Woman. The association was brought home to her when, while visiting an older couple for tea, the wife remarked on hearing of her new interest that "it was like a goddess come to earth!"—thinking of Nina, the only "goddess" she had ever met, on a bicycle, was dreadful to her.[43] She also experimented with tobacco, telling Redcliffe that she had joined Helen Bentwich and Cécile Hartog in smoking a cigarette one night and asked him whether he was horrified.[44] (Before the war, only libertine or bohemian women smoked. The attitude changed during the war, and in the 1920s tobacco companies began to market cigarettes to women.) On one occasion, she even ventured—ever so gingerly—into politics. In December 1918, with a parliamentary election approaching, Lord Robert Cecil, a Liberal, came to Barley to campaign. Impressed by what he said, she wrote out questions to be submitted to him when he spoke the next day at nearby Royston: Did he support the Balfour Declaration? Would he bring his influence to bear in Parliament to stop the pogroms still raging in Poland? When she wrote to Redcliffe in Palestine to tell him about her venture, she was sensitive to what he would think. "Tell me if I ought or not—though too late to stop me!"[45] In the end, then, she felt empowered to do what she wanted—but not without some wavering. Still, she did not hesitate to question Redcliffe when he used a double standard in judging women doctors. "Why," she asked, "is it worse—or more unsuitable for a woman doctor to attend to a man's wounds in certain parts than for a man [doctor] to do the same for a woman?"[46] By the time he returned home, she was aware that the war had changed her. On the eve of his departure from Palestine, she wrote him, "I have had to be more self-reliant, to deal with things and decide about them all on my own, and I suppose that is a training and makes me stronger in a sense. Physically I doubt if I feel quite as strong, but the strain of these years would account for that."[47]

The confidence that Nina acquired during the war years contributed to her most public break with the gender regime of traditional Judaism. On Friday evening, December 5, 1919, she became the first—and only—woman to preach in an Orthodox synagogue in Great Britain when she spoke on the weekly portion (the story of Jacob's wrestling with an angel) in the Cambridge Hebrew Congregation, a traditional synagogue but one independent of the authority of the chief rabbi. The occasion for the sermon was a weekend visit that she and Redcliffe were making to Cambridge to meet the Jewish students there and to assess how Judaism was faring at the university. (They had visited Oxford the previous weekend for the same purpose.) The sermon caused a stir, not in Cambridge, but elsewhere in Anglo-Jewry and even beyond, the *Times* remarking that on this point Judaism was in advance of Christianity. When asked whether Jewish law permitted women to speak from the pulpit, Chief Rabbi Hertz sidestepped the controversy. He ruled that, since she did not enter the pulpit until *after* the concluding prayer, she did not preach *during* the service and thus she did not speak *in* the synagogue, since, at that moment, it was not being used for religious worship. Hertz's waffling led the editor of the *Jewish Chronicle*, Leopold Greenberg, to remark that the chief rabbi was "evidently able to walk round a subject he does not like with agility, if not with courage" and that his "piece of pilpul [strained logic] . . . might have caused many a Medieval rabbi to turn green with envy."[48] The students in the congregation, the *Jewish Guardian* reported, saw her address as "a memorable close to a memorable term." At the end of December, the same newspaper, in an editorial calling for the independence of British synagogues from the control of the chief rabbi and the United Synagogue, cited her sermon as the kind of innovation such independence would make possible.[49] When news of her sermon reached the United States, the weekly *American Israelite*, a voice for Reform Judaism, sarcastically remarked that Judaism in England had escaped from "a terrible peril." After reporting the chief rabbi's tortured logic, which allowed him to avoid condemning Nina, it concluded that Judaism was "once more saved."[50]

It is also possible that the examples of two pioneer women preachers strengthened her resolve. One was Ray Frank, the so-called Girl Rabbi of the Golden West, whose preaching electrified Jewish congregations and audiences up and down the Pacific Coast of the United States in the 1890s. Frank's pathbreaking activities were widely reported in the press, and Nina met her in London in summer 1898, after which they corresponded intermittently for more than twenty years.[51] Closer to home was the example of Lily Montagu, one of the founders of Liberal Judaism in England. In 1918, Montagu preached for the first time at the Liberal Jewish Synagogue in Hill Street, Marylebone, at the urging of the congregation's first rabbi, the US-raised and US-educated Israel Mattuck. She continued to deliver sermons from the pulpit there and at other Liberal synagogues throughout her life. While Nina and she knew each other, they were not friends, but they both belonged to the upper tier of Anglo-Jewry and had friends and acquaintances in common. Nina would certainly have known of her activity. What distinguished her from Frank and Montagu is that the latter were closely identified with movements to reform Jewish worship while Nina was a traditionalist. In addition, neither Frank nor Montagu was a Hebraist and able to draw on postbiblical Hebrew texts.

Nina's and Redcliffe's dual visits to Oxford and Cambridge on consecutive weekends in late 1919 were not casual outings. They were well-planned sorties to explore the state of Jewish affairs at the ancient universities. They attended synagogue on Friday nights and Saturday mornings and dined with students in their rooms afterward. At Oxford, the future Jewish historian Cecil Roth hosted them and a few students for lunch in his rooms in Merton College. The young Roth struck Nina as a character—learned beyond his years, overly confident, and eccentric in speech and dress. "When he talks with you alone you discover, with all his rather queer stilted way of speaking and intensely rolling r's, how great is his enthusiasm for Hebrew poetry and how really remarkable for a boy of 19 or 20 is his knowledge of it." She was impressed that he could recite whole poems of Yehudah Ha-Levi by heart and predicted that, "if he could tone down his mannerisms and a certain slovenliness of appearance," he would turn out to be "an interesting character." After lunch, she spoke to Roth and the students on medieval Hebrew poetry. She and Redcliffe remained with them until they made *havdalah* and recited the evening service. That evening, after dining with the historians of medicine Charles and Dorothea Singer at their home, Redcliffe lectured to the Jewish student society on heredity and Jewish types.

At Cambridge, they dined much better. Phillip Samuel, Herbert and Beatrice's middle son, gave them lunch in his rooms. For the occasion, he borrowed the manservant of his cousin Stuart Montagu, the eldest son of the second Lord Swaythling, to wait on them. The servant, whom Montagu had wrested from his mother and brought to college with him, had "the most funnily prim and perfect manners" Nina had ever seen. After lunch, she again spoke on the Spanish Hebrew poets. Montagu hosted them for dinner that evening, and the meal was "such as few undergrads—except the princes—would ever dream of." That night they hosted a reception for the whole congregation—coffee and cakes—at Columba Hall, at which Redcliffe spoke on his experiences in Palestine. The next morning, she sat in on a Hebrew conversation circle in Pembroke College, conducted by Saul Wassilevsky (later Wassey), son of the Manchester Hebraist Isaiah Wassilevsky; she was impressed by the teacher's patience but not by the level of the students' knowledge.[52]

After Redcliffe and Nina returned to Barley, she wrote reports on her visits to Oxford and Cambridge. I doubt that they were intended to be circulated or to serve any public purpose, for her tone is both candid and casual, and she is often critical of individuals. For example, she described the future philosopher Leon Roth of Exeter College (older brother of Cecil Roth) as ruthlessly insensitive to students less observant than he, and she faulted him for making no effort to draw the less observant into the life of the synagogue or the Adler Society, the Jewish student group. She was even

162 | *The Last Anglo-Jewish Gentleman*

more scathing when it came to the Singers. In her view, they were "doing no good whatever from a Jewish point of view in Oxford." In fact, she thought, they were doing harm, not because of their antiorthodox views (recall that Charles was the son of Simeon Singer of the New West End Synagogue) but because they did not care at all about the students' Jewish interests. They were entirely absorbed in their work and seemed to care for little else. The most they would do was to invite the students in pairs to "dull" breakfasts and tread on their "cherished beliefs," as Edwin Samuel, oldest son of Herbert and Beatrice, told her. She ended her report with the observation that there was a striking difference between the Jewish students at Oxford and those at Cambridge. At Oxford, there was a small devout Orthodox group with a remarkable knowledge of classic Hebrew literature and a much larger group who took practically no part in Jewish life at all. The former did not benefit from general university life as much as they might, while the latter were almost entirely absorbed in the stream of general interests. At Cambridge, in contrast, interest in Jewish matters was far more widespread, "almost everyone taking his part to some extent," and some were well versed in modern Hebrew literature. Yet none of the Cambridge students, in her view, lived "such an absorbingly Jewish life as the little group in Oxford."[53]

What motivated Redcliffe and Nina's visits to the universities? There is no indication, not even a hint, in their correspondence. One might speculate that, as Myer would be matriculating in two years, they were naturally curious about Jewish life at the ancient universities. Another possibility is that Redcliffe, who was then immersed in a campaign to transfer Jews' College from London to either Oxford or Cambridge, wanted to familiarize himself with student Jewish life. The goal of the latter project was to produce clergy who were both able officiants and Oxbridge-educated gentlemen. The chapter that follows takes up the full story of the effort, which absorbed him for several years after the war.

Notes

1. NDS to RNS, December 9, 1918, Add. MS 8171, Wedderburn Deposit, RNS CUL.
2. Raphael Salaman, diary, week of April 25 to May 2, 1929, in possession of Jenny Salaman Manson, London.
3. On the impact of the war on the liberation of women from traditional roles, see Arthur Marwick, *The Deluge: British Society and the First World War* (New York: W. W. Norton, 1970), ch. 3, and Adrian Gregory, *The Last Great War: British Society and the First*

World War (Cambridge: Cambridge University Press, 2008). The memoir of Helen Bentwich is a striking account of how the war offered new opportunities to women: Helen C. Bentwich, *If I Forget Thee: Some Chapters of Autobiography, 1912–1920* (London: Elek, 1973). Bentwich was a niece of Herbert Samuel, the wife of Norman Bentwich, and by birth a member of the Franklin clan.

4. RNS to L. M. Westall, January 2, 1915, Add. MS 8171/3, RNS CUL.

5. Myer Salaman to RNS, July 11, 1915, Add. MS 8171, Wedderburn Deposit, RNS CUL.

6. NDS, diaries, May 1915, in possession of Jenny Salaman Manson.

7. NDS to RNS, July 5 and 31, 1915, Add. MS 8171, Wedderburn Deposit, RNS CUL.

8. NDS to RNS, May 31, 1915, Add. MS 8171, Wedderburn Deposit, RNS CUL.

9. NDS to RNS, June 23, 1915, Add. MS 8171, Wedderburn Deposit, RNS CUL.

10. NDS to RNS, September 25, 1915, Add. MS 8171, Wedderburn Deposit, RNS CUL.

11. NDS to Dr. William H. D. Rouse, December 29, 1915, Add. MS 8171, Wedderburn Deposit, RNS CUL.

12. NDS to RNS, February 12, 1918, Add. MS 8171, Wedderburn Deposit, RNS CUL.

13. NDS to RNS, July 13 and 16, 1918, Add. MS 8171, Wedderburn Deposit, RNS CUL.

14. NDS to RNS, February 18, 1918, Add. MS 8171, Wedderburn Deposit, RNS CUL.

15. Alec Waugh, 1954 Preface to *The Loom of Youth* (London: Bloomsbury Reader, 2012), xiii.

16. NDS to RNS, February 18, 1918, Add. MS 8171, Wedderburn Deposit, RNS CUL.

17. NDS to RNS, July 19, 1918, Add. MS 8171, Wedderburn Deposit, RNS CUL.

18. NDS to RNS, August 21, 1918, Add. MS 8171, Wedderburn Deposit, RNS CUL.

19. NDS to RNS, June 10, 1918, Add. MS 8171, Wedderburn Deposit, RNS CUL; Monk Gibbon, *Netta* (London: Routledge and Kegan Paul, 1960), 118.

20. NDS to RNS, February 27, 1918, Add. MS 8171, Wedderburn Deposit, RNS CUL.

21. The correspondence between Nina and Netta Franklin is in Add. MS 8171, Wedderburn Deposit, RNS CUL.

22. NDS to RNS, September 14, 1918, Add. MS 8171, Wedderburn Deposit, RNS CUL.

23. NDS to RNS, January 16 and 24, 1919, Add. MS 8171, Wedderburn Deposit, RNS CUL.

24. NDS, diaries, June 1915.

25. NDS, diaries, May 1917 and June 1919.

26. NDS, diaries, October 1911.

27. NDS to RNS, January 24, 1919, Add. MS 8171, Wedderburn Deposit, RNS CUL.

28. NDS to RNS, September 14, 1918, Add. MS 8171, Wedderburn Deposit, RNS CUL.

29. Herbert Loewe to RNS, January 7, 1921, Add. MS 8171, Wedderburn Deposit, RNS CUL.

30. NDS to RNS, November 10, 1917, Add. MS 8171, Wedderburn Deposit, RNS CUL.

31. NDS to RNS, July 19, 1918, Add. MS 8171, Wedderburn Deposit, RNS CUL.

32. NDS, "Marching Song of the Judeans," in *Songs of Many Days* (London: Elkin Matthews, 1923), 33.

33. NDS, "The Daybreak," in *Songs of Many Days*, 30.

34. NDS, "The Requittal," in *Songs of Many Days*, 36.

35. NDS to RNS, December 15, 1917, Add. MS 8171, Wedderburn Deposit, RNS CUL.

36. NDS to RNS, December 9, 1918, Add. MS 8171, Wedderburn Deposit, RNS CUL.

37. NDS to RNS, January 4, 1918, Add. MS 8171, Wedderburn Deposit, RNS CUL.

38. RNS to NDS, June 9, 1916, Add. MS 8171/4c, RNS CUL.

39. NDS to RNS, August 11, 1916, Add. MS 8171/103, RNS CUL.

164 | *The Last Anglo-Jewish Gentleman*

40. NDS to RNS, June 23, 1917, Add. MS 8171, Wedderburn Deposit, RNS CUL.

41. NDS to RNS, November 11, 1916, Add. MS 8171/103, RNS CUL.

42. NDS to RNS, June 23, 1917, Add. MS 8171, Wedderburn Deposit, RNS CUL.

43. NDS to RNS, June 22, 1917, Add. MS 8171, Wedderburn Deposit, RNS CUL.

44. NDS to RNS, December 22, 1917, Add. MS 8171, Wedderburn Deposit, RNS CUL.

45. NDS to RNS, December 13, 1918, Add. MS 8171, Wedderburn Deposit, RNS CUL.

46. NDS to RNS, March 5, 1917, Add. MS 8171/103, RNS CUL.

47. NDS to RNS, March 15, 1919, Add. MS 8171, Wedderburn Deposit, RNS CUL.

48. Mentor, "In the Communal Armchair," *Jewish Chronicle*, January 9, 1920.

49. *Jewish Guardian*, December 12 and 26, 1919.

50. *American Israelite*, February 19, 1920.

51. Ray Frank Littman Collection, AJHS CJH.

52. NDS, "Our Visit to Oxford, 28–30 November 1919" and "Our Visit to Cambridge, 5–7 December 1919," Add. MS 8171/74, RNS CUL.

53. Ibid.

8

COMMUNAL WORK AND PERSONAL LOSS

1

Redcliffe Salaman was not a religious man in the common sense of the term, that is, a person with spiritual interests, concerned with matters that transcend the material world. He was very much a typical twentieth-century man of science. He was certainly skeptical of fundamental doctrines of classical Judaism, such as the omniscience of God, the efficacy of prayer, and the revelation of the Written and Oral Law simultaneously at Mount Sinai. Nonetheless, like many Anglo-Jewish notables, he was profoundly concerned with the health of Judaism and found comfort in Jewish rituals and services (at least some of the time). In other words, the bonds of race did not exhaust his sense of Jewishness. Consequently, at various times in his life, he took a role in efforts to revive or energize Judaism in Britain. For him it was not a matter of more scrupulous observance. It was a much less tangible project. Some of his goals were concrete—for example, the creation of a genteel Anglo-Jewish clergy that was equally at home in the world of Torah and the culture of the West—but much of what he wanted was more nebulous, indeed, sufficiently so that at times it is difficult to know exactly what he had in mind.

An early expression of his discontent with the religious circumstances in Anglo-Jewry appears in a letter he wrote to Nina in 1913 after reading Arthur Ruppin's *Jews of To-day*.[1] (First published in German in 1904, Margery Bentwich's English translation appeared in 1913.) Ruppin, who shared Redcliffe's racial assumptions, was known for his sociological work on the corrosive impact of modernity on Jewish loyalties and for his advocacy of Zionism as the solution to what ailed the Jewish people. But Redcliffe was looking for something else, something that spoke to both his passionate sense of Jewishness and his scientific understanding of the world. As he wrote to Nina, "What surprises me in Ruppin & [Maurice] Fishberg on the one hand & the Orthodox outlook on the other is their utter hopelessness & despair in the face of modern culture. If Judaism is any good it must surely meet the needs of a 20th century man as well as a 19th & if it can't there is something radically wrong with it. To lead the double life of complete orthodoxy & modern culture à la [Herbert] Loewe is merely a tour de force & one that does not seem to lead anywhere."[2]

His idiosyncratic reading of Ruppin and Fishberg aside—neither was concerned with Judaism as a religion—it is clear that what troubled Redcliffe was the timeworn question of how to reconcile, in theory and practice, tradition and modernity. Herbert Loewe managed to do so, but Redcliffe saw his reconciliation as something few other Jews could achieve. Moreover, it was a reconciliation that did not lead anywhere, that is, was incapable of influencing the future of Anglo-Judaism.

Two months later, Redcliffe again expressed his sense of discontent with the state of Judaism in Britain in a letter to Nina. In this letter, however, he saw himself and his friends as critical figures in any Jewish awakening. "I feel the time is coming when those Jews who have a feeling of what is fit & right must stand up & say so & not countenance this ever spreading rot in our midst." (Again, it is not clear what was "fit & right" and what was "rot".) Even though the ground was "quietly crumbling away," he was somewhat optimistic: an ever growing number of intellectuals who adhered to "the old standards" (?) and despised "this sloppy characterless slide" were willing to stand forth. Among them he included his friends Charles Myers and Charles Seligman, neither of whom, in fact, shared his interest in the religious side of Jewish life. Redcliffe even went as far as to imagine that he and Nina might play a central role in reversing the decay around them, telling her that Barley might become "a second Modin."[3] (Modi'in, the usual spelling, was home to the priestly family, the Maccabees, who led the successful Jewish revolt against Seleucid rule in the second century BCE.)

Redcliffe found a vehicle for his interest in religious renewal in the campaign to revitalize Jews' College, which began before World War I but which moved ahead only after the war. The object of his interest, Jews' College, established in London in 1855, trained young men to serve mainstream Orthodox synagogues in Britain and the empire as preachers, ministers, and teachers.[4] Housed in Queen Square, Guildford Street, it was neither an East European–type *yeshivah*, with an almost exclusive focus on the study of the Talmud, nor a Central European–type seminary, with a combination of classical textual study and modern critical scholarship (*Wissenschaft des Judentums*). The level of instruction at Jews' College was not high nor its graduates intellectually distinguished, with a few exceptions. It produced officiants who were able to lead services, read Torah, deliver sermons, instruct children, and, in some cases, fulfill the duties of congregational secretary. It did not award the title of rabbi to its graduates, who were called, instead, "reverends." Starved of funding from its founding, it lived a hand-to-mouth existence, and by the early twentieth century, it was having difficulty attracting a sufficient number of qualified students.

For Redcliffe and those notables who shared his outlook, there was another problem: most students at Jews' College lacked the social polish, cultural sensitivity, and Western learning that would enable them to mix comfortably in genteel circles. As I pointed out earlier, most Anglo-Jewish clergymen came from lower-middle-class or immigrant homes and lacked a university degree—in striking contrast, for example, to their counterparts in Germany, where a university education counted far more. They were not, by the standards of British society, gentlemen, nor were they, by the standards of German Jewry, scholars, which explains, in part, why *Wissenschaft des Judentums* did not flourish in Britain. Their status and their salaries were low and they were at the beck and call of synagogue officers and wealthy congregants. In addition, they were subject to the authority of the chief rabbi, an arrangement that allowed them little room to exercise their own judgment or initiative.

The lay communal leadership recognized that Jews' College was in need of reform. The election in 1913 of a new chief rabbi, the Hungarian-born and American-educated Joseph H. Hertz, who, like his predecessors in the office, was not English, provoked comment about the lack of home-grown talent. After his election, for example, the greeting-card manufacturer Sir Adolph Tuck sent a printed memorandum to the council of the United Synagogue lamenting that the community was forced to go to New York City to find a chief rabbi. The lesson to him was that it needed to expand its own stock of rabbinical talent. He told the council that Jews' College was inadequately funded and widely ridiculed because "the raw material on which the College authorities have to work is derived practically without exception from a certain class in the community." By drawing students from only that class, it was impossible "to evolve the best type of Minister." The well-to-do and the cultured did not send their sons to Jews' College because the lay leadership did not much respect its ministers and because they viewed the college as a second-rate charity rather than a great seat of learning.[5]

The council of Jews' College, of which Redcliffe was a long-serving member, was acutely aware of the problems it faced. In November 1912, the council appointed a committee to investigate how the college recruited students and to consider means of improving the intake. The committee, on which Redcliffe also served, issued two reports in February 1914, a majority report, signed by seven members, and a minority report signed by three—Redcliffe, Robert Sebag-Montefiore, and Robert Waley Cohen.[6] The most significant difference between the two reports was that the minority proposed the transfer of Jews' College to either Oxford or Cambridge. It argued that a minister of religion must be "a man of character, broad education, and profound knowledge of human nature" in order to "rescue the minds and lives of his congregants from the engulfing materialism of our time." He needed to be able to expound Judaism to congregants who possessed general culture and education but were "lamentably deficient" in their knowledge of Judaism. Only the ancient universities were able to provide academic instruction, mold character, and encourage the study of human nature. The minority report also included remarks about the "repellant character" of the external features of the college in Queens Square, such as the "dingy" building and the locked library.[7] Most of the debate about the reports at two council meetings in February focused on the question of transferring the college. In defending the minority recommendation, Waley Cohen specifically extolled the nonacademic advantages of an Oxbridge education. The mere acquisition of knowledge was not the only end of education, he stressed. "The study of human nature, the close contact with other men's minds, which people had an opportunity of experiencing in the old resident universities, were not to be obtained anywhere else."[8] For Redcliffe and Waley Cohen, this was the chief reason to transfer Jews' College: Oxbridge would produce gentlemen rabbis who, by virtue of their polish and tact, would be instrumental in revitalizing Anglo-Jewry.

The majority report was carried by a vote of seventeen to twelve. The outbreak of the war, however, prevented the implementation of any steps to revitalize the college and, specifically, to enhance the student intake. Then, in the final months of the war, Waley Cohen and other like-minded notables launched a project, known as the Jewish War Memorial Trust, into which the proposal to revitalize the college was folded. They shared the not uncommon desire at the time to create something new and better out of the wreckage of the war, in part as a memorial to those who gave their lives in the conflict. The lay backers of the fund conceived of creating an educational trust to secure the future of "traditional Judaism" in Britain. What they meant by "traditional Judaism" was not, however, *Frömmigkeit* (piety and strict observance), but rather a Judaism that, while acknowledging the authority of the chief rabbi and respectful of tradition, actively promoted ethical behavior and combated crass materialism.

Waley Cohen launched the plan in June 1919 and, from the start, the proposal to reform the college was an essential part of it. The effort was overly ambitious, with the goal of raising a £1 million endowment. Its backers envisioned that it would fund a revitalized Jews' College, improve the compensation of synagogue officiants, and expand elementary and secondary religious and Hebrew education. The project was a spectacular failure: at the end of 1921, it had taken in only £218,000 in pledges and had actually collected only £113,112.[9] One year later, the fund closed with a capital of £147,000.[10] (These figures include pledges and funds that Chief Rabbi Hertz collected during an eleven-month pastoral tour of the English-speaking Jewish communities of the empire—from October 1920 to August 1921. Of the £68,000 in pledges that he received, only £20,000 was eventually collected.)[11] As the *Jewish Guardian* editorialized in December 1921, "the extravagant hopes and extreme views" that found "universal expression" at the end of the war were "now being revised in all directions."[12] The shortcomings in raising money, however, did not dampen Redcliffe's enthusiastic support for the campaign to move the college and his eagerness to produce gentleman rabbis.

2

Having supported the transfer of Jews' College from London before the war, Redcliffe was a natural ally of Waley Cohen in the campaign to establish the Jewish War Memorial. After a well-attended public meeting at Central Hall, Westminster, on June 11, 1919, to launch the project, Redcliffe wrote to the *Jewish Chronicle* to clarify its three goals, which he did not think had been adequately set out at the meeting. The first was to enlarge the entire system of elementary and secondary religious and Hebrew education. Where once ignorance of Judaism was confined to the well-to-do, he noted, it was now "a factor pregnant with danger to the whole Community, where its nakedness makes it hideous to both Jews and Gentile." While he did not explain why such ignorance was "dangerous," clearly there was a connection here to his prewar concern about "the spreading rot in our midst." The second goal was to improve the pay and status of the Anglo-Jewish ministry, a matter that struck close to home because of Myer's flirtation with the idea of becoming a rabbi. He lamented "the horrid bond of servility that at present exists in so many places between the minister and his congregation." By raising the standing of the ministry, he hoped to transform it into "an honourable career into which honourable men [like himself] will gladly encourage their sons to enter." He hoped that this would end the anomalous situation that no Jewish clergyman ever placed his son in the same profession. Young men who would have been "worth their weight in gold to the Community" refused to follow in their fathers' footsteps because they had seen how much their fathers had struggled in their congregational positions. Here it is likely that he was thinking of his friend Charles Singer, the son of Simeon Singer of the New West End Synagogue. Improving the status of the Anglo-Jewish clergy was linked to the third goal—the reconstitution of Jews' College and its transfer from London. As Redcliffe envisioned it, students for the rabbinate, "culled from every class of society," would take a degree at an Oxford or Cambridge college before pursing their rabbinic studies at the relocated Jews' College. The War Memorial fund would provide financial aid to those students whose parents could not afford an Oxbridge education. Both the second and third goals were designed to create gentlemen rabbis. In promoting the War Memorial, Redcliffe also introduced another theme that became increasingly important to him in coming decades—the defense of Anglo-Jewish latitudinarianism, or inclusiveness, the notion that the community ideally embraced diverse streams of Judaism and privileged harmony and solidarity over theological and ritual rectitude. In this vein, the reconstituted Jews' College would not be a boundary-setting sectarian institution but a center for Jewish scholarship open to students of every shade of Jewish thought. In addition to training ministers and the like, it would also function as a center for advanced Jewish scholarship.[13]

In November 1919, Waley Cohen, who chaired the War Memorial executive committee, appointed Redcliffe to its committee on the future of Jews' College. The chair was Philip Magnus, former minister of the West London Synagogue (Reform) and at this time a member of parliament for the University of London. The committee met for the first time on November 16, and, over the next six months, heard testimony from and interviewed students, faculty, scholars from other institutions, and members of the college's governing board. The picture they painted of the state of the college, irrespective of their views on its transfer, was depressing. Only six full-time students were at the college, three of whom had entered with an advanced knowledge of Talmud, having studied previously at *yeshivot* in London or abroad. One of them was already a fully qualified rabbi. According to the principal, Adolph Büchler, who had himself studied at the Budapest and Breslau seminaries, only one student between 1912 and 1919 "proved to be of great ability" (he had immigrated from Galicia at age twenty, already possessing a good knowledge of rabbinic and other Hebrew literature) but he was not adept at delivering sermons or leading prayers. Some students left after one or two terms, others after a year, and still others after obtaining a bachelor's degree from University College, using their time at Jews' College "as a cheap and easy road to a degree" (in the words of Herbert Loewe). Some even accepted congregational positions without finishing their coursework. The five members of the faculty, four of whom were born and educated on the Continent and whose scholarship was not a matter of dispute, were poorly paid. The library was starved for funds, and the governing board resorted to private collections to subsidize faculty publications.[14]

The most ardent advocates of transferring the college were academics from other institutions—Israel Abrahams (Cambridge), Herbert Loewe (Oxford), and Philip Hartog (University of London). Despite different religious outlooks, all three argued that Anglo-Jewry could no longer depend on foreign-born officiants with little secular education. Those students who were born abroad or who came from immigrant homes required "westernizing." Their mastery of the Hebraic needed to be balanced with their mastery of the Hellenic. The ideal candidates were men of the world "in the best sense of the term" (Hartog's phrase). An Oxbridge degree prior to their enrollment at Jews' College would produce reverends who could associate with the professional men in their congregations on equal terms and whose sermons, by invoking current affairs and contemporary literature and thought, could invoke their sympathy. In particular, they wanted religious leaders who could stem the drift of well-educated youth. The old-fashioned ministers were unable to solve their doubts, to show how the old and the new could be reconciled. And they wanted leaders who were able to defend the Jewish cause outside the Jewish community—that is, well-spoken gentlemen, not *yeshivah bokherim*.

As proof of the civilizing effect of an Oxbridge education, Waley Cohen frequently cited the case of Israel Brodie, later Hertz's successor as chief rabbi (1948–65). The son of a Lithuanian-born traveling salesman in Newcastle, he studied at Jews' College and University College concurrently, graduating in 1915 with a first-class degree in Hebrew, Arabic, and Syriac. He then proceeded to Balliol College on an Alfred Louis Cohen Scholarship (for British-born candidates for the rabbinate who had studied at Jews' College). In 1921, when Brodie was looking for employment in congregations in the United States and elsewhere, Waley Cohen worked behind the scenes to find him a post in London, not wanting to lose a rabbi whose education at Oxford had given him not only "a much broader outlook" but also "what one may call a social education, of which he has taken the fullest advantage."[15] (Brodie went to Melbourne in 1923 but returned to England in 1937 to pursue a doctoral degree at Oxford.)

The tone of the committee meetings was civil, but in private the advocates of transfer were more outspoken and even impolitic. When Loewe complained to Waley Cohen that the two War Memorial representatives coming to Oxford to meet with undergraduates would be arriving on Friday evening after sundown, which Loewe thought would prejudice the undergraduates against the project, Waley Cohen attacked the "silly, priggish ideas of ignorant young men" who wanted to impose their ideas on others and insisted he would not dream of altering the arrangements that had been made. In the intemperate, haughty tone that he often assumed, he replied to Loewe, " If there are any undergraduates at Oxford so narrow and silly to have their faith in the great Jewish War Memorial shaken by the fact that those who are keen on it have to reach Oxford on Friday night after Sabbath has begun, then it only shows how desperately badly we need religious education because people at Oxford should be better and not worse educated than their fellows."[16]

Waley Cohen was also candid in private about the need to require an Oxbridge undergraduate degree. Those who ministered to the community came from "impossible homes." The social and academic advantages of a residential college education—which were to be had nowhere else—would act as a corrective.[17] He was also frank about the consequences of rejecting the transfer plan: The spiritual well-being of the next generation depended on it. Unless it was acted on, the young would grow up to be "gross materialists," without any spiritual ideals whatever. The poorer classes would become "hooligans" and the richer "a blatant and ostentatious class which is much and rightly resented by the general public."[18]

Redcliffe was, apparently, as intemperate as Waley Cohen. Although little of his correspondence about the work of the committee survives,

Waley Cohen refers to their tone in a letter he wrote to Charles Myers, also a member of the committee. Urging Myers to be patient while he (Waley Cohen) built support for the transfer, he recognized nonetheless the advantage of letting people sound off, Redcliffe in particular: "I am sorry you did not let Redcliffe send along his torrent of abuse. I always love to read these things from him: they are so fresh and exuberant and they make him feel so much better when he has got them off and they do not do any harm at all to our mutual relations. He is one of the few people who really cares about the future and is prepared to work for it, and when the moment comes we shall need him badly with his extremely vigorous mind."[19]

Still, Waley Cohen felt he had to restrain Redcliffe's public utterances at times. When the campaign to raise funds for the War Memorial was first launched, Redcliffe toyed with the idea that it should be used for "a regular cleaning up of all our troubles," including repeal of the 1870 act of Parliament that established the United Synagogue and made the chief rabbi the arbiter of its rituals and practices. Waley Cohen responded to Redcliffe's musings with alarm: "For heaven's sake, don't overload our Memorial scheme with all your clean sweep ideas." He urged him to move slowly, as he was depending on him to be one of the main speakers in the campaign. If they were to accomplish something, however, Redcliffe had to "bottle up" his "violent radicalisms."[20]

While denominational affiliation influenced support for or opposition to transferring Jews' College, it was not always decisive. Both Israel Abrahams, a supporter of Liberal Judaism, and Herbert Loewe, a defender of Orthodoxy, argued for the move, as did Chief Rabbi Hertz initially. The West London Synagogue (Reform) favored it, but Philip Magnus, its assistant minister from 1866 to 1880, opposed it. The most adamant opposition came from the two extremes of the religious spectrum—the Liberal Jewish Synagogue and the newly created Organization of Observant Traditional Jews—and from the faculty of Jews' College, who feared a loss of influence or drop in status if the college were to be moved. They also feared that a move would expose their students to ideas that would corrode their faith. The head of the college, Adolph Büchler, told the committee that this was already a problem for students who were simultaneously pursuing an honors Semitics degree at University College, where they were exposed to critical biblical scholarship. The lectures they heard at Jews' College did not "invariably succeed in correcting the impressions of destructive criticism" they absorbed at University College. Often the students ended by viewing

174 | *The Last Anglo-Jewish Gentleman*

all attempts to counterbalance critical scholarship as "deliberate apologetics." Büchler found that restoring their faith in tradition and revelation was not always possible and that some left the college for that reason. Others remained but simply ceased to believe.[21] For their part, advocates of the move welcomed the challenges that the college's students would meet. Herbert Loewe told the committee that Jews' College students were completely out of touch with current theological thinking and that exposure to heretical views would strengthen and sharpen their faith. "The Cotton Wool policy is hopeless. No faith is worth anything until it is tested and proved."[22]

At the end of its deliberations, the Magnus committee was hopelessly divided. As a result, three reports (one majority and two minority) were forwarded to the executive committee of the War Memorial project in early summer 1921. One of the minority reports was written by Redcliffe and signed as well by Charles Myers, Robert Waley Cohen, the merchant banker and horticulturist Frederick C. Stern, the physician N. S. Lucas, the barrister Samuel H. Emanuel, and Joseph Polack, master of the Jewish house at Clifton College.[23] Redcliffe's minority report, while still endorsing the unparalleled benefits of an Oxbridge education, was willing to accept a reinvigorated Jews' College that remained in London—with the proviso that it become a postgraduate institution and that its students first have completed an arts degree at Cambridge. It stipulated, moreover, that, in their first year, students would study subjects other than Semitic languages, the intention being to broaden their intellectual horizon.[24]

In the end, Jews' College was not rejuvenated. Its transfer from London received insufficient support. Equally important, the War Memorial lacked the funds to undertake anything ambitious and instead provided the college with modest annual subsidies. The composition of the student intake remained more or less the same. Although Redcliffe continued to sit on the council of the college for many years, he never again took up the cause of creating gentlemen rabbis. As we will see, however, he continued to feel that something was wrong with the state of Anglo-Judaism and, from time to time, lent his name to abortive campaigns to address the problem. Waley Cohen, on the other hand, continued to pursue small measures on his own to make the Anglo-Jewish clergy more genteel. In 1923, for example, he arranged elocution lessons for an Oxford student, a Jews' College man, for whom he and Claude Goldsmid Montefiore were providing a scholarship. The student's enunciation struck Waley Cohen as "rather deficient."[25]

Five years later, he and Goldsmid Montefiore considered supporting another Jews' College student at Oxford. After meeting him, Goldsmid Montefiore wrote to Waley Cohen that the student looked unhealthy—"his face is spotty, he looks weedy"; he was weak and overworked and had not taken enough exercise. He also worried that the program the student had devised for himself at Oxford was too demanding, for it would leave him no time for exercise and no time for social intercourse with other students who were not Jews. He told Waley Cohen that it was self-defeating to sponsor a future minister who was "at Oxford, but, in no real sense, in Oxford and of Oxford."[26] When Waley Cohen learned that the history master at Portsmouth Grammar School, which the boy had attended, was planning on taking him to Italy over the summer, he remarked that this was an enormous stroke of good fortune, for coming from a very "limited" home he naturally lacked "savoir vivre." If he did not acquire that before going up, he might "miss a good deal at Oxford."[27]

Had Redcliffe's vision of an Oxbridge-educated Anglo-Jewish clergy been realized, would it have rejuvenated Jewish religious life in Britain? Redcliffe's focus on the educational and cultural gap between rabbis and congregants as an impediment to the former's effectiveness was undoubtedly well founded. It is a problem that has persisted to the present and has probably grown more acute as the percentage of British Jews with university degrees has soared. Also widening the gap has been the growing dependence of mainstream Orthodox congregations on rabbis trained in *yeshivot* in Israel and the United States. (Jews' College ceased to function as a seminary in the late twentieth century.) Yet, however acute Redcliffe's insights about the communication gulf between rabbis and congregants, he was probably mistaken in thinking that well-educated, well-spoken, up-to-date rabbis would be able to slow or rout the powerful inroads that secularization and integration were making in modern Anglo-Jewry. Drift and defection would have continued to chip away at communal solidarity whatever direction Jews' College took.

3

In the midst of the campaign to reform Jews' College, tragedy struck the Salamans. In early 1920, Nina was diagnosed with colon cancer and in March she underwent two operations in London, spending almost seven weeks in a nursing home in Manchester Street.[28] After her surgery, she received radiation therapy. For several years she was able to continue her work, to travel to London, and to visit friends. While she was aware that she was seriously ill, it is difficult to know whether she understood how ill she really was. When Herbert Samuel saw her at Homestall in May 1920, he was surprised at how well she looked and urged her and Redcliffe to "come out [to Palestine], perhaps next spring, to look round and decide about coming out for good."[29] In June she wrote to her friend Ray Frank in the United States that, while Redcliffe was enthusiastic about the new Jewish settlements in Palestine and their friends the Samuels were happy to be living in Jerusalem, she and Redcliffe felt that it was not the time for them and the children to go but that they might consider it in the future.[30] That summer, she was well enough to participate in the compilation of *Elegies for the Ninth of Av*, a small book of translations and notes prepared for a Jewish summer school in Oxford in July.[31] She and Redcliffe traveled to London in September to hear Zangwill speak to the University League of the Jewish Students' Union and in December she was present when Redcliffe delivered the lecture "The Racial Origins of Jewish Types" at the Hampstead Conservatoire in Swiss Cottage. In 1921 and 1922, she was still able to continue her translating, writing of articles and book reviews, and lecturing. In June 1921, for example, she spoke to the Adler Society at Oxford on the Jewish poets as historians and in July she gave one of ten lectures on the history of the Jews in the sixteenth century at Toynbee Hall in the East End, a series presented by the extension division of the University of London and the Jewish Historical Society of England.[32] In February 1922, she was again in London, making the usual round of social calls,[33] and in July she spent a few days with Israel and Edith Zangwill at their home in East Preston, Sussex.[34] In early August she delivered the lecture "Rachel Morpurgo and Contemporary Hebrew Poets" at a Jewish summer school at Cambridge and, a few days later, she hosted a garden party for the students at Barley, complete with a treasure hunt, tea, dancing, and musical performances by her children Ruth and Myer.[35] But, by the end of the month, she no longer had the strength to keep up that kind of routine. When she and the children were away later that month, near Scarborough, she was not up and about much.[36] She had another operation in London in June 1923,[37] but her health continued to deteriorate. Two weeks later, Arthur, who was at Bedales, received a letter from his father expressing his anxiety about Nina's prospects.[38] From this point on, she no longer left the house and eventually spent her time in bed or in a sledlike contraption that Redcliffe had built for her and in which

Communal Work and Personal Loss | 177

Figure 8.1. Ruth and Esther Salaman in the garden of Homestall. Courtesy of Jenny Salaman Manson.

she was carried about.[39] But she remained mentally alert, almost to the very end, and Israel Abrahams traveled from Cambridge to continue their study of Hebrew texts.[40] Another frequent visitor from Cambridge was the poet Frances Cornford, wife of the classicist Francis Cornford.

Arthur thought that, as death approached, her unquestioning faith seemed to be a great help. Aware that the end was near, she said goodbye to the three boys on the morning of February 21, 1925, making them promise that they would not marry out of the faith. She also told Arthur that she would give his love to his twin Edward if she met him. She then fell unconscious and died at 9:40 in the morning the next day at the age of forty-seven.[41] She had been sick for five years. Ruth and Esther, fifteen and ten years old, who had not been told how serious their mother's illness was, were almost immediately sent to stay with their aunt Isabelle, Redcliffe's sister, in London. Nina died on a Sunday. Three days later, on Wednesday, she was buried in the Salaman family plot at Willesden Cemetery, London, with Chief Rabbi Hertz delivering the eulogy. The girls did not attend the

178 | *The Last Anglo-Jewish Gentleman*

funeral. (Women in general were not present at graveside funerals under the authority of the United Synagogue at the time.) A memorial service was held at the Cambridge synagogue on Sunday, March 1, at which Israel Abrahams spoke and Myer sang some of mother's favorite liturgical melodies.

Nina's death was emotionally wrenching for everyone in the family, even if its impact was not immediately apparent in every case. Redcliffe was bereft; he could not endure the solitude in which her death left him. He also panicked and felt himself incapable of taking care of the girls. Ruth returned to Bedales and seemed to get on with life while Esther went to live with the Herbert Loewes in Oxford, where she attended Wynchwood School. In sending her there, Redcliffe felt he was acting in accordance with Nina's wishes. As he explained to Esther's older sister Ruth at the time, "Mother several times had spoken about her desire that E. should, if possible, follow in her footsteps; to do that you must learn your Hebrew continuously and not in odd fits and starts. . . . The only person who could give her that amount of teaching and at the same time was really nice was Mr. Loewe."[42]

For Esther, the experience was a horrific disaster: she was very unhappy and cried frequently. When Redcliffe realized that the arrangement was not working out, he then sent her to Bedales for two years (1926–28), where she was unhappy as well. In 1928, she transferred again—to a progressive girls' school, Maltman's Green, Gerrard's Cross, Buckinghamshire, where, for the first time since her mother's death, she was happy. She remained there until 1933.[43] At the time of Nina's death. Myer and Arthur were at Cambridge and Raphael was due to start there in October. Myer, who received a natural sciences degree in June 1925, intended to spend a fourth year at Cambridge, doing research, but his father found living alone so unbearable that Myer agreed to live at home and commute daily to Cambridge on a motor bike.

Overwhelmed by loneliness and grief, Redcliffe began to look for a second wife. Most of the women he considered were preselected by his sisters in London. It was, in this sense, an arranged marriage. We know very little about the candidates. There was a Winifred, to whom he proposed but who turned him down, to his later relief.[44] There was also a Frau Hahn, whom he dismissed as a good, intelligent woman "but sentimental and flabby to the point of nausea."[45] And there were others as well. Before he succeeded in finding a suitable mate, however, he fell in love with a much younger woman whom he had just met—Esther Polianowsky (1900–95), a

Figure 8.2. Esther Polianowsky Salaman before her marriage to Myer Salaman.

Ukrainian-born graduate student in physics at Cambridge whose family lived in Haifa and who had been educated in Berlin.[46] (See fig. 8.2.) Her appearance in Redcliffe's life was of enormous long-term consequence, since, after a tumultuous courtship, she eventually married his eldest son, Myer. Her sister Miriam (1914–2013) later married his third son, Raphael.

The Polianowskys' background was as different from the Salamans' as one could imagine. Born in Zhitomir, Ukraine, in the Pale of Settlement, into a comfortable (but not wealthy) Russified home, Esther received a Russian-language education at a local gymnasium. During World War I, when she was in her teens, she was exposed to the ideological currents then

180 | *The Last Anglo-Jewish Gentleman*

sweeping through East European Jewry, and, in her last year at school, she became a member of Dror, a left-wing Zionist student movement. In March 1919, after Ukrainian nationalists murdered Jews and looted Jewish shops in Zhitomir the previous December, Esther and her boyfriend, Shlomo Bardinstein [later Bardin], left for Palestine, where they arrived in January 1920. In 1921, she returned, clandestinely, to Ukraine to bring out her family, which she succeeded in doing at great risk to her own life. Her roundabout path to England began when she enrolled at the University of Berlin in 1922 to study mathematics and physics. Having decided after three years that she wanted to study for a doctorate in physics—but not in Germany—Albert Einstein, with whom she had studied, recommended that she go to the Cavendish Laboratory in Cambridge.[47] In September, she and Shlomo—she had been living with him ever since he had followed her to Berlin—left for England, Shlomo having arranged to teach Hebrew in Newcastle.

In December Esther went to see Chaim Weizmann (perhaps again on the recommendation of Einstein), president of the World Zionist Organization, who told her about the Education Aid Society, which awarded grants to talented Jewish students. Weizmann contacted David Eder, a member of the World Zionist Organization Executive, and Eder, in turn, contacted Redcliffe, active in the Education Aid Society from before the war. Redcliffe arranged to meet Esther, who was living in Newnham College, for lunch in Cambridge. He was immediately and thoroughly smitten. He invited her to spend the weekend at Barley, but her college would allow her to spend time in an unmarried man's house only if there were a chaperone present. And so, Redcliffe invited his sister and brother-in-law Dorothy and Fred Samuel to join them for the weekend. Before then, he took her to tea at his old friends' the Cornfords' and, later that evening, while dining alone with her in Cambridge, he asked her to marry him, telling her that he had made up his mind to do so within two minutes of first meeting her. He also told her to take her time in deciding, since they would be seeing each other on the weekend.

At Barley, Esther was plunged into English country-house life. The men dressed for dinner, as was customary, and she, who must have been forewarned, managed to purchase an appropriate dress in Cambridge beforehand. After breakfast the following morning, while the two were out walking, Redcliffe asked her whether she had decided. She reminded him that she had told him the first time they had met that she was already as good as married (that is, to Shlomo Bardinstein). Redcliffe seemed to have taken her refusal in good spirits, for he told her he would like to meet Shlomo, who then came to Barley for dinner the following weekend. Then, within a matter of weeks, Myer and Esther, whose paths in Cambridge began to cross ever more frequently, fell in love with each other. To muddle matters, Esther was also still in love with Shlomo, with whom she had a long-standing sexual relationship. Above all, she did not want to hurt Shlomo. Extracting herself from that relationship was an arduous, emotionally fraught monthslong process, described at length in surviving correspondence. In July 1926, while Esther, Shlomo, and Myer were in Berlin (their being there together is a story in itself), Esther made up her mind and she and Myer decided to marry and went off to Chamonix, a skiing and mountaineering resort at the base of Mount Blanc, to give themselves time to be alone together and to allow Esther to recover from the emotional stress of the past months. Myer was fully aware of how scandalous their behavior was by the standards of respectable English society and told only his father what they were doing. They intended to marry in Chamonix on August 2, 1926 (Myer's birthday), but Redcliffe convinced them to return to England and marry there.

It was not the end of the drama, however. On her return, Esther was still distraught about the pain she was inflicting on Shlomo. She was also scared to write her mother in Haifa, whose heart was set on her marrying Shlomo. She finally wrote the letter after much badgering from Redcliffe. Her wedding with Myer was scheduled for September 19. It was to be a quiet wedding, performed by the chief rabbi, at Barley; only close relatives were invited. Then, on September 2, Esther received a telegram from her brother in Haifa that her mother was dangerously ill and wanted to see her before she died. Redcliffe thought that Esther was too weak to travel to Palestine alone. While Myer was willing to accompany her, Redcliffe was adamant that he would not allow Myer to go unless they married beforehand. If they traveled to Haifa as man and wife, without marrying, they would "cover their names and *mine* [my emphasis] with scandal." He would also not allow Raphael to accompany her. And so, Myer and Esther were hastily married on Sunday, September 5, in the registrar's office in Royston. With some effort, Redcliffe obtained a British passport for her and, that Sunday evening, Raphael drove the newlyweds to London. They crossed the English Channel the next morning and from Paris took the train to Marseille, from which they intended to sail to Haifa. After they had left Barley, on Monday morning, Redcliffe received a telegram from Shlomo, who was in Haifa, saying that Esther's mother was not ill and that the telegram from her brother was a ruse to prevent her marriage to Myer. When Shlomo had told her family that his relationship with Esther was at an end, her mother had been terribly upset and had schemed with her son to get Esther back to Haifa. Redcliffe tried to recall the two, dispatching telegrams that chased them from Victoria station to Marseille, where, finally, they received his frantic telegram. Rather than returning immediately to England, they decided to first spend a few days at Juan-les-Pins.[48]

In the letters that Redcliffe wrote to Myer in the summer and fall of 1926, as the above events were unfolding, he revealed a side of himself that was usually not visible.[49] Esther's arrival in Cambridge had introduced a new kind of emotional intensity into his life and had challenged both him and Myer to cope with situations that they never could have imagined. In his letters, Redcliffe repeatedly reassured Myer of his unconditional love, while at the same time counseling him not to take steps that he would later regret. His life to that date had not prepared him for Esther's openness to premarital sex nor for his son's willingness to flaunt respectability as well, and he let them know of his disapproval. After they arrived in Chamonix, he wrote to them of his fears: "The world may be foolish and cruel but in the end it embodies in its customs all the stored up wisdom of mankind and those who transgress will suffer and the finer they are the more they suffer—I would give much my dears to save you from that."[50]

Myer had reassured his father that his relationship with Esther would remain platonic until they were married, but Redcliffe told him that he had no idea how impossible the task was that he had set himself. A "passionate platonic love" was a "tour de force" and no one would credit him and Esther with such self-control. When the couple decided to marry in Chamonix— presumably so that they might consummate their love sooner rather than later—Redcliffe counseled them to wait and marry in England and meanwhile to continue living as they had resolved, "so that neither your own consciences nor the sting of what others may say or think will harm you."[51] In his letters, Redcliffe referred to his own loneliness and his frustration and sorrow at having no one with whom to talk about Myer and Esther. During this crisis, Nina's death haunted him even more acutely. After attending Rosh Ha-Shanah services at the New West End in early September, he wrote to Esther and Myer how he had sensed Nina's presence in synagogue: "the simple majesty of her bearing as she stood in the gallery eclipsing everyone—it all came back, usually I get only memories and dreams of the days of illness but this was in the great past days when we had joy

Communal Work and Personal Loss | 183

of life—And you my dears enjoy life and each other while you may—Fate, please God, may be kinder to you than it has been to me."[52]

Throughout these weeks of crisis, Redcliffe remained in contact by mail with Shlomo Bardin. Although Bardin was his son's rival, Redcliffe expressed sympathy for the position in which he found himself, even telling him, in late July, before Esther had made up her mind, that he was on Bardin's side and not to lose hope—victory might still be his. At that point, he probably reasoned that Myer would be better off without Esther. He explained, however, that there was nothing he could do. He then took the opportunity to remind Bardin that if he and Esther had lived more conventionally—that is, if they had been married—then he would not have found himself competing with Myer. However progressive his views in some areas, Redcliffe remained a prisoner of his conventional upbringing when it came to sex. He wrote Bardin, as he had told Myer, that he would not help them financially unless they married. He also expressed to Bardin views that he probably did not share with Myer. He was clearly fed up with Esther's inability to make up her mind. She had "captained the team too long"—even though she was "no captain of life's ship"—a task for which he thought Shlomo was a hundred times better suited.[53] (Bardin later became a prominent figure in the American Jewish summer camping movement.)

Remarkably, it was during this turbulent period, while Myer and Esther were in Germany and France, that Redcliffe found his second wife—Gertrude Lowy (1887–1982), the eldest daughter of Ernest Lowy, a stockbroker, and his wife, Henrietta, a sister of the painter Solomon J. Solomon. The go-betweens were Redcliffe's sisters Bessie (Mrs. Hermann Cohen) and Jennie (Mrs. Herbert Cohen), who were friends of Henrietta Lowy. Jennie, the wealthiest of the Salaman siblings, and Henrietta were patrons of the poet and painter Isaac Rosenberg when he was at the Slade School, and Henrietta, along with four of her daughters and several of Redcliffe's sisters, were active in the women's suffrage movement. Bessie brought Gertie, as she was called, to Homestall on Thursday, September 16, and she and Redcliffe became engaged on Sunday morning, September 19. As Redcliffe wrote Myer immediately afterward, it took about ten seconds to settle.[54] They were wed on Wednesday afternoon, October 13, 1926, at the New West End Synagogue.

Gertie was thirty-eight years old when she married Redcliffe and still living at home; he was fifty-two. It was a marriage of convenience, not of love. It may have grown into something deeper over time, but the evidence that survives does not seem to support such a conjecture. They were married

184 | *The Last Anglo-Jewish Gentleman*

to each other for almost thirty years, but Gertie appears infrequently in his correspondence. There was more to her, however, than her absence from the archive suggests. While not learned in a bookish sense, she was clever and accomplished in other ways. She was a talented photographer who had exhibited her work at the Royal Photographic Society and worked professionally before her marriage. She also spoke French, German, and Italian fluently and had served as a volunteer X-ray assistant with a Red Cross unit in Italy from 1917 to 1919. Before the war, she had been a militant suffragette and, in March 1912, had been sentenced to two months of hard labor for her participation in the Women's Social and Political Union's window smashing in Kensington. Her niece, Livia Gollancz, believed that neither Redcliffe nor his children appreciated her and that, in effect, Redcliffe viewed her in the beginning as a housekeeper and then later as a caregiver.[55]

It is not surprising that Gertie's relations with Redcliffe's children, especially Esther, were rocky. Any woman seeking to replace Nina at Homestall, especially less than a year and a half after her death, would have found her position challenging vis-à-vis her husband's children. There is some disagreement among Redcliffe's grandchildren about how uncomfortable the situation was, but the consensus is that their parents never established a warm or affectionate relationship with their father's new wife. The one exception was Ruth, who, according to her daughter Jane Miller, welcomed her like "a breath of fresh air." But Ruth, Miller recalled, "always warmed to fellow outsiders, and her stepmother's discomforts and uncertainties may have chimed with her own. Her 'Well, here we all are, I suppose,' pronounced with anxious formality at a family gathering, expressed all too well her shaken sense of the place she occupied there."[56]

The other children were not very kind about Gertie, but Esther, who was only ten at her mother's death, could not bear her.[57] In a more cryptic vein, Arthur noted in his diary in 1929 that he did not consider his father's second marriage a success: "She's what I call a bad stock, that is, she is somehow fundamentally unsound. Ignorant yet would be wise. Her family [the Lowys] explains all."[58] What the problem was with the Lowys remains a mystery.

The emotional turmoil that accompanied Redcliffe's search for a second wife also owed something to his ties to a deteriorating Israel Zangwill, caught in a crisis of his own at the time. Zangwill, who had remained a warm friend of Nina's (despite her earlier rejection of his overtures), suffered from acute depression and anxiety in the last years of his life. The trigger for his breakdown was the failure of a West End season of his plays, which he launched in 1925. Redcliffe told a biographer of Zangwill that he was completely burned out from his exertions on the venture, on which he lost thousands of pounds: "His insomnia was terrible. His nerves were torn to shreds. He quarreled with the dramatic critics; he fought grueling law suits over stage scenery; he worried everyone dreadfully. He was a weary man, thinner and frailer than ever before. He used to lie in a chaise lounge in the sunshine. He drank hot water. Nothing could relieve his terrible insomnia. He could find no rest."[59] Zangwill's visits to Homestall added to Redcliffe's stress and unhappiness in the wake of Nina's death and the unfolding of Myer's pursuit of Esther. As he wrote to his brother Clement in August 1925, an "appalling" long weekend with Zangwill, who was in "a state of intense and ceaseless excitement," left him "nearly dead," "a complete wreck for the time."[60]

4

Throughout the 1920s, Redcliffe continued his breeding experiments with potato varieties, gaining the recognition of government agriculturalists and academic scientists. Before the war he had been concerned primarily with the inheritance of dominant and recessive traits and the breeding of blight-resistant hybrids, but in the twenties and thirties his focus shifted to the question of the source of potato blight. When Redcliffe began his work in the first decade of the twentieth century, he knew little about viruses—"pathogenic agents so small as to be invisible by ordinary microscopic methods and not retained by fine porcelain filters," as he described them in a 1939 essay.[61] Scientists did not become aware of the existence of viruses until the late 1890s, when the work of the Dutch microbiologist Martinus Beijerinck revealed them. In the early years of Redcliffe's research, while potato growers and breeders were obviously aware of the destructiveness of potato viruses, they did not understand their microbiological nature. They referred to them as "miffiness," which they attributed to the senescence of the plants. Their reasoning was connected to the ability of potatoes to reproduce in two ways—vegetatively, from tubers, or seed potatoes (the usual commercial practice), and sexually, from seeds contained in berries produced by the potato plant's flowers. Thus, they thought, commercial breeders, in forcing a method of reproduction (by tuber) on a plant with male and female generative organs that were able to produce healthy offspring, were sinning against nature and weakening their crops. As Redcliffe explained,

186 | *The Last Anglo-Jewish Gentleman*

"What could one expect but a rapid decay of vigour in such unnaturally begotten offspring? Vigour and sexuality are cognate, and the psychological complex they induced managed to retard for the best part of a century the investigation of a problem in pathology."[62]

After World War I, plant-virus research entered a new productive phase in Western Europe and North America. Fully convinced now that some diseases of the potato were due to viral infections, Redcliffe urged his views on the Ministry of Agriculture, which by 1921 embraced them. At the International Potato Congress that the Royal Horticultural Society convened in November 1921, Redcliffe delivered "The Degeneration of Potatoes." He provided a historical sketch of the subject and showed that degeneracy was not due to gradually increasing senility but rather to a viral infection. He also lobbied the Ministry of Agriculture to do more, pointing out that the United Kingdom suffered annual losses from blight in the millions of pounds. In 1924, the Ministry of Agriculture appointed a special committee to foster research on plant-virus diseases, and, in summer 1925, after spending a weekend at Barley and touring Redcliffe's experimental plots, Sir Daniel Hall, scientific adviser to the ministry, asked him to head a new government-funded research institute at Cambridge. Redcliffe was surprised, never having imagined that he would return to a research institution.[63] He should not have been surprised, however, since he had become the authority on everything connected with the potato in the years after the war. In 1927, he appointed Kenneth Smith, senior lecturer in entomology at the University of Manchester, to join him at what was now the Potato Virus Research Station at Cambridge. Smith had been investigating potato leaf curl at Manchester, and, in particular, the role of insects in transmitting the virus. Smith brought to their research the technique he had developed for studying the transmission of viruses by insects. At the research station, Redcliffe began studying the virus known universally as potato virus X and was one of the first scientists to demonstrate that plants infected with the virus acquired immunity against the entry of another, similar, virus or virus strain. By means of mechanical transmission, he built up a collection of strains of virus X, ranging from the most virulent to one that was completely symptomless, from which subsequent researchers greatly benefited.[64]

Before the move to Cambridge, Redcliffe's laboratory was his own garden. After his appointment, he transferred his breeding stock to the Cambridge research station, which was an improvement but still physically primitive. It had facilities to store potatoes and greenhouses to grow experimental plants. The laboratory was housed in one end of a small barn. It consisted of

Communal Work and Personal Loss | 187

an eighteen-foot bench, a cold-water tap, and an electric hotplate for sterilizing mortars and pestles used to crush leaves when preparing inocula. A researcher at the station from 1929 to 1936 later remembered that "the most sophisticated piece of apparatus was a recalcitrant Primus stove."[65]

In the early 1920s, Redcliffe also first took an interest in the historical and anthropological side of potato cultivation. The catalyst was a lecture he attended in Cambridge in 1922 by Julio C. Tello, "the father of Peruvian archaeology." Tello remarked that, in excavating sites in the northern coastlands of Peru, he had come across clay pots that, while molded more or less in the form of potatoes, still represented human figures, and that mutilations of the mouth and nose characterized some of them. Tello admitted he was at a complete loss to explain their meaning. But Redcliffe sensed that they referred to human sacrifices intended to increase the fertility of the potato crop, a thesis he later developed at length.[66] More generally, he came to realize the importance of the potato in molding the lives of the people who made the pottery. As a result, he began to pay attention "not only to discovering the progress of the potato in time and space" but to collecting evidence—written and visual—that would "throw light on its influence in shaping the social structure of a people to whom it was sufficiently important to justify human sacrifice."[67] This, then, was the genesis of *The History and Social Influence of the Potato*. While he did not begin writing the book until after he retired as director of the research station in 1939 and it only appeared in 1949, he began to gather material for the book in the 1920s.

5

By the 1920s, Redcliffe's reputation as a leading figure in plant virology in Britain was well established. Similarly, within Anglo-Jewry, he was recognized as a stalwart of communal life, whose standing within the community was certainly enhanced by his accomplishments outside it. While he was not the central figure that his friend Robert Waley Cohen was and, even more, would become in the next decade, he was a well-known and respected leader. "Men of Mark in 1921," a four-page, end-of-year supplement in the *Jewish Guardian*, included him among the thirty-seven Jewish men of note whose photographs it published.[68] His inclusion was no doubt due to a well-publicized visit of King George V and Queen Mary to the National Institute of Agricultural Botany in Cambridge in October of that year. During their visit, Redcliffe was presented to the royal couple and the king looked over his experimental plantings.[69]

Figure 8.3. George Kruger Gray's proposed design for a family crest for Redcliffe Salaman (1922). Courtesy of William Salaman.

The following year, Redcliffe asked George Kruger Gray, a London artist well known for his designs for stamps, coins, stained-glass windows, and coats of arms, to design a coat of arms for him (see fig. 8.3).[70] Kruger Gray sent him a design, based on suggestions made by Redcliffe. The design is ingenious, highlighting the two foci of Redcliffe's life work—Jews and potatoes. The crest at the top is a seven-branched *menorah*, a reference to the Temple in Jerusalem and a common symbol in Zionist iconography. The shield is divided into two parts. Two potato plants occupy the upper half; a salamander surrounded by flames the lower half. The heraldic symbolism of the latter is the mastery of passion in extreme situations, for the salamander emerges from the flames unblemished. The motto—"Let there be Light"—comes from the biblical account of creation (Genesis 1:3) and probably also alludes to Redcliffe's work as a scientist, enlightening humankind. Perhaps sensing that bearing arms would be seen by some as pretentious,

Figure 8.4. Chattie Salaman, oil portrait of Redcliffe Salaman (early 1920s), with the badge of the Jewish Legion and the family crest in the upper left corner, now hanging in the boardroom of the National Institute for Agricultural Botany, Cambridge.

he never petitioned the College of Arms in London to use Kruger Gray's design.[71] Only once, as far as I know, was the design displayed publicly. It appears, slightly modified, in the upper left corner of an oil portrait by his sister-in-law Chattie Salaman, Michel's wife, a one-time art student at the Slade (fig. 8.4). She painted it sometime in the 1920s and it now hangs in the boardroom of the National Institute of Agricultural Botany in Cambridge.

190 | *The Last Anglo-Jewish Gentleman*

What prompted him to commission the design is unclear. Perhaps, having been designated a "man of mark" by the *Jewish Guardian* in December 1921, he thought it appropriate to acquire a heraldic mark of distinction. If so, it was uncharacteristic, for, while certainly a snob, he was not a social climber.

Notes

1. Arthur Ruppin, *The Jews of To-Day*, trans. Margery Bentwich (New York: Henry Holt, 1913).

2. RNS to NDS, August 16, 1913, Add. MS 8171, Wedderburn Deposit, RNS CUL.

3. RNS to NDS, October 13, 1913, Add. MS 8171, Wedderburn Deposit, RNS CUL.

4. There is no critical historical scholarship on Jews' College. The only account is Albert M. Hyamson, *Jews' College, London, 1855–1955* (London: Jews' College, 1955).

5. Adolph Tuck, "Memorandum to the Members of the Council of the United Synagogue," March 12, 1913, MS 175/61/2, Papers of Chief Rabbi J. H. Hertz, HL US [hereafter, Hertz Papers].

6. *Jewish Chronicle*, February 20, 1914.

7. Jews' College Special Committee Report, January 1914, MS 175/7/4, Hertz Papers.

8. *Jewish Chronicle*, February 20, 1914.

9. *Jewish Guardian*, December 23, 1921.

10. Alexander Rosenzweig, *The Jewish Memorial Council: A History, 1919–1999* (London: Jewish Memorial Council, 1998), 32.

11. Rosenzweig, *Jewish Memorial Council*, 31–32.

12. *Jewish Guardian*, December 23, 1921.

13. *Jewish Chronicle*, June 27, 1919.

14. The minutes of the Magnus committee meetings are in the papers of the Jewish Memorial Council, Acc 2999/A1/1, LMA.

15. RWC to Ferdinand Spielmann, July 5, 1921; to Alfred Eicholz, July 15, 1921; and to Robert Solomon, August 12, 1921, MS 363/A3006/1/3/33, RWC Papers, HL US [hereafter, RWC Papers].

16. RWC to HL, February 10, 1920, MS 363/A3006/1/3/187, RWC Papers.

17. RWC to Philip Magnus, December 20, 1920, MS 363/A3006/1/3/188, RWC Papers.

18. RWC to A. Collin, March 21, 1921, MS 363/A3006/1/3/188, RWC Papers.

19. RWC to Charles S. Myers, February 10, 1921, A3006/1/3/188, RWC Papers.

20. RNS to RWC, July 5, 1919; RWC to RNS, July 8, 1919—both in MS 363/A3006/1/3/131, RWC Papers.

21. Minutes of the Jews' College Committee, December 28, 1919, Acc 2999/A1/1, Papers of the Jewish Memorial Council, LMA.

22. Minutes of the Jews' College Committee, May 3, 1920, Acc 2999/A1/1, Papers of the Jewish Memorial Council, LMA.

23. RNS to NDS, June 15, 1921, Add. MS 8171, Wedderburn Deposit, RNS CUL.

24. A printed copy of the report is in MS 363/A 3006/1/3/131, RWC Papers.

25. RWC to E. D. Lowy, February 23 and March 16, 1923, both in MS 363/A 3006/1/3/135, RWC Papers.

26. Claude Goldsmid Montefiore to RWC, May 16, 1928, MS 363/A 3006/1/3/140, RWC Papers.

27. RWC to Rev. W. J. Barton, April 2, 1928, MS 363/A 3006/1/3/140, RWC Papers.

28. NDS, diaries, August 1920.

29. NDS to RNS, May 24, 1920, Add. MS 8171, Wedderburn Deposit, RNS CUL.

30. NDS to Ray Frank, June 9, 1920, Ray Frank Litman Papers, AJHS CJH.

31. *Elegies for the Ninth of Ab according to the Ashkenazi Rite: Translations and Notes* (n.p.: Union of Hebrew and Religion Classes, 1920).

32. *Jewish Guardian*, September 24, 1920, November 19, 1920, May 6, 1921.

33. NDS to RNS, February 28, 1922, Add. MS 8171, Wedderburn Deposit, RNS CUL.

34. NDS to RNS, July 11, 1922, Add. MS 8171, Wedderburn Deposit, RNS CUL.

35. *Jewish Guardian*, July 7 and August 4 and 11, 1922.

36. NDS to RNS, August 23, 1922, Add. MS 8171, Wedderburn Deposit, RNS CUL.

37. Arthur Salaman, diaries, June 1, 1923, in possession of William Salaman, Cambridge.

38. Arthur Salaman, diaries, June 13, 1923.

39. Arthur Salaman, diaries, March 24, 1924.

40. Herbert M. Loewe, "Nina Salaman, 1877–1925," *Transactions of the Jewish Historical Society of England* 11 (1924–27): 231.

41. Arthur Salaman, diaries, February 21 and 22, 1925.

42. RNS to Raphael Salaman, March 1, 1925, Esther Salaman Papers, in possession of Peter Salaman, Tibberton, Gloucestershire.

43. Esther Salaman Hamburger, interview by the author, Highgate, London, May 17, 2002; program, Esther Salaman memorial, Royal Academy of Music, February 11, 2007, in possession of author.

44. RNS to Esther Polianowsky Salaman, September 20, 1926, in *The Autobiography of Esther Polianowsky Salaman*, ed. Thalia Polak (privately published, 2012), 291.

45. RNS to Esther Polianowsky Salaman, September 13, 1926, in *Esther Polianowsky Salaman*, 286.

46. Esther Polianowsky told the story of her life before her marriage in her autobiography. She also published two autobiographical novels: *Two Silver Roubles* (London: Macmillan, 1932) and *The Fertile Plain* (London: Hogarth, 1956). Her firsthand account of the Zhitomir pogrom, which she wrote in Russian and Alter Druyanov translated into Hebrew, "Bein zevim" [Among Wolves], was published in the third volume (1923) of the ethnological journal *Reshumot* that Druyanov and Hayim Nahman Bialik edited. It also appeared in German in three installments in the *Frankfurter Zeitung*.

47. Esther Polianowsky Salaman, "Memories of Einstein," *Encounter*, April 1979, 19–23.

48. RNS to Shlomo Bardin, September 7, 1926, Shlomo Bardin Papers, in possession of David Jonas Bardin, Washington, DC. The telegrams are included in Salaman, *Autobiography*, 275–79.

49. The letters are included in Salaman, *Autobiography*, 260–61, 263–64, 285–86.

50. RNS to Myer Salaman and Esther Polianowsky, July 21, 1926, in Salaman, *Autobiography*, 260.

51. RNS to Myer Salaman and Esther Polianowsky, July 24, 1926, in Salaman, *Autobiography*, 263.

52. RNS to Myer Salaman and Esther Polianowsky, September 13, 1926, in Salaman, *Autobiography*, 286.

53. RNS to Shlomo Bardin, July 23, 1926, Shlomo Bardin Papers.

54. RNS to Myer Salaman and Esther Polianowsky, September 20, 1926, in Salaman, *Autobiography*, 291.

55. Livia Gollancz, interview by the author, September 13, 2014, Highgate, London. Livia's father was the left-wing publisher Victor Gollancz (1893–1967), who married Gertie's sister

192 | *The Last Anglo-Jewish Gentleman*

Ruth (1892–1975) in 1919. In 1927, when Gollancz started his own publishing firm, Redcliffe, his new brother-in-law, took up some shares. According to Livia, Redcliffe's heirs did very well when the firm was sold in 1990.

56. Miller, *Relations*, 13.

57. Jane Miller, interview by the author, Chelsea, London, June 1, 2011.

58. Arthur Salaman, diaries, February 23, 1929.

59. Quoted in Joseph Leftwich, *Israel Zangwill* (New York: Thomas Yoseloff, 1957), 123.

60. RNS to Clement Salaman, August 4, 1925, Add. MS 8171/1/1, RNS CUL.

61. RNS, "Outlines of the History of Plant Virus Research," in *Agriculture in the Twentieth Century: Essays on Research, Practice, and Organization to Be Presented to Sir Daniel Hall* (Oxford: Clarendon Press, 1939), 261.

62. RNS, "Outlines," 266.

63. RNS, "Chance at the Helm," lecture, 1950, Add. MS 8171/27, RNS CUL.

64. Kenneth M. Smith, "Redcliffe Nathan Salaman," in *Biographical Memoirs of Fellows of the Royal Society* 1 (1955): 241–42.

65. Basil Kassanis, "Kenneth Manley Smith," in *Biographical Memoirs of Fellows of the Royal Society* 28 (1982): 455. The researcher was Sir Frederick Bawden, FRS, later director of Rothamsted Experimental Station.

66. RNS, "Deformities and Mutilations of the Face as Depicted in the Chimu Pottery of Peru," *Journal of the Royal Anthropological Institute of Great Britain and Ireland* 69, pt. 1 (1939): 109–22.

67. RNS, "Chance at the Helm."

68. *Jewish Guardian*, December 30, 1921.

69. *Jewish Guardian*, October 21, 1921.

70. The correspondence, along with the design, is in the possession of William Salaman, Cambridge.

71. Mark Scott, research assistant, College of Arms, London, email to author, February 14, 2019.

9

THE JEWISH HEALTH ORGANISATION OF GREAT BRITAIN

1

After the failure of the project to transform Jews' College, Redcliffe took the lead in a more successful initiative, a plan to improve the health of East European immigrant families in London's East End. The vehicle for the plan was the now largely forgotten Jewish Health Organisation of Great Britain (JHOGB), which he headed from its inception in 1923 to its formal demise in 1946. It embodied two distinct impulses, one long-standing and the other very much of the moment. The communal elite had long worried that the behavior of the Jewish poor—whether criminal or merely foreign—endangered the standing of the community as a whole in Christian eyes. In the Victorian period, West End Jews repeatedly intervened in the lives of East End Jews to promote their embourgeoisement. During the period of mass migration, communal leaders came forward with new ideas for promoting their rapid anglicization, as well as for bolstering existing institutions that promoted this goal, such as the Jews' Free School. The JHOGB was also the outgrowth of native Jewish anxiety about East End Jewish poverty, in this case focusing specifically on hygiene, sanitation, and physical and mental health. But the organization was concerned with much more than the perpetuation of negative images of Jews and the danger that they posed to the community as a whole. There was a racial or eugenicist dimension to the JHOGB's activities, for the Anglo-Jewish medical men who led it also believed that the Jews constituted a race and that their racial health was in peril.

2

The story of the JHOGB begins not in the East End of London but in Eastern Europe at the start of the previous century, with the establishment of the

194 | *The Last Anglo-Jewish Gentleman*

Society for the Protection of Jewish Health (Obshchestvo Zdravookhrane-nia Evreev; OZE) in St. Petersburg in October 1912. Its founders—medical men and communal workers—were motivated by both professional dedication and nationalist fervor. At a time when public debate about the fate and future of Jews often took an explicitly biological turn, by focusing on the health of the Jews, they sought to promote the bodily rehabilitation of what they considered a physically degenerate Jewish nation. Fundamental to their outlook was the belief that the Jews possessed a unique demographic, biological, and psychological profile, which was a result of their religious traditions, their persecution and marginalization, and their confinement in cities, far from nature. Their goals were twofold. First, they promoted research on the physical development of contemporary Jewry and the history of medicine and hygiene among the Jews, thus offering a counterweight to scientific writing that stressed Jewish "otherness." Second, they worked to improve the physical condition of the Russian Empire's Jews, primarily by remolding attitudes and practices about hygiene, especially with regard to the health of children. They focused not on strengthening or replicating existing medical facilities but, rather, on encouraging what would today be called preventive medical measures. In the broadest sense of the term, their program was eugenicist, seeking to combat physical degeneration by raising a new generation of healthy Jewish children. In its earliest years, for example, the OZE opened playgrounds and summer camps for children, provided school meals, operated clinics and hospitals, provided maternity and early childhood advice, and published public health pamphlets in Yiddish.[1]

The outbreak of World War I forced OZE to set aside temporarily its initial emphasis and to focus instead on emergency relief work in the Pale of Settlement, where disease, starvation, and marauding armies were devastating the Jewish population. It resumed its preventive medical activities after the war, but, in 1919, the Bolsheviks took control of it in their campaign against autonomous Jewish organizations. It limped along under Soviet direction until early 1921, when it was completely liquidated. By then, however, there were OZE branches in other East European countries—most notably Poland, where the OZE branches united in 1921 to form their own Society for the Protection of Jewish Health (Towarzystwo Ochrony Ludnosci Zidowskiej, or TOZ)—and even in some West European countries. In early 1922, OZE supporters who had found refuge in Berlin formed a relief committee for victims of the pogroms in Ukraine and succeeded in obtaining the financial backing of international Jewish organizations. In December of that year, the committee convened a conference with representatives from Poland, Lithuania, London, and Berlin, from which emerged a central bureau for OZE.

In London a group of physicians and communal leaders, with Redcliffe at the helm, met on June 10, 1923, at Jews' College to establish a London affiliate of OZE. In his opening remarks, Redcliffe explained that OZE was working to halt the biological degeneration of East European Jewry and that Anglo-Jewry was obligated to take a lead in supporting its work financially. The keynote speaker was an OZE veteran, the Odessa-born physician Mikhail Schwartzman, head of the radiology department at the London Jewish Hospital, who stressed that the main aim of OZE was reviving and improving the Jewish race and thus saving it from biological degeneration. Much of his talk was taken up with statistical evidence about Jewish mental and physical health in the newly independent successor states. Cast in the language of Jewish nationalist medical discourse, it spoke of "the great national worth" of OZE. At this initial meeting, there was no discussion of health and sanitation conditions in the East End.[2]

At first, the group functioned as the London committee of the OZE, disseminating information about its work and seeking donations to support its East European projects. Early on, however, in September 1923, the decision was made to attend as well to the public health of Anglo-Jewry (East End Jewry, in effect). But its initial purpose—raising funds for the central office in Berlin—did not go well. In fact, in 1924 and 1925, the London group was unable to cover its own office expenses. In minutes and other documents from 1924, it still called itself the London affiliate of OZE, but by the spring and summer of 1925 it was referring to itself as the Jewish Health Organisation.[3] The change in self-description matched a shift in programmatic focus to the health of East End Jewry. Despite the shift and change of name, the JHOGB continued to affiliate with the Berlin-based OZE and, until the end of the decade, it continued to seek financial aid for OZE. In autumn 1926, with the backing of Lord Rothschild (Lionel Walter Rothschild), it successfully solicited the support of the American Jewish Joint Distribution Committee, then headed by Felix Warburg.[4] Redcliffe himself served as a vice president of OZE until World War II.

It is not surprising that Redcliffe took a leadership role in the JHOGB, in light of his long-standing interest in the biological history of the Jews, his racial understanding of Jewish cohesion, and his concern with East End public-health issues, which began when he was a medical student at the

196 | *The Last Anglo-Jewish Gentleman*

London Hospital in Whitechapel Road. Moreover, like other Jewish race scientists—and unlike most doctrinaire racial ideologues—he believed that the Jews were capable of biological regeneration. For him, biology was destiny but only up to a point. Preventive medicine, as well as the restorative powers of physical labor in the Land of Israel, also had the potential to reinvigorate Jewish bodies.

European and American medical circles, Jews and Christians alike, shared his concern about the physical health of the Jewish people, a concern that for non-Jews was tied to fears of racial pollution and degeneration. The biological turn in the formulation of the Jewish Question, which began in the late nineteenth century, raised questions about whether there were diseases or other medical conditions to which Jews were especially prone, whether they were a matter of racial inheritance and thus innate, and whether they constituted a public-health threat.[5] Allied to such questions were concerns about Jewish intelligence, temperament, and susceptibility to mental illness. In Britain, in particular, the conversation took place against a background of highly charged worries about the racial fitness of Britons, worries that were stoked by the British army's poor showing in the Boer War (1899–1902). Uncertain about the future of the empire and keen to halt the adulteration and decline of Britain's racial stock, social reformers, medical professionals, and political figures on both the left and the right embraced eugenicist ideas.[6] The East End of London as a whole (rather than its Jewish residents alone) was a particular focus of concern, since it had long been viewed as a site of moral and social contamination, a veritable swamp of immorality, that posed a danger to London as a whole. For more than a half a century, it was "firmly established in the public mind . . . as a nursery of destitute poverty and thriftless, demoralized pauperism, as a community cast adrift from the salutary presence and leadership of men of wealth and culture, and as a potential threat to the riches and civilization of London and the Empire."[7] The movement of its economically successful Jewish residents to leafier districts in north and northwest London, moreover, left the Jewish residential areas of the East End more homogeneously poor and working-class than they had been before the war—and, thus, more than ever, in need of improvement and reformation in the view of the communal elite.

3

Like OZE, the JHOGB focused on preventive health measures. Its first foray into the public-health field was a series of Saturday night lectures on public health at the Whitechapel Art Gallery during the winter months of 1923–24. The series, which included lectures by noted physicians like the pediatrician and gynecologist Liba Zarchi, the psychoanalyst David Eder, and the pediatrician William M. Feldman, drew appreciative crowds and was repeated in the years that followed. One series—at Toynbee Hall in Whitechapel in spring 1930—appeared in print as *The Difficult Child: A Medical, Psychological and Sociological Problem*. In a preface to the volume, F. C. Shrubsall, senior medical officer at the London Country Council, articulated the racial assumption that undergirded much of the JHOBG's work: "The old idea that the mind of the child is like a smooth wax tablet on which anything can be impressed is not correct—there is a certain inherited background and certain traits derived from the ancestors which will come to the surface in some form; these facts must be considered by the wise parent or teacher that the best may be intensified and the less satisfactory elements reduced."[8]

The JHOGB targeted groups in the East End whose future it considered essential to the health of the Jewish people (children and adolescents) or whose work environment attracted adverse comment (garment workers and after-school Hebrew teachers [*melammedim*]). In its first year, Redcliffe's friend, the psychologist Charles Myers, along with W. Spielman, an investigator for the JHOGB, lectured to members of Jewish trade unions on industrial psychology with special reference to the tailoring trade.[9] Other speakers lectured on elementary hygiene and preventive medicine to Jewish-friendly societies and youth clubs. In 1926, it sponsored four lectures on social hygiene at the Jews' Free Reading Room in connection with the British Social Hygiene Council, an organization that worked to control venereal disease, regulate prostitution, and promote sex education. One lecture was for men only and one for women only.[10]

From the start, the JHOGB took an interest in health and sanitary conditions in the East End's Hebrew schools (both private *hadarim* and communally supported Talmud Torahs). These were a long-standing irritant in relations between West End and East End Jews. For decades, the Hebrew schools of the East End were notorious for the unhealthy, shabby conditions in which they operated. Filthy, poorly lit and badly ventilated, overcrowded, lacking basic sanitary facilities, they were regarded as incubators of disease and corrupters of youthful bodies. From its first year, the JHOGB sponsored lectures for Talmud Torah teachers to improve "the racial physique" of their students.[11] The range of topics that the lecturers covered was broad: the hygienic condition of books, water supply, ventilation, sanitation, artificial and natural light, personal cleanliness, student posture (especially the correlation between eyestrain and crooked backs), mental and physical fatigue, adolescence-related problems (including sex education), and the maintenance of discipline and order. In time, the JHOGB undertook the hygienic supervision of the Talmud Torahs and those London County Council schools in the East End with largely Jewish enrollments, as well as the medical inspection of their children. By May 1937, seventy-four schools were under its supervision. The intervention of the JHOGB led some Talmud Torahs to improve conditions and some to even move to better premises. Concerned that two to three hours of attendance daily (except on the Sabbath) placed too much strain on the health of the students, the JHOGB convinced the Talmud Torahs to give them two weeks off during the summer vacation. The *hadarim*, on the other hand, which met in private homes, were beyond its reach, for they received no community financial support.[12]

Few texts of the lectures survive. But from the popular Yiddish- and English-language pamphlets that the JHOGB made available for free at East End sites, such as the London Jewish Hospital, the Jewish Reading Room, the Jewish Day Nursery, and the Jewish Infant Welfare Center, it is possible to recover how they presented their message.[13] In the early years of their work, they issued eight pamphlets. The first, *Your Baby*, was a list of dos and don'ts. It warned mothers against drinking beer, wine, and spirits while pregnant and sleeping with their baby in the same bed lest it smother; it urged them to breast-feed their baby, to bathe it every day, and to give it as much sunshine as possible. The second, *Guides to Good Health*, stressed the importance of good nutrition, fresh air, exercise, and regular bowel movements for raising healthy children. The contents of the third, *Der weg tsum gezunt*, were similar to the second, but in Yiddish. The fourth, also in Yiddish, *Eier kind*, offered twelve rules for raising a healthy child. The fifth was dedicated to the care of the eyes. The sixth, *The Training of Children*, advised parents to avoid corporal punishment, to be firm but not overly strict, to avoid favoring one child over another, and to inculcate habits of orderliness, neatness, punctuality, and cleanliness. It also discussed good health habits for children. The seventh, *Jewish Health Sayings*, was a compendium of pithy sayings from classical Jewish texts, grouped under the rubrics Diet, Fresh Air, Sunlight, Bodily Cleanliness, Clothing, Sleep, Work, and Exercise. For example, Sleep included advice from *Avodah Zarah* (20b)—"a sick person sleeps better when the room is dark" and *Yoma* (78b)—"do not sleep in your clothes." The eighth, *Household Pests*, advised how to deal with fleas, lice, rats, mice, cockroaches, mites, mosquitoes, beetles, ants, and flies.[14]

The advice that the JHOGB offered was, by and large, practical and uncontroversial. Much of it would qualify as sound even today. The way in which Redcliffe and some of the other physicians who supported the organization framed their efforts, however, was eugenicist: their aim was collective—improving "the racial physique" of the Jews. The aim was implicit in the preventive medicine programs that OZE was sponsoring in Eastern Europe and the JHOGB in the East End. When preventive medicine is assigned a national purpose, it is eugenicist by definition, even if it never embraces such extreme measures as enforced sterilization or controlled breeding. While their eugenicist perspective is not obvious in the JHOGB popular pamphlets, it is clearly discernible in reports and lectures in which its leaders reflected on their goals.

In a lecture that Redcliffe delivered at the Whitechapel Art Gallery on December 5, 1925—"Heredity: A Factor in Public Health"—he was explicit about his own eugenicist perspective. Though environment contributed to the formation of the individual, he explained, many troubles were hereditary in nature. Public-health policy, he went on, failed to recognize hereditary factors and worked, in effect, "to preserve the less fit," allowing imbeciles and undesirables "to produce, with dread monotony, their like." Eliminating from human stock "faulty hereditary strains" would far outstrip in effectiveness improving the external conditions of life, whether by public action or by charitable and individual effort. "Surely the time has come when the serious workers have a right to say to such people [imbeciles and undesirables], we will keep you alive but we must deny to you the privilege of reproducing your kind." Implementing such a program would relieve society of a financial burden and eliminate "a potential mass of criminal and anti-social individuals." The Jewish community, he advised, needed to undertake "new methods." Sterilization of mental defectives was one possibility, but he conceded that public opinion opposed it as a violation of personal liberty. Still, he thought that much could be done without legislation and that it was the responsibility of parents to prevent damaged children from marrying. In his view, this was an especially acute problem in the Jewish community, since Jews regarded marrying as a *mitsvah* and forced their children into marriage regardless of their hereditary defects—with the result that "there were more mental deficiencies among the Jews than among the Gentiles."[15] To address the problem, Salaman proposed that the Jewish community establish a register of mental defectives, whom it would keep under surveillance, in order that any defective children to whom they gave birth could immediately be segregated and observed. That same year, the JHOGB discussed the establishment of a voluntary system of "anthropometric and medical" registration and consultation for Jewish youth groups—whose aim, it would appear, was to detect those young persons who should be cautioned not to marry and reproduce.[16] It does not seem that the JHOGB ever acted on the matter, for this was the last mention of it.

Redcliffe's concern with Jewish mental defectives had another dimension to it as well. His younger brother Harry (1877–1901), who distinguished himself in boxing and fencing at Cambridge, suffered from "melancholia" and committed suicide in 1901. Redcliffe never mentioned his death in any of his memoirs or later correspondence. His youngest brother Archibald (b. 1875), known as Archie, was mentally unstable from late adolescence and a source of ongoing concern to the family until his institutionalization during World War I.[17] Later, while confined at an institution in Virginia Water, Surrey, he impregnated a caregiver, who gave birth to a boy. Contrary to eugenicist fears, this son turned out just fine. Moreover, because Archie, who was under care until his death, never lived lavishly, unlike his siblings, this son, his only heir, received a considerable inheritance at his father's death. On Nina's side of the family as well, there was also a child with a developmental or emotional disability. Rosalind, one of her sister Elsie's two daughters, also was institutionalized.[18] Mental deficiency among Jews was not an abstract issue for Redcliffe.

It is difficult to know how many physicians who supported the JHOGB shared Redcliffe's enthusiasm for eugenics and race science. Most of them, while comfortable in speaking about the Jews as a race, which was commonplace at the time in scientific and medical circles, did not seem to embrace eugenicist ideas. That said, one other physician on the executive committee—Jacob Snowman—was an enthusiastic advocate of measures to bolster the health of the Jewish people. Like Redcliffe, Snowman, the son of a Polish-born art dealer, was a public figure. He was the author of two popular surveys, *Jewish Law and Sanitary Science* (1896) and *A Short History of Talmudic Medicine* (1935), both of which served as counternarratives to the medicalized representation of Jews as diseased and a source of disease.[19] In the first, which initially appeared as two articles in the *Medical Magazine* in 1896, he argued that, over the centuries, Jewish law had worked

The Jewish Health Organisation of Great Britain | 201

to preserve the health of the Jews, rendering them immune from many diseases and raising "the standard of [their] national health to a high degree." Thus, poor Jews in overcrowded slums—he cited statistics from Manchester and New York—contracted tuberculosis at a lower rate than their Christian neighbors because they were "the better fitted to resist it." Their resistance derived from their ancestors having lived for centuries in accord with the sanitary provisions of Jewish law.[20] In the second, Snowman identified a "hygienic consciousness" among the rabbis of antiquity in the public-health regulations that he found scattered throughout the Talmud. For example, the rabbis praised "the tonic effect" of the air of the Land of Israel. They used the cinnamon wood that abounded around Jerusalem for fuel because they assumed that "the vapours which arose from the combustion exercised a salutary effect on the atmosphere of the surrounding districts," and they fumigated their rooms daily with "various perfumes after meals as a forerunner of ventilation."[21] Snowman also served as medical officer for the Jewish Initiation Society from 1904 to 1931 and wrote and periodically revised *The Surgery of Ritual Circumcision.*[22] In December 1948, he was called to circumcise Prince Charles at Buckingham Palace.

The fullest exposition of Snowman's eugenicist perspective on Jewish health is found in an essay that he wrote for the short-lived *Jewish Review* just before World War I. In it he envisioned the task of Jewish eugenics as endowing future generations with the physical stamina, the intellectual acumen, and the moral courage to carry on the perpetual Jewish struggle for survival. Unlike full-blown ideologues of race, Snowman believed that whatever defects the Jewish people exhibited were the result of persistent persecution, not heredity. For example, he traced the frequency of insanity among Jews to their past confinement to ghettos and to their present concentration in cities. Indeed, because of his adherence to environmentalism, he, like the other medical members of the JHOGB, was an enthusiast for measures to improve Jewish health. Thus, the eugenic response to Jewish insanity was to encourage Jews to take up agricultural life. In his essay, as in his survey of the health consciousness of Jewish law, Snowman pointed to ways in which traditional Jewish practice embodied eugenicist concerns long before the modern period. In this regard, he singled out the care Jews had always devoted to selecting marriage partners, thus promoting unions among the best types of men and women in the prime of their lives.[23]

202 | *The Last Anglo-Jewish Gentleman*

Redcliffe shared Snowman's enthusiasm for traditional Jewish match-making as practical eugenics. In his December 1925 lecture at the White-chapel Art Gallery, while acknowledging the large number of "mentally unfit" among the Jews, he also noted that the community contained an abnormally large number of "highly gifted," whose existence he attributed to heredity as well. The old Jewish custom of marrying the rich man's daughter to the most promising *yeshivah* student (a custom that was never as widespread as he imagined) was one of the most successful eugenics experiments ever conceived. He told his audience that they could never be too grateful to their ancestors for thus "artificially breeding an aristocracy of brains."[24]

One other key figure in the history of the JHOGB—the psychiatrist Emanuel Miller—was also sympathetic at the time to eugenics and the attribution of cognitive and emotional states to racial inheritance.[25] The son of illiterate East European–born immigrants, Miller attended Cambridge on a scholarship and received his medical training at the London Hospital before serving in the Royal Medical Corps in World War I. In 1927, he became one of two medical officers at the child guidance clinic that the JHOGB established that year (discussed later) and soon became the chief medical officer, a post he held until 1940, when he resigned to serve in the Royal Medical Corps. Miller was a member of the Eugenics Society, and, while little is known about his eugenicist views other than his membership, he was interested at this time in race-oriented psychological research. An early project of his at the clinic was a study of mental disorders of Jews. Unfortunately, there are few archival traces of the research. There is a note that the statistical committee of the JHOGB awarded him £50 in July 1929 to cover his out-of-pocket expenses.[26] The organization's annual report for 1931 noted that he was in the process of completing his investigation, and the minutes of a meeting of the statistical committee in January 1933 reported that he had completed his clinical research and now proposed to collect statistical data for England and Wales.[27] No report or summary ever appeared. But in May 1930, while ostensibly at work on the study, Miller offered a glimpse into his views in the lecture "The Jewish Mind in Health and Disease" at a JHOGB-sponsored meeting at Conway Hall titled "Physical and Mental Aspects of the Jew." Having acknowledged the difficulties of assessing temperamental differences between Jews and non-Jews and having noted that "the same laws which operate in the Jew are found to operate in diverse races who have been subject to the same type of investigation," he endorsed the view, popular at the time, that "the Jewish child thinks verbally and a non-Jewish child pictorially." In observing Jewish and non-Jewish children with borderline neuroses and behavior problems, he told the audience, he had noticed that visual imagery disappeared quickly in Jewish children at a comparatively early age, but verbal expression (imitating the linguistic habits of the adult) came easier to them. This explained, he added, why musical ability was found more frequently among Jewish children, for it was nearer to the world of mathematics and logical relationships than the visual world of concrete things. This tendency toward realism also explained, in his view, why Jews were such striking contributors to the sciences.[28]

The most innovative initiative of the JHOGB was the establishment in 1927 of the first children's mental health clinic in Britain. From the start, the organization had "viewed with apprehension the growth of the nervous disorders amongst the children of this thickly populated district [the East End]," where there was not only "an increase of psychological maladjustment in home and school producing emotional disturbance and educational disorders, but an increase in disorders of behaviour from simple refractoriness to delinquency."[29] More pointedly, the annual report for 1931 declared that "the prevalence of mental disorder alone" in the East End was "a standing menace" to the Jewish community as a whole.[30] In response to concerns such as these, in January 1926, the health committee of the JHOGB urged the establishment of a clinic for difficult and delinquent children. Planning started the following year, and the clinic opened in October 1927 in three rooms in the Jews' Free School in Bell Lane. This "temporary" arrangement lasted for ten years until the JHOGB acquired a building of its own in Rampart Street, Commercial Road, in 1937. At that time, the JHOGB, which had been headquartered in Woburn House, moved its office into the Rampart Street building as well. The clinic, known as the East London Child Guidance Clinic from 1932, remained there until the JHOGB's demise during World War II. The clinic outlived its parent, however, and continued its work elsewhere in East London, where, now renamed the Emanuel Miller Centre for Families and Children, it treats disturbed children to this day.

The approach of the clinic to the treatment of children with "nervous disorders" was innovative from the start. Borrowing from methods practiced in the United States, where the first child guidance clinic was established in Boston in 1921, it embraced the notion of cooperative, multidimensional treatment. It employed psychiatrists, psychologists, social workers, play therapists, speech therapists, and research psychologists who, as a team, treated the totality of their patients' needs. Treating the child in the context of his or her home setting and family background was also critical to its method. As Miller explained, often a grandparent was found to be "a potent force, perhaps a hidden one" in the working of a family and, unless his or her role was addressed, it was often "impossible to make headway in the elucidation and removal of the child's difficulties."[31] Children were referred to the clinic by school doctors, head teachers, probation officers, hospitals and clinics, private doctors, and parents. The presenting symptoms included backwardness, lack of concentration, nervousness, excitability, restlessness, depression, bedwetting, temper tantrums, speech impediments, aggressiveness, theft, masturbation, night terrors and sleepwalking, truancy, solitary behavior, reading disability, breathing difficulty, cyclic vomiting, photophobia, headache, temporary lapses of consciousness, and eating disorders—a list that, with one or two exceptions, would be familiar to health-care professionals today.[32]

To judge by the number of children who were seen at the clinic and by the professional praise it garnered, it was a success. In its first two years, the clinic treated 104 children,[33] and soon there was a waiting list, leading the clinic to forgo advertising its services to local practitioners.[34] In its first six years, it treated 735 children,[35] and, in its first ten years, according to Emanuel Miller, about 1,500 children.[36] Its work attracted attention outside the Jewish community. A speaker at the fourth annual meeting in 1928 boasted that it was referred to at science and education congresses.[37] In January 1931 Sir George Newman, chief medical officer in the Ministry of Education, wrote approvingly in his annual report of the work of the clinic, which he described at length. He emphasized that the primary aim of the clinic was similar to that of the school medical service of the Ministry of Education: the diagnosis and treatment of early and slight departures from normal behavior to prevent them from becoming major abnormalities, leading to "gross aberrations of conduct, delinquency and crime."[38] That same year, ten county medical officers of health visited the clinic as a group and, in May 1936, the Austrian émigré psychologist Alfred Adler visited and demonstrated his technique and method of diagnosis before a large audience.[39] Medical dignitaries graced the programs at fundraising events. In 1931, for example, Lord Moynihan, president of the Royal College of Surgeons, told a gathering at a private home that strictly observant Jews were more resistant to the diseases of urban degeneracy than those who were lax or indifferent.[40]

The establishment of the clinic and then its expansion taxed the financial resources of the JHOGB. In March 1936, for example, a year before the launch of a major fundraising campaign, it had £61 in its bank account and £500 in unpaid bills.[41] A financial statement prepared for that campaign estimated annual income at £1,650 and annual expenditure at £2,390—plus an existing deficit of £800.[42] The problem was both the increase in JHOGB work and the niggardliness of wealthy English Jews. From the start, Redcliffe complained about the challenges of fundraising. In one notably angry outburst in 1934, he scathingly observed that "We seem to need a German crisis, a pogrom, or a Rothschild to be evicted from a restaurant before the community wakes up." Why, he asked, does Anglo-Jewry allow its schools and religious classes to be so badly equipped and ventilated? "Are we really humbugs or do we really care for the children's health and education?" He noted that Jews took pride in how well they cared for their children (whom he described as the most overfed in the world). Yet, he lamented, it was difficult to raise money to remedy the underfeeding of poor children.[43]

It is surprising, what with the nationalist ethos of the JHOGB and the race thinking of its president, that the clinic accepted children for treatment on a nondenominational basis. When it first opened, the majority of patients were Jewish—sixty-three Jewish children and forty-one non-Jewish children in the first two years[44]—but the ratio shifted within a few years and, by the early 1930s, more than half the patients were non-Jews.[45] Because the JHOGB targeted Jews exclusively in its other activities, it is reasonable to ask why the clinic, which received no state funds, served Jewish and Christian children alike. Unfortunately, little documentation survives that sheds light on this question. A few, frustratingly brief notes in the minutes of the clinic committee prior to the opening of the clinic reveal that the question was discussed early on. Alfred Eicholz, chief medical inspector to the Board of Education, chair of the newly created Central Committee for Jewish Education, and son-in-law of Chief Rabbi Hermann Adler, expressed the view that the clinic should not be limited to Jews. Redcliffe's friend Charles Myers wondered whether non-Jews would be reluctant to send their children for treatment if the clinic was housed in the Jews' Free School—to which G. Chaikin responded that the London Jewish Hospital was very popular with non-Jews.[46] Other than these few remarks, there is no record of how or why the decision to treat non-Jewish children was reached.

In the absence of documentation, we can only speculate. One possibility is that most of the physicians who were active in the JHOGB did not

206 | *The Last Anglo-Jewish Gentleman*

share the eugenicist views of Redcliffe and others and thus did not view the rehabilitation of the health of the Jews as a priority. For them, the clinic was a humanitarian project to improve the health of children in a well-known deprived quarter of London where Jews and non-Jews lived in close proximity to each other. Another possibility is that the clinic's backers, whatever their views, saw the benefits of sponsoring a project that would cultivate goodwill outside the Jewish community. One hint that the latter was the case to some extent appeared in a report for the period January 1933 to June 1934. After noting that more than half the clinic's intake was not Jewish, the report added that "this practical philanthropy" promotes "a better understanding with our neighbours in the most populous Jewish district in England."[47] Whatever the case, it was the nondenominational character of the clinic that allowed it to survive the demise of its parent organization.

4

In addition to its preventive medicine programs and its clinical work with disturbed children, the JHOGB also sponsored research on the physical and mental health and demographic profile of London Jews. This dimension of its work was largely due to Redcliffe's initiative. His interest in the demography of the Jews, which predated the establishment of the JHOGB, grew out of and was integral to his work on the biological history of the Jews. The linkage was commonplace in Central Europe among the pioneers of Jewish social science research—Arthur Ruppin, Ignaz Zollschan, Bruno Blau, Felix Theilhaber, and others—whose work Redcliffe knew. There Jewish social science went hand in hand with Jewish race science.[48] Both were responses to the racialized treatment of Jews in scientific literature. They were efforts to appropriate the methods and concepts of social science for Jewish ends, usually but not always nationalist. Armed with statistical data, these researchers fashioned Jewish narratives of Jewish health, crime, family life, and fertility to counter existing, frequently hostile, ones. Their statistical research also served communal leaders as a weapon to rebut the slanders, distortions, and falsehoods of antisemitism. Convinced that Jew-hatred stemmed from ignorance and primitive ways of thinking, Jewish leaders everywhere thought it was possible to combat it with the truth, as revealed in the work of Jewish social scientists. The assumption drew on liberal ideas about human nature and perfectibility and reflected a starkly pre-Freudian view of the sources of human sentiments and behavior.

No well-developed tradition of demographic research on Anglo-Jewry existed when Redcliffe first entered the field. Joseph Jacobs had published a series of seven studies in the 1880s,[49] but he had left behind no disciples to carry on his statistical work when he moved to New York in 1900. Redcliffe first ventured into the field of Jewish demography in 1921, when he published, in five consecutive monthly supplements to the *Jewish Chronicle*, a pamphlet-length article, "Anglo-Jewish Vital Statistics: A Survey and Consideration."[50] The article showed his indebtedness to both Jacobs and German-Jewish social scientists, especially Felix Theilhaber. His wide-ranging article commented on conditions that were specific to the sociology of Anglo-Jewry (questions about social class and economic mobility), but it also highlighted concerns about demographic decline that were a hallmark of Theilhaber and his associates: falling birth rates and increasing conversion and intermarriage rates, as well as the threats that urban life, economic competition, and modernity in general posed to Jewish continuity. Though acknowledging that German Jewry was in a more perilous position than British Jewry, Redcliffe felt that the fate of the latter was, nonetheless, uncertain and hung in the balance. Echoing the pessimism of Theilhaber, he asserted that if British Jews, "bewitched by the syren [*sic*] of assimilation and turning their back on the trusted lights which have illumined Jewish life throughout the ages[,]. . . cast from them their ancient weapons, then surely here [in Britain] the race will pass out with the tide and, like some wreck cast on the bottom of the ocean, leave but a few scattered spars to mark the scene of its undoing."[51] Note that for Redcliffe, writing at the start of the 1920s, the threat to Anglo-Jewry was internal decay, not external enmity. He was mobilizing statistics at this date not to combat antisemitism but to determine which Jewish characteristics were racial in origin and which were situational and environmental.

However, mounting hostility to Jews in the 1920s moved Redcliffe to appreciate the value of statistical work for defense purposes. The JHOGB's first statistical intervention on behalf of Anglo-Jewry was triggered by the publication of research on Jewish intelligence.[52] The biostatistician Karl Pearson, Galton Professor of Eugenics at University College, London, and his assistant, Margaret Moul, published a long article on immigration and the intelligence of alien children in the first volume of the *Annals of Eugenics* (1925–26), using data that Pearson had gathered years earlier, in 1913, at the Jews' Free School. Pearson and Moul found that the immigrant children were inferior, mentally and physically, to their native English peers and attributed their inferiority to their racial background. Because, in their view, Jews were not assimilable, being resistant to external cultural and social influences, they concluded that further Jewish immigration would not benefit the British nation.[53]

Some historians argue that Moul and Peterson's research was not representative of British scholarship on race at the time and that it influenced few other researchers. They also point out that this was a period in which once-conventional assumptions about racial difference were being challenged.[54] It may be true that the significance of the article has been exaggerated, but the lay leaders of Anglo-Jewry did not enjoy the benefit of historical hindsight. They well remembered the antialien agitation of the first years of the century and the Jews-as-Bolsheviks agitation in the aftermath of the Russian Revolution. The appearance of Pearson and Moul's article alarmed them, even though no new immigration legislation was before Parliament. Jacob M. Rich, assistant secretary of the Board of Deputies, sent Redcliffe an extract from the Pearson and Moul article in late 1925. Redcliffe, in turn, referred him to his friend, the distinguished psychologist Charles Myers. Myers was familiar with Pearson's work on the intelligence of Jewish schoolchildren, having heard him speak about it three years earlier, curiously, at a meeting of the Union of Jewish Literary Societies at University College, London. Myers had not been impressed, for neither Pearson nor those who administered the tests at the Jews' Free School were trained in experimental psychology and the tests did not correspond to those then recognized as tests of general intelligence. Indeed, when Myers had asked Pearson whether one of his assistants could see the tests he had used, the latter had made "some excuse of secrecy" and put him off from seeing them. Redcliffe and Myers then contracted with Cyril Burt, an educational psychologist and a pioneer of intelligence testing, to supervise a new study, whose costs the Board of Deputies met with a grant (£30) to the JHOGB. Burt believed that "mental defect" was rare among Jewish schoolchildren, noting that a disproportionate number of scholarships went to them at the age of ten and a half. For him, the exclusion of Jews from Britain was bad eugenics policy.[55]

The new study, conducted by the psychologists Mary Davies and Arthur G. Hughes, tested children in three schools (the first in a good district in North London, the second in a moderately poor district in East London, and the third in a very poor district in East London). In their study, only 3.1 percent of the Jewish children were foreign-born, in contrast with 28.3

percent in the Pearson and Moul study, which tested children only from the Jews' Free School. The difference in the social composition of the Jewish sample in the new study, which included children from middle-class homes, unlike the Pearson and Moul study, helped to produce very different results: Jewish children, boys and girls alike, at all age levels, outperformed non-Jewish children in three sections of the Northumberland standardized intelligence text, regardless of the type of school.[56] Pleased with the results of the investigation, the Board of Deputies ordered fifty offprints of the report, which was published in the *British Journal of Psychology*. It noted that Jews suffered collectively from the prejudices of non-Jewish investigators, whose casual observations about Jews, which were often take as authoritative, were merely incidental to their interest in some broader problems.[57] The JHOGB's sponsorship of the research marked a reversal of almost three decades of Anglo-Jewish statistical neglect, which dated to Joseph Jacob's departure for New York in 1900.

Research that was harnessed to the needs of communal defense, like the Hughes and Davies study, carried with it a strategic risk. There was always the possibility that, even when the investigators were sympathetic to the Jewish community, the result would be inconclusive or undesirable and the Jews who supported the project would be disappointed. Such had been the case with Pearson, who had not been sympathetic. At the start of his investigation, as Gavin Schaffer discovered, he had obtained financial support from Lord Rothschild and other leading Jewish figures who appreciated "the gravity" of the research and hoped that its results would bolster the position of Jews in Britain (which it did not).[58]

The second foray of the JHOGB into the intelligence debate yielded results that were not well suited to apologetic ends. Several years after the Davies and Hughes report, it commissioned a review of the literature on "the psyche of the Jew" and "his intelligence" by the budding sociologist Judah Rumyanek, then a doctoral student at the London School of Economics.[59] Rumyanek's review, which appeared in the *British Journal of Psychology* in 1931, analyzed nineteen comparative studies of the intelligence of Jewish and non-Jewish children in Europe and the United States.[60] (He did not undertake testing of his own.) While critical of the Pearson and Moul study, he was also critical of the Davies and Hughes study, largely because the investigators were unsuccessful, in his view, of holding constant the role of environment. His overall conclusion was that claims of innate psychological differences among groups were unfounded and that no technique existed to evaluate either the alleged intellectual superiority of Jews or their allegedly unique psychological faculties. He acknowledged that Jews tended to outscore non-Jews on intelligence tests, but he stressed that there was no way to prove that the result was due to innate, hereditary differences and argued that environment was of overwhelming and pervasive importance. More likely, he believed, their performance was rooted "in the traditions, education, and general superiority of the Jewish environment."[61] Similarly, he also found unproven the claim that certain nervous diseases—neurasthenia, hysteria, and melancholia—that were disproportionately found among Jews were the result of their racial character. They were, he explained, urban diseases, common to all city dwellers who were daily consumed by ambition and anxiety, diseases that, in the case of the Jews, were exacerbated by their long history of exile and persecution. Yet, despite his stress on the primacy of nurture over nature and his awareness that "prejudice rather than scientific acumen or dispassionate analysis" shaped most assessments of temperamental and emotional racial differences,[62] Rumyanek did not question the meaningfulness of the very concept of race. Thus, he concluded: "An exact technique which will eliminate or make allowance for nurture, and will secure really random samplings, will have to be devised before we range the various races in a hierarchy."[63] In 1931, Rumyanek and his sponsors, including Redcliffe, were not prepared to jettison the utility or validity of the notion of racial difference.

5

In the mid-1930s, the triumph of Nazism in Germany, the outbreak of Blackshirt violence in the East End, and the escalation of anti-Jewish agitation across Britain more generally provoked a flurry of communal responses to what was increasingly seen as a crisis. As organizations mobilized to meet the new challenges, Redcliffe, characteristically, devoted increasing time and effort to communal defense work. Much of what he did will be discussed in the following chapter, where it can be incorporated into an account of his work on behalf of refugee scientists and academics. Here, however, it makes sense to explore one dimension of his activity: his efforts, as president of the JHOGB, to generate more data with which to mount a credible defense campaign.

In November 1932, the JHOGB, with the support of B'nai B'rith, convened at Woburn House a meeting of representatives of Jewish organizations to consider establishing a permanent statistical bureau, to be communally funded and to be supervised by the statistical committee of the organization. The Woburn House conference attracted twenty-three organizations. The immediate spur to action was the failure of a similar proposal that B'nai B'rith had submitted to the Board of Deputies in 1931. Redcliffe and other leading figures of the JHOGB had been alarmed at the time, believing that any research work that the board, a lay, nonprofessional body, undertook would be amateurish. Redcliffe had declared that the JHOGB was ready to set up a bureau but that it lacked the money to do so.[64] In his opening remarks, Sir Philip Hartog highlighted the benefits of statistical research for communal defense. Anglo-Jewry, he said, "never knew when there was going to be an unfair attack made upon them." While he hoped that events in Germany were no augury for British Jewry—note that this was prior to the Nazi seizure of power—the community had to take precautions beforehand. As an example of the falsehoods then in circulation, he cited the claim that there were half a million Jews in London (the Jewish population of Greater London in 1933 was less than half that, about 234,000). Other voices at the conference pointed to the value of statistical research for communal planning. The Reform rabbi Maurice Perlzweig declared that "it was no use building new synagogues or new schools in districts which statisticians would tell them were dying districts from the Jewish point of view."[65] Despite the enthusiasm of the participants, contributions to launch the bureau were not forthcoming.

The following year, in 1933, the JHOGB offered an alternative scheme for financing the bureau. Having concluded that periodic public appeals would be ineffective in the current worldwide economic crisis and because of the financial demands of resettling German refugees, the organization proposed that established communal institutions commit themselves to funding the bureau with regular annual contributions. All Jewish bodies would be linked to it as subscribing members and would be able to take advantage of its services and, in turn, cooperate in supplying it with data. In its call for support, the JHOGB stressed that statistical data about "the fundamental conditions of Jewish life and progress" were needed for "assessing needs, requirements and resources in every department of communal life." It concluded its case by adding that "facts and figures are also needed in preparation for [responding to] anti-semitic misstatements." In recognition of "the extreme urgency" of the situation, the organizing committee had set up, prior to any fundraising, a provisional bureau and had taken steps to find a German-Jewish refugee scholar to act as communal statistician. It also suggested that the Central British Fund for German Jewry, which supported refugees, be tapped to be pay his salary.[66]

The proposal to establish a provisional bureau provoked a blistering critique of the JHOGB's statistical work from Simon Rowson (né Rosenbaum) in a letter to the Board of Deputies secretary in February 1934.[67] Rowson was a pioneer distributor and producer in the British film industry, a member of the Board of Deputies, a member of the statistical committee of the JHOGB, and himself a statistician of note.[68] (Before the establishment of the JHOGB, he had been associated with an abortive effort to create a Jewish statistical society.)[69] Rowson's critique identified two central problems in the statistical work of the JHOGB and, indeed, in any demographic study of Anglo-Jewry. First, the absence of a religious or racial question on the national census made it impossible to collect data that could be viewed in a comparative light, which he believed was the only measure of importance. All attempts to surmount this problem by using indirect estimates of the Jewish population and its age and sex composition were "mere second-rate makeshifts." In support of his claim, he cited the estimate of the Jewish population in London in 1929 by the JHOGB's newly hired refugee statistician, Miron Kantorowitsch, who had lost his position as librarian at the Social Hygiene Seminar at the University of Berlin in 1933 and found refuge in Britain in 1934. (In 1938, he settled in the United States and, under the name Myron K. Gordon, became one of the pioneers of Soviet demography in American social science.)

Second, and more fundamentally, he asserted that the collection and interpretation of statistical material was both a science and an art and that the work must be carried out in a scientific spirit without any concern that "the results might prove unpleasant and disagreeable." Knowing the statistical work of the JHOGB at first hand, he was convinced that the group did not meet that standard. Ironically, Redcliffe had earlier leveled the same accusation against the Board of Deputies. Whether or not Rowson's low opinion of Kantorowitsch's work was justified, he was correct in recognizing that statistical research is not the value-free scientific exercise that Redcliffe thought it was. Rowson was also reluctant to entrust the work of communal statistics to a body whose concerns were first and foremost medical and hygienic. It is unclear whether he was worried about the eugenicist agenda of Redcliffe and some of the other medical men. In any case, after he first made known his views about the appropriate agency to gather and analyze the data (at the 1933 conference), Redcliffe removed Rowson as the chair of the JHOGB's statistical committee. Redcliffe, confident by virtue of his upbringing, education, and social status that his way was the correct way, was unaccustomed to being challenged, especially by a newly rich businessman, the son of a Manchester butcher from Suwalki, Poland. Neither of them prevailed, however, since no communal support was forthcoming.

Meanwhile, communal wrangling over the best means of fighting domestic antisemitism continued, reaching a new intensity in late 1935 and early 1936.[70] In early 1936, the Board of Deputies, driven by a deep sense of alarm and fearful that it would lose control of the defense campaign to left-wing East End activists, ramped up its educational antidefamation activity, under the direction of a newly created body, the Co-ordinating Committee. The activity led to renewed contact in summer 1936 between the board and the JHOGB, the only body committed to generating numbers for counterpropaganda work. In July, the JHOGB, with the financial support of the board, commissioned Jay Rumney (formerly Judah Rumyanek) to investigate antisemitic publications in Britain, with a view to compiling a list of the allegations made about Jews and rebuttals to them. Rumney thought it would take four to five weeks to do the research, for which he would be paid £20.[71] (There is no evidence that he completed or even started the report.) In August, Neville Laski, president of the board, suggested to Redcliffe that he gather material on Jewish contributions to science. Redcliffe responded that the best strategy would be for him and the historian of medicine Charles Singer to draw up a research plan and engage "a younger man" to do the work.[72] He also used the opportunity to urge Laski once again to fund a permanent statistical bureau, not a one-off committee to carry out the project. He complained as well that, despite the good work that the JHOGB's statistical committee had done, it had received "no recognition whatever," even speculating that the Anglo-Jewish leadership exhibited "a peculiar dislike for all scientific data."[73] His lament—about the anti-intellectualism of Anglo-Jewry—was a familiar one in the twentieth century. Still, Sidney Salomon, the press officer of the board, did include a chapter on Jewish contributions to medical science in the substantial apologetic volume that he published in 1938, *The Jews of Britain*.[74]

The Board of Deputies, however, was no more interested in funding a permanent statistical bureau in 1936 than it had been earlier, but it did agree to give the JHOGB £500 to study the Jewish presence in the professions, hoping the data would counter claims that Jews were overrepresented in

214 | *The Last Anglo-Jewish Gentleman*

and even "controlled" certain fields. In its request for funding, the JHOGB reviewed its previous work, stressing the utility of statistics in antidefamation work. Referring to the communal conference it had convened in November 1932, it emphasized that it had "endeavoured to make the delegates see that the events on the Continent created a situation which must give the greatest concern to all." It also pointed out that the JHOGB's response in the mid-1920s to Pearson's study of intelligence (the first time that it and the board had cooperated) demonstrated why such charges could not be left unanswered, pointing out that it could be even more widely appreciated "in the face of current racial policy" than it was in the 1920s.[75] The new, Russian-born chair of the JHOGB's statistical committee, Leon Isserlis, statistician at the Chamber of Shipping, sounded the same note of urgency in a letter to Redcliffe at the time. The lack of numerical data in normal times hampered Anglo-Jewry's handling of everyday problems, but now, he believed, with events in Germany very much on his mind, Anglo-Jewry should be on "a war footing." As he told Redcliffe, "Anti-semitism in this country may at the moment appear to be a cloud no bigger than a man's hand, but so it appeared to the casual observer in Germany six years ago."[76]

With funding from the Board of Deputies, the statistical committee of the JHOGB investigated the percentage of Jews in medicine, dentistry, law, architecture, surveying, the civil service, and teaching and research in England, Wales, and Scotland. It completed its work in February 1937, but I was unable to locate its report in any archive. Nor does the economist Sigbert Prais even mention it in his 1962 survey of Anglo-Jewish statistical research, although he was aware of earlier surveys of the JHOGB.[77] A few tantalizing references to it are all that remain. An internal board memorandum suggested that the information would be helpful in responding to hostile remarks in the press. The memorandum then added that the study would also be useful in counseling young Jews who were thinking of entering the professions by discouraging them from entering fields in which Jews were already heavily represented. For example, it advised that in Manchester, where 108 of the 761 doctors were Jews, "no further entrants into the profession should be encouraged."[78] The assumption was that reducing Jewish "overrepresentation" would remove one source of hostility toward Jews. Behind this assumption was another assumption: that Jewish behavior (or misbehavior) created and fed antisemitism and that Jews were thus, to some extent, responsible for the hostility directed toward them.

The memorandum also recognized that statistical research could be a double-edged sword, a concern to which I referred earlier. It advised that certain occupational statistics should not be disseminated because "they reveal the weak points in our armour." The example it cited was the number of Jews in the Territorial Army (the volunteer reserve force of the British army): there were only thirteen Jewish officers and only forty-two Jews in other ranks in an army of 123,000.[79] In this regard, it is telling that Sidney Salomon, when discussing Jewish patriotism and military service in *The Jews of Britain*, mentioned only Jews who served in World War I, including those who died and were wounded and those who were decorated with honors like the Victoria Cross. The realization that there was a downside to publishing data had surfaced before in the deliberations of the board. In 1934, when Neville Laski had solicited the opinion of Leonard G. Montefiore, president of the Anglo-Jewish Association, about funding statistical research, Montefiore had cautioned that antisemites could exploit such research for their own end. He gave as an example the propaganda use the Nazis had made of Heinrich Silbergleit's *Die Bevölkerung- und Berufsverhältnisse der Juden im Deutschen Reich* [The demographic and occupational profile of Jews in the German Empire, 1930].[80] (Silbergleit was director of the statistical office of the city of Berlin from 1906 to 1923 and one of the pioneers of Jewish social science in Germany.) The last public reference to the study came in Redcliffe's address at the annual meeting of the JHOGB in December 1938, when he cited its usefulness to encourage, once again, the creation of a permanent statistical bureau.[81]

6

The start of World War II ushered in the decline and collapse of the JHOGB and its statistical committee. Its financial condition had never been robust and, after 1933, the demands of refugee resettlement on the communal purse made it even more precarious. In 1934, it ran a deficit of £666; it had no investments and no ability to borrow money. Its position was "one of great embarrassment."[82] At a reception in London in April 1937 for potential contributors, Redcliffe announced that the organization's current appeal for £6,000 had raised only £2,700. A fundraising dinner scheduled for later in the month was canceled when it failed to elicit sufficient support.[83] Donations dried up as war approached. With the onset of the Blitz, the evacuation of children to safer parts of the country, as well as the bombing of homes, schools, and businesses, reduced the Jewish population of the East End, accelerating a demographic trend that was already underway before the bombing. With East End Jewry becoming a shadow of its former

216 | *The Last Anglo-Jewish Gentleman*

self, the concerns that led to the establishment of the JHOGB became less significant. From the start of the war, some figures within the organization were pressing to close it and the clinic.

The coup de grâce was an unpleasant blowup between Redcliffe and David Cheyney, the long-serving salaried secretary of the JHOGB. The conflict, the details of which are murky, began in 1941 when Cheyney charged that Mikhail Schwartzman, vice chair of the organization, had misappropriated funds. Redcliffe acknowledged his discovery of some financial irregularities, but he told Cheyney that the evidence would not stand up in a court of law and told him to drop the matter, particularly since the accusations concerned Schwartzman's fundraising for East European Jewish relief schemes associated with ORT and OZE. There is no doubt in my mind that Redcliffe was eager to keep the whole affair out of the public eye. The *Jewish Chronicle*, for example, never ran an article about it. Cheyney, however, was incapable of letting the matter drop. He became obsessed with it and eventually suffered a mental breakdown. In August 1943, Redcliffe ordered Cheyney to close the child guidance clinic and cancel all appointments forthwith. The next month, Redcliffe wrote him saying that Cheyney's health rendered him unfit to fulfil his duties as secretary and that the JHOGB was granting him sick leave with full pay on condition that he be examined by the king's physician, John Jeeves Horder, who was known for his diagnostic skills. Cheyney refused to abandon his post, and in October Redcliffe showed up at the office in Rampart Street, accompanied by the organization's solicitor, and ejected him. He took away Cheyney's keys and had the building's locks changed.[84] By then the JHOGB was largely moribund. It was formally wound up in July 1946; Redcliffe transferred its remaining funds—£356—to the Jewish Board of Guardians.[85]

The end of the JHOGB was a squalid affair that did not reflect well on Redcliffe, Cheyney, Schwartzman, or anyone else. Still, the child guidance clinic managed to survive and eventually flourished, independent of any Jewish communal ties. Even statistical studies of the Jewish community made a comeback, although not until the 1960s. In 1965, almost a decade after Redcliffe's death, the Board of Deputies established a research unit to provide statistical data on the Anglo-Jewish community. Then, in the early twenty-first century, the initiative for demographic research passed to the Institute for Jewish Policy Research, an independent policy-oriented think tank and research institute. Unlike the statistical work of the interwar period, however, its body of research aimed to provide communal leaders with data to address pressing internal problems, such as the increase in intermarriage, the decline in mainstream Orthodoxy, and the shrinking of provincial communities. The demographers and sociologists who designed its studies did not view the data they produced as tools with which to fight antisemitism. Indeed, in retrospect, it is doubtful whether numbers ever convinced anyone to abandon his or her hostility to Jews. If antisemitism were rooted in mere ignorance about its targets, it would have faded away long ago. Redcliffe's trust in the power of numbers and their utility in dislodging prejudice was typical of Jewish leaders everywhere before the Holocaust. Their faith in reason, science, and education was unshakable.

Notes

1. Nadav Davidovitch and Rakefet Zalashik, "'Air, Sun, Water': Ideology and Activities of OZE (Society for the Preservation of the Health of the Jewish Population) during the Interwar Period," *Dynamis* 28 (2008): 128–35; Marina Mogliner, "Toward a History of Russian Jewish 'Medical Materialism': Russian Jewish Physicians and the Politics of Jewish Biological Normalization," *Jewish Social Studies*, n.s. 19, no. 1 (Fall 2012): 70–106; Mikhail Beizer, "OZE," *The YIVO Encyclopedia of Jews in Eastern Europe*, accessed March 31, 2016, www.yivoencyclopedia.or/article.aspx/OZE.

2. "Di grindung-ferzamlung fon OZE in London," *Buletin fon zentral biro fon der gezelshaft zur ferhiten di gezuntheit fon der idisher befolkerung OZE* no. 2 (June 1923): 10–13. I am grateful to Zvi Gitelman for his help in translating this article.

3. Finance committee, minute book of meetings, February 1, 1924, February 25, 1925, and July 9, 1925, Acc. 3090/2, JHOGB Papers, LMA. The Latvian-born general practitioner Benjamin William Lowbury, one of the founders of the JHOGB, wrote in the *Jewish Chronicle* on March 25, 1927, that the group decided to turn its attention to needs nearer home when one of its chief sources of funding, the Jewish War Victims Fund, ceased its activities. Lowbury, *né* Loewenberg, anglicized his name at the start of World War I, as did many British Jews with German-sounding names. He was the father of the poet Edward Lowbury.

4. Finance committee, minute book of meetings, October 17, 1928, Acc. 3090/2, JHOGB Papers, LMA; Lord Rothschild et al. to Felix M. Warburg, October 8, 1926, and A. H. Levy to Felix M. Warburg, October 24, 1926, JDC Archives, New York; *Jewish Chronicle*, October 7 and 14, 1927.

5. See, for example, Sander Gilman, *The Jew's Body* (New York: Routledge, 1991), chs. 2, 7, and 9; John M. Efron, *Medicine and the German Jews: A History* (New Haven, CT: Yale University Press, 2001), ch. 4; Mitchell B. Hart, *The Healthy Jew: The Symbiosis of Judaism and Modern Medicine* (New York: Cambridge University Press, 2007).

6. Richard A. Soloway, *Demography and Degeneration: Eugenics and the Declining Birthrate in Twentieth-Century Britain* (Chapel Hill: University of North Carolina Press, 1990).

7. Gareth Stedman Jones, *Outcast London: A Study in the Relationship between Classes in Victorian Society* (London: Penguin, 1992), 15–16.

8. Jewish Health Organization of Great Britain, *The Difficult Child: A Medical, Psychological and Sociological Problem* (London: JHOGB, 1930).

9. Jewish Health Organization of Great Britain, *Report and Accounts, 1923–24* (London: JHOGB, April 1925).

10. Jewish Health Organization of Great Britain, *Report and Accounts, 1926* (London: JHOGB, September 1927).

11. Jewish Health Organization of Great Britain, *Report and Accounts, 1923–24* (London: JHOGB, April 1925); Jewish Health Organization of Great Britain, *Report and Accounts, 1925* (London: JHOGB, May 1926); Jewish Health Organization of Great Britain, *Report and Accounts, 1927* (London: JHOGB, September 1927); Jewish Health Organization of Great Britain, *Public Health Work in the Jewish Community: Annual Report of the JHOGB for the Year 1927–28* (London: JHOGB, 1928).

12. Gerry Black, "Health and Medical Care of the Jewish Poor in the East End of London, 1880–1939," PhD diss., University of Leicester, 1987, 113.

13. G. Black, "Health and Medical Care," 112.

14. The British Library has the set of eight pamphlets. They are undated and catalogued under the name of the JHOGB.

15. RNS, "Heredity: A Factor in Public Health," *Jewish Friendly Societies Magazine*, February 1926, 4. The article is based on RNS's lecture at the Whitechapel Art Gallery on December 5, 1925. It did not reproduce the entire lecture. Additional remarks were included in the reports of the lecture in the *Jewish Guardian*, December 11, 1925; the *Jewish Chronicle*, December 11, 1925; and the *Lancet*, December 12, 1925.

16. Jewish Health Organization of Great Britain, *Report and Accounts for 1925* (London: JHOGB, May 1926).

17. RNS, return questionnaire for BBC program "The Changing Family," February 17, 1932, Add. MS 8171/12/2, RNS CUL; Sarah Salaman to RNS, April 19, 1918, Add. MS 8171/4, RNS CUL.

18. Esther Salaman Hamburger, Nina Salaman Wedderburn, and Miriam Polianowsky Salaman, interviews by the author, Highgate, London, May 22, 2000; Esther Salaman Hamburger, interview by the author, Highgate, London, June 22, 2000, and June 29, 2003; Nina Salaman Wedderburn, interview by the author, East Finchley, London, May 31, 2011.

19. On Jewish efforts to counter medicalized and racialized antisemitism in Europe and the United States, see Hart, *Healthy Jew*. There is a brief discussion of Snowman on 99–101.

20. Jacob Snowman, *Jewish Law and Sanitary Science* (London: Medical Magazine, 1896), 21, 24.

21. Jacob Snowman, *A Short History of Talmudic Medicine* (London: J. Bale, Sons, and Danielsson, 1935), 31.

22. Jacob Snowman, *The Surgery of Ritual Circumcision* (London: Medical Board of the Initiation Society, 1904).

23. Jacob Snowman, "Jewish Eugenics," *Jewish Review* 4, no. 19 (1913–14): 159–74.

24. *Jewish Chronicle*, December 11, 1925.

25. On Miller, see Kate Bassett's biography of his polymath son, *In Two Minds: A Biography of Jonathan Miller* (London: Oberon, 2012), 11–16. Coincidentally, Jonathan Miller married one of Redcliffe's granddaughters, Rachel Collett, a daughter of Ruth.

26. Finance committee, minute book of meetings, July 10, 1929, Acc. 3090/2, JHOGB Papers, LMA.

The Jewish Health Organisation of Great Britain | 219

27. Jewish Health Organization of Great Britain, *Public Health Work in the Jewish Community: Annual Report of the Jewish Health Organization of Great Britain for the Year 1931* (London: JHOGB, 1932), 15; JHOGB statistical committee, minutes, January 25, 1933, BD Papers, LMA. The survival of the JHOGB documents in the archives of the BD was a result of JHOGB soliciting financial support for its statistical program. Because of the incompleteness of JHOGB's own records, the BD's JHOGB files are invaluable.

28. *Jewish Guardian*, November 1, 1929.

29. Quoted in George Renton, "The East London Child Guidance Clinic," *Journal of Child Psychology and Psychiatry* 19, no. 4 (1978): 309.

30. Jewish Health Organization of Great Britain, *Public Health Work in the Jewish Community for the Year 1931*, 7.

31. Quote in Renton, "East London Child Guidance Clinic," 311.

32. Clinic committee, minute book of meetings, May 24, 1934, Acc. 3090/4, JHOGB Papers, LMA.

33. *Jewish Guardian*, November 1, 1929.

34. Clinic committee, minute book of meetings, July 2, 1928, Acc. 3090/4, JHOGB Papers, LMA.

35. Jewish Health Organization of Great Britain, *Report for the Period January 1st, 1933, to June 30th, 1934* (London: JHOGB, 1934), 11.

36. Clinic committee, minute book of meetings, July 1, 1937, Acc. 3090/4, JHOGB Papers, LMA.

37. Jewish Telegraphic Agency, *Jewish Daily Bulletin*, December 9, 1928.

38. Jewish Telegraphic Agency, *Jewish Daily Bulletin*, January 15, 1931.

39. East London Child Guidance Clinic, "Honorary Director's Report for 1936." The late Sarah Miller, Emanuel Miller's daughter, kindly gave me a copy of this report. See also Renton, "East London Child Guidance Clinic," 311.

40. Jewish Telegraphic Agency, *Jewish Daily Bulletin*, March 4, 1931.

41. Executive committee, minute book of meetings, March 10, 1938, Acc. 3090/1, JHOGB Papers, LMA.

42. This document, dated January 11, 1937, was given to me by Sarah Miller.

43. Jewish Telegraphic Agency, *Jewish Daily Bulletin*, October 25, 1934.

44. *Jewish Guardian*, November 1, 1929.

45. Jewish Health Organization of Great Britain, *Report for the Period January 1st, 1933, to June 30th, 1934*, 11.

46. Clinic committee, minute book of meetings, June 22, 1927, Acc. 3090/4, JHOGB Papers, LMA.

47. Ibid.

48. Mitchell B. Hart, *Social Science and the Politics of Modern Jewish Identity* (Stanford, CA: Stanford University Press, 2000).

49. These studies were later collected in Joseph Jacobs, *Studies in Jewish Statistics: Social, Vital and Anthropometric* (London: D. Nutt, 1891).

50. *Jewish Chronicle*, April–August 1921.

51. *Jewish Chronicle Supplement*, August 26, 1921.

52. Gavin Schaffer, "Assets or 'Aliens'? Race Science and the Analysis of Jewish Intelligence in Inter-war Britain," *Patterns of Prejudice* 42, no. 2 (2008): 191–207.

53. On the article by Pearson and Moul and the response to it by Hughes and Davies, see Schaffer, *Racial Science and British Society, 1930–62* (Houndmills, Basingstoke: Palgrave Macmillan, 2008), 17–21.

54. See, for example, Elazar Barkan, *The Retreat of Scientific Racism: Changing Concepts of Race in Britain and the United States between the World Wars* (Cambridge: Cambridge University Press, 1992).

55. Charles Myers to Jacob M. Rich, December 7, 1925, and RNS to Jacob M. Rich, February 9, 1926, Acc. 3121/C08/002/001, BD Papers, LMA. Burt's post–World War II studies of the inheritability of intelligence were widely discredited after his death and he was accused of deliberate fraud, at worst, and gross, but unintentional, carelessness, at best.

56. Mary Davies and Arthur G. Hughes, "An Investigation into the Comparative Intelligence and Attainments of Jewish and Non-Jewish School Children," *British Journal of Psychology* 18, no. 2 (1927): 134–46.

57. Jewish Health Organization of Great Britain, *Public Health Work in the Jewish Community: Annual Report of the JHOGB for the Year 1927–28* (London: JHOGB, 1928), 9.

58. Schaffer, "Assets or 'Aliens'?," 201.

59. Rumyanek was the son of the Leeds Hebraist Aaron Rumyanek. He changed his name to Jay Rumney when he became an instructor at the London School of Economics in 1934 and, after emigrating to the United States in 1938, spent most of his career teaching at what later became the Newark campus of Rutgers University.

60. Judah Rumyanek, "The Comparative Psychology of Jews and Non-Jews: A Survey of the Literature," *British Journal of Psychology* 21, no. 4 (1931): 404–26.

61. Ibid., 416.

62. Ibid., 422.

63. Ibid., 423.

64. RNS to Jacob M. Rich, March 1931, Acc. 3121/E01/,052, BD Papers, LMA; "The Statistical Bureau Conference," *Jewish Chronicle*, November 11, 1932.

65. "A Jewish Statistical Bureau," *Jewish Chronicle*, November 25, 1932.

66. Mimeographed documents prepared for distribution at the 1933 conference, ACC/3121/E03/011/054, BD Papers, LMA; Miron Kantorowitsch, "Estimate of the Jewish Population of London in 1929–1933," *Journal of the Royal Statistical Society* 99, no. 2 (1936): 378.

67. Simon Rowson to B. Zaiman, February 12, 1934, Acc. 3121/E01/052, BD Papers, LMA.

68. In 1936, he published an invaluable, much-cited study of the British film industry: Simon Rowson, "A Statistical Survey of the Cinema Industry in Great Britain in 1934," *Journal of the Royal Statistical Society* 99, no. 1 (1936): 67–129.

69. *Jewish Chronicle*, April 9, 1923.

70. The response of Anglo-Jewry to domestic antisemitism and the British Union of Fascists in the 1930s is a much-contested subject. Major contributions to the debate include Henry Felix Srebrnik, *London Jews and British Communism, 1933–1945* (London: Vallentine Mitchell, 1995), ch. 4; Elaine R. Smith, "But What Did They Do? Contemporary Jewish Responses to Cable Street," *Jewish Culture and History* 1, no. 2 (Winter 1998): 48–55; Geoffrey Alderman, *Modern British Jewry* (Oxford: Clarendon Press, 1992), 282–95; David Rosenberg, *Battle for the East End: Jewish Responses to Fascism in the 1930s* (Nottingham: Five Leaves, 2011); Daniel Tilles, *British Fascist Antisemitism and Jewish Responses, 1932–40* (London: Bloomsbury, 2015). The Board of Deputies commissioned a history to mark its 250th year—Raphael Langham, *250 Years of Convention and Contention: A History of the Board of Deputies of British Jews, 1760–2010* (London: Vallentine Mitchell, 2010), but, as is often the case with commissioned histories, its treatment of the topic is anodyne.

71. Defense committee minutes, July 26, 1936, 1658/1/1/1, BD Papers, Wiener Library, London.

The Jewish Health Organisation of Great Britain | 221

72. RNS to Neville Laski, August 1, 1936, Acc. 3121/B04/JHO, BD Papers, LMA.

73. RNS to Neville Laski, August 17, 1936, Acc. 3121/B04/JHO, BD Papers, LMA.

74. Sidney Salomon, *The Jews of Britain* (London: Jarrolds, 1938), 136–43.

75. Hugh Gainsborough, Leon Isserlis, and David Cheyney to Neville Laski, September 10, 1935, Acc. 3121/B04/JHO, BD Papers, LMA.

76. Leon Isserlis to RNS, undated, uncatalogued box, file 3, correspondence 1920–1943, JHOGB Papers, LMA.

77. Sigbert J. Prais, "Statistical Research: Needs and Prospects," in *Jewish Life in Modern Britain: Papers and Proceedings of a Conference Held at University College, London, on 1st and 2nd April, 1962*, ed. Julius Gould and Shaul Esh, 111–26 (London: Routledge and Kegan Paul, 1964).

78. "Memorandum on Report of the Statistical Investigation Conducted by the Jewish Health Organization," April 23, 1937, Acc. 3121/B04/JHO, BD Papers, LMA.

79. Ibid.

80. Leonard G. Montefiore to Neville Laski, January 15, 1934, Acc. 3121/E03/011/01, BD Papers, LMA. The German race scientist Hans F. K. Günther, an unrepentant Nazi and Holocaust denier after the war, made use of Redcliffe's work in his *Rassenkunde des jüdischen Volkes*, 2nd ed. (Munich: J. F. Lehmann, 1930), 215, 252, 285–87, 329.

81. *Jewish Chronicle*, December 16, 1938.

82. *Jewish Chronicle*, November 22, 1935.

83. *Jewish Chronicle*, April 16, 1937.

84. For the conflict between RNS and Cheyney, I have relied on the letters and memoranda in the uncatalogued box, file 3, correspondence 1920–1943, in the JHOGB Papers, LMA. The documents were apparently in the possession of Cheyney and reflect his perspective on what happened.

85. RNS to the secretary of the Jewish Board of Guardians, July 19, 1946, Add. MS 8171/51, RNS CUL.

10

CONFLICTS AT HOME AND ABROAD

1

The triumph of Nazism in Germany in 1933 ushered in twelve years of death and destruction in Europe. For most Britons, however, the war became an immediate threat only in September 1940, with the start of the Blitz, the German campaign of mass bombing of London and other British industrial cities. Anglo-Jewry, in contrast, became aware of the ferocity of the Hitler regime earlier. Soon after the Nazi seizure of power, a stream of Jewish refugees began to reach Britain. Their arrival reintroduced an old problem. With a few notable exceptions, Britons were either unenthusiastic about or hostile to absorbing foreign-born Jews, whatever their qualifications. Nervous that the new arrivals would fuel domestic antisemitism, the communal elite saw the refugees, however sympathetic they were to their plight, as a threat to the settled community. Indeed, as we saw in the previous chapter, even before January 1933, some British Jews worried that events in Germany might herald a deterioration in their own status. The emergence of the British Union of Fascists (BUF) in 1932 and its embrace of Nazi-style antisemitism a few years later confirmed their fears, further undermining their sense of security. In light of the strength of anti-immigrant feeling, communal representatives pledged to Home Office officials in April 1933 that the community would bear the expenses of refugee accommodation and maintenance, without any charge to the state. It was an extraordinary undertaking. It reintroduced the political notion of collective Jewish responsibility—at a time when no corporate, all-inclusive Jewish community in Britain existed and Jewish distinctiveness was a matter of religion alone, at least in theory. It also imposed a heavy financial burden on Jewish institutions. For the British Jewish community—and very much for Redcliffe— "the war against the Jews" (Lucy Dawidowicz's formulation) was, indeed, a twelve-year war. It consumed Redcliffe, taking over his life at times, leaving him emotionally drained and eventually physically incapacitated as well.

2

Support for Zionism spread among Jews everywhere in the 1930s as Jewish status deteriorated in Central and East Central Europe. The spread was not surprising: two central postulates of political Zionism from the start were the eternality of Jew hatred and the necessity for a sovereign state as a safe haven. While Redcliffe endorsed the goal of Jewish sovereignty, his support for Zionism drew more on a social and cultural analysis of the impact of Jewish marginalization in the Diaspora than on political concerns about the shortcomings of emancipation. For example, when he spoke at a Friends of the Hebrew University luncheon in Manchester in 1934, he focused on the lack of awkward self-consciousness among the Jews of Palestine that he had observed on a recent visit there. Everywhere in the world, he told his audience, the Jew was aware that he was a little bit different and not 100 percent normal. But in the Land of Israel, he was in harmony with his surroundings. As an example, he noted that in Jerusalem's cafés both waiters and customers were Jewish and that this was the first time in the Christian era that a Jewish population had ever been "normal" or almost "normal."[1] That the attainment of statehood was not uppermost in his mind may help explain why he was not *politically* active in the Zionist movement in the interwar years or during the war itself. As he wrote Chaim Weizmann in 1949, he had never been "a real worker" in the Zionist cause.[2] Still, from time to time, he helped on an ad hoc basis in small ways. In 1940, for example, the historian Lewis Namier, then serving as liaison officer between the British government and the Jewish Agency, asked him to check on the pamphlet that Redcliffe's neighbor James Parkes was writing on the Jewish Question for the series Oxford Pamphlets on World Affairs. Worried that Parkes was insufficiently pro-Zionist, he wanted Redcliffe to "keep an eye on it." Redcliffe reassured him that Parkes had shown drafts of the pamphlet to both him and Norman Bentwich and had incorporated some of their suggestions, although he added that he was not completely satisfied.[3]

While not active on the political front, Redcliffe took a lead role in supporting the growth and welfare of one pillar of cultural Zionism, the Hebrew University in Jerusalem, whose ceremonial opening he had attended in July 1918. In the interwar period, he spoke frequently at events in support of the

224 | *The Last Anglo-Jewish Gentleman*

university and regularly sent the library on Mount Scopus books, pamphlets, and government reports on agriculture. In 1926, when Arthur Ruppin was working to establish an institute for Jewish anthropology at the Hebrew University, he wrote to Redcliffe asking him to serve on a committee that would raise £1,000 a year to support it. Redcliffe consulted with his anthropologist brother-in-law Charles Seligman, who had no interest in it and told him that it was difficult to raise money in Britain for anthropology of any kind.[4]

In winter 1933–34, Redcliffe was thrust into a controversy that rocked the university and its overseas supporters when he served on a three-person external committee, known as the Survey Committee, to review its administration and to propose reforms. The background to the storm was a long-standing conflict between Albert Einstein, an early supporter of the university, and Judah Magnes, its American-born chancellor from 1925. Magnes, a Reform rabbi who lacked academic experience but was close to German-Jewish donors in the United States, never enjoyed the warm support of either Einstein or Weizmann. As Magnes's authority grew, so did Einstein's animus. He thought that the university required a chief academic officer of scholarly repute and administrative experience and in 1928 withdrew from taking an active role in its governance.

The dispute between the two men was reignited in 1933, when the university faced a new challenge: creating positions for Jewish researchers and academics whom the Nazi regime had forced out of German universities. Einstein, who resigned his position at the Prussian Academy of Science in Berlin, was offered a visiting position at the university in Jerusalem in April 1933. He declined the offer, in letters to the *Jewish Chronicle* and the *Palestine Post*, harshly attacking what he saw as Magnes's incompetence and malfeasance. (At the time he was in negotiations with the Institute for Advanced Study in Princeton about a position there.) As his public criticism was damaging to the university's fundraising work in Britain and the United States, its supporters tried to placate him. In June 1933, Philip Hartog, a non-Zionist but a backer of the university, hosted a conciliation meeting with Einstein at his house in London. Also present were David Eder; Selig Brodetsky, professor of applied mathematics at the University of Leeds and later second president of the Hebrew University; Abraham Fraenkel, professor of mathematics at the Hebrew University; and Leo Kohn, political secretary of the Jewish Agency. Einstein agreed to cease criticizing the university in public if an impartial committee to investigate its administration were appointed and its recommendations brought to the university's board of governors. In October, the board agreed to his demand. It named Hartog, who had served as registrar of the University of London and vice chancellor of the University of Decca (now Dhaka) in India (now Bangladesh), to head the committee. The other two members were Redcliffe, whose appointment was probably the idea of his old friend Hartog, and Louis Ginzberg, who taught Talmud and Midrash at the Jewish Theological Seminary of New York.[5] In effect, most of the work fell to Hartog and Redcliffe.

Redcliffe and Hartog, accompanied by their wives, sailed from Genoa on November 18 and arrived in Jerusalem on November 23. From December 8 to December 21, the committee, working long hours, often late into the night, interviewed faculty and listened to their complaints. The committee kept its distance from Magnes until it completed its interviews, thus straining relations with him. Redcliffe and Hartog then spent about two months formulating the report, which they submitted to the board of governors in April 1934. Their conclusions were devastating and created a sensation. The report faulted the university's handling of almost every facet of academic and administrative matters. It singled out, in particular, the grievances of the junior faculty in the science departments, who claimed that they were treated poorly and left by Magnes to the mercy of department and institute heads who embodied the authoritarian ethos of German universities.[6] The economist Eli Ginzberg, in his biography of his father, believed these men were concerned primarily, "as academics frequently are, with their little empires which they ruled as tyrants," embittering the careers of many young scientists.[7] Privately, Hartog referred to "the Magnes dictatorship"—in truth, a fair description of Magnes's monopolization of authority—and both he and Redcliffe thought Magnes should resign.[8] The Survey Committee's recommendations were sweeping. They urged that the chancellor's unchecked powers be curbed and that a rector be appointed to oversee academic matters. They also recommended the dismissal of one senior zoologist and the possible dismissal of a professor of hygiene and bacteriology (if he did not mend his ways within six months). Both Redcliffe and Hartog attended the board of governors meeting in Zurich in August 1934, when their report was discussed. The board adopted most of the recommended reforms. While it neither dismissed Magnes nor forced his resignation, it substantially curtailed his authority. When the board met in London in October 1938, Redcliffe and Hartog were among those elected as governors.[9] Redcliffe continued to serve on the board until late in life, often traveling to Jerusalem (after the establishment of the state) to attend its annual meetings.

226 | *The Last Anglo-Jewish Gentleman*

During his stay in Jerusalem, Redcliffe also delivered a public lecture at the university on the racial origins of the Jewish people.[10] In retrospect, his topic seems to be an inappropriate choice, given the brutal progress of Nazism in Germany over the previous eleven months. To the three hundred people who filled the lecture hall in the Chemistry Institute—"everyone in Jerusalem was there"[11]—however, the subject was timely. The fundamental ideas of racial thinking were not yet widely discredited, even if its extreme German articulation was increasingly under fire. Nodding to events in Germany, Redcliffe prefaced his lecture by rejecting the notion of pure races as an abstraction that did not correspond to anything in the real world. He also rejected the notion that a distinctive physical type characterized each race. Instead, he explained, a single people might contain several types. This was consistent with his reconstruction of the biological history of the Jews, the focus of his lecture, with its emphasis on the mixed racial origins of the Jews—Semitic, Hittite, and Philistine—prior to the time of Ezra and Nehemiah. He ended the lecture by explaining how the distinguishing physical characteristics of each constituent race passed from one generation to the next in accordance with the principles of Mendelian inheritance.

This was Redcliffe's last public lecture on the racial character of the Jewish people. He never again appeared before the public as a race scientist, lecturing and writing on racial themes, and when he spoke of race he did so in a new way, with a new sensitivity to the political consequences of racial discourse. For example, in a lecture on communal governance that he prepared for delivery at Jews' College in May 1939, he initially included a few brief references to racial themes. He wrote that the Jews were a group "united by a common tradition and welded by the reaction of their neighbours into a family," in which a "community of blood" was no greater than that among the citizens of the British Isles. "Racialism," as he called it, was "a component in the complex of factors determining Jewish behaviour, but a weak one compared to the force of a common tradition and a similarity of environment." But when he delivered the speech, he omitted even these weak affirmations of the racial element in the Jewish character.[12]

In private, however, Redcliffe was more inclined to voice his earlier views. In an unpublished twenty-one-point statement of his beliefs about Judaism and the Jews, written in 1943 and marked "confidential," he declared that the genetic composition of the Jews was still conditioned by that of the original elements from which they derived and that contemporary Jews were "kaleidoscopic regroupings of the qualities, physical and mental, introduced by their . . . forefathers." Their genetic stability was such that they presented "a certain degree of physical uniformity"—enough to enable him "to 'spot' a Jew even from behind, certainly nine times out of ten." Of the three elements that shaped the Jews—race, nation, and religion—he saw the racial component as the strongest, the most stable, and the most likely to persist.[13] These views, however, he kept to himself.

3

The fate of refugees from Germany, especially academics and professionals, occupied Redcliffe from the start. He joined the Academic Assistance Council (the Society for Protection of Science and Learning [SPSL] after 1937) soon after its founding in spring 1933. An initiative of William Beveridge, then director of the London School of Economics and Politics, and other prominent, mostly non-Jewish academics, the group worked to find places in universities and research institutes in Britain and elsewhere for displaced scholars. As in the United States, both antisemitism and the fear of competition on the part of existing staff combined to hamper their efforts. Thus, the society framed its work as a humanitarian mission that would simultaneously enhance the status of British universities. It also avoided identifying the displaced scholars as Jews, portraying them more neutrally as victims of German persecution. Among the limited number of universities and research institutes in the United Kingdom, few full-time positions were open. To ease the problem, the SPSL provided grants to university and other laboratories to make research facilities available to refugee scientists for their work until they found permanent positions or emigrated (usually to the United States). It also provided maintenance grants to those for whom it was unable to find immediate openings and aid to graduate students who wished to pursue degrees at British universities.

Redcliffe was a stalwart of the organization. He joined its executive in 1935, served as treasurer, and did not resign until 1945, when ill health forced him to curtail his public and communal work. During his years of service, he took responsibility for more than 250 refugees. He interviewed them, sometimes more than once, before trying to place them, or arranged for them to be interviewed by specialists in their fields. He wrote hundreds of letters on their behalf and drew on a network of friends and acquaintances to give him advice or to use their connections to help them. Those to whom he turned most frequently were Charles Seligman, Philip Hartog,

228 | *The Last Anglo-Jewish Gentleman*

Emmanuel Miller, Chaim Weizmann, Cyril Burt, Charles Myers, Lewis Namier, and Alfred J. Makower, chair of the electrical engineering department at Chelsea Polytechnic. He also tapped his own relatives, including his sister Brenda and her husband Charles Seligman and his sister Bessie Cohen, for financial contributions. In addition, he drew on endowments that he had helped to establish and that he more or less controlled—the Arthur Davis Memorial Fund and the Israel Zangwill Memorial Fund.[14] He also served as a member of the Professional Committee, which served Jewish professionals (rather than academics) who were no longer able to practice in Germany. As a rule, they faced more obstacles to finding employment than academics. The British Medical Association, for example, was unsympathetic to refugee physicians, whom it characterized as economic opportunists.

Among those whom Redcliffe assisted through the SPSL were scholars and researchers who later achieved distinction in their respective fields. They included the pioneering social psychologist Kurt Lewin; the mathematician Richard Courant, founder of the highly respected Institute for Mathematics and Mechanics at New York University (now known as the Courant Institute for Mathematical Sciences); Aaron Steinberg, German translator of Shimon Dubnov's *History of the Jewish People* and long-time director of the cultural department of the World Jewish Congress in London; the political scientist Franz Neumann, a member of the Institute for Social Research at Columbia University and author of *Behemoth* (1942), an early study of the theory of Nazism; the biochemist Ernst Chain, who shared the Nobel Prize for Medicine for producing penicillin by chemical synthesis; the Jewish historian Moredecai Wilensky, who taught for many years at Boston's Hebrew College; the philosopher David Baumgardt; the historian and Talmud scholar Samuel Krauss, rector of the Israelitisch-Theologische Lehranstalt in Vienna before his escape to England; and the historian and sociologist of literature Ernst Kohn-Bramstedt, later Ernest K. Bramsted, author of *Aristocracy and the Middle Classes in Germany: Social Types in German Literature, 1830–1900* (1937). In many cases, Redcliffe's familiarity with the refugee scholars' fields was slight, but somehow he was able to find places for them, whether in Britain, the United States, or even Palestine. But on one occasion, he failed miserably to take the measure of the man. In May 1935, after interviewing the thirty-something Leo Strauss, later an eminent political philosopher and classicist at the University of Chicago, he described him as "very shy" with "poor presence," dismissing him as a *schlemiel.*

With his agricultural experience, Redcliffe also vetted refugee boys for training at Oaklands, the Hertfordshire Institute of Agriculture, near St. Albans. Curiously, in his interview notes he usually noted whether a boy was "Jewish looking," whether he kept the dietary laws (to which he, Redcliffe, was becoming increasingly hostile), or both. Some of the boys who finished their training found work at Waddesdon, James de Rothschild's Buckinghamshire estate.

Redcliffe's work for the SPSL continued throughout the war. But once it became possible to envision the war's end—after the German defeat at Stalingrad (January 1943) and eviction from North Africa (October 1942 to May 1943)—he and other communal leaders began to think ahead to the task of providing relief to those who managed to survive the Nazi onslaught. Toward the end of 1942, the Joint Foreign Committee of the Board of Deputies and the Anglo-Jewish Association began discussing the creation of a new organization dedicated to postwar relief and rehabilitation. It convened a conference in February 1943 that gave birth to the Jewish Committee for Relief Abroad. Redcliffe was named chair at the time, a post he held until ill health curtailed his communal work in 1945. During the period he headed the Jewish Committee for Relief Abroad, it confined itself, of necessity, to recruiting and training volunteers for service, most of whom were drawn from Zionist youth movements and the Jewish boys' and girls' clubs of East London. The volunteers learned first aid, studied the history of the continent's Jewish communities, and received Yiddish lessons. In February 1944, the first Jewish relief unit (ten persons, including two non-Jews) reached Cairo. It hoped to be sent to the Balkans to begin work there, but the British authorities, fearing it would encourage refugees to make their way to Palestine, delayed their leaving Egypt for months. Only in late 1944 did they allow the first Jewish relief workers to leave for Italy and then Greece.[15]

4

The British public's wariness about welcoming German (and later Austrian and Czech) Jews and the government's policy of admitting as few Jews as possible and treating them as temporary transmigrants rather than potential citizens shaped Jewish communal policy from 1933 to 1945. Together they fueled Anglo-Jewish insecurity and left communal leaders feeling unsure about the extent to which British Jews were seen as indisputably British (or English). At the same time, the growth of domestic

230 | *The Last Anglo-Jewish Gentleman*

fascism and, in particular, violence in the East End reinforced this lack of communal self-confidence. It would not be an exaggeration to say that in this period the Jewish Question once again loomed large in Britain, as it had during the period of mass migration from Eastern Europe before World War I.

Some historians believe that the return of the Jewish Question sapped the resolve of mainstream Jewish leaders, leaving them overly cautious in responding to the challenges of the time.[16] In their view, mainstream communal leaders were too restrained in confronting domestic antisemitism, fearing that militancy would backfire and provoke even more hostility. They also quietly accepted the government's rationale for immigrant restriction (the more Jews, the more antisemitism) while failing to challenge its refusal to rescue Jews in Nazi-occupied Europe and admit them to Palestine. There is some truth in this accusation, but also a surfeit of ahistoricity. It assumes that in the 1930s Anglo-Jewry's leaders foresaw Nazism's Final Solution (which, of course, they did not). Above all, it assumes that these leaders, whose moral claims were certainly strong, were sufficiently powerful to reverse policies rooted in the harsh realities of *Realpolitik*. To offer a full critique here would take us too far afield; suffice it to say that even if Lords Rothschild and Swaythling, along with the chief rabbi, had taken their lives on the doorstep of 10 Downing Street to protest the unwillingness of officials to save Jewish lives, the government would not have changed its course.

We do not know whether Redcliffe harbored misgivings about the government's refugee policy or whether he was even aware of how actively it was working to prevent Jews trapped in Europe from reaching Palestine (much of this became known only decades later). After 1945, certainly, he was a bitter critic of British policy in Palestine, even defending Jewish attacks on British officials there, as we will see. But in his refugee work before then, he seems to have tacitly accepted the terms on which Jewish refugees entered Britain: that the Jewish community would fully support them and that it would cooperate with the Home Office in selecting those to be admitted, favoring those who would contribute to British cultural and economic life and who would rapidly fit in. His work for the SPSL was predicated on the notion of selectivity, although he himself was not involved in the vetting of refugees for admission. The decision to admit the scientists and academicians whom he assisted was made long before they came into his orbit.

As for domestic antisemitism, Redcliffe continued to believe in the power of reason and numbers, as embodied in apologetic pamphlets, books, speeches, and letters to the press, to correct slanderous misinformation. This belief, after all, underpinned his appeals to establish a communal statistical bureau in the 1930s. It was also the assumption that underpinned the defense work of the Board of Deputies at the time. While he did not contribute to their creation of counterpropaganda, he took part in their heightened monitoring of antisemitic activity, when in 1937 he agreed to serve, along with his neighbor James Parkes, as a vigilance correspondent for Cambridgeshire for the board's newly created Co-ordinating Committee.[17] He also acted on his own initiative to counter pro-Hitler opinion. In November 1937, he told Leonard Montefiore that he had been meeting from time to time with the pro-German merchant banker and industrialist Ernest Tennant, whose country home in Essex was near Barley. Tennant was enthusiastic about the Nazi regime from the start. He was a frequent visitor to Germany, a close friend of Joachim von Ribbentrop (ambassador in London, 1936 to 1938, and foreign secretary, 1938 to 1945), and a founder of the Anglo-German Fellowship. But he was not a virulent, Nazi-style antisemite. Redcliffe wrote to Montefiore asking him for accurate data about German Jewry that he could feed to Tennant.[18] He also provided his friend Charles Singer with information and counsel about antifascist counterpropaganda he was preparing. The rise of Nazism had awakened Singer's sense of solidarity with Jews and he was soon in the thick of the intellectual battle to discredit Nazism. He and Redcliffe's brother-in-law Charles Seligman spearheaded the writing of *We Europeans* (1935), whose aim was to undermine the Nazi concept of race in regard to the populations of Europe. (The book was attributed to the evolutionary biologist and popularizer of science Julian Huxley and the anthropologist Alfred C. Haddon because Singer and Seligman, as Jews, it was thought, would be considered biased observers. In fact, most of the book was written at Singer's house on the south Cornish coast.)[19] In 1937, Singer began working closely with his brother-in-law Robert Waley Cohen, who a year earlier had set up his own defense operation when he became exasperated by the Board of Deputies' inability to respond effectively to antisemitic attacks. Funded by contributions from a handful of wealthy individuals, including Rothschilds and the second Viscount Bearsted, the secret enterprise was unaccountable to anyone, not even its financial supporters. Among other initiatives, Waley Cohen provided Singer with a fund for the subvention of the publication of antiracist books and pamphlets.[20] In April 1937, Redcliffe, the historian Cecil Roth, and the sociologist Morris Ginsberg met with Singer to discuss defense work.[21] In 1941, Singer again wrote an antiracist publication under Julian Huxley's name, a Macmillan pamphlet on German race science, *Argument of Blood*.

The intensification of Blackshirt attacks on Jews in the East End of London and in Leeds and Manchester in 1935 and 1936 raised questions about the adequacy of the Board of Deputies' defense activities, especially among those outside the communal establishment. Communists, socialists, trade unionists, Zionists, members of Jewish friendly societies, and small traders and workers who experienced BUF violence at first hand wanted a more militant, confrontational approach. The board's reliance on issuing pamphlets and books, monitoring antisemitic activity, and lobbying government officials behind closed doors and its insistence on framing its response solely as a fight against antisemitism rather than as a broader fight against fascism (the board did not want to take what it saw as a politically partisan stand) struck many as timid and even spineless. To the dismay of the board, which saw itself (unjustifiably) as the official voice of Anglo-Jewry, more confrontational defense groups sprang up, cheered on in some cases by the *Jewish Chronicle* and a handful of notables who thought the board was bungling and overly cautious. The largest of these groups was the left-wing Jewish People's Council against Fascism and Anti-Semitism (JPC), which emerged in late summer 1936. While not a communist front, Jewish members of the Communist Party of Great Britain were instrumental in its formation and running. This, too, heightened its unacceptability to the officers of the Board of Deputies.[22]

The bitter dispute that broke out between the board and the JPC over who represented the authentic voice of Anglo-Jewry and how to respond to BUF attacks dismayed Redcliffe. Increasingly a champion of pluralism in Jewish life, he regretted the sparring and name-calling of the two groups in the face of an unprecedented, common threat. In November 1936, he and James Parkes wrote jointly to the *Jewish Chronicle* deploring the internecine squabbling and urging the two warring parties to recognize the legitimate role that each had to play at the moment, calling for "mutual recognition and understanding." Redcliffe and Parkes accepted the board's view that it must remain impartial and avoid entanglement in partisan politics. They attributed the board's past successes in part to that policy and to the fortunate historical circumstance that Britain's mainstream parties had never embraced antisemitism. Leaving aside the accuracy of their understanding of the political uses that both Liberals and Conservatives had made of anti-Jewish sentiment (the Liberals at the time of the Eastern Crisis [1875–78] and the Conservatives at the time of mass migration from Eastern Europe), the merit of this reading was that it allowed them to argue that there was room for both the board and the JPC to act. The emergence of the BUF necessitated political action. Since this response was outside the purview of the board, it was natural, yea, inevitable, that Jews "from those areas directly affected by the new alignment of forces" (East London) would want to respond with direct political action. Redcliffe and Parkes did not suggest that the board and the JPC should merge their efforts, but counseled, rather, that each should continue to operate independently in its own sphere of activity.[23]

The precipitate of Redcliffe's intervention was an open letter by Neville Laski, president of the Board of Deputies, on November 5, 1936, urging its readers to have nothing to do with a conference that the JPC had scheduled for November 15. In the letter, Laski declared that the board's Co-ordinating Committee had neither authorized nor approved the activities of the JPC. Their convening of the conference was "as example of the independent, sporadic and undisciplined effort which the Co-ordinating Committee was set up to quash and prevent."[24] After attending a meeting of the Schechter Society in Cambridge on November 22, at which the students debated the respective policies of the board and the JPC, Redcliffe wrote to the press officer of the board, Sidney Salomon, asking for more information about the board's stance. Salomon responded that the JPC was a self-appointed body created by East End extremists who wanted to take action against the Blackshirts and that the board could not be party to a movement that was to all intents and purposes political. Representatives of the two groups had met (in August 1936), he told Redcliffe, and the board had offered to co-operate with them under two conditions: that the JPC remove the word "Anti-Fascism" from its name and that it dissociate itself from communists, who, in fact, supplied much of the JPC's leadership. Needless to say, both conditions were nonstarters.[25]

In response to the letter of Redcliffe and Parkes in the *Jewish Chronicle* in late November, Laski came to Barley to meet with them on January 6, 1937. As a result of their conversation, Laski agreed to meet with representatives of the JPC on neutral ground. He stipulated that Adolph Brotman, executive secretary of the board, accompany him and that Redcliffe and

234 | *The Last Anglo-Jewish Gentleman*

Parkes also be present. He also wanted it clearly understood that he was meeting with the JPC representatives not as president of the board but in a private capacity.[26] Then, having committed himself, Laski reconsidered and delayed fixing a date for the meeting, claiming he had a very busy schedule.[27] Tired of being put off, Redcliffe wrote to Brotman on February 1 that, if he now had to write to the JPC that Laski had withdrawn his offer and would not meet with them, they would regard Laski's withdrawal as "a breach of faith" and they would infer from his unwillingness to respond to their arguments that they were, in fact, unanswerable. Redcliffe told Brotman that Laski's presence at the meeting could do no harm while "a breach of faith" might be "fatal" (to whom? the reputation of the board? to the campaign against fascism?). He also added that he was not a partisan of either organization and that he had sent the letter to the *Jewish Chronicle* in the first place because he had seen clearly the chasm between them widening.[28] On February 3, Laski agreed to meet but insisted that the meeting be kept secret, that Parkes not be included (he was uncomfortable with the presence of an outsider at the resolving of an internal Jewish dispute), and that there be written acknowledgment that he would be speaking for himself, without any mandate from the board.[29]

The meeting was held on February 11, 1937, at the Salaman Estates offices, 7 Southampton Street, and lasted two hours. Brotman was not able to attend, as he was in Paris, so the barrister Arthur S. Diamond, chair of the board's law and parliamentary committee, took his place. Representing the JPC was Lazar Zaidman, a prominent figure in the Communist Party of Great Britain and the Workers' Circle friendly society; Julius Jacobs, an official in the largely Jewish East End cabinetmakers' union and also a communist; and Jack Pearce, secretary of the JPC. The participants reached agreement on five points: one, that the JPC would reconsider the title of the organization, the chief objection now being the word *people* (rather than *fascism*); two, that the JPC would not lobby any government bodies without prior consultation with the board; three, that the JPC would restrict itself to organizing public meetings and functions and distributing literature; four, that the JPC would not promote parliamentary legislation; and five, that the JPC would consult with the board before taking action on major questions. Those present agreed to submit the five agreed-on points to their respective bodies. A further meeting took place on February 15.[30] The five points suggest that underlying the dispute about the best way to confront the BUF was the question of the board's claim to exclusive representation of the interests of British Jewry in the public sphere. What is not clear is why the representatives of the JPC went so far in acknowledging the board's claim.

While those who attended the two meetings agreed to work together, when they returned to their respective constituencies they failed to follow through on the freshly signed agreement. Sensing, it would seem, that their rank-and-file were less willing to compromise than they were, they never presented the terms of the agreement to them. On February 25, Zaidman wrote to Redcliffe in his capacity as go-between, complaining that a week had passed and with no sign from the board of any willingness to cooperate with the JPC. At the same time, however, he reneged on one of the five points, telling Redcliffe that cooperation should not be tied to the JPC changing its name and adding that the proposed change would never get a hearing at the JPC. The week before, Zaidman had suggested to Diamond that the best way to initiate cooperation would be for Laski or Diamond to say something friendly about the JPC in reporting about the Co-ordinating Committee at a meeting of the board. Diamond had agreed with him, but, when the board met a few days later, no one said anything about the JPC. For Zaidman, another opportunity was lost, and nothing could happen at least until the board's next meeting, in a month's time. Zaidman's letter infuriated Redcliffe, who told Zaidman that if he could not get the name change through, he had no reason to blame the board for its inaction. Zaidman responded that there was no possibility of even raising the name issue in the JPC without a gesture from the board. He explained his problem to Redcliffe thus: "What would my fellow members of the JPC think if we were to suggest such a change in the absence of the slightest evidence of a change of heart on the part of the Board toward the JPC?"[31] In short, neither Zaidman nor Laski was willing to risk making the first move.

In early March, Redcliffe tried to break the stalemate. He spoke to Diamond, who reassured him that there was a good chance that the Board of Deputies would issue a statement in the near future that would be a first step. But when Laski heard of their conversation, he let Redcliffe know, via Brotman, that the board would not make any statement until the outspoken members of the Co-ordinating Committee, vigorous critics of the JPC, could be won over—which was not likely to happen.[32] Replying to Brotman,

236 | *The Last Anglo-Jewish Gentleman*

in what was his last comment on the matter, Redcliffe condemned the board for its failure to engage with the JPC:

> When I said that if you did not make some announcement soon you would be too late, you would lose the bus, or that the position might get out of hand, I was deducing what I think is the obvious. You only have to put yourself in the position of these young men to realise their struggles and experiences, and their position vis-à-vis their followers and "wild men" and you will see that the betting is not far off 10 to 1 that if you do not make good friends you will make bitter enemies; and what form that enmity may take I do not know.[33]

Redcliffe's prediction that the split between the board and the JPC would end in bitter, irreconcilable conflict was wrong. After the abortive negotiations between the two organizations, the board's position on antifascist activity moved closer to that of the JPC. It began to identify the fight against antisemitism with the fight against fascism and took steps to combat the BUF more directly. In parliamentary elections, it supported candidates who faced BUF opponents. It also established an East End outpost, the London Area Committee, to challenge the BUF in the areas where anti-Jewish violence was at its worst. Most important, it monitored and infiltrated the BUF and smaller fascist organizations and fed, via Laski, the information it gained to officials in the Home Office. The board's embrace of a more activist policy from 1937 on thus helped to reduce the tension between it and East End Jewish organizations.[34]

If Redcliffe was wrong about the immediate outcome of the failure, his grasp of the mood of East End Jewry was correct. Moreover, his sense that their views mattered and that the communal notability ignored them at their own risk set him apart from other Jews like himself. Perhaps his time in the East End—as a medical student, a newly minted physician, and long-time president of the JHOGB—allowed him to transcend the cultural blinders that upper-middle-class status so frequently imposed. In time— that is, after the war—Redcliffe became acutely aware that the hegemony of the old elite, to which he belonged, was collapsing and that the future lay with Jews of East European background. His sense that the Anglo-Jewish landscape was changing unalterably was not widely shared. In his controversial Lucien Wolf Lecture of 1953, which I will discuss in a later chapter, he described at length and accounted for this transformation.

During World War II, Zaidman and Redcliffe again worked together, when, likely at Zaidman's recommendation, Redcliffe was named president of the Jewish Fund for Soviet Russia (JFSR).[35] The JFSR was the successor to a number of left-wing, pro-Soviet fundraising organizations that emerged in Britain in the wake of the German invasion of the Soviet Union in June 1941 and the hastily forged alliance between the Soviet Union and the Western powers. Most of its supporters were Jews of East European background who were sympathetic to the Soviet Union even before the war—communists, trade unionists, socialists—but they also included some prominent Jews whose politics were not radical, like the historian Cecil Roth, the social worker Basil Henriques, the former attorney general in the Mandate administration Norman Bentwich, and the Labour politician Barnett Janner. Seeking to broaden support for the Soviet Union, to mobilize Jews of every description, regardless of their politics, Jewish communists created a new charity, the JFSR, in December 1942 to collect contributions for Clementine Churchill's Red Cross Aid-to-Russia Fund. Its aim was to collect £50,000 to purchase twenty-five mobile X-ray units for the Soviets.[36] Although members of the Communist Party of Great Britain controlled the organization, it enjoyed broad communal support, in part because those who fronted it—Redcliffe and the Labour politician Lord Nathan of Churt, who chaired its appeal—were not radical activists, and, in part, because pro-Soviet enthusiasm had gained respectability, having become identified with the overall war effort. Even Zionists were willing to cooperate with it. In addition, revelations about Nazi atrocities, which communist-front organizations like the JFSR publicized, also linked the Soviet cause with Jewish suffering. In his foreword to a JFSR pamphlet, *Calling All Jews to Action!*, which the then-communist-activist Chimen Abramsky edited and published in May 1943, Redcliffe urged Jews to support the Soviet Union for bearing the brunt of the fighting burden and thus saving Britain and "the Jewish National Home in Palestine" from "the horrors of Nazi invasion."[37] When funding for the first X-ray unit was in hand, the JFSR marked the occasion with a meeting at Grosvenor House in Park Lane on February 28, 1943. Redcliffe presided and handed a check for £2,000 to Clementine Churchill. The roster of speakers included Lord Nathan, the presidents of the Board of Deputies and the Anglo-Jewish Association (Selig Brodetsky and Leonard Stein), and the Labour member of Parliament and outspoken Zionist Sydney Silverman.[38] Even Chief Rabbi Joseph Hertz lent his support to the JFSR. He ordered his ministers to recite a prayer for the victory of Soviet forces at the Sabbath morning service on February 20, 1943, and told them to encourage donations to the JFSR.[39] While the JFSR failed to meet its goal, it came very close. Lord Nathan

238 | *The Last Anglo-Jewish Gentleman*

told the Board of Deputies in late November 1944 that the fund had raised between £43,000 and £44,000.[40]

The acme of JFSR activity was its hosting of the visit of Shloyme Mikhoels, director of the Moscow State Yiddish Theater, and Itsik Feffer, a Soviet Yiddish poet, in November 1943. Mikhoels was the chair and Feffer a member of the Jewish Anti-Fascist Committee, which Stalin had set up to rally support for the Soviet war effort in Western Jewish communities. Their visit to Britain came at the tail end of a tour of Canada, the United States, and Mexico. They spoke, in Yiddish, to overflow crowds in London, Glasgow, and Manchester and attended numerous receptions, where they were feted by both establishment and left-wing figures. Such was the pro-Soviet euphoria they generated that Chief Rabbi Hertz publicly told them that no Jew, even the most pious, could object to the sentiments they had expressed. At their last public appearance, a meeting sponsored by the JFSR at the Stoll Theatre on November 21, Hertz read Feffer's poem "Ich bin a yid" and broke into tears.[41]

5

In his letter to the *Jewish Chronicle* in November 1936 calling for cooperation between the JPC and the Board of Deputies, Redcliffe defended the principle of heterogeneity in Anglo-Jewish life. He argued that there was room for diverse approaches to fighting fascism and antisemitism and that subordinating one approach to another and one organization to another in order to achieve unity would be to follow a totalitarian path. From the mid-1920s on, this theme, encouraging diversity in Jewish life, increasingly preoccupied Redcliffe, especially in the sphere of Jewish observance and belief. Much of his commitment to heterogeneity was a vestige of the latitudinarian Judaism that characterized middle-class Anglo-Jewry in the Victorian and Edwardian periods when he was a young man. The commercial and financial magnates who then oversaw Jewish charities, synagogues, and schools displayed a relaxed, broad-minded approach to Judaism and its rituals. While more likely to attend the synagogue or observe the Sabbath and festivals than their counterparts in Germany or France, they were not punctilious in their own observance or concerned with imposing higher standards of observance on others. They admired and valued religious traditions because they were ancient and hallowed by the centuries. (This was one reason most of them opposed Reform Judaism.) They tolerated different degrees of ritual commitment, although they would not countenance doctrinal or political challenges to the authority of the religious establishment—the chief rabbinate and the synagogues under his authority. Their Judaism was a broad, big-tent Judaism—undemanding, nonsectarian, and polite. It stressed reasonable behavior, fraternal responsibility, charitability, civility, and courtesy. It was genteel—a religion for gentlemen and their families. There was little place in it for theological rigor, spiritual enthusiasm, or scholarly fervor.

The growth of more exclusivist and more demanding kinds of Judaism challenged (but did not vanquish) the old Anglo-Judaism in the decades after World War I. While their rise was not the result of any one cause alone, most were linked, in one way or another, to the increasing prominence of Jews of East European background in the community as a whole. Already in the first decade of the century, their numbers dwarfed those of previously settled, anglicized families. Their needs, expectations, and habits, in turn, influenced religious leaders, who gradually moved rightward to accommodate them, embracing a more demanding, doctrine-driven Judaism.

While Nina was alive, Redcliffe was more respectful of religious tradition than he might otherwise have been if he had married someone else. Her influence on him and their home life was profound in that regard. But after her death in 1925, he was more lax in his observance and more heterodox in his views. He spoke his mind, first among friends and later in public forums, about dimensions of traditional Judaism, like the dietary laws, that clashed with his sense of the core or heart of Judaism, however vague and ill-defined that was in his mind. Still, he never became a partisan of liberal forms of Judaism—his institutional commitments, formed in his youth, were too strong for that. But the inroads that strict Orthodoxy was making in communal life encouraged him to champion the tolerant, nonhectoring, genteel Judaism of the pre–World War I period. Indeed, in time he seemed to relish the opportunity to vent his opposition to rightward currents in establishment Orthodoxy. More and more he exhibited the characteristics of a communal gadfly and more and more expressed views that he might have moderated were Nina still alive.

An early expression of the change was his critique of Herbert Loewe's traditionalism, as evidenced in the way in which Loewe was raising his two sons, Raphael, the future Hebrew scholar, and Michael, the future Chinese scholar. In March 1930, after the two boys stayed at Barley with Redcliffe and Gertie, Redcliffe wrote to their mother, Ethel, that he wanted to talk with Herbert about the boys, especially Raphael, before "the trouble" with them became serious: "When your boys were here they had the most complete freedom to do whatever they liked in the matter of religious observance, and they did so. All that I did was to watch, and I am certain as I am standing here that Raphael is scared to death by religion. . . . Do not think for a moment that I want to see him de-Judaised; but what I do want to see is his soul unfettered—and that is the bottom of the whole trouble." The problem was, in Redcliffe's view, that "your own taboos, your silent, quiet, but very determined insistence" was "sapping the boy's vigour."[42] Redcliffe may have felt entitled to intervene in the matter, which was none of his business, after all, because he was helping Loewe financially at the time. As he told his sister Isabelle Davis, Loewe was shamelessly underpaid at Oxford and he and Claude Montefiore were making a serious effort to restore him to financial stability. After telling his sister that he was almost ashamed to say how much he had given him, he asked her to send him some money for Loewe.[43]

Herbert Loewe naturally thought that Redcliffe's analysis was without merit. Defending himself, he insisted to Redcliffe that he did not pump Judaism into the boys by force, that they did as they liked, and that they followed their own inclinations, which led them powerfully to Judaism. Moreover, he told him that the training that Nina had given their children was exactly the same as he was giving his boys and her training had certainly not "induced repressions." Loewe then went on the offense. Introducing politics into their disagreement, he blamed Redcliffe's attitude toward Orthodoxy on Zionism, claiming that he underwent a great change when he became a Zionist. (Loewe was anti-Zionist.) "You cannot see yourself back as you were before the war, before you went to Palestine." Zionism's privileging of nation above religion had completely altered his views, he wrote to him—which was not true, for Redcliffe had never identified with Judaism as a set of beliefs and practices deriving their meaning from divine revelation. As Loewe told Redcliffe, Judaism was more than a colonization scheme or a philanthropic project.[44]

By the early 1930s, Redcliffe was fully aware that his views placed him outside mainstream Orthodoxy. In early 1931, the Russian-born Asher Feldman, a *dayyan* on the London Bet Din, invited Redcliffe to lecture to the Conference of Anglo-Jewish Preachers on a subject of his choosing. Redcliffe hesitated to accept because he was concerned that if he spoke frankly he would express views that did not fall within the limits of ordinary Orthodoxy and thus offend many in the audience. He also was concerned about the probable presence of newspaper reporters, for he did not want to be "heckled afterward"—presumably after they printed what he had said. Despite his reluctance, the planning committee pushed him to accept the invitation. They told him that they could not very well exclude the press but that they trusted him "to carry out the rabbinic maxim of *hahamim tizharu be-divreikhem*" [wise men take care with their words] and therefore welcomed a frank paper. Redcliffe responded that the presence of the press would vitiate the main object, a "frank discussion of difficulties." In the end, pleading "too much work," he turned down the invitation.[45]

In private, Redcliffe was less reticent. When Chief Rabbi Hertz asked him in 1932 to comment on the proofs of his commentary on Genesis, Redcliffe's response was frank: it struck him "as thumbnail notes for a series of sermons" rather than scholarly, critical aids to understanding the historical significance of the text. "No! my dear Dr. Hertz, you are never going to recover young Israel by these methods." Any intelligent student, schooled in modern scholarship, would see through his commentary, whose method Redcliffe thought unsound and whose tone he found unattractive.[46] Concerned that his frankness might have hurt Hertz's feelings, Redcliffe wrote to him a week later to invite him to spend a weekend at Homestall.[47] While the gap between Hertz's and Redcliffe's view of the Bible was unbridgeable, Redcliffe did succeed in influencing him on one specific point: Hertz moderated his denunciation of homosexuality after receiving his comments. Redcliffe had urged him to avoid words like "hideous" and "execrable" in describing homosexuality, explaining that "homosexuals are born such" and that "they are no more responsible [for their sexual orientation] than they would be for being born black."[48] In January 1937, Hertz sent him his commentary on Numbers, Leviticus, and Deuteronomy and again asked for his comments—which, unfortunately, do not survive.[49]

Redcliffe's relationship with the notoriously difficult Hertz illuminates the conflicting commitments that shaped his stance toward Judaism and communal authority. While not a close friend of Hertz, he recognized the chief rabbi as the titular representative of mainstream Judaism in Britain, the Judaism into which Redcliffe had been born and raised and to which he remained formally attached until his death. It was also the Judaism of the social circles in which he had mixed since his youth. However maddening Hertz's behavior at times, however naïve his views on the text of the Bible, and however intolerant his attitude toward Liberal Judaism, Redcliffe never attacked the institution of the chief rabbinate. Moreover, he never hounded

242 | *The Last Anglo-Jewish Gentleman*

Hertz, belittling and opposing him, as did Robert Waley Cohen, whose disdain for Hertz was well known. Yet even Waley Cohen acknowledged the positive role the chief rabbi played "in keeping the ultra-orthodox within bounds." In his view, which Redcliffe would have shared, the chief rabbinate (in general) and Hertz (in particular) ensured that "the voice of the community . . . [did] not get into the hands in any way whatever of the wild men, who would certainly disgrace us."[50]

Thus, despite his heterodox views, Redcliffe remained on good terms with Hertz. In 1924, when Waley Cohen told Redcliffe that his relations with Hertz were beyond repair, Redcliffe counseled him to reach a modus vivendi with him, telling him frankly that he had tried to "push him farther than he wanted to go" and "unnecessarily hurt his feelings." He advised Waley Cohen that if he wanted Hertz to behave himself then he "must put him at his ease and not make him stand on his dignity." Waley Cohen objected to what Redcliffe wrote, and Redcliffe then responded, "I know the Chief Rabbi is a difficult person, but then you yourself are not always easy, and a mistake in the correct interpretation of another's point of view is often the worst form of blunder. I am sure it is that which has led to the mutual distrust between the Chief Rabbi and yourself."[51]

In 1933, when Hertz wanted to attack Cambridge University for having appointed Herbert Loewe to a readership in rabbinics—Hertz thought Loewe was incompetent—Waley Cohen turned to Redcliffe for help in dissuading Hertz. Redcliffe explained to Waley Cohen that Hertz's animosity was entirely personal: Hertz believed, incorrectly, that Loewe had written a devastating review of his Genesis commentary in the *Times Literary Supplement*, whose reviews at the time were published anonymously. Redcliffe offered to speak to Hertz ("a troublesome old fool," in his words) and to "try to get some sense into his head."[52]

What especially troubled Redcliffe about the new rightward swing in British Judaism was its hostility to the latitudinarianism of the Victorian and Edwardian eras. While Anglo-Jewry had not been immune to the religious strife that plagued Central European Jewry in the mid-nineteenth century, it had not been racked by the intense battles that raged there. The emergence of non-Orthodox congregations, primarily the West London Synagogue of British Jews in 1840 and the Jewish Religious Union (precursor to the Liberal Jewish Synagogue) in 1901, had provoked concern and controversy but not rage. Their growth had not disrupted communal life in the way that Reform Judaism had in Germany and Hungary. Hertz, sensing the changing religious climate in Anglo-Jewry, was less willing than his predecessor, Hermann Adler, to tolerate diverse forms of Judaism, especially the radicalism of Liberal Judaism. From the mid-1920s until his death in 1946, he waged war against Liberal Judaism, its ministers, and its doctrines in sermons and in print. (He was less hostile to Reform Judaism, which in Britain was more moderate than Liberal Judaism.) These attacks outraged the old communal notability. After the publication of two series of sermons attacking Liberal Judaism in 1926, Waley Cohen wrote him that Anglo-Jewry did not need polemics but "positive statements" to keep those who were drifting away within the fold of the United Synagogue.[53] Two decades later, when the London Bet Din abused Israel Mattuck, rabbi of the Liberal Synagogue and a frequent target of the recently deceased Joseph Hertz, in a letter to the *Jewish Chronicle*, Redcliffe responded with a letter of his own, bemoaning the decline of civility in religious life: "I would ask these gentlemen [the *dayyanim*] whether such an example of bad manners could be found issuing from any court in England, from that of Petty Sessions up to the House of Lords? How can we expect to retain the respect of our fellow citizens when our leaders find themselves unable to discuss technical and legal points without transgressing the conventions of normal behaviour?"[54]

Later, when Lily Montagu, one of the leaders of Liberal Judaism, thanked him for coming to Mattuck's defense, he replied, "It is always the same tale: bad manners and religious enthusiasm seem to be almost inseparable, and with bad manners there is almost invariably bad logic too."[55] For Redcliffe, bad manners and religious enthusiasm were the antithesis of the genteel Judaism of the New West End Synagogue he had known as a young man.

In 1939, Redcliffe had used the opportunity of an invitation from the council of Jews' College to deliver the principal address at its annual Speech Day to sharpen his critique of the very Orthodoxy that Jews' College embodied. (The invitation was a testament to the standing of the old notability in the wider community, for, on the face of it, it made no sense—Redcliffe was not Orthodox in either belief or practice.) His title was "What of the Laity?" and its theme the ever-widening gap between the clergy and the laity. Some of the gap he attributed to the ignorance of the laity about the content and meaning of Judaism, "its honesty towards life, and the noble catholicity of its teachings." But he also blamed the rabbis as well. They had failed to present Judaism to a Western, sophisticated people in terms that they could absorb into their lives. In particular, their insistence on the strict observance of the dietary laws had alienated Jews who were unaware of Judaism's spiritual treasures. They had made Judaism into a religion of the stomach rather than of the soul.[56]

Although Redcliffe was never attracted to Reform or Liberal Judaism, he shared their understanding that contemporary Orthodoxy was fixated on *kashrut*—to the point that it marginalized the spiritual and ethical dimensions of Judaism. Like their spokesmen, he embraced the idea that Judaism should nourish and guide the ethical behavior of its adherents. While there is nothing in this notion that is in doctrinal conflict with Orthodox Judaism, in practice, Orthodox Judaism in Britain tended to privilege correct observance over ethical behavior. In the decade before and during World War II, as the Jewish Question once again captured the British imagination, Jewish conduct in commercial and social life (for example, black marketeering during the war) became a frequent target of critics of the Jews. Some prominent communal figures, most of them outside conventional Orthodox circles, believed that Anglo-Jewry was suffering a spiritual-ethical crisis, which they attributed, in part, to the synagogues' neglect of Judaism's social-justice tradition. In fall 1942, in the midst of the war, a small group who shared that perspective convened two private conferences in London to discuss the matter and consider steps to give more prominence to the non-ritualistic side of Judaism.[57] Twenty-three persons attended the first conference; eighteen the second. They were, in the main, well-known communal leaders associated with the Reform and Liberal movements (Lily Montagu, Basil Henriques), intellectuals (Norman Bentwich, Philip Hartog), Liberal and Reform rabbis (Harold Reinhardt, Israel Mattuck, Werner van der Zyl), and members of long-established families who remained within the United Synagogue (Ewen Montagu, Henrietta Adler). Redcliffe was among those who were invited but unable to attend. But he, like Cecil Roth, sent a letter of support to the first conference, setting forth his views.

Redcliffe's interest in the health of Judaism in Britain was long-standing, and so it is not surprising that he signed on with this new campaign. Recall his work in the War Memorial project to transfer Jews' College to either Oxford or Cambridge in the hope of producing gentlemen rabbis. From the start, however, his concern with the state of Judaism was not a concern with its ritual and worship as with its ability to strengthen character and inspire high-minded behavior among Jews. In his letter to the first conference, he rooted Judaism's call for social justice in its teachings about the sanctity of life and then offered an unusual explanation of what social justice demanded: it required "the repression of our own aggressive and possessive instincts." Channeling Freud, he wrote, "For three thousand years the Jew has been taught, and not without success, to practice those restraints on his individualism which in the aggregate spells civilization." He then related an anecdote, from twenty years earlier, when George Bernard Shaw, then a guest at Barley, remarked to Nina that "the Jew is born civilised." Having achieved prosperity, contemporary Jews did not always live up to their own ideal; before it was too late, they needed to "accept the self-discipline which that ideal calls for."[58]

Redcliffe's focus on self-discipline is revealing. He was himself a tireless communal worker and polemicist, a productive natural scientist, a voracious reader, a man of broad intellectual interests, and a diligent correspondent. He could have been none of these without remarkable self-discipline. But while his own emotional needs made him a champion of internally imposed control and restraint, there were currents in Jewish life as well that encouraged his emphasis. It was an article of faith among communal leaders that Jewish excess fed or even created antisemitism. The targets of their criticism were the East European–born nouveaux riches—their speech loud, their dress flashy, their manners crude, their carriage awkward, and their commercial ethics dodgy—or so it was alleged. For those attending the conference, the link between antisemitism and Jewish excess was self-evident. The revitalization of Jewish ethical and social-justice traditions, they believed, was a way to curb the kind of behavior that attracted unwanted hostile attention. Ewen Montagu, son of the second Lord Swaythling and at the time a lieutenant commander in Naval Intelligence, made this explicit. His concern was "the enormous number of Jews who regarded themselves as Jews but who had not the slightest idea what Judaism meant. These people lived under the influence of the herd instinct congregating in districts [in north and northwest London] with Jews with similar flashy habits invoking the antipathy of their neighbours. In this way they roused the problem of anti-Semitism and we must appeal to them to try and get a real Jewish spirit."

In April 1941, when Chief Rabbi Hertz became aware of the beginnings of the effort that eventually convened the two conferences, he sent a circular letter to friends and supporters, Redcliffe among them, warning that a scheme was afoot to subvert all Orthodox teaching and replace it with Waley-Cohen-like liberalism. He asked those who received the letter to join him in a campaign against this scheme, which he described only in vague terms. Redcliffe delayed answering the letter and only replied on May 5, saying that he had heard nothing about such a movement. Hertz responded by sending him a copy of a letter that he (Hertz) had sent to Frank Samuel, vice president of the United Synagogue, specifically denouncing Waley Cohen, Norman Bentwich, and Lily Montagu as the instigators. Redcliffe then wrote to Bentwich on May 11 to find out what was going on. The latter explained that the three had invited about twenty people in London to a private meeting to discuss religious education in relation to Jewish institutions, the attitude of Judaism to social and international questions, and Judaism and personal conduct. Then, once again, Redcliffe acted to calm the chief rabbi. He met with him in London in late May and showed him Bentwich's notes about the aims of the group. But he was not successful. Hertz was so on edge that Redcliffe was unable to get him to look at anything objectively. As Redcliffe wrote to Bentwich on May 26, "I tried very hard to persuade him to distinguish between his personal troubles with R.W.C. and the big problems ahead of us, but I honestly do not think he is capable of that kind of statesmanship." Redcliffe was equally scathing about Waley Cohen (who, incidentally, was not publicly associated with the conferences in the fall). In an assessment from which no historian of Anglo-Jewry would dissent, Redcliffe wrote that Waley Cohen was not qualified to be a spiritual or philosophical guide to anyone. All that he understood was the "practical organization of men and material." He closed his letter with a swipe at Orthodoxy: "I was always impressed by the conception that Judaism is 'a way of life,' but who, out of Bedlam, thinks that life stands still? Yet the orthodox would petrify the 'way' and hamper all adaptation."[59] In the end, nothing came of the two conferences. Their goals were too amorphous and their ability to influence the community too limited, even assuming the possibility of sparking the kind of revival they envisioned.

Redcliffe's one great success in fostering Jewish culture before World War II was his work to secure the readership in rabbinics at Cambridge University—at a time when Jewish scholarship was poorly represented in British academia. The teaching of rabbinic literature at Cambridge, which began in 1866, was due to the initiative of Christian scholars at the university who appreciated the importance of rabbinic literature for understanding the formative years of Christianity. The university funded the first incumbent of the position, Solomon Marcus Schiller-Szinessy, and Claude Goldsmid Montefiore supported the position with an annual benefaction from 1892 until 1925, when the readership was held by Solomon Schechter and then Israel Abrahams. After the latter's death in 1925, the readership lapsed. For the next few years, Herbert Loewe, who had been Abrahams's student and who was then teaching at Oxford, traveled to Cambridge to provide some instruction. But the arrangement was not ideal, for, among other reasons, Loewe suffered from Hodgkin's lymphoma, which made the travel difficult. Meanwhile, with the support of the university, Redcliffe took the lead in raising funds to reestablish the readership permanently, launching an appeal in 1929. He was successful and, in October 1931, Herbert Loewe, Abrahams's acknowledged successor, took up the position at Cambridge.[60]

Redcliffe's experience in raising funds for the readership confirmed a frequent complaint of his: British Jews, on the whole, were indifferent to Jewish scholarship and learning. He raised a little less than £9,000 (the equivalent of £617,824, or $829,923, in 2021) for the endowment—the great bulk of which came from Jews outside Britain. The single biggest donor was Julius Rosenwald, the Chicago businessman and philanthropist who headed Sears, Roebuck, who gave £5,000; the second, N. M. Rothschild and Sons, which gave £2,000; and the third, the Mosseri family, bankers and businessmen in Cairo, who gave £1,000. (The Mosseri gift was in memory of Lionel Mosseri, one-time president of the Cambridge Hebrew Congregation.) In other words, two-thirds of the funds came from overseas. Redcliffe and three other family members contributed £500, of which £350 came from the Arthur Davis Memorial Fund, which Redcliffe controlled.[61] While not himself well educated in matters Jewish (which did not stop him, of course, from making sweeping assertions about Jewish culture and civilization), he valued—and was willing to support—Hebrew scholarship. In this sense, he was atypical of the Anglo-Jewish elite, who directed their philanthropy toward charities for the care of the Jewish poor or to cultural institutions that enhanced their status in British society at large.

Notes

1. *Manchester Guardian*, March 5, 1934.
2. RNS to Chaim Weizmann, April 21, 1949, Add. MS 8171/5, RNS CUL.
3. Lewis Namier to RNS, April 8, 1940, and RNS to Lewis Namier, April 9, 1940, MS 60/9/6/4/3–4, James Parkes Papers, HL US.
4. Arthur Ruppin to RNS, April 5, 1926, and RNS to Arthur Ruppin, May 27, 1926, both in Add. MS 8171/5, RNS CUL.

248 | *The Last Anglo-Jewish Gentleman*

5. Uri Cohen, "Mosdot nihul ha-universitah ha-ivrit, 1925–1948," in *Toldot ha-universitah ha-ivrit bi-yerushalayim*, ed. Hagit Lavsky, vol. 2, pt. 1, *Hitbassut ve-tsemihah* (Jerusalem: Magnes Press, 2005), 28–30.

6. Norman Bentwich, *For Zion's Sake: A Biography of Judah L. Magnes* (Philadelphia: Jewish Publication Society, 1954), 166–69; Mabel Hélène Kisch Hartog, *P. J. Hartog: A Memoir* (London: Constable, 1949), 127–28; Herbert Parzen, "The Magnes-Weizmann-Einstein Controversy," *Jewish Social Studies* 32, no. 3 (1970): 188.

7. Eli Ginzberg, *Keeper of the Law: Louis Ginzberg* (Philadelphia: Jewish Publication Society, 1966), 211.

8. Philip Hartog to Louis Ginzberg, April 5 and May 26, 1934, Louis Ginzberg Papers, ARC 42, Jewish Theological Seminary, New York.

9. *Palestine Post*, October 11, 1938.

10. *Palestine Post*, December 6, 1933.

11. Arthur A. Dembitz, letter to the editor, (Philadelphia) *Jewish Exponent*, January 5, 1934.

12. *Jewish Chronicle*, May 12, 1939; RNS, "What of the Laity," typescript, May 7, 1939, Add. MS 8171/10c, RNS CUL. The typewritten text of the speech he actually delivered includes the words, in his own hand, "these pages omitted" just before the references to race.

13. RNS, typescript, October 14, 1943, Add. MS 8171/10c, RNS CUL. From internal evidence, it appears that Redcliffe was responding to a list of questions from his friend Charles Singer.

14. Documents on refugees whom Redcliffe assisted are in MS SPSL 83/2, the Archive of the Society for the Protection of Science and Learning, Special Collections, Bodleian Library, Oxford, UK.

15. Norman Bentwich, *They Found Refuge: An Account of British Jewry's Work for Victims of Nazi Oppression* (London: Cresset, 1956), chap. 9.

16. See, for example, Tony Kushner, *The Persistence of Prejudice: Antisemitism in British Society during the Second World War* (Manchester: Manchester University Press, 1989), ch. 9; Richard Bolchover, *British Jewry and the Holocaust* (Cambridge: Cambridge University Press, 1993); and Meier Sompolinsky, *The British Government and the Holocaust: The Failure of Anglo-Jewish Leadership* (Brighton: Sussex Academic, 1999). The behavior of the American Jewish leadership at the time of the Holocaust is an equally contentious subject.

17. Sidney Salomon to RNS, July 22, 1937, Add. MS 8171/51, RNS CUL.

18. RNS to Leonard G. Montefiore, November 26, 1937, Add. MS 8171/51, RNS CUL.

19. Gavin Schaffer, *Racial Science and British Society, 1930–62* (Houndmills, Basingstoke: Palgrave Macmillan, 2008), 32–39; Elazar Barkan, *The Retreat of Scientific Racism: Changing Concepts of Race in Britain and the United States between the World Wars* (Cambridge: Cambridge University Press, 1992), 296–308.

20. Daniel Tilles, *British Fascist Antisemitism and Jewish Responses, 1932–40* (London: Bloomsbury Academic, 2015), 180–82.

21. Charles Singer to Robert Waley Cohen, April 8, 1937, MS 363/A3006/1/3/61A, Robert Waley Cohen Papers, HL US [hereafter, RWC Papers].

22. Henry Felix Srebrnik, *London Jews and British Communism, 1933–1945* (London: Vallentine Mitchell, 1995), ch. 4; Tilles, *British Fascist Antisemitism and Jewish Responses*, pt. 2.

23. RNS and James Parkes, "The Deputies and the People's Council," *Jewish Chronicle*, November 27, 1936.

24. A copy of Laski's letter is in a binder labeled "Jewish People's Council and Board of Deputies," in Add. MS 8171, RNS CUL [hereafter, JPC binder].

Conflicts at Home and Abroad | 249

25. RNS to Sidney Salomon, November 23, 1926, and Sidney Salomon to RNS, November 25, 1936, both in JPC binder.

26. Neville Laski to RNS, January 6, 1937, JPC binder.

27. Neville Laski to RNS, January 19, 1937; RNS to Adolph G. Brotman, January 27, 1937; Adolph G. Brotman to RNS, January 28, 1937—all in JPC binder.

28. RNS to Adolph G. Brotman, February 1, 1937, JPC binder.

29. Neville Laski to RNS, February 3, 1937, JPC binder.

30. RNS, minutes of the February 11 meeting, JPC binder.

31. Lazar Zaidman to RNS, February 25, 1937; RNS to Lazar Zeidman, February 26, 1937; Lazar Zeidman to RNS, March 3, 1937—all in JPC binder.

32. RNS to Lazar Zeidman, March 8, 1937, and Adolph G. Brotman to RNS, March 9, 1937, both in JPC binder.

33. RNS to Adolph G. Brotman, March 10, 1937, JPC binder.

34. Tilles, *British Fascist Antisemitism*, 163–80.

35. Srebrnik, *London Jews*, ch. 5.

36. *Jewish Chronicle*, October 13, 1944.

37. Srebrnik, *London Jews*, 86–94.

38. *Jewish Chronicle*, February 3, 1943.

39. *Jewish Chronicle*, February 19, 1943.

40. *Jewish Chronicle*, November 24, 1944.

41. Srebrnik, *London Jews*, 94–98.

42. RNS to Ethel Loewe, March 19, 1930, Add. MS 8171/1/2, RNS CUL.

43. RNS to Isabelle Davis, May 12, 1930, Add. MS 8171/1/2, RNS CUL.

44. Herbert Loewe to RNS, March 21, 1930, Add. MS 8171/1/1, RNS CUL.

45. Asher Feldman to RNS, January 26 and February 13, 1931; RNS to Asher Feldman, January 30, 1931; Isaac Livingstone to RNS, March 27, 1931; RNS to Isaac Livingstone, March 9 and 25, 1931—all in Add. MS 8171/1/2, RNS CUL.

46. RNS to Joseph H. Hertz, February 19, 1932, Add. MS 8171/1/1, RNS CUL.

47. Harvey Warren Meirovich, *A Vindication of Judaism: The Polemics of the Hertz Pentateuch* (New York: Jewish Theological Seminary, 1998), 234n26.

48. RNS to Joseph H. Hertz, February 19, 1932, quoted in Meirovich, *Vindication of Judaism*, 214n121.

49. RNS to Joseph H. Hertz, January 15, 1937, Add. MS 8171/1/1, RNS CUL.

50. RWC to Osmond d'Avigdor Goldsmid, May 20, 1929, MS 363/A3006/1/3/41, RWC Papers.

51. This correspondence is quoted in Robert Henriques, *Sir Robert Waley Cohen, 1877–1952: A Biography* (London: Secker and Warburg, 1966), 343.

52. RNS to RWC, February 21, 1933, MS 363/A3006/1/3/147, RWC Papers.

53. RWC to J. H. Hertz, April 20, 1926, MS 363/A3006/1/3/138, RWC Papers.

54. RNS to the editor, *Jewish Chronicle*, January 31, 1947.

55. RNS to Lily Montagu, February 8, 1947, Add. MS 8171/1/6, RNS CUL.

56. *Jewish Chronicle*, May 12, 1939.

57. Needless to say, there was no press coverage of the meetings. In Redcliffe's papers, there are mimeographed copies of the minutes of the two conferences, marked "PRIVATE AND CONFIDENTIAL," in Add. MS 8171/51, RNS CUL. The minutes of the first meeting reprint his letter.

58. Ibid.

250 | *The Last Anglo-Jewish Gentleman*

59. RNS to Norman Bentwich, May 11 and 26, 1941, and Norman Bentwich to RNS, May 12, 1941, Add. MS 8171/51, RNS CUL.

60. Nicholas de Lange, "Books and Bookmen: The Cambridge Teachers of Rabbinics, 1866–1971," *Transactions of the Jewish Historical Society of England* 44 (2012): 139–63. When de Lange retired from the position in 2011, the university failed to appoint a successor, citing financial reasons.

61. A complete, typed list of donors is in Add. MS. 8171/51, RNS CUL.

11

THE POTATO BOOK

1

In the twenties and thirties, while devoting much time and energy to Jewish institutions and causes, Redcliffe continued his own research, directing the Potato Virus Research Station at Cambridge and publishing extensively in scientific journals. World War I had effectively brought research on potato blight in Britain and elsewhere to a standstill. When it resumed after the war, there was greater awareness, although not consensus, that the threat to the potato was not due to senescence—the gradual and accelerating aging of the plant (as commonly believed in the nineteenth century)—but to specific infections. In an essay on the history of plant virus research that appeared in 1939 in a *Festschrift* for Sir Daniel Hall, a noted agricultural educationist, Redcliffe reminded his readers that there was still confusion within the scientific community on the matter. As an illustration, he quoted one researcher who, in a 1918 publication, described curly dwarf potato as "a physiological disorder resulting in a permanent deterioration of the potato stock . . . perhaps senescence of the particular race of potato attacked, or in other words a varietal decline."[1] By 1939, this view was discredited, but Redcliffe urged his readers to be charitable to those who had held it earlier, since the views they now held true might be discredited twenty years thence.

As I explained in an earlier chapter, when Redcliffe began breeding potatoes before the war, he knew little of viruses. His focus then was the inheritance of characteristics (including, of course, immunity to disease). His focus changed after the war. In 1920, two researchers at the University of Manchester, an entomologist and a mycologist, launched the study of potato virus in England. From that time, they and their colleagues elsewhere expanded their work to include the spread of virus diseases among other crops. They also began to focus on how insects—mites and aphids, for example—transmitted viral infections to healthy plants. In 1926, Redcliffe transferred his stocks from Barley to Cambridge, when he became director of the Potato Virus Research Station. By that time, he had developed a score of economically profitable seedling varieties that were resistant to disease most of the time. As research revealed more about the character of viruses that attacked potatoes, it became clear that the control of aphids, which transmitted the virus, would combat its spread. English potato breeders had known for more than a century that potato-seed tubers that came from the moors of the Scottish Highlands produced healthier plants on the whole than those grown in sheltered enclosures in England. Further work showed that regions exposed to sea air and enjoying high rainfall produced even healthier seeds than sheltered inland areas where the rainfall was lower. (Heavy rainfall can more or less completely destroy colonies of aphids while strong winds prevent them from flying.) Still, from time to time, there would be outbreaks of virus disease even in such areas when weather conditions allowed the rapid multiplication of aphids.

In 1925, Redcliffe set out to acquire small nuclear stocks of virus-free seed, visiting growing areas in western Ireland and Scotland. He removed immature tubers from the healthiest plants he could find and replanted them, at first in insect-proof cages at Barley and then in insect-free greenhouses at Cambridge. Testing them periodically for infections, he then replanted and multiplied the healthiest in pots in the greenhouses, maintaining them from year to year. In 1934, he proposed to the Potato Marketing Board a scheme, based on this work, to produce on a commercial scale sufficient virus-free seed to supply the potato-growing areas of Scotland. The hope was that the potato growers of eastern Scotland would import their seed from approved culture areas with climate conditions that hampered the multiplication and spread of aphids and that breeders in approved areas would renew their stocks with regularly inspected virus-free stock from the greenhouses at Cambridge. (See fig. 11.1.) The proposal languished for five years but, after a conference of government officials, agricultural experts, scientists, and breeders finally convened in June 1939, it was approved. The outbreak of war, however, postponed any immediate trial. Redcliffe, meanwhile, searched for areas in Scotland where tubers would be safe from contaminated aphids. A visit to the west coast and the Inner and Outer Hebrides convinced him that the islands, in particular, where green flies are rare, would provide ideal conditions. In 1941, the National Institute of Agricultural Botany adopted the scheme, and Redcliffe located the ideal

Figure 11.1. Redcliffe Salaman, potato in hand (sometime after World War II). Collection of the author.

place for the trial on the Isle of Islay. In 1949, when he published his potato book, there were fifty acres of reclaimed peat and other lands there growing virus-free stock.[2] By this time, however, he was no longer actively researching potato blight.

In the 1930s, the scientific community formally recognized the importance of his work. He was elected a fellow of the Royal Society in 1935, an honor he valued more than any other he received. The following year, he delivered the Masters Memorial Lectures of the Royal Horticultural Society. In October 1937, as director of the Potato Virus Research Station, he was invited to attend the Twelfth International Horticultural Congress to be held the following year in Berlin, but, as is no surprise, refused the invitation in a sharply worded letter.[3] From November 1937 to February 1938, he visited India, accompanied by Gertie, as part of a delegation of English scientists attending the twenty-fifth Indian Science Congress at Calcutta.[4] Addressing the agricultural section of the congress, he remarked that scientists in India

254 | *The Last Anglo-Jewish Gentleman*

took little interest in the potato and that there was great scope for work in this area. The outstanding problems, he told his audience, were establishing the purity of varieties, eliminating degenerate stocks, and selecting and propagating clean seed.[5] And in 1943, he delivered the prestigious Finlay Memorial Lecture at the University of Dublin. The annual lecture, which was devoted to themes in political economy, was a central intellectual event in the life of the university. His topic was "The Influence of the Potato on the Course of Irish History," a preview of the book he was then writing.

2

In 1939, Redcliffe turned sixty-five and was required to resign his position as director of the Potato Virus Research Station. "The abrupt closure of my career," he wrote in the early 1950s, "produced a feeling of frustration, tempered, I must admit, with resentment." He felt that the powers that be had no use for his services as a scientist.[6] While refugees and other matters continued to occupy him during the war, he now had the leisure to devote himself to scholarship, and he began to research and then write what would become his magnum opus, *The History and Social Influence of the Potato*. When it appeared in 1949, some reviewers mistakenly assumed that he had devoted forty-plus years of his life to its writing, that is, that his work on the book went back to the time of his earliest genetic work on potatoes, in the first decade of the century. As reviewers are wont to do, they failed to read carefully what the author wrote. In the book, he clearly described the genesis of his initial scientific research and his later historical research. The potato book was the product of his "retirement" years—a period when, in fact, he was as busy with communal business as before the war. With its length (685 pages) and its chronological sweep, geographical scope, multidisciplinary method, and sheer novelty (all of which I will have more to say about further on), it is extraordinary that it took him less than a decade to research and write the book. Moreover, at the end of the war, but before the book was finished, he fell seriously ill with "a fulminating attack of lumbago, complicated with bronchial pneumonia." (Lumbago was a general term used to describe pain in the lumbar region of the back. It could have been caused by a number of conditions: muscle strain, spinal stenosis, degenerative disk disease, or herniated disks.) The fatigue and exhaustion overwhelmed him. He had never been so sick and spent much of December 1945 and January 1946 in the Evelyn Nursing Home in Cambridge. During the first weeks of the attacks, he experienced "bouts of almost unimaginable pain" and for a long time dreaded their recurrence. He felt he was near death and resigned from most of the posts he held. When he left the nursing home, he was hobbling on two sticks, but the pain was much less than it had been. Several months passed before he could attempt any kind of work. Characteristically, in a passage written a few years later, he described the fatigue and exhaustion as breaking through his psychological defenses "like a flood," sweeping everything else before it. He attributed the erection of those defenses to the unending strain and work of the Hitler years. He thought that the nerve-wracking, exhausting, and "heart-breaking job" of singlehandedly winding up the affairs of Jewish Health Organization also took a toll.[7]

3

The History and Social Influence of the Potato is the work of a gifted amateur whose method, style, and knowledge were anything but amateurish and whose perspective was never antiquarian. It draws on the disciplines of anthropology, archaeology, botany, history, and psychology and his intimate familiarity with potato breeding. While the twenty-first-century academy celebrates multidisciplinary work, the potato book's disciplinary range and competence eclipse the work of contemporary historians who pride themselves on their ability to cross the borders of their own academic specialization. In a formal sense, of course, Redcliffe was woefully unprepared to write the book he did. He lacked formal training in any of the above fields of scholarship. To the best of my knowledge, the fact never gave him pause or inhibited him. The tradition out of which he wrote was that of the independent, highly disciplined amateur scholar or scientist, free of institutional or professional constraints. Indeed, his amateur status was critical for what he accomplished. I cannot imagine an academic historian then or now with the self-assurance or learning to range so widely. His self-assurance was also a product of his financial independence and class position. Redcliffe was accustomed to having his way, within the family and the neighborhood and at communal charities, and to having others defer to him. He was supremely self-confident in the correctness of his views in all manner of things, even when not justified. For example, he, like Robert Waley Cohen, was quick to pontificate about the correctness of this or that path in Jewish life, although, in fact, his knowledge of Jewish culture and

256 | *The Last Anglo-Jewish Gentleman*

civilization was not extensive (Waley Cohen's was even less). The upside of this trait, however, was his incapacity to be daunted by a project of such scope and complexity. His status inoculated him against doubts that might have plagued other researchers.

The title of Redcliffe's book often provokes amusement. The potato is a humble foodstuff—unattractive and inexpensive, and rarely the focus of gastronomic attention. It is an unremarkable accompaniment—roasted, boiled, fried, or mashed—to meat and fish in Western cooking. Redcliffe knew well that many of his contemporaries would regard his project "as having no more scientific value or importance than a cookery book."[8] Even today one might ask whether such a ubiquitous and prosaic vegetable can have a "history." Or, in what way it can have a "history." After all, potatoes are not social institutions; they lack agency, let alone consciousness. In the mid-twentieth century, when Redcliffe was at work, there were no other examples of the history of a single foodstuff. There was no model or template on which he could draw. It was the first book of its kind—"a scholarly rhapsody on a single cultivar," in the words of the cultural anthropologist Sidney Mintz, himself the author of the pioneering *Sweetness and Power: The Place of Sugar in Modern History* (1985). For Mintz, it was "a tour de force of a kind"—"a beacon, a model, a *point de repère.*"[9] This kind of history became more common several decades later, as the field of history continued to broaden, a process underway since the 1960s. In the years since the publication of Mintz's book, salt, cod, oysters, milk, corn, wheat, rice, bananas, saffron, and chocolate (to name only a few) have also found their historians.

Redcliffe did not dwell on the novelty of his project in *The History and Social Influence of the Potato.* He was, however, fully aware of its methodological character (that is, its historiographical assumptions or underpinnings) and clearly and self-consciously articulated them. For him, the history of the potato was a study of the interplay between a plant and variable social environments—in particular, its initial adoption as a foodstuff in its home, the Andes, its diffusion in the Americas and then Europe, and its influence on the social structures of the people who adopted it. During his fourteen years as the director of the Potato Virus Research Station, he was occupied in the main with the genetics, morphology, and pathology of the potato. But it had occurred to him even then that "the potato—or rather its employment as an item of diet—offered a unique opportunity for the study of the social and economic reactions which might ensue from the adoption by the masses of the people of a new, cheap, efficient and easily produced foodstuff."[10] His *magnum opus* studies "the reactions set up between a plant which, under cultivation, is relatively stable, and the social environment often unstable and variable, into which it has been introduced." It is surprising, in one who had expounded the racial history of the Jews for decades, that race, as a category of analysis, was completely absent in his account. One searches in vain for any hint that the dependence of the Irish on the potato was a consequence of their "race." His understanding of the history of the potato was political and socioeconomic in nature, even materialist, and he approvingly quoted the well-known aphorism of the nineteenth-century German philosopher Ludwig Feuerbach (the so-called intellectual bridge between Georg Wilhelm Friedrich Hegel and Karl Marx), "Der Mensch ist was er isst" [Man is what he eats].[11]

It is hard to know what to make of the absence of race in *The History and Social Influence of the Potato*. While Redcliffe ceased writing and lecturing about the racial character of the Jews in the 1940s, he never abandoned the idea that there was a racial component to Jewishness, as we will see in the following chapter. Perhaps all that can be said by way of explanation is that Redcliffe was inconsistent, that he was not obsessive in his attachment to the categories of race, and that his thinking about the two major foci of his life—Jews and potatoes—was compartmentalized.

4

The History and Social Influence of the Potato begins with the question of the origins of the potato as a foodstuff. In the Andes, their native habitat, they grow wild, but their value for food is not obvious. Ancient species were scraggly and small, their foliage filled with poisonous glycoalkaloids. The tubers of some species were also poisonous. What, then, led the people of the Andes to experiment with and then cultivate them? (Scientists now date their earliest cultivation to about 4000 BCE.) The author of a recent history of the potato finds it difficult to imagine what might initially have encouraged them to do so.[12] Redcliffe proposed a solution rooted, once again, in the emotional life of human beings. He argued, not unreasonably, that the original inhabitants of the Peruvian Andes were migrants from forests at lower elevations, where potatoes were unknown. Noting that European travelers in the great rain forests of the Amazon often experienced feelings of terror, becoming "as frightened children" in its "dark solitudes," the "nightmare terrors" of their childhood reawakened, he proposed that

258 | *The Last Anglo-Jewish Gentleman*

the "terrors of the jungle" conditioned the mentality of the earliest cultivators of the potato.[13] In the secluded valleys and the more fertile portions of the high tablelands of the Andes to which they had fled to escape the threats of their old home, they had to find foodstuffs that would grow under largely unfavorable conditions, plants that were hardier than those they had known in the forest. Hence, the necessity to experiment—to take risks—as a consequence of which humans "solved the problem of how to live at great altitudes, and thereby attained the mastery of a continent."[14] Redcliffe's evocations of the "terrors of the jungle" are among the liveliest, most vivid passages in the book. To cite one example: "The dense, impenetrable rain-soaked jungle through which a way must needs be hacked yard by yard, the only guide a network of rivers, the air swarming with savage insects, the land haunted by jaguar and boa constrictor, the waters infested by alligators and voracious fishes, all create a picture which is not merely one of hardship and difficulty, but one which inspired then, as it does to-day, a feeling of terror, even in the hardiest explorers."[15] Passages like these were the product of wide reading, not personal experience. He actually never set foot in South America.

In the following chapter, more an extended aside really, Redcliffe considered the archeological record—specifically the representation of the potato in pre-Columbian Peruvian and Bolivian pottery. After systematically categorizing and dating the potato pots (pots in the shape of potatoes, rather than pots for storing or serving potatoes), Redcliffe took up a question that fascinated him (and about which he had written earlier)[16] but that was, in fact, marginal to his story. He noted that the spherical bodies of the pots often represented the potato as a human being whose face was mutilated to appear like a person born with a cleft lip and palate. Drawing on anthropology and Freud (whether directly or indirectly), he connected the mutilation to ancient rites of human sacrifice intended to strengthen the spirit of the potato to ensure the success of the crop in the field. Since a good crop required seed tubers "with big mouths and prominent teeth," the end of the noses of the sacrificial victims were cut off and their lips removed. Hence, "the mouth was enlarged, the teeth made prominent, the god both strengthened and instructed, and the people eventually saved."[17] Redcliffe also assumed that, in its origins, the rite was associated with cannibalism. Over time "the reality and strength of those ancient rites" were sublimated, recorded, so to speak, only in the subconscious and preserved materially in the potato pots of later generations. Perhaps, he speculated, "in the sacrificial rites themselves we have the sublimated expression of the fears and anxieties which harried man during the period of his early struggle with nature in his new environment, that struggle in which he must win the first round of the combat, or perish."[18] Once again "fears and anxieties" drove human history.

Having accounted for the earliest cultivation of the potato, Redcliffe turned to the European encounter with the potato in South America in the early sixteenth century, its introduction to Europe, and its reception in learned and ruling circles. Here he was on firmer evidentiary ground, for there was an extensive paper trail. The details of his account need not detain us, but it is worth noting that it has stood the test of time in the main. He painstakingly explored how tubers could have traveled, literally, from Peru to Spain—which sailings, under what conditions, at what times of the year. His extensive correspondence with historians and social scientists around the world also allowed him to date, with some precision, the arrival of the potato. From Earl J. Hamilton, an economic historian at Duke University, who studied the impact of South American gold and silver on prices in early modern Spain, he learned of the earliest mention of the use of the potato as a foodstuff: the inmates of a charitable institution in Seville were regularly served potatoes from December 1573 on. Allowing three years for the seed tubers to grow and develop into a crop that could be marketed profitably, this meant that they had to have been shipped from South America no later than 1569. On the basis of this calculation, Redcliffe was credited with having discovered the arrival of the potato in Europe. Subsequently, in the 1990s, the botanist John G. Hawkes, a specialist in the taxonomy of wild potato species at the University of Birmingham, and Javier Francisco Ortega, a plant biologist at Florida International University, discovered that potatoes were being grown as a commercial crop in 1567 in the Canary Islands—from which they were shipped to Spain. By positing the Canary Islands as the steppingstone for the introduction of New World plants to Europe, Hawkes and Francisco Ortega resolved a problem that Redcliffe did not fully acknowledge: on the long passage from South America to Europe, tubers would have been too shriveled and sprouted to have had any commercial value.[19]

Redcliffe's tone shifted when he proceeded to what is, for most readers, the heart and soul of the book—the arrival of the potato in Ireland, its absolute conquest of the Irish diet, and the terrible consequences when blight struck several years in succession in the mid-nineteenth century

260 | *The Last Anglo-Jewish Gentleman*

(chapters 11 to 18). His chapters introduced a bevy of morally freighted historical questions about responsibility for the Great Famine (1845–49), an issue that still haunts English-Irish relations today. Redcliffe gave impassioned descriptions of the poverty of Irish rural life before the famine, the deaths of one million persons from starvation and disease, and the social structures, ideological convictions, anti-Irish sentiments, and government ineptitude and ill will that encouraged dependence on the potato and then failed to respond humanely when the crops in the field failed. In reviewing the second edition of 1985 in *The London Review of Books*, the novelist and essayist Angela Carter wrote of its "inflammatory humanism."[20] Drawing on firsthand accounts of the suffering, the tone of his writing was engaged and sympathetic, not at all reluctant to pass judgment. Here is his characterization of Irish landowners, both resident and absentee:

> Amongst the gentry replete though it was with the external trappings of cultured London and the exotic experiences of the European tour, we see a moral irresponsibility, not to say dishonesty, which was far more sinister than the boorish simplicity of the peasant. In the one, the spirit of enterprise and the hope of betterment had spent themselves in a featureless existence, dominated by the potato and its culture; in the other, the same causes which had led to this unique dominance, had allowed the landowner to regard his estate, and those whose lives depended on its cultivation, as so many tools, designed by Providence, for the production on his behalf, of an assured income.[21]

On occasion, Redcliffe was withering. England's policy of crippling and destroying Irish industries (woolens, brewing, linen, glass) in the eighteenth century, which left the population even more dependent on the potato, was "an incredible drama of spite and imbecility."[22] The government's initial decision to require recipients of relief in Ireland, who were starving and ill, their strength depleted, to labor at public works projects to qualify for aid was "stupid and brutal."[23] When the potato became the food of one class in Ireland (the laboring class), it automatically became "an instrument of class exploitation," whether or not either party was conscious of the role it was playing.[24]

Angela Carter attributed the impassioned tone of the Irish chapters to "the sensibility of the period of welfare socialism voted in at the end of the Second World War."[25] (She referred to the period "as the only time in the history of Britain [excepting 1949] when the great majority of British people actively demonstrated that they knew what was good for them.") There may be some truth in this, but there were sentiments of another kind stoking Redcliffe's anger as well, perhaps even more. His sympathy for Irish suffering and scorn for English arrogance and indifference were not the typical views of country gentlemen in Hertfordshire. I think it is likely that the rage that drove his writing about the Great Famine stemmed from his sense that the government had betrayed the promises made to the Jewish people when it issued the Balfour Declaration in 1917 and when it assumed the mandate for Palestine in 1920. Redcliffe's sense of English perfidy went back decades. While still serving in Palestine, he complained bitterly to Nina and other correspondents about military officials who repeatedly undermined the Zionist position. Their shabby treatment of the Jewish units affected him directly. The White Paper of 1939, which in effect repudiated the Balfour Declaration, trapping hundreds of thousands of Jews in Nazi-occupied countries, furthered angered him, as did the Labour government's blatantly pro-Arab policies after 1945. Knowledge of the extent of European Jewry's destruction, which came after the war, heightened his perception of Albion's perfidy. Even though he disapproved of the terrorist campaigns the Irgun and the Stern Gang waged against the British in Palestine after 1945 and worried about their negative impact on public opinion toward Jews in Britain, he could not bring himself to denounce them publicly because they were "so understandable."[26] The government, he wrote to his brother-in-law Harold Rubinstein in August 1948, was in "tacit agreement" with the Arab states to drive the Jews into the sea.[27]

The most compelling evidence of a Jewish subtext to Redcliffe's sympathetic account of Irish history is the explicit linkage he made between the Jews and the Irish in his *History and Social Influence of the Potato*. He connected them as outstanding examples of peoples, "the major part of whose long history is a record of suffering and tragedy."[28] In describing the English campaigns under Elizabeth to subdue the Irish, he compared English cruelty—the mass executions and torching of houses—to that of Hitler and the Germans. To those who wondered whether he was sketching conditions in Ireland "in too sombre a hue," he replied, "the picture of Hitler's Europe is probably no more tragic than was that of Ireland in 1603."[29] And, as with the German case, he noted that "men of noble character and high culture" (William Pelham, Philip Sidney, and Edmund Spenser, for example) participated and "were induced to behave as ravening monsters."[30] In recounting the potato's arrival in Ireland in the early seventeenth century—it offered the people "a sporting chance of warding off the famine and pestilence which hammered at their doors"—Redcliffe also evoked a Jewish precedent: "The fall of manna in the desert was not more opportune than the coming of the potato to Ireland."[31]

262 | *The Last Anglo-Jewish Gentleman*

Whether he was conscious of it or not, Redcliffe's linkage of Jewish and Irish history echoed a well-established theme in nationalist Irish discourse.[32] Writers and agitators noted repeatedly that the Irish and the Jews had suffered more than other peoples. Beyond evoking this shared victimization, they also analogized the history of the biblical Israelites, borrowing the themes of enslavement and redemption from slavery. They drew on the biblical exodus to narrate their hopes for Irish national liberation. This analogy was strong throughout the nineteenth century but weakened when flesh-and-blood Lithuanian Jews arrived in Ireland at the end of the century, for their unheroic presence—peddling clothing and dry goods—complicated and weakened the analogy.

Redcliffe's portrayal of the fate of the Irish was unrelentingly "dolorous," as one reviewer wrote,[33] and, at times, his effort to capture the depth of their degradation ran the risk, ironically, of dehumanizing them. For example, he frequently compared the living condition of the peasantry in the eighteenth and nineteenth centuries to that of animals. Thus, "In Ireland the potato had reduced the art of living to that of the beast in the field. At that level it is superfluous to talk of the customs and inclinations of the people, for their customs had been determined and their inclinations limited by an enforced subservience to a single source of food, the cultivation of which dictated the whole economy of their lives. At that level, they were but helpless victims of the social and political forces of their environment."[34]

Describing the domestic life of the peasantry, Redcliffe several times remarked that the hovels in which they lived also sheltered their livestock (if they were fortunate to own any), usually a pig or cow, and that humans and livestock were fed "out of the same cauldron, cooked on [an] open hearth of burning turves."[35] "What pride," he asked rhetorically, "could be taken in the home, or what call was there for ceremony, however elementary, to welcome a meal that was about to be shared with the pigs and the poultry and from the same cauldron?"[36] The physical degradation of the Irish, which the potato enabled, and their lack of hope for the future left them, he believed, sunk in lethargy and bereft of ambition. "The more the potato fulfilled the requirements of the household, the sooner was endeavor tamped down, and sloth and slovenliness exalted."[37]

According to Victorian political economists, the "laziness" of the Irish peasantry was the root of their distress. Redcliffe conceded the truth of the claim but framed it in a nonaccusatory way. The potato, he explained, required the minimum from its cultivators. The actual time the cottier spent in preparing the ground and in sowing, earthing up, and harvesting his crop totaled less than three months. He had no other urgent task, other than feeding his pig or cow and cutting his turf. This regime demanded neither "haste nor energy," while the impossibility of socioeconomic mobility stifled any thoughts of self-improvement. As he concluded, "If inertia in human affairs ranks as laziness, then the Irishman was lazy, and with good reason."[38] Still, even if the intent of this formulation was to undermine racial and other essentialist explanations of Irish behavior, it nonetheless unwittingly reinforced widely held beliefs about Irish character in the English imagination.

Redcliffe's presentation of Irish life was so bleak that Angela Carter wondered in her review whether he was suggesting that Irish peasants were victims without any agency whatsoever, incapable of achieving anything, whose only role in history was to be battered and beaten. She complained that even the well-intentioned Redcliffe could see "only a degraded peasantry sunk in sloth and intellectual darkness, locked in a hopeless symbiosis with the tuber." What he did not mention, she wrote, was that "these peasants retained their impenetrable language, concealed within it a vast and continually refreshed tradition of oral poetry, and continued to make music of a beauty and complexity to be found nowhere else in Western Europe except Spain."[39] Carter's concern—that Redcliffe stripped the dispossessed of all agency (and thus dignity)—was not a common theme in history writing when she reviewed the second edition of his book in 1986. Since then, however, the assumption that the victimized retain agency even in the depths of their victimhood has become a dogma in the academy. The need to identify and celebrate resistance—among slaves, Jews, peasants, workers, and other victimized groups—is strongly felt, certainly by those who hope to change the world. Whether Carter's complaint is valid, however, is another matter. It is possible that Redcliffe's more tragic understanding of Irish history before the twentieth century was closer to the mark.

5

The role that Redcliffe attributed to the potato in the suffering of the Irish became a matter of contention in the aftermath of the book's publication. Some reviewers, questioning Redcliffe's focus on the potato, offered

264 | *The Last Anglo-Jewish Gentleman*

alternative explanations for Ireland's troubles, emphasizing, for example, the explosive growth of Ireland's population, which doubled between 1780 and 1840; its land tenure system, which discouraged tenants from improving their holdings; and landlord rapacity (dispossessions, rent increases, and other impoverishing acts). In many cases, their criticism was the result of misunderstanding the exact role he assigned the potato, a misunderstanding for which he was, in part, responsible. For *The History and Social Influence of the Potato* is a long book, sometimes repetitious, often prolix, its argument woven into its thirty-plus chapters. The most egregious misunderstanding was the idea that Redcliffe had demonized the potato. The *Manchester Guardian* complained that he "had put the potato in the dock and made it responsible for almost half the social evils of the early nineteenth century." *Time* magazine was more reductionist, claiming that he made the potato "the root of most evil," while the *Washington Post* headlined a report of a lecture of his following the book's publication "British Scientist Says Potato Makes Irish Hate the English."[40] (What he said, in fact, was that the Irish who migrated to the United States as a result of the Great Famine carried with them a hatred of England that was alive one hundred years later.) Even those with knowledge of the subject, like the University of Chicago historian William H. McNeill, believed that Redcliffe occasionally exaggerated "the role of the potato in fixing the lines of social development."[41] The Irish historian K. H. Connell, as well, thought that he attributed to the potato greater influence than it really exercised, elevating it almost "to the position of constructor and source of power of the social system." While Connell admitted that the failure of the potato crop in the 1840s "shattered" Irish society, he believed that it was destined to collapse anyway by "the instability bred of its injustice."[42]

A careful reading of *The History and Social Influence of the Potato* shows that Redcliffe's treatment of Irish history was subtler than his critics charged. His argument was that the potato *enabled* the Great Famine by virtue of the dominant position it gained in the diet of the Irish peasantry. It won this place, among other reasons, because of its positive qualities: its nutritional value, its cheapness, its few demands on human labor, its high yield per acre, and the ease with which it can be made edible. It is no mystery why the Irish peasantry embraced it so completely in the seventeenth century and remained wed to it long after. For three centuries, Redcliffe wrote, the potato "both stabilized and perpetuated the misery of the Irish masses."[43] It played a twofold role: it was a cheap, easily cultivated, nutritious food and, at the same time, "a weapon ready forged for the exploitation of a weaker group." The more valuable and acceptable the potato was, "the richer nature's gift," the more effective it was as "an instrument of exploitation." That is, if the potato was sufficient to sustain the peasantry nutritionally, the landlords were able to ignore their degradation more generally. Human wisdom—or its absence—decided how "the richest of nature's gifts" was put to use, whether it was a blessing or a curse.[44]

Another way to frame the question of the role of the potato is to introduce the distinction between a necessary cause and a sufficient cause. The blight-induced crop failures of the 1840s would not have been catastrophic if the potato had not been the mainstay of Irish subsistence. The potato, then, was a necessary cause of the Great Famine. In this sense, Redcliffe did not overstate its importance. But he was careful to stress that the potato was not "the *fons et origo* of Ireland's misfortune."[45] The English conquest of Ireland robbed the Irish of their freedom long before the introduction of the potato. "An inequitable land system allied to an aggressive Protestant policy of Ascendancy" having degraded the Irish, they were receptive to this new, nutritious, cheap, and efficient foodstuff.[46] It then sustained a social structure divided by "an impermeable vertical wall, which cut the entire people into two unequal groups, between which there was little or no communication. On the one side stood the vast majority of the people, Celtic in blood, Erse in tradition and speech, Roman Catholic in faith; on the other, the English and Scottish settlers, with a wholly different tradition, speaking what to the majority of the Irish was a foreign tongue, and professing variants of the Protestant faith."[47]

In counties where social relations were less inequitable and strained and a diversity of crops cultivated, the population was not reduced to subsisting on the potato. In these more favorable circumstances, the potato became a welcome addition to a diversified diet. In itself, it was neither good nor bad.

6

The History and Social Influence of the Potato was well received, both in scholarly and in mass-circulation periodicals. Even specialists in Irish history who challenged Redcliffe's chronology of the diffusion of the potato in Ireland—he claimed it was rapid and they thought it was slower—were generous in their praise for his erudition and vision. His book has also stood the test of time, even gaining in stature. The first edition went out of print in

266 | *The Last Anglo-Jewish Gentleman*

the 1950s, and in the 1960s it was difficult to find a secondhand copy for less than £4.[48] (When first published, it cost 50 shillings—about £106 in current prices.) In 1970, Cambridge University Press reissued it. The text was unchanged, but the page size was smaller, the paper quality inferior, and the cost higher—£8. When the reissue appeared, P. M. Austin Bourke of the Irish Meteorological Service, the world expert on the fungus that causes potato blight, gave it an enthusiastic welcome in *Irish Historical Studies*. He wrote that he found it "almost as great a joy to re-read" as when he first came upon it years earlier. Duly noting where he thought Redcliffe had erred, he concluded with unqualified praise: the monumental stature of the book dwarfed every criticism. "For all its imperfections, the book remains a unique work of scholarship, by an author whose breadth of authoritative interest is unlikely to be matched in this field for a long time to come."[49]

The 1970 printing was exhausted in a matter of years. Acquiring a copy again required searches in "second-hand book stores and exorbitantly-priced book lists."[50] In 1985, Cambridge University Press brought out what they called "a revised impression" and what I have referred to as a "second edition." It appeared only in soft covers. Redcliffe had been dead for thirty years by this time, and so the text remained more or less the same. The editor, John G. Hawkes, professor emeritus of plant biology at the University of Birmingham, was a specialist in the taxonomy of wild potato species who had started his doctoral work at Cambridge and whom Redcliffe had mentored there. He did not rewrite any sections of the book but confined himself to correcting small textual errors and adding footnotes, many of them based on Redcliffe's manuscript notes, which had been deposited at Cambridge University Library, and on his interleaved copy of the book, which contained notes and corrections. Hawkes also wrote a useful introduction in which he indicated points in the book that more recent work had made out-of-date—for example, Redcliffe's chronology of Peruvian cultures. He also explained how the work of Irish researchers—P. M. Austin Bourke, Kenneth H. Connell, Cormac Ó Gráda, and others—had corrected Redcliffe's claim about the rapid adoption of the potato as the main item of the Irish diet. He concluded his introduction with the closing line of Austin Bourke's review of the 1970 reprinting, which I quoted above.[51] In 2020, Cambridge University Press was selling this edition for £40.99 in the United Kingdom and $54.99 in the United States.

The press sold 7,500 copies of the second edition from 1985 to 2019. It has no record of how many copies of the first edition it sold. The publisher

Michael Manson, a grandson-in-law of Redcliffe, estimated that the first edition sold, at a minimum, 7,700 copies. The basis for his calculation was that, if the second edition sold on average 220 copies a year, the first edition must have sold at least at the same rate—220 copies per annum over 35 years. Manson thus estimates lifetime sales have reached at least 18,000 copies.[52] By academic standards, Redcliffe's potato book was a bestseller.

Notes

1. John William Harshberger, *A Text-book of Mycology and Plant Pathology* (Philadelphia: P. Blakiston's Son, 1917), quoted in RNS, "Outlines of the History of Plant Virus Research," in *Agriculture in the Twentieth Century: Essays on Research, Practice, and Organization to be Presented to Sir Daniel Hall* (Oxford: Clarendon Press, 1939), 268.

2. On RNS's scientific research in the interwar years, see his "History of Plant Virus Research" and The *History and Social Influence of the Potato*, rev. ed. (Cambridge: Cambridge University Press, 1985), 174–84.

3. Councillor's File, MS 25/2/101, Special Collections, Bodleian Library, Oxford.

4. RNS, "Biographical Notes Prepared for the Records of the Royal Society," July 1947, Add. MS 8171/27, RNS CUL.

5. *The Times of India*, January 17, 1938.

6. RNS, "Boyhood and the Family Background," Add. MS 8171/27, RNS CUL.

7. RNS, "Boyhood and Family Background"; Edith Haggar to Joseph B. Skemp, December 31, 1945, and January 21, 1946, MS 25/2/151 and 25/2/154, SPSL Papers, Special Collections, Bodleian Library, Oxford.

8. RNS, *History of the Potato*, xxxiii.

9. Sidney Mintz, "Heroes Sung and Unsung," *Nutritional Anthropology* 25, no. 2 (2002): 5.

10. RNS, *History of the Potato*, xxxi.

11. Ibid., 338.

12. John Reader, *Potato: A History of the Propitious Esculent* (New Haven, CT: Yale University Press, 2008), 4.

13. RNS, *History of the Potato*, 7.

14. Ibid., 11.

15. Ibid., 5.

16. RNS, "Deformities and Mutilations of the Face as Depicted in the Chimu Pottery of Peru," *Journal of the Royal Anthropological Institute of Great Britain and Ireland* 69, no. 1 (1939): 109–22.

17. RNS, *History of the Potato*, 25.

18. Ibid., 33.

19. John G. Hawkes and Javier Francisco Ortega, "The Early History of the Potato in Europe," *Euphytica* 70, no. 1 (1993): 1–7; Reader, *Potato*, 88–91.

20. Angela Carter, "Potatoes and Point," *London Review of Books* 8, no. 9 (May 22, 1986): 11.

21. RNS, *History of the Potato*, 271.

22. Ibid., 245.

23. Ibid., 310.

268 | *The Last Anglo-Jewish Gentleman*

24. Ibid., 503.

25. Carter, "Potatoes and Point," 11.

26. RNS to Helen Melchior, March 3, 1948, Add. MS 8171/1/6, RNS CUL.

27. RNS to Harold Rubinstein, August 11, 1948, Add. MS 8171/1/6, RNS CUL.

28. RNS, *History of the Potato*, 190.

29. Ibid., 214.

30. Ibid., 211.

31. Ibid., 221.

32. Abby Bender, "British Israelites, Irish Israelites, and the Ends of an Analogy," in *Irish Questions and Jewish Questions: Crossovers in Culture*, ed. Aidan Beatty and Dan O'Brien (Syracuse, NY: Syracuse University Press, 2019), 17–30.

33. Carter, "Potatoes and Point," 11.

34. RNS, *History of the Potato*, 262.

35. Ibid., 215.

36. Ibid., 338.

37. Ibid., 343.

38. Ibid., 265.

39. Carter, "Potatoes and Point," 11.

40. *Manchester Guardian*, September 5, 1950; *Time*, September 18, 1950; *Washington Post*, September 5, 1950.

41. William H. McNeill, review of *The History and Social Influence of the Potato*, by Redcliffe Nathan Salaman, *Journal of Modern History* 22, no. 4 (December 1950): 366.

42. Kenneth H. Connell, review of *The History and Social Influence of the Potato*, by Redcliffe Nathan Salaman, *Economic History Review*, n.s., 3, no. 3 (1951): 390.

43. RNS, *History of the Potato*, 343.

44. Ibid., 600, 602.

45. Ibid., 338.

46. Ibid., 319.

47. Ibid., 335–36.

48. P. M. Austin Bourke, review of *The History and Social Influence of the Potato*, by Redcliffe Nathan Salaman, *Irish Historical Studies* 17, no. 67 (March 1971): 410.

49. Ibid., 412–13.

50. D. E. Yen, review of *The History and Social Influence of the Potato*, by Redcliffe Nathan Salaman, *Canberra Anthropology* 11, no. 1 (1988): 104.

51. John G. Hawkes, "Introduction to the Revised Impression," RNS, *History of the Potato*, xxi.

52. Michael Manson, email to the author, February 14, 2020.

12

COMMUNAL GADFLY

1

In the few years between the publication of his potato book in 1949 and his death in 1955, Redcliffe returned repeatedly to two topics that had occupied him for much of his life—the nature of Jewishness and the state of Anglo-Jewry. While he avoided publicly discussing the biological history of the Jews in the explicit way he had before World War II, the racial component in Jewishness was never absent in his thinking. In essays and lectures, he worked to clarify the respective roles of biology, religion, and nationalism in forming the character of the Jews. He also continued to champion the ideal of a latitudinarian Anglo-Judaism at a time when fundamentalism and intolerance were on the rise within the community. His opposition to the growing power of strict Orthodoxy transformed him, in turn, into a vigorous and often intolerant critic of the Anglo-Jewish religious establishment, especially in his Lucien Wolf Lecture of 1953. The furor that the lecture created drained him emotionally and sapped his strength. He changed in another way in the years before his death. He shed some of the reserve and propriety that he inherited from his Victorian upbringing. In particular, he came to enjoy the visits to Barley of his many grandchildren, romping about with them on the floor, something he never did with any of his children, and taking them on walks in the countryside.

2

As we saw, race is absent as a category of analysis in *The History and Social Influence of the Potato*. Nonetheless, during the decade Redcliffe was at work on the book, he continued to believe that biological descent influenced the fate of persons and peoples. In two essays on the Jewish Fellows of the

Royal Society, he addressed and offered an explanation for the incidence ("overrepresentation" in popular parlance) of Jews in the Royal Society.[1] The first, based on a lecture he delivered to the Jewish Historical Society of England on December 15, 1947, opened with a reaffirmation of an assumption that guided all his writing about Jews: it was a "travesty of truth" to think that the Jewish community was merely a group of persons with common religious beliefs and practices who differed from their fellow citizens in no other way. Avoiding the term *race*, he chose to describe Jews as "a group united by a common ancestry and a long tradition of suffering, but divided more or less acutely by divergent variations of a basic Judaistic faith."[2] He restated this pillar of his thinking at the outset of the article because, in tallying the number of Jewish Fellows, he included all those with two Jewish parents regardless of whether they (the Fellows) identified with the Jewish community in any way. His concern was not their religious outlook but rather their "intellectual powers" and the relation of their powers to the community in which they and their forbears were raised. He thus included Benjamin Disraeli and a host of others who had divorced themselves from Judaism. (In all, they numbered about one-third of those he designated as Jewish.) In the eighteenth and nineteenth centuries, the number of Jews among the Fellows was not striking. In the period 1900 to 1947, however, forty-nine Jewish Fellows were elected, eighteen more than the total elected between 1723 and 1900 and three and a half times as many as those elected in the previous fifty-two years. In this period, Jews were more than 5 percent of the Fellows, at least five times as many as their proportion in the population.[3]

For Redcliffe, the figures revealed "a phenomenon so striking and provocative" that it demanded close investigation.[4] His explanation, however, was not biological, which we might have expected, but historical and sociological in the main. The rise in the number of Jewish Fellows was a consequence of the influx of talented refugees from Nazism and of the anglicization of the children from the mass migration from Eastern Europe and their exposure to Western scientific education. For centuries, he argued, the Jews of Europe had satisfied "their acute intellectual thirst" at "the subtle waters of the Talmud and Cabbala" (without, however, explaining the origins of this thirst). These texts "sharpened and refined the students' minds to a degree scarcely equaled by any other discipline." With the dissolution of the traditional community in the age of emancipation, there was "a veritable army of young men with highly trained minds waiting, ready and eager, to absorb the new learning." Brandishing the new weapons of Western scholarship, they fought their way to its highest citadels.[5]

Redcliffe's explanation of Jewish scientific achievement in the twentieth century was not novel. It was and remains commonplace in popular and academic books that seek to explain the overrepresentation of Jews in elite circles, such as lists of Nobel Prize winners and captains of commerce and finance. Its appeal is obvious: it explains the phenomenon of Jewish achievement in a nonbiological way that links that achievement with specific developments in Jewish history. Long after Redcliffe addressed it, this question—why are Jews overrepresented in cultural, scientific, and economic life in the modern world?—continues to generate speculation.

Toward the end of the article, however, without acknowledging the move, Redcliffe resurrected biological inheritance as a determinant of Jewish achievement. After noting that the number of Jewish Nobel Laureates was much greater than the Jewish share of the population, he added that there was "a definite bias" in the way in which Jewish "genius" exhibited itself. Between 1901 and 1946, he noted, Jews won 10 percent of the prizes in physics and chemistry and 14 percent of those in medicine but only 2 percent of those in literature. The figures led him to speculate that there were "certain innate or inherited paths along which Jewish genius tends to develop." Jews excelled in mathematics and in the interpretation of classical music and as "the greatest dreamers and the most profound teachers of mankind" (Moses and Marx, for example) but were less distinguished in the realms of literature and art than non-Jews.[6] However much the latter assertion reflects Redcliffe's own limited knowledge of art and literature outside the English-speaking world, it does testify to the persistence of his faith in the inheritability of creativity and intelligence.

Redcliffe concluded his first essay on an elegiac note: in the wake of World War II, the only asset left to European Jews, whom the Germans had stripped of homes, possessions, and human rights, was "this peculiarity of intellectual development." There was a danger, however, that this asset too could be lost. If through intermarriage the Jews let themselves melt into the mass of people among whom they lived, they would lose their distinctive inheritance. English Jewry, for example, could no longer expect reinvigoration from immigration from Central and Eastern Europe. It was living on its intellectual and spiritual capital, "a fund which is steadily being drained away by intermarriage." The only way to preserve the distinctive distribution of intellect among the Jewish people for the benefit of themselves and all mankind was the establishment of "a Jewish Reserve—a homeland where this precious gift may be conserved."[7] He delivered this lecture, with its plea for the creation of "a Jewish Reserve," six months before the establishment of the State of Israel.

In December 1949, Redcliffe returned to the topic of Jews in the Royal Society in a brief essay in the society's *Notes and Records*. Its subtitle, "A Problem in Ecology," suggested a nonracial approach to understanding the incidence of Jewish Fellows, and he repeated his earlier argument that over the centuries the regimen of Talmudic study had prepared Jews to distinguish themselves in mathematics and the sciences. But here again, as before, he introduced the idea that "genetic factors" may have played a part, and he reintroduced the claim, which he had made before the war, that traditional Jewish marriage practices "favoured the selection and survival of hereditary tendencies towards higher intellectual attainment."[8] In the isolated Jewish communities of Eastern Europe before World War I, where hygiene was lacking, poverty endemic, and overcrowding the rule, only the physically sound survived. In these conditions, there was also little room for "the simple-minded" and "the intellectually feeble." Brains trumped muscle, intelligence trumped money. Thus, relatively well-off fathers married their daughters to the ablest Talmud students, whom they agreed to support for several years. "The eugenic capital unconsciously acquired as a result of centuries of suffering . . . remained a hidden asset."[9] Those who inherited it later triumphed as Fellows of the Royal Society, Nobel Laureates, and titans of industry. As in 1947, he concluded with the observation that European Jewry, three-quarters of whom Hitler had murdered, was now exhausted and that the hopes of the Jewish people for renewed vigor were now centered on the Land of Israel.

The essays were not Redcliffe's last word on the role of race in the making of the Jews. In December 1950, he addressed the Anglo-Jewish Association on the theme "The Jews—Race, Nation, Religion" and invoked a new metaphor to describe the links among the three elements. The Jews were like a Russian troika, drawn, animated, and given life by the three horses of race, nation, and religion. In regard to the first, race, he asserted, as he had for decades, that the Jews were a mix of three distinct historic peoples. But, apparently reluctant to call them a race, he labeled them instead "an inbreeding family," one that had continually reshuffled the genetic counters that had come together early in its history. The Jews throughout the world were physically related to each other, sharing a recognizable group of facial and other features. Thus, "this tie of blood" was "the basis and enduring bond" that cemented together the scattered Jewish people. Race, in other words, was "the indispensable and central member of the troika."[10]

Redcliffe's weakened but lasting commitment to the notion of race was overdetermined. First, it owed something to the length of his connection to it. Having embraced the notion as a young man and having devoted his scientific career to studying the inheritance of characteristics (in potatoes, to be sure), Redcliffe was emotionally incapable of jettisoning biology as an analytical category in discussing the Jews. He no longer vested the concept of race with the explanatory power that he had earlier, but he never relinquished it altogether. Second, as the historian Dan Stone suggests, without biology, he lacked a firm foundation to undergird his sense of Jewishness. As a late adolescent, he had rejected the supernaturalism of traditional Judaism and, whereas other secular Jews were able to replace their lost faith with the bonds of ethnicity, nation, or cultural inheritance (or some combination thereof), he was unable to do so. In Stone's words: "Without his racial self-identification, there would have been nothing left, in his eyes, to distinguish him and the Jews in general from the rest of the British population." And finally, Stone also suggests, Redcliffe did not keep abreast of developments in the field of genetics. On the eve of the identification of the molecular structure of DNA by Francis Crick and James Watson in Cambridge in 1953, he remained a Mendelian, regarding Jewishness as a Mendelian trait. His ideas about the inheritance of traits were still rooted in the breeding of potatoes, work that had occupied him for four decades and earned him scientific recognition.[11]

3

In the last five years of his life, Redcliffe was also more openly critical of Orthodox Judaism than he had been previously. Some of it may have been due to age. He was seventy-five in 1949, and perhaps crotchetier than earlier. But he was also provoked by changes in the religious tone of the British Jewish community. The rule of the old notability was over. High death duties and income tax had eliminated that pool of young men of ability and wealth who in earlier generations had devoted themselves to communal affairs. Well-to-do East European Jews, who were more likely to be observant than Jews whose families had lived in Britain for several generations, were becoming more visible in positions of influence and power. Zionists

274 | *The Last Anglo-Jewish Gentleman*

gained control of the Board of Deputies during World War II. Robert Waley Cohen died in 1952, and while his two immediate successors as president of the United Synagogue, Frank Samuel and Ewen Montagu, shared his background, Montagu's successor in 1962 was the self-made retail magnate Isaac Wolfson, the first fully observant Orthodox Jew and the first East European Jew to head that institution in the twentieth century. In addition to an increase in the number of observant Jews in leadership positions in the postwar period, the number of those among the observant who were strictly Orthodox also increased. Their insistence on imposing more rigorous standards pushed mainstream Orthodoxy to the right. Centrist or mainstream Orthodox rabbis, graduates of Jews' College, themselves called for more exacting standards, not wishing to be outflanked by the ultra-Orthodox. This shift to the right fed Redcliffe's anti-Orthodox criticism in the postwar period and sharpened its tone.

One pillar of the new Orthodox outlook in particular infuriated him: its obsession with the laws of *kashrut*, including the procedures for slaughtering animals in accordance with Jewish law (*halakhah*). Redcliffe was no enemy of ritual and observance per se. In his talk to the Anglo-Jewish Association in 1951, he described the Sabbath (that is, "a sanely observed Sabbath") as the most valuable gift Judaism had given to the world and the mounting of a *mezuzah* at the doorpost of the house "a practice of much beauty." In fact, he was critical of Britain's rabbis for rarely referring to the practice, blaming them in effect for its decline. Moreover, he remained a member of the Orthodox New West End Synagogue, and on the infrequent occasions he was present, "it was in the main to bathe afresh in the traditional atmosphere which I knew in my youth. It is to feel myself once more a mere Jew amongst my fellow Jews and to hear the prayers chanted as they have been for so many centuries."[12] He admitted that the appeal of the service was sentimental and that he did not care what the prayers meant. The traditional melodies were soothing, and being there represented a return to the peaceful, satisfying, friendly days of his childhood.

But "the fungus-like overgrowth of Kashruth" was another matter. While he himself did not eat pork, an abstention that led some in the younger generation to consider him highly Orthodox and old-fashioned, he thought that the new exaggerated emphasis on *kashrut* was turning Judaism into "a religion of the stomach rather than the heart." In his lecture to the Anglo-Jewish Association, he blamed "the ecclesiastical mind" for this trend, for thinking that *kashrut* was "the most powerful weapon at their disposal for maintaining cohesion within the community." The rabbis had transformed it into a burdensome and soulless imposition, so much so that the majority of educated Jews in the country had abandoned Jewish practice altogether. (He may have been correct.) Like the leaders of Reform and Liberal Judaism, he pointed out that there was no positive correlation between the observance of *kashrut* and ethical behavior.[13]

When the slaughter of animals in accordance with *halakhah* became a public rather than an intracommunal issue in the postwar years, he was drawn even further into the battles over *kashrut*. Understanding the issue requires some context. While the Hebrew Bible enumerates animals that Jews are permitted and forbidden to eat, the Talmud elaborates these lists and, in addition, requires that permitted animals be slaughtered in a prescribed manner. The main features of these requirements are that a highly trained pious Jew (*shohet*), using a razor-sharp, perfectly smooth, nick-free knife, perform the act of slaughtering, that he cut both the windpipe (trachea) and the food pipe (esophagus) in one quick motion, without delay or pause, and that he then inspect the beast, especially its lungs, for physical blemishes and pathological defects. If present, they render the meat unfit for Jewish consumption. Because the flesh and organs of the animal must not be bruised or otherwise injured, rabbinic authorities do not permit the animal to be stunned before its slaughter.

Before the nineteenth century, Christians took little interest in the Jewish method of slaughter. Their attitude changed across Europe and in North America in the modern period with the secularization of hostility to Jews and the rise of the animal welfare movement. In Britain, the first signs of Christian criticism appeared in the 1850s, but there was no institutional opposition until the 1880s, when the Royal Society for the Prevention of Cruelty to Animals (RSPCA) began to attack the method. Although expressive of concern about the mistreatment of animals, these protests were rooted in ignorance about *shehitah* and animal physiology and, most critically, in hoary anti-Jewish sentiments. Christian critics consistently framed their case around the well-established trope of Jewish cruelty and bloodthirstiness. They contrasted Christian humanitarianism to innate Jewish cruelty. They represented the Jewish method of slaughter as barbarous, abnormal, and extraordinary, while considering the Christian method as normal and ordinary. There was humane slaughter and then there was the Jewish mode.[14] *Shehitah*'s most intemperate opponents associated it with the blood libel and ritual circumcision and, thus, by extension, with fears of castration by stony-hearted, knife-wielding, revenge-seeking father figures. In the 1910s, 1920s, and 1930s, animal welfare advocates in Parliament attempted to include *shehitah* in bills requiring stunning before slaughter, but Jewish lobbying efforts succeeded in excluding the Jewish and Muslim methods from their provisions. *Shehitah*'s opponents, the *Jewish Chronicle* charged in 1914, were "far less imbued with the care for or the love of animals than with the desire to harm our people."[15]

Because opposition to *shehitah* was shot through with antisemitism, Jews across the religious spectrum, Orthodox and Reform alike, united in its defense. For the latter, who observed the dietary laws only in part or not at all, defending *shehitah* was equivalent to defending religious liberty and combating antisemitism. Before the 1940s, Redcliffe was a strong defender of the Jewish method of slaughter. As a physician and a scientist, he had believed that a swift, sure cut was more humane than the uncertainties of the methods then used for stunning. After watching both Jewish and non-Jewish slaughterers at work in Chicago in 1911, he had written to Nina that "the kosher [method] was the better."[16] But when electrical stunning became available in the 1930s, he had reconsidered his position. In 1932 and 1933, he had discussed scientific data on stunning with Chief Rabbi Joseph Hertz, at the latter's request. He had told Hertz that electrical stunning, unlike more primitive methods, produced immediate insensibility but left the animal fully alive, a requirement of *halakhah*. According to Redcliffe, Hertz had replied, "If you can prove to me that by electric stunning no rupture of blood vessels, not even of the minutest capillary, and no destruction of any organ or structure results, I shall be satisfied." If Redcliffe quoted him accurately, Hertz was being remarkably open-minded. In any case, Redcliffe had responded that this could not be proven, especially in regard to minute capillaries, but that the time was ripe for a "reconsideration" of *shehitah*; otherwise, there would be "trouble," that is, antisemites would exploit the issue.[17] In 1934, Herbert Samuel, then leader of the parliamentary Liberal party, had also warned the chief rabbi that "at any time there might arise a strong agitation in this country with regard to Shechita" and had advised him "to forestall such an eventuality" by pushing ahead with an investigation of the compatibility of electric stunning with Jewish law.[18]

The fear that antisemites would exploit the stunning issue had been a reasonable one. The RSPCA, for example, had suggested to the Board of Deputies in June 1939 that, if the Jews discarded their method of slaughter, their relations with other Britons would improve.[19] During the war, attacks on *shehitah* as a cruel, primitive, un-English practice continued. In a debate on antisemitism in the *News Chronicle* in 1943, opposition to *shehitah* featured prominently in letters that were hostile to Jews, and, in a symposium at the end of the war, the left-wing journalist Hamilton Fyfe urged Jews to "give up their kosher meat and their worship of a bloodthirsty, revengeful anthropomorphic deity" and "melt into the population"—just as Scots in England had abandoned their porridge and Presbyterianism.[20]

After the war, when Redcliffe returned to the subject of the dietary laws, another issue as well was provoking hostility to Jews. In postwar Palestine, right-wing Zionist paramilitaries, infuriated by the government's renewed hostility to the establishment of a Jewish state and incensed by British indifference to the plight of survivors of Nazism, mounted a campaign of terror to drive the government to abandon the Mandate. Between May 1945 and October 1947, the Irgun and the Stern Gang killed 127 members of British security forces and wounded another 331.[21] As violence escalated in Palestine, hostility to Jews in Britain did as well. The Irgun's bombing of the King David Hotel in Jerusalem in July 1946, noted the *Jewish Chronicle*, allowed British antisemitism to flourish, providing "a pretext for . . . a sudden spate of letters—mostly anonymous or pseudonymous—which, not satisfied to denounce the outrages and their perpetrators, wander off into the usual brutalities of the anti-semite."[22]

In October 1946, an Irgun bomb wrecked the British embassy in Rome. Writing in *Commentary* in May 1947, Chaim Raphael captured the domestic impact of this anti-British campaign: "Day after day, the ordinary Briton reads in his newspaper and hears over the radio that British forces—their own sons and brothers—have been attacked (or killed) by Jews or are in active operation against them."[23] Then, in spring 1947, the Stern Gang took its terror campaign to London, planting bombs at a club for servicemen and students from the West Indies and Africa and at the Colonial Office (only the latter was found before it detonated). In early June, the same group sent eleven letter bombs to leading political figures, all of which were discovered before inflicting any damage. And in late June, when a considerable amount of gelignite and five hundred detonators were stolen from two quarries near Exeter, the police began searching for two "foreign-looking" Jews who were seen in the vicinity. Hostility to British Jews boiled over in early August 1947, following the Irgun's hanging of two British sergeants in an orange grove near Netanya (in retaliation for the British hanging of three Irgun fighters in Acre prison). For four days, anti-Jewish rioters in Liverpool, Manchester,

278 | *The Last Anglo-Jewish Gentleman*

and Glasgow attacked synagogues, Jewish-owned businesses, and Jewish passersby. There were attacks in nine other cities and throughout London.[24]

That same year, animal-welfare groups launched a new anti-*shehitah* campaign, perhaps intending to exploit the hostility generated by Jewish terrorist activities. Then, in January 1948, the Council of Justice to Animals and Humane Slaughter circulated a leaflet condemning the Jewish method of slaughter to the press, members of Parliament, and all local authorities in England and Wales. The next year, questions were asked in the House of Commons and an anti-*shehitah* motion was introduced in the House of Lords. Whether intentional or not, the two sources of hostility fed each other: Jews in Palestine and Jews at home were viewed as cruel, bloodthirsty killers. The link between the two did not escape the attention of English Jews. After the appearance of letters critical of *shehitah* in his local newspaper in March 1948, two months before Britain's withdrawal from Palestine, Redcliffe wrote to a member of the London Bet Din, "The country is in a mood which is, to say the least of it, extremely irritable as far as Jewish matters are concerned."[25]

The volume of the anti-*shehitah* clamor and the mood of the country alarmed Redcliffe and, in tandem with his animosity to the new Orthodox assertiveness, led him to seek changes in the Jewish method of slaughter. He met in 1948 with the new chief rabbi, Israel Brodie, Elsley Zeitlin, a barrister and chair of the *shehitah* committee of the Board of Deputies, and Rabbi Solomon D. Sassoon, a bibliophile and Hebrew scholar, to convince them of the need for change, but he made no headway. In spring 1950, he again met with communal leaders, including Dr. Abraham Cohen, president of the Board of Deputies; Adolf G. Brotman, executive secretary of the board, Zeitlin, and officials of the Board of Shechita—to no avail. In May of that year, he privately published a five-page pamphlet, *Observations on Shechita*, which he circulated to communal leaders. In that tract, after expressing pride that Jewish law had always evinced compassion toward animals, he declared that "a rigid and unquestioning compliance with mediaeval custom" was "bringing our community into disrepute" and was "disheartening the more enlightened thinkers amongst our own people." He recounted his public support of *shehitah* before the advent of electrical stunning, when he believed it "could hold its own." Now, with the availability of a reliable, compassionate form of stunning, it was time to reconsider the Jewish method. He concluded on an uncharacteristically melodramatic note, asking, "Would you prefer to have your throat cut when you are conscious, or unconscious?"[26] (His old friend Charles Singer upbraided him for this remark, reminding him that animals had no idea of the nature of death. They might feel fear, but not the fear of death. If so, he concluded, what did it matter if they felt fear for three seconds or seven seconds?)[27]

Redcliffe's campaign to introduce electrical stunning was quixotic. It revealed how distant he was from the Orthodox camp, how poorly he understood their sentiments and values, and, perhaps, how much he exaggerated his own powers of persuasion. Most of those to whom he sent the booklet failed to acknowledge even receiving it. The only communal leader who showed any interest was the rabbinic head (*haham*) of the Spanish and Portuguese congregation Solomon Gaon, whose outlook in general was more liberal than that of his Ashkenazi counterparts.[28] Redcliffe persisted, however. In late May, soon after publication of the pamphlet, he met with Waley Cohen, still president of the United Synagogue, and Cohen and Brotman from the Board of Deputies. While Waley Cohen was not an observant Jew—despite heading Britain's largest Orthodox body—he was incensed about the circulation of the pamphlet and wanted it withdrawn. His reason was strategic. The pamphlet inflicted "a most unfair stab in the back to Judaism and an entirely unjustified support to that section of 'public opinion' which has always been, is still and always will be anxious to create ill-feeling towards Jews." Waley Cohen, who usually saw eye to eye with Redcliffe, viewed the pamphlet as an attack on the Jewish community. It put his old friend "in the same camp as the anti-semitic gutter press," offering encouragement to the enemies of the Jews.[29] The May meeting, which began pleasantly enough, with Waley Cohen and Redcliffe meeting on the street and walking arm in arm, rapidly degenerated. Waley Cohen began criticizing the pamphlet, "at first quietly, then more warmly." Redcliffe stood his ground while Waley Cohen "worked himself up into a terrible state, . . . lost control of himself and could hardly get to his feet." Redcliffe feared that Waley Cohen was going to "collapse" at any moment— it was "the most painful scene I have ever witnessed," he later recalled. When Waley Cohen suffered a heart attack the following year, Redcliffe did not visit him, lest the subject of *shehitah* arise and an enraged Waley Cohen suffer another attack.[30]

Waley Cohen's fury is striking. He did not observe *kashrut*, "nor cared a damn about it" (Redcliffe's words); of Judaism, he "understood nil."[31] According to Waley Cohen's son Bernard, he did not even know what *shehitah* meant. The reason that he turned on Redcliffe on this occasion was that he saw any attack, whatever its source, on a Jewish practice that was already the target of antisemites as lending support to the enemy. It is ironic then that what infuriated him—the fear of strengthening antisemitism—was the same concern that had moved Redcliffe to write the pamphlet in the first place. For Redcliffe, the introduction of stunning was not an animal welfare issue but a way to deny critics of the Jews an issue that they had been exploiting for decades. A country gentleman who had hunted when he was younger, he took no interest in animal welfare issues other than this. Waley Cohen was also motivated by another concern that at one time had been important to Redcliffe. Respecting tradition qua tradition (for social and cultural rather than theological reasons), he thought it critical to defend and support long-established mainstream communal institutions, like the United Synagogue and the chief rabbinate. In his mind, if *shehitah* was integral to establishment Judaism, then it required defending. Waley Cohen knew, Redcliffe wrote, that *kashrut* was "one of the most important supporting pillars of the Jewish façade" of communal Orthodoxy. "His general outlook was to keep up a clean, strong-looking façade and not worry too much about what happened behind it."[32] In this sense, both men were products of Victorian Anglo-Judaism—tolerant of heterodoxy, latitudinarian, devoted to respectability and civility—although Redcliffe was increasingly less so.

After the tumultuous meeting with Waley Cohen, Redcliffe agreed to withhold his pamphlet from further circulation if the Board of Deputies would address the *shehitah* issue—which, however, it failed to do. (In truth, it had no authority to act, since *shehitah* is a matter of religious law and subject to rabbinic, not lay, regulation.) He was becoming an increasing irritant in the eye of the religious establishment. In spring 1952, when he was invited to visit a religious Zionist training farm in Essex, he asked, before accepting, for a guarantee that Rabbi Alexander Altmann, a vice president of the organization that sponsored the farm, would not harangue him about his views on *shehitah*.[33] In early 1953, Redcliffe notified the board that, having kept his part of the bargain, he was now prepared to distribute the booklet. His letter jolted the board into action. It began to discuss with him and the Universities Federation for Animal Welfare a scientific investigation of electrical stunning. While this matter was under consideration, Redcliffe delivered the Lucien Wolf Memorial Lecture, which further enflamed his relations with the religious establishment.

Figure 12.1. Redcliffe Salaman (sometime after World War II). Collection of the author.

4

In July 1952, the council of the Jewish Historical Society of England invited Redcliffe to deliver the seventeenth Lucien Wolf Memorial Lecture the following spring. He was a natural choice, a scholarly veteran of communal service who had served as the society's president (1920–1922). Moreover, as he later told his audience, he was "old enough to remember the hey-day of the Lucien Wolf epoch and the part he played in steering the Community thorough the late Victorian and Edwardian times."[34] He chose for his subject the transformation of Anglo-Jewish life in the first half of the twentieth century, with a focus in particular on shifts in religious behavior to which he was eye witness. His title—*Whither Lucien Wolf's Anglo-Jewish*

Community?—was wistful in tone, expressing a sense of loss for a system of communal government and religious latitudinarianism that was no more. He knew beforehand that what he would say would be provocative, for he wrote to the historian Albert M. Hyamson, soon after receiving the invitation, that his choice of subject was "dangerous."[35] In the end, it ruffled feathers more than he could have imagined.

The date of the lecture was May 18, 1953; the venue, the hall of the West London Synagogue of British Jews, the "cathedral" synagogue of Reform Judaism in England. Among the eighty or so persons present[36] were the president of the society, Bertram B. Benas, a Liverpool barrister; its secretary, Arthur Barnett, minister of the Western Synagogue; and Chief Rabbi Israel Brodie, who was to propose a vote of thanks to the lecturer.

Redcliffe's lecture was a groundbreaking contribution to the history of British Jewry. It was the first description of the system by which the old Anglo-Jewish notability, of which he was one of the last representatives, governed the community before World War II, and of the kind of Judaism—its tone and its priorities—that they represented and fostered. His approach was analytical on the whole and only polemical here and there. But it was also frank, offering few consolations to those seeking inspiration and uplift. He described the English-born section of the community as "clusters of families, rather than groups selected on a basis of religious observance or belief." They took as their model the standards of English gentility, esteeming "manners, good taste, tolerance, ease and elegance above specialized learning." If some held heretical views, few advanced them publicly: "In the community at large there was, if not religious peace, at least an atmosphere of kindly make-believe and gentlemanly behaviour which for long had been no inadequate substitute. That it covered much indifference and more ignorance, distressed neither leaders nor led. A sense of brotherhood and the acceptance of collective responsibility was then, as now, a firmer bond than religion in our time is ever likely to be."[37]

The years before World War I were "days of security at home and the god of respectability reigned supreme." During the long tenure of Chief Rabbis Nathan Adler and Hermann Adler, relaxed Orthodoxy dominated the scene. Their "character, secular learning and dignified bearing" raised them to the social level of archbishops and cardinals, or so some English Jews believed. "Of them it might be said that if their crest was 'an eagle [*Adler*, in German] stirring up a nest,' their motto might have been 'let sleeping dogs lie.'"[38]

Redcliffe's characterization of the reign of the Adlers, dripping at times with sarcasm, rattled some in his audience. It is a characterization, however, that many historians of Anglo-Jewry accept as an accurate description of the centrist Orthodoxy of the period. Most are probably not aware of its origins in the Lucien Wolf Lecture of 1953. At the time, it was provocative, and for some historians, usually Orthodox in their own commitments, it remains so. These historians take umbrage at descriptions of the Adlers that suggest that they were more flexible than Chief Rabbis Israel Brodie, Immanuel Jacobovits, and Jonathan Sachs, who held office from 1948 to 2013. Their investment in the defense of Orthodoxy in their own time, especially the United Synagogue and the chief rabbinate, led them to construct an unbroken line of unswerving Torah-true Judaism from Nathan Adler to Jonathan Sachs. Derek Taylor's hagiographic biographies of Nathan Adler and Joseph Hertz and Benjamin Elton's more scholarly account of Britain's chief rabbis from 1880 to 1970 are examples of this apologetic genre.[39]

When Redcliffe next discussed shifts in religious behavior, including observance of the dietary laws, in the previous half-century, he entered even more sensitive territory. He acknowledged that in his youth the observance of the dietary laws had functioned as "a bond of union whilst not hindering intercommunal relations." But now, he noted, the bond had declined. In accounting for the decline, he offered several reasons, including the observation that "with the enforcement of humane methods of slaughter the Jewish method no longer has, from this point of view, its former unique primacy." While it is doubtful that more humane slaughtering laws caused British Jews to eat unkosher meat—this linkage tells us more about Redcliffe's preoccupations than about British Jewry's priorities—the brief mention of *shehitah* caused him much aggravation in the aftermath of the lecture, as we will see further on. He even suggested that "a much simplified formulation" of the dietary laws might be designed to stimulate Jewish consciousness in the Diaspora.[40] In tandem with *kashrut*, he also took up the decline in Sabbath observance. At the turn of the century, the Friday-night family dinner, with "the beauty of its ceremonies," was among the strongest bonds uniting those sections of the anglicized community who were neither "ostentatiously orthodox nor irritatingly schismatic." In his circles, even the "linkest" of the "link" [the laxest of the lax] would not be seen in a London theater on a Friday night. He attributed the decline in large part to economic mobility, Anglicization, and the automobile. In Lucien Wolf's day, he recalled, a mere handful of wealthy Jews owned country houses.

284 | *The Last Anglo-Jewish Gentleman*

Even those who were able to afford one saw it as a non-Jewish luxury. "Since then, with the aid of the motor car, the country house, the rural cottage, the riverside bungalow, the weekend visit to the seaside has become a habit with a large and increasing section of the general as well as the Jewish community, and thus strikes at the heart of Jewish observance."[41]

Associated with the decline in observance, Redcliffe continued, was "the change which has overtaken the relation between the Community and its religious leaders." Before World War I, religious leaders (and lay leaders as well) were not "unduly concerned with the attitude of the individual towards religious observance or belief." As secularism and apathy eroded Jewish practice in the interwar years and beyond, conservative groups within the community reacted by demanding a return to the (often imagined) traditional discipline of earlier generations. They represented a minority of British Jews, but they were vocal and assertive. Moreover, mainstream Orthodox rabbis, fearful of being seen as insufficiently Orthodox and afraid of antagonizing the ultra-Orthodox, who were often foreign-born and lacked a secular education, yielded to many of their demands—even at the cost of offending the general public—a dynamic that continues to this day. Redcliffe then listed policies and proposals that he felt were out of harmony with the spiritual aspirations of cultured Jews: the plan to create a bureau to certify garments free of *shatnez* (cloth made with a mixture of wool and linen, whose wearing *halakhah* forbids); the imposition of impossible standards on Christians wishing to convert to Judaism; the refusal to allow newly established Liberal synagogues to perform state-recognized marriages; the ban on cremation, forcing the family of the deceased to inter his or her ashes in a coffin and masquerade them as a corpse in order to bury them in a Jewish cemetery; the ban on the sale of even porged hindquarters in kosher butcher shops;[42] and the exclusion of children from United Synagogue religious classes if their mothers were not halachically Jewish.[43]

At the end of his lecture, Redcliffe turned to what he deemed "the most destructive force" in Anglo-Jewry—intermarriage—not a topic that received much serious discussion in the 1950s. To be sure, it was occasionally denounced from the pulpit, but there was no serious consideration of its extent and its causes. One reason for its neglect was undoubtedly its low rate of incidence *overall*. The children of immigrants, the overwhelming majority of Jews who were marrying at the time, were marrying other Jews. By virtue of their upbringing and their limited integration into non-Jewish social circles, they were not candidates for intermarriage. But in the highly anglicized social stratum to which Redcliffe belonged, among comfortably well-off families whose ancestors had come to Britain one or two centuries earlier, that was no longer true. He drew attention to the almost complete absorption of Sephardi families who had come to England in the seventeenth and early eighteenth centuries and the Ashkenazi families who had come in the eighteenth and early nineteenth centuries. Even the Russo-Polish wave showed "signs in places of wearing thin." There were no more demographic reservoirs to reinforce the losses the older families were experiencing, and, thus, he bleakly concluded that "we may foresee our own near demise in a not very distant future."[44] Anglo-Jewry was past its prime and on the decline.

In retrospect, Redcliffe's prognosis was both right and wrong. He was correct that, over time, toleration, integration, and secularization erode Jewish attachments (not just in Britain, but everywhere). By the end of the twentieth century, it was universally acknowledged that intermarriage was a threat to the future of Anglo-Jewry, for by this time the forces that eroded Jewish cohesion among the descendants of the earliest waves of migration were at work among the descendants of the East European wave. What he did not foresee was the resurgence of strict Orthodoxy in the late twentieth century, itself part of a worldwide explosion of fundamentalist forms of religion more generally, and the astoundingly high birthrate among the most observant sections of the community. He also did not foresee how Jewish refugees from the Middle East and North Africa would strengthen the declining non-Ashkenazi element of the community.

Intermarriage for Redcliffe was not an abstract issue. Three of his siblings had married out, Michel, Clement (though Clement's wife underwent a pro forma Reform conversion), and Louise (b. 1876). While four of his five children had married within the fold, his daughter Ruth had not. She had met Robert Collet, her future husband, when he was at school at Bedales with her brothers Arthur and Raphael and began to spend parts of the school holidays with them at Barley. After he had known her for several years as the sister of his friends, he began to notice her in a different way. When he was twenty-six and she twenty-two, they began an affair. In 1932, thinking she was pregnant (it turned out she was not), they ran off to Paris, where they married quietly in the British Consulate, sparing Redcliffe the embarrassment of an interfaith wedding in England. As a son-in-law, Collet had three strikes against him in Redcliffe's eyes: he was not Jewish; he loved men, perhaps more than women; and he was a lackluster breadwinner. In

286 | *The Last Anglo-Jewish Gentleman*

1935, Ruth and her husband returned to London. While Redcliffe made the best of it, others in his circle shunned them, including Herbert and Beatrice Samuel, whose daughter Nancy was married to Redcliffe's son Arthur. The Samuels never invited the couple to their home.[45] Among his many nieces and nephews, intermarriage was common; in the next generation, among his grandchildren and grandnieces and -nephews even more common. Or, as he told the Anglo-Jewish Association in 1951, "To-day a greater number of the younger generation of both sexes of my acquaintance marry non-Jews rather than Jews."[46] So when Redcliffe spoke about intermarriage, he did so as a close observer.

But let us return to the Lucien Wolf Lecture. There was much in it to offend Chief Rabbi Brodie and his supporters. Soon after Redcliffe commenced speaking, the chief rabbi began "evincing signs of disapproval." He spoke once or twice to Benas, the society's president, who, with Barnett, its secretary, did his best to quiet him. But eventually, pale and furious, he sprung to his feet before Redcliffe finished and blurted out, "I find this most intolerable. We were invited to hear a Lucien Wolf Memorial Lecture, but all we have heard has been one sheer castigation of Orthodoxy, one which is painful to those of us who hold dear everything Jewish."[47] Redcliffe shot back "I must speak the truth as I find it" and continued with his lecture. Several members of the audience, including Wilfred Samuel, a stalwart of the society, along with his son Edgar, noisily walked out, while cheers and countercheers punctuated the remainder of the talk. When the chief rabbi rose to speak at its conclusion, ostensibly to propose a vote of thanks, he launched into a further attack on Redcliffe. Leonard G. Montefiore, son of Claude Montefiore, who was to second the vote of thanks, complained that the lecturer had "trodden on my toes also." One member called for a division, explaining that some in the audience wished to disassociate themselves from the vote of thanks. That course, however, was not pursued.[48]

The ill-mannered conduct of the chief rabbi and his supporters was unusual. As a rule, the meetings of the Jewish Historical Society were (and are) tranquil and staid. What then provoked this behavior? The remark that immediately triggered Brodie's intervention was Redcliffe's reference to a letter from Brodie in the *Jewish Chronicle* of January 16, 1953, protesting the attendance of children who were not Jewish according to Jewish law in United Synagogue religion classes.[49] But this was simply the spark that ignited his already smoldering anger. What inflamed him and his supporters was Redcliffe's account of the decline of moderate traditionalism and the ascendance of right-wing views and standards and his suggestion that the new strict Orthodoxy was alienating many in the community. In particular, Brodie was furious about his remarks about *shehitah*. That this, above all, was what most troubled him and his allies became clear when, in the months after the lecture, they mounted a vigorous campaign to prevent its publication.

It was the practice of the Jewish Historical Society to publish the Lucien Wolf Lecture as a standalone pamphlet and to distribute it to its members. When the council of the society met in late June, however, there was strong opposition to the publication of Redcliffe's talk.[50] Seeking a compromise, the council appointed a subcommittee of three—James Parkes, Oskar K. Rabinowicz, a refugee banker and Revisionist Zionist from Czechoslovakia, and Alfred Rubens, a property developer and noted collector and student of Anglo-Jewish caricatures. As a Christian, Parkes had no stake in either the state of Jewish practice or the manner in which *shehitah* was performed; his concern was to prevent the society, which he served as president from 1949 to 1951, from splitting apart. Rabinowicz, on the other hand, was a veteran defender of *shehitah*, having published a ninety-three-page vindication of the practice in Vienna before escaping to Britain. The dominant figure on the subcommittee, he worked to block publication of Salaman's lecture and, when that failed, to eliminate material offensive to the chief rabbi. Rubens, it seems, was inactive.

Redcliffe's strongest supporters on the council were professional men, former civil servants, and men of letters—Norman Bentwich, Cecil Roth, the solicitor Arthur Arnold (a nephew of Rubens), Charles Singer, and the jurist Lionel Cohen, Baron Cohen of Walmer. As a group, they were critical of the intellectual poverty of Anglo-Jewry and the mounting conservatism of its religious leadership. Some, like Singer, were utterly hostile to *shehitah*, to which he referred in private as "a mass of highly sophisticated bosh, based on practices of a low anthropological order." In his eyes, it was "degrading in itself . . . part of a detestable literalism that, separated from its original content, humiliates the very word 'religion.'"[51] Redcliffe's most outspoken critics, aside from the chief rabbi himself, were businessmen—Rabinowicz and Samuel, for example—and other rabbis, like Isidore Epstein, editor of the first English-language translation of the Babylonian Talmud. Their opposition was surprisingly bitter. For example, Wilfred Samuel, himself not an observant Jew, claimed that Redcliffe suffered from "a trace of senility as well as megalomania" and dismissed his views as those of a "a Jew who

288 | *The Last Anglo-Jewish Gentleman*

has inherited wealth and has lived his life remote from Jewry." He lacked, in Samuel's view, "the necessary knowledge that might entitle him to pontificate & to prophesy about Judaism in England."[52] Samuel's words suggest that resentment of the old communal elite fueled his anger as much as religious fervor.

Twelve months passed (from June 1953 to May 1954) before a compromise satisfactory to both Redcliffe and his critics was reached. Redcliffe agreed to moderate the tone and the language of the text, but not its substance. He removed, for example, several warnings about "the capacity of a fanatically minded minority capturing the machine of [communal] government."[53] Parkes saw the changes as "generous" and "reasonable," but not Rabinowicz, who, less than aboveboard in his negotiations with Redcliffe, schemed to delay the vote on publication and even convened a meeting of the council when Parkes was out of the country. He remained adamant that Redcliffe eliminate his discussion of the decline in the observance of *kashrut* and, above all, the inhumanity of *shehitah*. At Parkes's urging, Cecil Roth worked with Redcliffe to modify the contested sentence so that it read "One reason [for the decline] is that with the enforcement of humane methods of slaughter the Jewish method no longer has, from this point of view, its former unique primacy."[54] In the end, the council voted, at an unusually well attended meeting on May 26, 1954, to publish the controversial but now amended lecture, with fifteen voting in favor of publication and the other four or five, who accepted the compromise without enthusiasm, abstaining.

This controversy was the first of several in the 1950s and 1960s over the future direction of Anglo-Jewry. Those who supported Redcliffe were, at the time, acutely aware of the high stakes. Harry Sacher, a solicitor, newspaper editor, and later Marks and Spencer executive, warned Redcliffe that the rabbinate was "in danger of capture by the ultra-Orthodox element which is out of tune with the times," while Leon Simon, a civil servant and Hebraist (who had known Nina), saw the hullabaloo over the lecture as "sad evidence of the reactionary character of the 'spiritual' leadership which is doing its best to drag Anglo-Jewry back into the Middle Ages."[55]

5

While the council of the Jewish Historical Society debated whether to publish the Lucien Wolf Memorial Lecture, Redcliffe continued his fight. When he had first approached the Board of Deputies about a scientific investigation of the impact of electrical stunning in February 1953, it had expressed interest, and, during the following month, letters had passed between Redcliffe and Adolf Brotman, the board's secretary (executive director) over how such an inquiry might be conducted.[56] His May lecture, however, ended any possibility of cooperation. Within a few weeks, Brodie convened a meeting of rabbis from everywhere in the United Kingdom to discuss whether they should participate in any scientific investigation of electrical stunning. They unanimously decided that they would not participate.[57] Meanwhile, Redcliffe arranged with the Department of Veterinary Clinical Studies at Cambridge to send a researcher to Sweden to examine electrical stunning, which was in use in the small Jewish community there. He reported in October 1953 that careful examination of all the animal's organs failed to reveal any internal bleeding from electrical stunning.[58] Redcliffe then sent the report to Brodie, who became worried that it could be used to justify the introduction of electrical stunning in Britain. After all, if the report demonstrated that stunning was not injurious, the halakhic bar to its introduction weakened, perhaps even disappeared. Fearing the consequences of the report, Brodie and Elsley Zeitlin flew to Israel in early November to obtain a ban on stunning from the chief rabbinate there, a ban that foreclosed further discussion of the issue as far as the Board of Deputies and the chief rabbi were concerned.[59]

A few months later Cecil Roth confided to Redcliffe that Chief Rabbi Brodie was actually sympathetic to change (he offered no evidence) but deferred to his bet din—in his words, "the Arch-beard [chief rabbi] agrees with the likes of me, but doesn't dare to say so." This charge continued to echo during the terms of subsequent chief rabbis—the charge that, because their expertise in Jewish law was inferior to that of the strictly Orthodox rabbis on their batei din, they repeatedly deferred to them, fearing to appear insufficiently staunch in their defense of Torah-true Judaism. Roth also suggested that Redcliffe continue his campaign by offering scientific evidence that the casting pens approved by the bet din (pens that immobilized animals before their throats were slit) also caused tissue damage. Then, he told Redcliffe, "you would put the Beards in a pretty quandary: they would logically either have to withdraw their objection to stunning or admit that they have been feeding the community terefa [unkosher] meat for the past quarter of a century."[60]

"The Great Turbot Affair" the following year exposed the same communal rift and drew Redcliffe's intervention once again. In October 1954,

290 | *The Last Anglo-Jewish Gentleman*

the Anglo-Jewish Association hosted a dinner in honor of a former president, Ewen Montagu, second son of the second Lord Swaythling. The main course of the meal, which was under the supervision of the Kashrus Commission, was listed on the menu as *le turbot poché*. Its presence caused consternation at the head table, where Chief Rabbi Brodie was seated, since it was believed that turbot lacked scales, which would render it unkosher. Brodie consulted Haham Gaon, rabbinic head of the Sephardi community, who in turn consulted his wife, who said she had always thought turbot was forbidden.[61] He then left the table to interrogate the *shomer* (*kashrut* supervisor). Meanwhile, "the diners hotly (but good humouredly) debated whether their consciences would allow them to consume the main dish of the meal. With few, but eminent, exceptions, it was an easy win for material over moral forces." The *shomer* told the chief rabbi that there were two kinds of turbot, one with scales and one without, and that the turbot on which they were dining was kosher.[62]

When Redcliffe read the *Jewish Chronicle*'s tongue-in-cheek account of the turbot incident, from which I quoted, he went on the attack. He told a reporter, "There is no such thing as two kinds of turbot," explaining that all turbot have scales, but some have different kinds of scales. He thought it "monstrous and irresponsible" that communal authorities had issued a patently false statement and called for the establishment of a scientific advisory committee that the rabbis would be required to consult when problems like "this turbot nonsense" arose.[63] The strict Orthodox response was that, while there were not, zoologically speaking, two kinds of turbot, in the fish and catering trades, as well as in popular parlance, the name *turbot* was often applied to fish similar in appearance, like halibut.[64] The clerk of the bet din, Marcus Carr, then wrote to Denys W. Tucker, fish expert at the Museum of Natural History, asking him whether ling, plaice, turbot, flounder, snoek, and turbot had both fins and scales (as required in Leviticus 11:9). Regarding turbot, Tucker replied that it had "small tubercles of bone scattered over its skin" and that whether these were scales or not was a "theological matter."[65]

It was not the first time that turbot had bedeviled Anglo-Jewry's religious leaders. In the mid-eighteenth century, Hirschel Levin, rabbi of London's Great Synagogue from 1758 to 1764, had permitted turbot, basing himself on testimony of the bet din of Venice, which reported that Jews in the Venetian territories and the Ottoman Empire ate it (the Amsterdam rabbinate, on the other hand, forbade it).[66] In 1822, when Levin's successor,

Solomon Hirschell, received a query from Newcastle about turbot, he replied it was kosher. In the decades before the Great Turbot Affair, kosher caterers frequently served turbot as the fish course and Jewish housewives found it a perfect-size fish to serve at dinner parties.[67] During World War II, the bet din issued a list of kosher fish as an aid to Jewish housewives who were encountering unfamiliar fish in the shops under wartime conditions. Turbot was on the list. But when the bet din issued a list of permitted fish in October 1951—before the Great Turbot Affair erupted—the troublesome turbot was missing, as it was on another list issued in June 1954, again prior to the contentious dinner. But that was not the end of the matter. In 1960, because of an increase in the number of British Jews traveling on the Continent, the London Bet Din asked its counterparts in various countries to provide lists of fish they considered kosher, which would be made available to travelers who might encounter fish with unfamiliar names. The list from Paris included turbot as a kosher fish![68]

The Great Turbot Affair, which came soon after the row over the Lucien Wolf Lecture, revealed the same divisions within Anglo-Jewry. The Anglo-Jewish Association, the dinner's sponsor, was the last institutional stronghold of the old communal elite. Its members, while not indifferent to Jewish tradition, were indifferent to the strict Orthodox elaboration of the dietary laws. They went on eating their *turbot poché* while the chief rabbi made his inquiries; in their eyes, the fish was unproblematic. Redcliffe later told Ewen Montagu, the dinner's honoree, a story about turbot and Montagu's paternal grandfather, Samuel Montagu, first Lord Swaythling, which highlights the more flexible Orthodoxy of the late Victorian period. Samuel Montagu was an observant Jew by the standards of Victorian Orthodoxy, his adherence to traditional observance easily outstripping that of other communal notables. His son Edwin, the future Liberal politician, rebelled—or tried to rebel—against his father's Judaism from his youth. According to Redcliffe, one time when Samuel was laying down the law to Edwin, the latter whispered to his mother that if his father went on like this, he would tell him that turbot was not kosher. She begged him not to, the story went, "as there would soon be nothing left to eat."[69]

While not a landmark in Anglo-Jewish history, the Great Turbot Affair was symptomatic of the social and religious tensions that characterized the community in the postwar years. In this sense, it can be viewed as a precursor or run-up to the explosive events of the Louis Jacobs Affair (1961–64), which splintered the community and was reported in the national press

292 | *The Last Anglo-Jewish Gentleman*

in some detail. A clash between moderate traditionalism and strict Orthodoxy, it ended with the ejection from the United Synagogue and Jews' College of Rabbi Louis Jacobs, a gifted modern Orthodox scholar and religious thinker ("the greatest chief rabbi Britain never had," in the words of one pundit). Jacobs then spearheaded the establishment of a new branch of Judaism in Britain, the Masorti (traditional) movement, with which more than a dozen congregations were affiliated in 2020. Redcliffe was no longer alive at the time of the Louis Jacobs Affair but the affair would not have surprised him if he had been. The battles he had fought in the 1950s were tremors preceding the Jacobs earthquake.

6

The Great Turbot Affair was the last intracommunal quarrel in which Redcliffe intervened. In March 1955, he wrote to Lionel Loewe, Herbert's brother, "At present I am disengaged, i.e., I have no active quarrel on with anybody in the community."[70]

While strictly true, Redcliffe was not completely disengaged. The House of Commons was considering a bill in early 1955 to amend the Slaughter Act to require electrical stunning in *shehitah*, and he told a correspondent that he was doing all he could to assist in its passage.[71] He followed the progress of the amendment into the early spring,[72] but already in February he was too ill to do very much. An undiagnosed, slow-growing brain tumor was eating away at his life. On April 1, the *Jewish Chronicle* reported that he was seriously ill. He died on June 12, 1955, at his house in Barley and was buried at Willesden Jewish Cemetery in London next to Nina, who had died thirty years earlier.

Notes

1. RNS, "The Jewish Fellows of the Royal Society," *Miscellanies of the Jewish Historical Society of England* 5 (1948): 146–75; RNS, "Jews in the Royal Society: A Problem in Ecology," *Notes and Records of the Royal Society of London* 7 (1949): 61–67.

2. RNS, "Jewish Fellows," 146–47.

3. RNS, "Jewish Fellows," 148, 159–60, 164.

4. RNS, "Jewish Fellows," 160.

5. RNS, "Jewish Fellows," 174.

6. RNS, "Jewish Fellows," 173.

7. RNS, "Jewish Fellows," 175.

8. RNS, "Jews in the Royal Society," 65.

9. RNS, "Jews in the Royal Society," 66–67.

10. RNS, "The Jews—Race, Nation, Religion," address to the Anglo-Jewish Association, December 19, 1950, typescript, Add. MS 8171/1, RNS CUL.

11. Dan Stone, "Of Peas, Potatoes, and Jews: Redcliffe N. Salaman and the British Debate over Jewish Racial Origins," *Simon Dubnow Instititute Yearbook 3* (2004): 239.

12. RNS, "The Jews—Race, Nation, Religion."

13. RNS, "The Jews—Race, Nation, Religion."

14. Tony Kushner, "Stunning Intolerance: A Century of Opposition to Religious Slaughter," *Jewish Quarterly* no. 133 (Spring 1989): 16–20; Sebastian Poulter, *Ethnicity, Law and Human Rights: The English Experience* (Oxford, UK: Clarendon, 1998), ch. 4; Robin Judd, *Contested Rituals: Circumcision, Kosher Butchering, and Jewish Political Life in Germany, 1843–1933* (Ithaca, NY: Cornell University Press, 2007); David Fraser, *Anti-shechita Prosecutions in the Anglo-American World, 1855–1913—"A Major Attack on Jewish Freedoms"* (Boston: Academic Studies Press, 2018).

15. *Jewish Chronicle*, May 29, 1914.

16. RNS to NDS, May 4, 1911, Add. MS 8171/102, RNS CUL.

17. RNS to Joseph H. Hertz, February 5, 1932, RNS to Israel Feldman, October 11, 1933, both in Add. MS 8171/47, RNS CUL.

18. Herbert Samuel to Joseph H. Hertz, May 1, 1934, Acc. 2805/04/01/92, Office of the Chief Rabbi Papers, LMA.

19. Kushner, "Stunning Intolerance," 17.

20. Kushner, "Stunning Intolerance," 18; Hamilton Fyfe, "Assimilation or a Jewish State," in *Gentile and Jew: A Symposium*, ed. Chaim Newman (London: Alliance, 1945), 102.

21. Howard M. Sacher, *A History of Israel from the Rise of Zionism to Our Time*, 2nd ed. (New York: Alfred A. Knopf, 2000), 296.

22. *Jewish Chronicle*, August 2, 1946.

23. Mark Raven [Chaim Raphael], "British Jewry in Heavy Weather," *Commentary* 3, no. 5 (May 1947): 454.

24. David Cesarani, *Major Farran's Hat: The Untold Story of the Struggle to Establish the Jewish State* (Cambridge, UK: Da Capo, 2009), 43, 85–87, 115–16, 148–49; Tony Kushner, "Anti-Semitism and Austerity: The August 1947 Riots in Britain," in *Racial Violence in Britain, 1840–1959*, ed. Panikos Panayi, 149–68 (Leicester: Leicester University Press, 1993).

25. RNS to Harris (Hirsch) M. Lazarus, March 16, 1948, Add. MS 8171/47, RNS CUL.

26. A copy of the pamphlet is in Acc. 312/E02/133, Papers of the Board of Deputies, LMA [hereafter, BD Papers].

27. Charles Singer to RNS, April 11, 1954, Add. MS 8171/47, RNS CUL.

28. Beatrice Samuel to RNS, December 1, 1950, Add. MS 8171/1/7, RNS CUL; RNS to Adolf G. Brotman, January 16, 1953, Acc. 3121/E02/133, BD Papers.

29. Robert Waley Cohen to RNS, June 6 and 8, 1950, Add. MS 8171/47, RNS CUL.

30. RNS to Bernard Waley Cohen, December 6, 1952, Add. MS 8171/1/7, RNS CUL; RNS to Charles Singer, December 24, 1952, Add. MS 8171/5, RNS CUL.

31. RNS to Charles Singer, December 24, 1952, Add. MS 8171/5, RNS CUL.

32. RNS to Charles Singer, December 24, 1952, Add. MS 8171/5, RNS CUL.

33. Oscar Philipp to RNS, April 28 and May 5, 1952, Add. MS 8171/1/7, RNS CUL.

34. RNS, *Whither Lucien Wolf's Anglo-Jewish Community?* (London: Jewish Historical Society of England, 1954), 4.

294 | *The Last Anglo-Jewish Gentleman*

35. RNS to Albert M. Hyamson, July 10, 1952, Add. MS 8171/48, RNS CUL.

36. RNS to David C. Benn, May 22, 1953, Add. MS 8171/48, RNS CUL.

37. RNS, *Whither*, 7.

38. RNS, *Whither*, 10.

39. Derek Taylor, *Chief Rabbi Hertz: The Wars of the Lord* (London: Vallentine Mitchell, 2015); Taylor, *Chief Rabbi Nathan Marcus Adler: The Forgotten Founder* (London: Vallentine Mitchell, 2018); Benjamin J. Elton, *Britain's Chief Rabbis and the Religious Character of Anglo-Jewry, 1880–1970* (Manchester: Manchester University Press, 2009).

40. RNS, *Whither*, 10–11.

41. RNS, *Whither*, 11–12.

42. Jewish law forbids the eating of the sciatic nerve. Removing the sciatic nerve and the fat surrounding it (porging, *nikkur* in Hebrew) is a highly skilled, labor-intensive process. The chief rabbinate banned kosher butchers from selling porged hindquarters because they doubted they had the halachic knowledge and skills to carry it out correctly.

43. RNS, *Whither*, 13–14.

44. RNS, *Whither*, 23.

45. Jane Miller, *Relations* (London: Jonathan Cape, 2003), 12–13, 222–25.

46. RNS, "The Jews—Race, Nation, Religion."

47. *Jewish Chronicle*, May 22, 1953.

48. RNS to Leo Baeck, June 29, 1953, RNS to Bertram R. Benas, June 22, 1953, Add. MS 8171/48, RNS CUL; *Jewish Chronicle*, May 22, 1953. Montefiore later apologized to Redcliffe for "the rather poor part he played" that evening. See RNS to Albert M. Hyamson, June 9, 1953, Add. MS 8171/48, RNS CUL. The historian Vivian D. Lipman characterized Brodie as "a quiet, gentlemanly and conciliatory person" (*A History of the Jews in Britain since 1858* (New York: Holmes and Meier, 1990), 24. In light of Brodie's behavior in this and the Louis Jacobs controversy a decade later, Lipman's characterization is misleading, at best.

49. In contrast to the January 16 report in the *Jewish Chronicle*, Redcliffe recalled that the chief rabbi interrupted his lecture before he mentioned the religion classes (*Jewish Chronicle*, May 29, 1953). Perhaps he was thinking of Brodie's earlier remarks to Benas.

50. I have reconstructed the conflict within the council of the society from the correspondence and memoranda in the following two files: MS 60/13/24/2, James W. Parkes Papers, Hartley Library, University of Southampton, Southampton; and Add. MS 8171/48, RNS CUL.

51. Charles Singer to RNS, April 11, 1954, Add. MS 8171/48, RNS CUL. In a later letter, Singer characterized *shehitah* as "one of those odd survivals of savagery, like fox hunting, or caste, or suttee, or Christmas that have, in the ages, somehow gathered an emotional aura of pseudo-historical or religious associations" (Charles Singer to RNS, April 16, 1954, Add. MS 8171/48, RNS CUL).

52. Wilfred Samuel to James W. Parkes, June 17, 18, and 20, 1953, MS 60/13/24/2, James Parkes Papers, Hartley Library, University of Southampton.

53. This phrase appears in the unrevised text of the lecture, copies of which are in Add. MS 8171/48, RNS CUL, and in MS 60/39/24/1, James Parkes Papers, HL US.

54. RNS, *Whither*, 11.

55. Harry Sacher to RNS, June 24, 1953, and Leon Simon to RNS, September 15, 1953, Add. MS 8171/48, RNS CUL.

56. The letters are in ACC/3121/E02/133, BD Papers.

57. Israel Brodie to Israel Abrahams (chief rabbi of South Africa), July 28, 1953, ACC/2805/6/1, BD Papers.

58. J. Hickman, "Memorandum on the Electrical Stunning of Animals Prior to Slaughter," mimeographed report, October 7, 1953, ACC/2805/6/1/241, BD Papers.

59. RNS to Charles Singer, January 4, 1954, Add. MS 8171/1/7, RNS CUL; RNS to L. F. Newman, August 10, 1954; RNS to S. L. Last, January 24, 1955, Add. MS 8171/47, RNS CUL; *Jewish Chronicle*, October 30, 1953.

60. Cecil Roth to RNS, January 19, 1954, Add. MS 8171/47, RNS CUL.

61. Leonard Montefiore to RNS, November 6, 1954, Add. MS 8171/5, RNS CUL.

62. *Jewish Chronicle*, October 29 and November 5, 12, and 26, 1954.

63. *Jewish Chronicle*, November 5, 1954.

64. *Jewish Chronicle*, November 12, 1954.

65. Marcus Carr to Denys W. Tucker, November 29, 1954; Denys W. Tucker to Marcus Carr, December 8, 1954, Acc. 3400/2/5/49, Archives of the London Bet Din, LMA.

66. Charles Duschinsky, *The Rabbinate of the Great Synagogue, London, from 1756–1842* (London: Henry Milford, Oxford University Press, 1921), 292–93.

67. Hyman A. Simons, letter to the editor, *Jewish Chronicle*, September 2, 1977; Nicholas de Lange, email to the author, April 11, 2012.

68. Correspondence regarding fish, Acc. 3400/5/49, Archives of the London Bet Din, LMA.

69. RNS to Ewen Montagu, October 29, 1954, Add. MS 8171/5, RNS CUL. Redcliffe could not remember whether Edwin himself or Israel Abrahams had told him the story.

70. RNS to Lionel Loewe, March 15, 1955, Add. MS 8171/5, RNS CUL.

71. RNS to S. L. Last, January 24, 1955; RNS to Adolf G. Brotman, February 18, 1955, Add. MS 8171/47, RNS CUL.

72. A box of *shehitah* materials in his papers includes clippings from every issue of the *Jewish Chronicle* from February 25 to April 22, 1955.

AFTERWORD

THE WORLD THAT REDCLIFFE SALAMAN KNEW NO LONGER exists. Science research in the twenty-first century is a narrowly focused professional pursuit, requiring years of highly specialized academic training and generous funding from state agencies, private foundations, and industry. It is not, as it often was in Redcliffe's early years, a gentlemanly avocation to be pursued privately in the comfort of one's home or garden. The writing of history has also become a professional rather than a gentlemanly pursuit. In another sphere altogether, the governance of Jewish communal institutions, while hardly democratic, is not the preserve of men of leisure whose inherited wealth allows them to devote themselves to its time-consuming tasks. While men of property still influence communal priorities, they rely increasingly on an experienced cadre of professional workers—executive secretaries, programming directors, media specialists, accountants, and fundraisers. A country gentleman, an educated amateur, and a man of property, Redcliffe made his mark simultaneously in the worlds of science and Jewish communal affairs, moving with apparent ease between the two spheres of activity (as well as others, such as local public life). He contributed to each in a way that was possible during his lifetime but is rare today, when the specialist has replaced the amateur.

The racial assumptions that guided much of his thinking have also ceased to have currency in scientific and cultural life. They no longer dominate the thinking of anthropologists, ethnographers, archaeologists, and critics of literature and art and certainly have no place in the work of the natural sciences. In this sense as well, Redcliffe was a man of his time. To say so is not to excuse him—just as it would be beside the point to condemn him. Anachronism is always an obstacle to understanding the past. I have tried instead to emphasize, along with the ubiquity of notions of race before World War II, how the concept of race functioned in his thinking, that is, the work that it did for him (to borrow a turn of phrase from the study of literature). Defining the Jews as a race allowed Redcliffe to think about the collective life of the Jews in nonreligious terms. It allowed him to see that the bonds of affection, sociability, responsibility, and fraternity that held the Anglo-Jewish community together (and, by extension, other Western

Jewish communities) were not spiritual—that is, fidelity to the observance of the *mitsvot* and faith in their divine origin (*Torah mi-Sinai*). What historians and sociologists today call the ties of ethnicity Redcliffe called the ties of race. This way of thinking about Jewishness allowed him to understand better the transformation of Western Jewish communities between the mid-nineteenth century and the mid-twentieth century. It gave him a conceptual framework to understand the decline of observance and belief and the simultaneous continuation of social cohesion. The insights in his Lucien Wolf Memorial Lecture owed much to this way of thinking about Jewishness.

Redcliffe's devotion both to the well-being of the Jews and to the breeding of blight-free potato strains—the two foci of his life—rested on the financial foundation of the wealth he inherited from his father and his father's childless brother Nathan. It allowed him to pursue his passions rather than toil to support his family. Few persons, whether in England or elsewhere, enjoy such good fortune today. His social and economic position also contributed to his self-confidence, allowing him to speak and act with authority in diverse spheres of activity. The ethos of social deference, which still operated powerfully in his time, reinforced his confidence.

Although Redcliffe admired his father, even if from a distance, he did not follow him into the family business. (Recall that his father at one time hoped he would train as an architect and join him in the property business.) Free of the burden of earning a living, he was content, after illness made a career in medicine impossible, to enjoy the life of a country squire, a gentleman scientist, and a communal notable. Like many children of successful Jewish businessmen in the modern world, he absorbed the priorities and prejudices of the social stratum with which he identified and clearly thought that there were better things to do with his life than make money. After the deaths of his older brothers Euston (1916) and Elkin (1919), who had run the family business after the death of their father in 1896, he showed no interest in taking their place. Of necessity, his younger brother Michel took on some responsibility for the family's London properties, but he, as well as another elder brother, Clement, essentially did little with his life other than live well. To his credit, Michel, who had studied at the Slade School of Fine Art in the mid-1890s, was a generous host and patron of the arts, best known for his support for Augustus John, whom he knew at the Slade. (For a time in the mid-1890s, John's future wife, Ida Nettleship, was engaged to Clement.)[1]

298 | *The Last Anglo-Jewish Gentleman*

What is striking is how little of Myer Salaman's business drive and acumen his sons inherited. (His six daughters were not expected to be active as breadwinners.) None of his sons, other than Elkin and Euston, showed any spark of commercial talent. They were good at spending money but not at making it. Redcliffe rarely discussed it with his children. His daughter Esther recalled that, as a young woman, she did not know the first thing about earning money and budgeting it. As a child and then an adolescent, she was given whatever she needed.[2] Redcliffe's only encounter with the world of business was not a success. When he retired from the directorship of the Potato Virus Research Station in 1939, he worked briefly for Marks and Spencer on problems of quality control in fruits and vegetables, but he hated the routine of traveling to London and working in an office, quarreled with management, and left not long after starting. As Esther remembered, he did not like the business of doing business.[3]

As adults, his children (with the exception of Raphael) pursued careers in which they were not likely to become wealthy. Myer, the eldest, having abandoned the idea of becoming a rabbi after his mother's death, followed Redcliffe into medicine. Trained as a pathologist, like his father, he devoted himself to cancer research, ending his career as director of the cancer research department at the London Hospital Medical College from 1948 to 1967. Serving in the Royal Army Medical Corps during World War II, he did important work on jaundice, a common and disabling disease among servicemen receiving injections for syphilis. Arthur, who was also at Cambridge, was less focused as a young man. He toyed with becoming an actor, which Redcliffe strenuously opposed, and tried his hand at banking before settling on medicine. He practiced as a country doctor his entire life and was an avid participant in amateur theatrical groups. In 1935, he married Nancy Samuel, the only daughter of Herbert and Beatrice Samuel, who were old friends of his mother and father. Some of his nieces believe that the match was arranged, as they were both beyond the usual age of marrying. Although Arthur lived only twelve miles from Barley, he and Redcliffe were not close.

Raphael, the youngest son, studied engineering at Cambridge, at the insistence of Redcliffe, who opposed his first choice, archaeology. After Cambridge, he worked for a theatrical lighting firm, inventing a hydraulic dimmer used to simulate daybreak and nightfall on the stage. In 1929, he set up a light engineering works in southeast London, specializing in pumps. This choice offered the possibility of material success, but during the Depression the business failed. In 1938, he went to work for Marks and Spencer, taking charge eventually of the engineering aspects of their business. During the war, for example, he organized the firm's fire-fighting and air-raid procedures. Of all of Redcliffe's children, Raphael was the only one with a foot in the world of commerce, but it never captured his imagination or sparked his ambition. His true passion was the collection and study of tradesmen's tools.[4] As a boy in Barley, he had come to know the work of the skilled craftsmen in and around the village. When visiting his father in 1946, he realized that economic and technological change had virtually wiped out their trades. He then began collecting the tools of the major trades and recording how they were used, building up a vast museum-quality collection, which eventually was split between the Science Museum in London and the Museum of St. Albans. He took early retirement from Marks and Spencer in 1963 to devote himself to his collection and eventually published two celebrated works, *Dictionary of Tools Used in the Woodworking and Allied Trades, c. 1700–1970* (1975) and *Dictionary of Leather-Working Tools, c. 1700–1950, and the Tools of Allied Trades* (1986). As his entry in the *Dictionary of National Biography* states, "These are his monuments: substantial but concise, copiously illustrated, authoritative, thoroughly comprehensive, and unlikely to be superseded, now that the trades themselves are gone."[5]

Redcliffe's daughter Ruth studied at the Slade after leaving Bedales. She exhibited paintings, drawings, and linocuts throughout her life but was not commercially successful. Her musician husband made ends meet with various teaching positions and miscellaneous work for the British Broadcasting Company. They lived for half a century in a small, semidetached house "at the distinctly 'lower' end" of the late Victorian London suburb of Northwood.[6] The youngest child, Esther, was more successful, but again not in a way that ever allowed her to live in the manner to which she was accustomed as a child. She studied singing at the Royal Academy of Music in 1937–38 and then launched a career as a mezzo-soprano, becoming known for collecting and singing English folk songs. During the war, she met the Viennese-born Paul Hamburger (1920–2004), a pianist, chamber musician, and accompanist, and, in 1947, they married, but the marriage did not last. In later life, she achieved worldwide fame for developing a new method of teaching singing, detailed in her 1989 book *Unlocking Your Voice: Freedom to Sing*, and for helping singers who developed vocal problems.

If none of the children lived privileged lives, as Redcliffe and Nina had, they lived comfortable lives, nonetheless. Moreover, they lived lives that were neither ordinary nor unremarkable. Like their parents, they set themselves goals that transcended the basic requirement of keeping their heads above water. They were, in short, people who mattered (as were many of their children in turn). Their achievements left less of a footprint than those of their parents, but saying so does not minimize the character of what they did with their lives. Where they differed was the stage on which they played a role. None of the children shared Nina's religious and Hebraic commitments or Redcliffe's communal and Zionist interests. Religious observance played little or no role in their lives. Nor did they give their children the kind of intensive Hebrew education that they had received from their mother. Even the Hebrew-speaking wives of Myer and Raphael did not raise their children to read or speak the language. Nor were they active in communal life, with the exception of Esther, who sang frequently at services at the West London Synagogue and then at the Westminster Synagogue, after its establishment in 1957. This is not to say that the other children were radical assimilationists. Far from it, but for them Judaism, Jewishness, and Jewish nationalism were not priorities that governed their thinking and set the agenda for their lives. Moreover, even if they had been inclined to play the kind of role their father had, they would not have been able to do so, for they lacked the inherited wealth that allowed him to serve and govern. Most of those at the helm of Anglo-Jewry since Redcliffe's death have been self-made men of East European descent, not the descendants of the old notability.

To some extent, Redcliffe's attachments to Jewish life were exceptional even in his lifetime. I am speaking here not of the racial construction he gave to Jewishness but of the place of communal commitments in his day-to-day activities. While the intensity of his connection was not unique among Jewish men of his background—his friend Robert Waley Cohen devoted even more time to Jewish matters than he—it was, broadly speaking, uncommon. The remarkableness becomes clear when one compares Redcliffe's commitments with those of his siblings, whose interest in Jewish affairs was either mild or perfunctory or even hostile. His brother Euston took no interest, while his brother Elkin was a socially ambitious radical assimilationist who baptized his children and whose wife Florence and famous aviatrix daughter Peggy later refused to acknowledge their Jewish origins.[7] Clement and Michel both married non-Jews and lived in the country, as did Redcliffe's sister Louise Bishop. His sisters Isabelle Davis, Bessie Cohen, and Jennie Cohen, all of whom lived in London, were less distant from Jewish life. Jennie, in particular, came closest to Redcliffe in the depth of her Jewish commitments. She was an enthusiastic Zionist, a generous supporter of East End charities, especially the Jewish Free Reading Room in Whitechapel, and a tireless communal worker. In the years before World War I, she was active in the Jewish League for Woman Suffrage and in the movement to enhance the role of women in the synagogue. She even tried her hand at writing dramatic sketches and plays with Jewish themes. Her younger sisters (by almost a generation) Brenda Seligman and Dorothy Samuel were completely disengaged. Brenda devoted her life to anthropological research, teaming with her husband Charles in writing about communities in Sri Lanka, Sudan, Egypt, China, and Japan. His career overshadowed hers, but, in fact, their working relationship was so close that it is difficult to distinguish their individual contributions to their published work. Her stature was such that in 1959 she succeeded Alfred Radcliffe-Brown as president of the Association of Social Anthropologists. She made no attempt to do anything Jewish and prided herself on once having served ham to Nina (whom, I assume, refused it).[8] Dorothy Samuel was not as aggressively antireligious as her sister, but she too did not share Redcliffe's enthusiasms. And Archie, of course, suffered from mental illness and Harry killed himself.

In the context of his own sprawling family, Redcliffe was then a singular figure in his Jewish commitments. He was well aware of this. His description of the demise of the old Anglo-Jewish notability in his Lucien Wolf Memorial Lecture at the end of his life was as much a history of his own family as it was a history of the social group from which his family emerged. From close observation, he knew how prosperity, acculturation, integration, and secularization eroded old attachments and made new ones possible. While he would have preferred another outcome, he was neither outraged nor disconsolate. Perhaps he thought the decline of Jewish particularism was an inevitable consequence of material progress and growing toleration—a development that he accepted but did not celebrate. In any case, the *embourgeoisement* of the East Europeans and their conquest of communal life, which was well underway by midcentury, ensured Anglo-Jewish continuity. What Redcliffe did not foresee was that the fundamentalist Orthodoxy that he fought in the last three decades of his life would go from strength to strength, its adherents multiplying and its influence expanding. The tolerant, latitudinarian Orthodoxy of Anglo-Jewry that he knew in his youth and early adulthood would fall by the wayside—and in some cases would be routed—in the course of the twentieth century.

Notes

1. Ida John, *The Good Bohemian: The Letters of Ida John*, ed. Rebecca John and Michael Holroyd (London: Bloomsbury, 2017), 29; Alison Thomas, *Portraits of Women: Gwen John and Her Forgotten Contemporaries* (Cambridge, UK: Polity, 1994), 38–40.

2. Esther Salaman Hamburger, interview by the author, March 25, 1999, Highgate, London.

3. Ibid.

4. Desmond Painter, "Redcliffe and Raphael Salaman: A Memoir," *History Workshop Journal*, no. 40 (Autumn 1995): 276–82.

5. *Oxford Dictionary of National Biography*, s.v. "Salaman, Raphael Arthur (1906–1993)."

6. Miller, *Relations*, 3.

7. *Jewish Telegraphic Agency Bulletin*, November 6, 1931.

8. Rachel Miller, email to the author, March 20, 2014.

GLOSSARY

amora (s.), amoraim (pl.) (Aramaic) The rabbinic sages in the Land of Israel and Babylonia from ca. 200 to ca. 500 CE. Their teachings constitute the second level of text in the Talmud, the basis of rabbinic Judaism.

bet din Jewish court of law.

birkat ha-mazon Hebrew blessing at the conclusion of a meal.

dayyan Judge on a bet din.

divrei Torah Comments on a passage from the Hebrew Bible, often delivered at a public religious gathering.

gemara (Aramaic) The second level of text in the Talmud, the record of the conversations and debates of the amoraim.

Haftarah (s.), Haftarot (pl.) The selection from either the Writings or the Prophets that follows the reading from the Torah in the synagogue on the Sabbath.

Haggadah (s.), Haggadot (pl.) The ritual text, in Hebrew, with some Aramaic, that accompanies the Seder meal on the first two nights of Passover.

halah A braided loaf of bread eaten, in particular, at Sabbath meals.

halakhah Jewish law.

halukah The Diaspora-financed system of charitable distributions that supported the impoverished, pre-Zionist, traditional Ashkenazi community of Jerusalem.

Hasid An adherent of Hasidism, the pietistic movement that began in eighteenth-century Poland.

havdalah The ceremony at the conclusion (sundown) of the Sabbath that marks the separation between the holiness of the Sabbath day and the mundaneness of the weekdays that follow.

heder (s.), hadarim (pl.) A private, one-room elementary school for boys in Eastern Europe and in East European immigrant quarters elsewhere.

ivrit-be-ivrit A method for teaching modern, spoken Hebrew in which instruction is in Hebrew rather than the language of the students.

kadimah An exclamation, "Forward!" or "Advance!"

kashrut The system of dietary laws that governs what Jews eat.

Magen David The shield of David (or, in common usage, the star of David).

melammedim Teachers, especially in hadarim.

meshugeneh (Yiddish) Crazy.

mezuzah Small box or cylinder, often decorated, attached to doorframe of a Jewish home, containing a piece of parchment with the Hebrew texts of Deut. 6: 4–9 and 11: 13–21.

minyan Minimum number of men (ten) required for prayer in traditional Judaism.

303

304 | *Glossary*

Mishnah The record of the conversations and debates of the earliest generations of rabbis in the Land of Israel from ca. 200 BCE to 200 CE. It functions as the first level of text in the Talmud.

mitsvah (s.), mitsvot (pl.) Divine commandment.

musaf The "additional" prayer service on the Sabbath and festivals, immediately following the morning service and the reading of the Torah.

neginah (s.), neginot (pl.) The system of cantillation for the Torah according to the musical accents in the Masoretic text.

or la-goyyim Literally, "a light unto the nations," that is, an example and inspiration for the gentile nations of the world.

Pirkei Avot The "chapters of the fathers," a tractate of the Mishnah that collects ethical teachings and maxims of the earliest generations of rabbinic sages.

piyyut (s.), piyyutim (pl.) Premodern liturgical poem in Hebrew and occasionally Aramaic.

Rosh Ha-Shanah The Jewish new year.

Sefer Torah Parchment scroll containing the Five Books of Moses.

shehitah The method of slaughtering animals according to Jewish law.

Shekhinah The visible manifestation, that is, dwelling or settling, of God's presence.

Shema Literally, the command "Hear!" or "Listen!," the first word of a central Jewish prayer, from Deut. 6: 4–9, proclaiming the unity of God and commanding the love of God and obedience to his commandments all the time.

Shulhan Arukh Literally, "the set table." The most widely consulted code of Jewish law, compiled in the sixteenth century by Joseph Karo in Safed.

sukkah Temporary, outdoor shelter or booth erected by Jews in which to eat meals during the fall harvest festival of Sukkot, symbolic of the temporary dwellings in which the biblical Israelites lived during the forty years of wandering in the wilderness following the exodus from Egypt.

Torah mi-Sinai The traditional Jewish belief that God gave the Torah, both the Written Law and the Oral Law, to Moses on Mount Sinai, that is, the belief that it was divinely composed and transmitted to the Jewish people.

tsaddik A righteous person; also, the leader of a Hasidic sect, whose authority is both charismatic and inherited.

yeshivah (s.), yeshivot (pl.) An academy for the study of the Talmud and other rabbinic texts.

yeshiva bocher (s.), yeshiva bocherim (pl.) (Yiddish) A yeshivah student (male), usually used to refer to a student with little or no secular education.

yishuv Literally, "settlement." The Old Yishuv refers to the traditional, strictly observant Jewish population in the Land of Israel prior to the beginnings of Zionist settlement; the New Yishuv refers to the largely secular, frequently ideologically driven Jewish population that began to settle there in the 1880s.

SELECT BIBLIOGRAPHY

Alderman, Geoffrey. *Modern British Jewry*. Oxford: Clarendon Press, 1992.

Barkan, Elazar. *The Retreat of Scientific Racism: Changing Concepts of Race in Britain and the United States between the World Wars*. Cambridge: Cambridge University Press, 1992.

Bassett, Kate. *In Two Minds: A Biography of Jonathan Miller*. London: Oberon, 2012.

Bender, Abby. "British Israelites, Irish Israelites, and the Ends of an Analogy." In *Irish Questions and Jewish Questions: Crossovers in Culture*, edited by Aidan Beatty and Dan O'Brien, 17–30. Syracuse, NY: Syracuse University Press, 2019.

Bentwich, Helen C. *If I Forget Thee: Some Chapters of Autobiography, 1912–1920*. London: Elek, 1973.

Bentwich, Norman. *For Zion's Sake: A Biography of Judah L. Magnes*. Philadelphia: Jewish Publication Society, 1954.

———. *They Found Refuge: An Account of British Jewry's Work for Victims of Nazi Oppression*. London: Cresset, 1956.

———. "The Wanderers and Other Jewish Scholars of My Youth." *Transactions of the Jewish Historical Society of England* 20 (1964): 51–62.

Biddiss, Michael D. "The Universal Races Congress of 1911." *Race* 13, no. 1 (1971): 37–46.

Black, Eugene C. *The Social Politics of Anglo-Jewry, 1880–1914*. Oxford: Basil Blackwell, 1988.

Black, Gerry. "Health and Medical Care of the Jewish Poor in the East End of London, 1880–1939." PhD diss., University of Leicester, 1987.

Bloom, Etan. *Arthur Ruppin and the Production of Pre-Israeli Culture*. Leiden: Brill, 2011.

Bolchover, Richard. *British Jewry and the Holocaust*. Cambridge: Cambridge University Press, 1993.

Brann, Ross. *The Compunctious Poet: Cultural Ambiguity and Hebrew Poetry in Muslim Spain*. Baltimore, MD: Johns Hopkins University Press, 1991.

Bruce, Anthony. *The Last Crusade: The Palestine Campaign in the First World War*. London: Thistle, 2013.

Cesarani, David. *Major Farran's Hat: The Untold Story of the Struggle to Establish the Jewish State*. Cambridge: Da Capo, 2009.

———, ed. *The Making of Anglo-Jewry*. Oxford: Basil Blackwell, 1992.

———. "The Transformation of Communal Authority in Anglo-Jewry, 1914–1940." In *The Making of Anglo-Jewry*, edited by David Cesarani, 115–40. Oxford: Basil Blackwell, 1990.

Chertok, Haim. *He Also Spoke as a Jew: The Life of the Reverend James Parkes*. London: Vallentine Mitchell, 2006.

Cohen, Stuart A. *English Zionists and British Jews: The Communal Politics of Anglo-Jewry, 1895–1920*. Princeton, NJ: Princeton University Press, 1982.

Cole, Peter. *The Dream of the Poem: Hebrew Poems from Muslim and Christian Spain, 950–1492*. Princeton, NJ: Princeton University Press, 2007.

Davidovitch, Nadav, and Rakefet Zalashik. "'Air, Sun, Water': Ideology and Activities of OZE (Society for the Preservation of the Health of the Jewish Population) during the Interwar Period." *Dynamis* 28 (2008): 128–35.

306 | Select Bibliography

Davis, Arthur. *La-menatseah bi-neginot maskil: The Hebrew Accents of the Twenty-One Books of the Bible.* London: D. Nutt, 1892.

Davis, Arthur, and Herbert Adler, eds. *Service of the Synagogue: A New Edition of the Festival Prayers with an English Translation; Day of Atonement.* 2nd ed. London: George Routledge and Sons, 1905.

Davis, Nina. "An Aspect of Judaism in 1901." *Jewish Quarterly Review* 13, no. 2 (January 1901): 241–57.

———. "The Ideal Minister of the Talmud." *Jewish Quarterly Review* 7, no. 25 (October 1894): 141–44.

———. *Jacob and Israel.* Cambridge Jewish Publications no. 5. Cambridge: Cambridge University Press, 1920.

———, trans. *Songs of Exile by Hebrew Poets.* Philadelphia: Jewish Publication Society, 1901.

De Lange, Nicholas. "Books and Bookmen: The Cambridge Teachers of Rabbinics, 1866–1971." *Transactions of the Jewish Historical Society of England* 44 (2012): 139–63.

Efron, John M. *Defenders of the Race: Jewish Doctors and Race Science in Fin-de-Siècle Europe.* New Haven, CT: Yale University Press, 1994.

———. *German Jewry and the Allure of the Sephardic.* Princeton, NJ: Princeton University Press, 2015.

———. *Medicine and the German Jews: A History.* New Haven, CT: Yale University Press, 2001.

Elton, Benjamin J. *Britain's Chief Rabbis and the Religious Character of Anglo-Jewry, 1880–1970.* Manchester: Manchester University Press, 2009.

Endelman, Todd M. *Broadening Jewish History: Towards a Social History of Ordinary Jews.* Oxford: Littman Library of Jewish Civilization, 2011.

———. *The Jews of Britain, 1656–2000.* Berkeley: University of California Press, 2002.

———. *Leaving the Jewish Fold: Conversion and Radical Assimilation in Modern Jewish History.* Princeton, NJ: Princeton University Press, 2015.

———. *Radical Assimilation in English Jewish History, 1656–1945.* Bloomington: Indiana University Press, 1990.

Feldman, David. *Englishmen and Jews: Social Relations and Political Culture, 1840–1914.* New Haven, CT: Yale University Press, 1994.

Fishberg, Maurice. *The Jews: A Study of Race and Environment.* New York: Scribner's, 1911.

Fraser, David. *Anti-shechita Prosecutions in the Anglo-American World, 1855–1913—"A Major Attack on Jewish Freedoms."* Boston: Academic Studies Press, 2018.

Freulich, Roman. *Soldiers in Judea: Stories and Vignettes of the Jewish Legion.* New York: Herzl Press, 1964.

Friedman, Isaiah. *The Question of Palestine, 1914–1918: British-Jewish-Arab Relations.* London: Routledge and Kegan Paul.

Gibbon, Monk. *Netta.* London: Routledge and Kegan Paul, 1960.

Glendinning, Victoria. *Leonard Woolf: A Biography.* New York: Free Press, 2006.

Glenn, Susan A. "In the Blood? Consent, Descent, and the Ironies of Jewish Destiny." *Jewish Social Studies* 8, nos. 2–3 (Winter–Spring 2002): 139–61.

Gregory, Adrian. *The Last Great War: British Society and the First World War.* Cambridge: Cambridge University Press, 2008.

Hart, Mitchell B. *The Healthy Jew: The Symbiosis of Judaism and Modern Medicine.* New York: Cambridge University Press, 2007.

———. *Social Science and the Politics of Modern Jewish Identity*. Stanford, CA: Stanford University Press, 2000.

Hartog, Mabel Hélène Kisch. *P. J. Hartog: A Memoir*. London: Constable, 1949.

Hawkes, John G., and Javier Francisco-Ortega, "The Early History of the Potato in Europe." *Euphytica* 70, no. 1 (1993): 1–7.

Hyamson, Albert M. *Jews' College, London, 1855–1955*. London: Jews' College, 1955.

Jabotinsky, Vladimir. *The Story of the Jewish Legion*. New York: Ackerman, 1945.

Jacobs, Joseph. *Studies in Jewish Statistics: Social, Vital and Anthropometric*. London: D. Nutt, 1891.

Jewish Health Organization of Great Britain. *The Difficult Child: A Medical, Psychological and Sociological Problem*. London: JHOGB, 1930.

Judd, Robin. *Contested Rituals: Circumcision, Kosher Butchering, and Jewish Political Life in Germany, 1843–1933*. Ithaca, NY: Cornell University Press, 2007.

Kantorowitsch, Miron. "Estimate of the Jewish Population of London in 1929–1933." *Journal of the Royal Statistical Society*, 99, no. 2 (1936): 372–79.

Keren, Michael, and Shlomit Keren. *We Are Coming, Unafraid: The Jewish Legions and the Promised Land in the First World War*. Lanham, MD: Rowman and Littlefield, 2010.

Kushner, Tony. "Anti-Semitism and Austerity: The August 1947 Riots in Britain." In *Racial Violence in Britain, 1840–1959*, edited by Panikos Panayi, 149–68. Leicester: Leicester University Press, 1993.

———. *The Persistence of Prejudice: Antisemitism in British Society during the Second World War*. Manchester: Manchester University Press, 1989.

———. "Stunning Intolerance: A Century of Opposition to Religious Slaughter." *Jewish Quarterly* no. 133 (Spring 1989): 16–20.

Langham, Raphael. *250 Years of Convention and Contention: A History of the Board of Deputies of British Jews, 1760–2010*. London: Vallentine Mitchell, 2010.

Leftwich, Joseph. *Israel Zangwill*. New York: Thomas Yoseloff, 1957.

Levene, Mark. *War, Jews, and the New Europe: The Diplomacy of Lucien Wolf, 1914–1919*. Oxford: Oxford University Press, 1992.

Leventhal, Fred, and Peter Stansky. *Leonard Woolf: Bloomsbury Socialist*. Oxford: Oxford University Press, 2019.

Lipman, Vivian D. *A History of the Jews in Britain since 1858*. New York: Holmes and Meier, 1990.

Litman, Simon. *Ray Frank Litman: A Memoir*. New York: American Jewish Historical Society, 1957.

Loewe, Herbert. "Nina Salaman, 1877–1925." *Transactions of the Jewish Historical Society of England* 11 (1929): 228–32.

Loewe, Raphael J. "The Bible in Medieval Hebrew Poetry." In *Interpreting the Hebrew Bible: Essays in Honour of E. I. J. Rosenthal*, edited by John A. Emerton and Stefan C. Reif, 133–55. Cambridge: Cambridge University Press, 1982.

Marcus, Ivan. "Beyond the Sephardi Mystique." *Orim* 1, no. 1 (1985): 35–53.

Marks, Lara V. *Model Mothers: Jewish Mothers and Maternity Provision in East London, 1870–1939*. Oxford: Clarendon Press, 1994.

Marwick, Arthur. *The Deluge: British Society and the First World War*. New York: W. W. Norton, 1970.

Mead, A. Hugh. *A Miraculous Draught of Fishes: A History of St. Paul's School, 1509–1990*. London: James and James, 1990.

308 | Select Bibliography

Miller, Jane. *Relations*. London: Jonathan Cape, 2003.

Mintz, Sidney. "Heroes Sung and Unsung." *Nutritional Anthropology* 25, no. 2 (2002): 3–8.

Mogliner, Marina. "Toward a History of Russian Jewish 'Medical Materialism': Russian Jewish Physicians and the Politics of Jewish Biological Normalization." *Jewish Social Studies* 19, no. 1 (Fall 2012): 70–106.

Myers, Charles S. "Is There a Jewish Race?" *Jewish Review* 2, no. 8 (1911–12): 120–25.

Oren, Elhanan. *Hibbat Tsiyyon be-Britanyah, 1878–1898*. Tel Aviv: Ha-kibbuts Ha-meuhad, 1974.

Painter, Desmond. "Redcliffe and Raphael Salaman: A Memoir." *History Workshop Journal* no. 40 (Autumn 1995): 276–82.

Parzen, Herbert. "The Magnes-Weizmann-Einstein Controversy." *Jewish Social Studies* 32, no. 3 (1970): 187–213.

Pennybaker, Susan D. "The Universal Races Congress, London Political Culture, and Imperial Dissent, 1900–1939." *Radical History Review* no. 92 (Spring 2005): 103–17.

Penslar, Derek J. *Jews and the Military: A History*. Princeton, NJ: Princeton University Press, 2013.

Pevsner, Nikolaus, and Bridget Cleary. *The Buildings of England: Hertfordshire*. Rev. ed. London: Penguin Books, 1977.

Poulter, Sebastian. *Ethnicity, Law and Human Rights: The English Experience*. Oxford: Clarendon Press, 1998.

Prais, Sigbert J. "Statistical Research: Needs and Prospects." In *Jewish Life in Modern Britain: Papers and Proceedings of a Conference Held at University College, London, on 1st and 2nd April, 1962*, edited by Julius Gould and Shaul Esh, 111–26. London: Routledge and Kegan Paul, 1964.

Reader, John. *Potato: A History of the Propitious Esculent*. New Haven, CT: Yale University Press, 2008.

Renton, George. "The East London Child Guidance Clinic." *Journal of Child Psychology and Psychiatry* 19, no. 4 (1978): 309–12.

Rich, Paul B. "'The Baptism of a New Era': The 1911 Universal Races Congress and the Liberal Ideology of Race." *Ethnic and Racial Studies* 7, no. 4 (October 1984): 534–50.

———. "The Long Victorian Sunset: Anthropology, Eugenics and Race in Britain, c. 1900–48." *Patterns of Prejudice* 18, no. 3 (1984): 3–17.

Richmond, Colin. *Campaigner against Antisemitism: The Reverend James Parkes, 1896–1981*. London: Vallentine Mitchell, 2005.

Rochelson, Meri-Jane. *A Jew in the Public Arena: The Career of Israel Zangwill*. Detroit: Wayne State University Press, 2008.

Rosenberg, David. *Battle for the East End: Jewish Responses to Fascism in the 1930s*. Nottingham: Five Leaves, 2011.

Rosenzweig, Alexander. *The Jewish Memorial Council: A History, 1919–1999*. London: Jewish Memorial Council, 1998.

Rubinstein, William. "Jewish Top Wealth-Holders in Britain, 1809–1909." *Transactions of the Jewish Historical Society of England* 37 (2002): 133–61.

Rumyanek, Judah. "The Comparative Psychology of Jews and Non-Jews: A Survey of the Literature." *British Journal of Psychology* 21, no. 4 (1931): 404–26.

Salaman, Esther Polianowsky. *The Autobiography of Esther Polianowsky Salaman*. Edited by Thalia Polak. N.p.: privately published, 2012.

———. *The Fertile Plain*. London: Hogarth, 1956.

Select Bibliography | 309

———. "Memories of Einstein." *Encounter*, April 1979, 19–23.

———. *Two Silver Roubles*. London: Macmillan, 1932.

Salaman, Nina Davis, ed. *Apples and Honey: A Gift-Book for Jewish Boys and Girls*. London: William Heinemann, 1922.

———, trans. *Selected Poems of Jehudah Halevi*. Edited by Heinrich Brody. Philadelphia: Jewish Publication Society, 1924.

———. *Songs of Many Days*. London: Elkin Matthews, 1923.

Salomon, Sidney. *The Jews of Britain*. London: Jarrolds, 1938.

Sarna, Jonathan D. *JPS: The Americanization of Jewish Culture, 1888–1988*. Philadelphia: Jewish Publication Society, 1989.

Schaffer, Gavin. "Assets or 'Aliens'? Race Science and the Analysis of Jewish Intelligence in Inter-war Britain." *Patterns of Prejudice* 42, no. 2 (2008): 191–207.

———. *Racial Science and British Society, 1930–62*. Houndmills, Basingstoke: Palgrave Macmillan, 2008.

Scheinberg, Cynthia. "'And We Are Not What They Have Been': Anglo-Jewish Women Poets, 1839–1923." In *Jewish Women Writers in Britain*, edited by Nadia Valman, 35–65. Detroit: Wayne State University Press, 2014.

Scheindlin, Raymond P. *Wine, Women, and Death: Medieval Hebrew Poems on the Good Life*. New York: Oxford University Press, 1999.

Schorsch, Ismar. "The Myth of Sephardi Supremacy." *Leo Baeck Institute Year Book* 34 (1989): 47–66.

Segev, Tom. *One Palestine Complete: Jews and Arabs under the British Mandate*. Translated by Haim Watzman. New York: Metropolitan, 2000.

Singer, Charles. *The Christian Failure*. London: Victor Gollancz, 1943.

Singer, Steven. "Orthodox Judaism in Early Victorian England." PhD diss., Yeshiva University, New York, 1981.

Smith, Elaine R. "But What Did They Do? Contemporary Jewish Responses to Cable Street." *Jewish Culture and History* 1, no. 2 (Winter 1998): 48–55.

Smith, Kenneth M. "Redcliffe Nathan Salaman, 1874–1955." *Biographical Memoirs of Fellows of the Royal Society* 1 (1955): 238–45.

Snowman, Jacob. "Jewish Eugenics." *Jewish Review* 4, no. 20 (1913–14): 159–74.

———. *Jewish Law and Sanitary Science*. London: Medical Magazine, 1896.

———. *A Short History of Talmudic Medicine*. London: J. Bale, Sons, and Danielsson, 1935.

———. *The Surgery of Ritual Circumcision*. London: Medical Board of the Initiation Society, 1904.

Soloway, Richard A. *Demography and Degeneration: Eugenics and the Declining Birthrate in Twentieth-Century Britain*. Chapel Hill: University of North Carolina Press, 1990.

Sompolinsky, Meier. *The British Government and the Holocaust: The Failure of Anglo-Jewish Leadership*. Brighton: Sussex Academic, 1999.

Srebrnik, Henry Felix. *London Jews and British Communism, 1933–1945*. London: Vallentine Mitchell, 1995.

Stedman Jones, Gareth. *Outcast London: A Study in the Relationship between Classes in Victorian Society*. London: Penguin Books, 1992.

Stein, Sarah Abrevaya. *Plumes: Ostrich Feathers, Jews, and a Lost World of Global Commerce*. New Haven, CT: Yale University Press, 2008.

Stepan, Nancy. *The Idea of Race in Science: Great Britain, 1800–1960*. Hamden, CT: Archon, 1982.

310 | Select Bibliography

Stone, Dan. "Of Peas, Potatoes, and Jews: Redcliffe N. Salaman and the British Debate over Jewish Racial Origins." *Simon Dubnow Institute Yearbook* 3 (2004): 221–40.

Summers, Anne. *Christian and Jewish Women in Britain, 1880–1949: Living with Difference*. London: Palgrave Macmillan, 2017.

Tanenbaum, Adena. "On Translating Medieval Hebrew Poetry." In *Hebrew Scholarship and the Medieval World*, edited by Nicholas de Lange, 171–85. Cambridge: Cambridge University Press, 2001.

Tilles, Daniel. *British Fascist Antisemitism and Jewish Responses, 1932–40*. London: Bloomsbury Academic, 2015.

Valman, Nadia, ed. *Jewish Women Writers in Britain*. Detroit: Wayne State University Press, 2014.

Waldstein, Charles. *The Jewish Question and the Mission of the Jews*. New York: Harper and Brothers, 1894.

Wasserstein, Bernard. *Herbert Samuel: A Political Life*. Oxford: Clarendon Press, 1992.

Watts, Martin. *The Jewish Legion and the First World War*. Houndmills, Basingstoke: Palgrave Macmillan, 2004.

Wendehorst, Stephan. *British Jewry, Zionism, and the Jewish State, 1936–1956*. Oxford: Oxford University Press, 2012.

Woolf, Leonard. *Sowing: An Autobiography of the Years 1880–1904*. Harvest Book ed. New York: Harcourt Brace Jovanovich, 1975.

INDEX

Abrahams, Freda, 149

Abrahams, Israel, 7, 36, 41, 70, 72, 74, 109, 127, 148, 154, 157, 158, 171, 173, 176, 178, 247

Abramsky, Chimen, 237

Academic Assistance Council. *See* Society for Protection of Science and Learning

Adler, Alfred, 204

Adler, Henrietta, 244

Adler, Herbert, 41–42

Adler, Hermann, 18, 41–42, 53, 282, 283

Adler, Michael, 127

Adler, Nathan, 282, 283

Adler family, 54

Aguilar, Grace, 104

Amery, Leopold, 124

Anglo-Jewish Association, 290–291

antisemitism: anti-Jewish riots of 1947, 277–278; in anti-*shehitah* polemics, 275–276, 278; at Bedales School, 151, 152–153; and the British Union of Fascists, 232–236; in British universities, 227; at Clifton College, 150; combatting, 206–215, 230, 231–238; in Hertfordshire, 64–65; at the London Hospital, 32–33; at St. Paul's School, 21, 148; at Trinity Hall, 65–66

Arabs in Palestine, 139–142

Arnold, Arthur, 287

Austin Bourke, P. M., 266

Bardinstein (Bardin), Shlomo, 180–183

Barley, Hertfordshire, 59–62, 70–72

Barnett, Arthur, 282, 286

Bateson, William, 66–67

Baumgardt, David, 228

Bedales School, 77, 151–153, 178

Benas, Bertram B., 282, 286

Bentwich, Herbert, 36, 41, 44

Bentwich, Norman, 41, 223, 237, 244, 246, 287

Bentwich family, 113

Berman, Hannah, 104–105

Bishop, Louise Salaman, 121, 285, 300

Bolau, Bruno, 206

B'nai B'rith, 210–211

Board of Deputies of British Jews, 37, 276–278; Co-ordinating Committee, 213, 231, 233; dispute with Jewish People's Committee against Fascism and Anti-Semitism, 232–236; funding of statistical research, 208, 209, 211, 212, 213–215, 216; response of to British Union of Fascists, 232–236; and *shehitah*, 276, 280, 288–289

Boas, Franz, 87

Bomberg, David, 44

Bramsted, Ernest K., 228

British Union of Fascists, 222, 232–236

Brodetsky, Selig, 224, 237

Brodie, Israel, 171–172, 278, 282, 283, 286–287, 289, 290

Brotman, Adolph, 233, 235, 278, 279

Büchler, Adolph, 171, 173–174

Burt, Cyril, 208, 220n55, 228

Cambridge Hebrew Congregation, 70, 159–160

Carr, Marcus, 290

Carter, Angela, 260, 263

Central British Fund for German Jewry, 212

Chaikin, G., 205

Chain, Ernst, 228

Cheyney, David, 216

chief rabbinate, 41, 239, 241–242, 280

Clifton College, Bristol, 77, 150–151

Cohen, Abraham, 278, 279

Cohen, Bessie Salaman, 20, 22, 24, 183, 228, 300

Cohen, Cecil Morris, 87, 88, 98n20

Cohen, Jennie Salaman, 107, 154, 183, 300–301

Cohen, Lionel, 287

Collett, Robert, 285–286, 299

311

312 | Index

Collett, Ruth Salaman, 70, 75, 115, 148, 176, 177, 178, 184, 285–286, 299
Communist Party of Great Britain, 232, 237
Connell, Kenneth H., 267
conversion. *See* radical assimilation
Cornford, Frances, 177, 180
Cornford, Francis, 177, 180
Courant, Richard, 228
Cowen, Joseph, 125

Davies, Mary, 208–209
D'Avigdor, Olga, 48
Davis, Arthur, 36, 39–45
Davis, Elsie, 42, 43, 45
Davis, Isabelle Salaman, 39, 107, 113, 177, 240
Davis, Louisa, 40
Davis, Marcus, 48
Davis, Nina. *See* Salaman, Nina
Davis family of Derby, 40
Diamond, Arthur S., 234, 235
Disraeli, Benjamin, 24–25, 81, 109
Doniach, Aaron, 108, 153–154

East End of London. *See* East European immigrants in Britain
East European immigrants in Britain, 31, 32, 34–35, 36, 193, 196, 197–199, 232, 233, 237, 238, 273–274
East London Child Guidance Clinic, 203–205
Eder, David, 125, 140, 180, 197, 224
Education Aid Society, 44–45, 180
Eicholz, Alfred, 205
Einstein, Albert, 224–225
Elton, Benjamin, 283
Emanuel, Samuel H., 174
Epstein, Jacob, 44–45
eugenics, 193, 199–203

Falk, Leib Aisack, 128
Feffer, Itsik, 238
Feldman, Asher, 240–241
Feldman, William M., 197
Feuerbach, Ludwig, 257
Fishberg, Maurice, 82, 86, 89, 166
Fraenkel, Abraham, 224

Francisca Ortega, Javier, 259
Frank, Helena, 104–105
Frank, Ray, 160, 176
Franklin, Henrietta, 114, 153
Franklin family, 105, 113, 153
Fyfe, Hamilton, 277

Gainer, John Rutherford, 65
Galton, Francis, 84
Gaon, Solomon, 279, 290
Gaster family, 113
genetics, 66–69, 84–85
gentility, 4, 282
Gertler, Mark, 44
Ginsberg, Morris, 232
Ginzberg, Louis, 225
Goldsmid Montefiore, Claude, 36, 157, 174–175, 240, 246–247
Gollancz, Alide, 113
Gollancz, Livia, 184, 191n55
Gordon, Myron K. *See* Kantorowitsch, Miron
Great Turbot Affair, 4, 7, 289–291
Greenberg, Leopold, 125, 160
Guinness, Alec, 122
Guinness, Merula Salaman, 122

hadarim, 197–198
Haddon, Alfred C., 231
Hamilton, Earl J., 259
Hartog, Cécile, 155
Hartog, May Marion, 48
Hartog, Philip, 171, 211, 224–225, 228, 244
Hawkes, John G., 259, 266
health and hygiene of the Jews, 194–195, 197–204
Hebrew poets of medieval Spain, 108–112
Hebrew University, Jerusalem, 130, 223–226
Henriques, Basil, 237, 244
Herbert, Solomon, 86, 91–92, 96
Hersch, Israel, 70
Hertz, Joseph, 159–160, 167, 173, 177, 237, 238, 241–242, 245–246, 276, 283
Hewitt, Emily, 17–18, 20
Hirsch, Samuel, 42
Hirschell, Solomon, 291

historiography of Anglo-Jewry, 7, 208, 230, 283, 294n48

History and Social Influence of the Potato, The: absence of concept of race in, 257; criticism of, 263–265; genesis of, 187, 254; Jewish subtext in, 261–262; reception and impact of, 1, 264–267; scope and method of, 255–257

Hochman, Joseph, 87

Homestall, 59–62, 68–69, 176, 185, 241

homosexuality at public schools, 150–151

Hopkin, Daniel, 114, 119, 128, 138, 148

Horder, John Jeeves, 216

Hughes, Arthur G., 208–209

Huxley, Julian, 231, 232

Hyamson, Albert H., 282

Institute of Jewish Policy Research, 216

intermarriage. *See* radical assimilation

Ireland, 259–265

Isserlis, Leon, 214

Jabotinsky, Vladimir (Zev), 3–4, 123

Jacobovits, Immanuel, 283

Jacobs, Joseph, 36, 40, 84, 87, 207

Jacobs, Julius, 234

Jacobs, Louis, 292

Janner, Barnett, 237

Jewish Battalions. *See* Jewish Legion

Jewish Committee for Relief Abroad, 228

Jewish Fund for Soviet Russia, 236–238

Jewish Health Organisation of Great Britain, 7; children's mental health clinic, 203–206; collapse of, 215–216, 255; financial travails of, 205, 215; origins of, 193–196, 217n3; pamphlets by, 198–199; preventive health measures of, 196–199; research agenda of, 206–215

Jewish Historical Society of England, 93, 158, 270, 281–288

Jewish League for Woman Suffrage, 105, 301

Jewish Legion: battle record of, 131–133; fitness of recruits to, 128–129; genesis of, 123–126; marching song of, 155–156; marginalization after World War I of, 140–141; opposition of communal notables

to, 127–128; Redcliffe's initial ambivalence about, 125–126; War Office hostility to, 126, 138–141

Jewish People's Council against Fascism and Anti-Semitism, 232–236

Jewish War Memorial Trust, 168–170, 172–174

Jews' College, 5, 7, 41, 244; campaign to reform, 162, 166–175

Joseph, Morris, 49

Kantorowitsch, Miron, 212

kashrut, 274–275

Kohn, Leo, 224

Krauss, Samuel, 228

Laski, Harold, 91

Laski, Neville, 213, 215, 233–236

Lazarus, Emma, 194

League of British Jews, 138, 156–157

Levin, Hirschel, 290

Lewin, Kurt, 228

Leys School, Cambridge, 149

Liberal Judaism, 153, 160, 173, 242–243, 244

Lipman, Vivian D., 294n48

Lloyd George, David, 123–124

Loewe, Herbert, 7, 37, 82, 149, 154, 155, 166, 171, 172, 173, 174, 178, 239–240, 242, 247

Loewe, Lionel, 292

Loewe, Michael, 149, 239–240

Loewe, Raphael, 149, 239–240

London Hospital, 57–58

Louis Jacobs Affair, 4, 7, 291–292

Lowbury, Benjamin William, 217n3

Lucas, N. S., 174

Lucien Wolf Lecture, 1–2, 4, 6, 7, 269, 281–288, 297

Maccabeans, 36

machzor, English translation of, 41–44

Magnes, Judah, 224–225

Magnus, Katie, 104

Magnus, Laurie, 20–21

Magnus, Philip, 104, 157, 170, 173, 174

Makower, Alfred J., 228

Maltman's Green School, Buckinghamshire, 178

314 | Index

Manson, Michael, 267
Marcousé, Sophie, 105
Margolin, Eliazar, 130
Masorti Judaism, 292
Mattuck, Israel, 243, 244
Mendel, Gregor, 66–67
Meninsky, Bernard, 44
Mikhoels, Shloyme, 238
Miller, Emanuel, 202–204, 228
ministry, Anglo-Jewish, 166–167, 170
Ministry of Agriculture, 186
Mintz, Sidney, 256
missions to the Jews, 36–37
Mocatta family, 54
Montagu, Edwin, 292
Montagu, Ewen, 4, 244, 245, 274,
   290–291
Montagu, Ivor, 113
Montagu, Lily, 157, 160, 243, 244, 246
Montagu, Louis, second
   Baron Swaythling, 157
Montagu, Samuel, first
   Baron Swaythling, 291
Montagu, Stuart, 161
Montagu family, 54, 113
Montefiore, Leonard G., 215, 231, 286
Mosseri family, 247
Moul, Margaret, 207–209
Moynihan, Berkeley, first
   Lord Moynihan, 205
Myers, Charles, 27, 31, 58, 86–87, 96, 119,
   120, 166, 173, 174, 197, 205, 208, 228
myth of Sephardi supremacy, 108–109

Namier, Lewis, 4, 223, 228
Nathan, Harry, first Baron Nathan of Churt,
   237, 238
Nathan, Lewis, 12
Neumann, Franz, 228
Newman, George, 204
New West End Synagogue, London, 5, 18,
   38–39, 72, 106, 154, 243

Ó Gráda, Cormac, 266
Organisation of Observant Traditional Jews,
   173
Ormsby-Gore, William, 142

Orthodox Judaism in Britain:
   bibliocentricity of, 44, 50, 100; eclecticism
   and latitudinarianism of in Victorian age,
   43–44, 49–50, 238–239, 280, 282; growth
   of strict Orthodoxy within, 239, 242–244,
   273–275, 286–287, 288, 301
ostrich feather trade, 10–13, 121–123
OZE. See Society for the Protection of Jewish
   Health

Palestine Exhibition and Bazaar, London,
   112–113
*Palestine Reclaimed: Letters from a Jewish
   Officer in Palestine*, 2, 127, 142
Parents' National Education Union, 114
Parkes, James, 65, 223, 231, 232–236, 287–288
Patterson, J. H., 123, 125, 138
Pearce, Jack, 234
Pearson, Karl, 207–209, 214
Perlzweig, Maurice, 211
Perse School, Cambridge, 70, 149–150
Phillips, Bloom, 11–12
piyyutim, 42–43
Polack, Joseph, 174
Polianowsky, Esther. See Salaman, Esther
   Polianowsky
potato: debate on role of in Irish famine,
   263–265; diseases of, 68–69, 185–187,
   251–253; famine in Ireland, 254, 259–260;
   history of, 187, 254–265; introduction
   of to Europe, 259–260; origins of as a
   foodstuff, 257–258; representation of in
   pre-Columbian pottery, 187, 258
Potato Virus Research Station, Cambridge,
   186–187, 251–253, 254
Prais, Sigbert, 214

rabbinate, Anglo-Jewish. See ministry,
   Anglo-Jewish
Rabinowicz, Oscar K., 287, 288
race science and racial thinking, 24–25,
   81–88, 90–97, 226–227, 296–297
radical assimilation in Britain, 40, 46, 47–49,
   77, 207, 284–286
readership in rabbinics at Cambridge,
   246–247
real estate business, 16–17, 121–123

Reform Judaism, 88–89, 192, 238, 239, 242–243, 244
refugees from Nazism, 222, 224, 227–229, 270
Reinhardt, Harold, 244
Rich, Jacob M., 208
Rosenblum, Morris, 83
Rosenwald, Julius, 247
Roth, Cecil, 7, 161, 232, 237, 244, 287, 288, 289
Roth, Leon, 161
Rothenstein, William, 44–45, 152–153
Rothschild, James de, 229
Rothschild, Lionel de, 157
Rothschild, Lionel Walter, second Lord Rothschild, 195, 209
Rothschild family, 231, 247
Rowson, Simon, 212–213
Royal Society, 269–272
Rubens, Arthur, 287
Rumney, Jay. See Rumyanek, Judah
Rumyanek, Judah, 209–210, 213, 220n59
Ruppin, Arthur, 165–166, 206, 224

Sacher, Harry, 86, 288
Sachs, Jonathan, 283
Salaman, Aaron, 11, 12–13
Salaman, Abraham, 11–12
Salaman, Archie, 87, 88, 200, 301
Salaman, Arthur, 57, 75, 113–115, 117n28, 149–150, 151–154, 176, 177, 178, 184, 286, 298
Salaman, Bessie. See Cohen, Bessie Salaman 20, 22, 24
Salaman, Betsy, 11, 12
Salaman, Brenda. See Seligman, Brenda Salaman
Salaman, Chattie Wake, 122, 189
Salaman, Clement, 22, 36, 48–49, 82, 121, 285, 297
Salaman, Edmund, 77
Salaman, Edward, 57, 76–77, 114–115
Salaman, Elkin, 22, 77, 121, 297–298, 300
Salaman, Esther, 2, 113, 148, 177, 178, 184, 298, 299, 300
Salaman, Esther Polianowsky, 178–183, 191n46, 300
Salaman, Euston, 20, 22, 121, 297–298, 300
Salaman, Fanny, 11

Salaman, Gertrude Lowy, 107, 183–184
Salaman, Harry, 200, 301
Salaman, Isaac, 10–11, 12
Salaman, Jane, 11
Salaman, Jennie. See Cohen, Jennie Salaman
Salaman, Louise. See Bishop, Louise Salaman
Salaman, Michel, 121–123, 285, 297
Salaman, Miriam Polianowsky, 179, 300
Salaman, Myer, 11, 12, 13–18, 27, 32
Salaman, Myer Head, 56, 72–74, 76, 77, 89, 113–115, 148–155, 176, 178, 180–183, 298
Salaman, Nancy, 286, 298
Salaman, Nathan, 11, 12, 16–17
Salaman, Nina: enthusiasm of for the Jewish Legion, 127, 129; family background of, 39–41; feminism of, 6, 103–108, 158–159; final illness and death of, 175–178; and Hebrew, 20, 45, 72–75,103–104, 108, 153–154; influence of on Redcliffe Salaman, 6, 38, 46, 70–71, 239; and Israel Zangwill, 1, 89, 148, 157–158; liberating impact of World War I on, 158–159; as mother, 74–77, 113–114; opposition to radical assimilation of, 49–50; religious views of, 45–46, 49–52, 70–72, 99–104; report on Jewish students at Oxford and Cambridge by, 160–162; as scholar and translator, 6, 42–43, 45–46, 70, 108–112, 176; schooling of children of, 147, 148–155; sermon in Orthodox synagogue by, 159–160; and Zionism, 102–103, 105, 112–113 127–128, 136–137, 155–157
Salaman, Peggy, 300
Salaman, Rachel, 11, 12, 13
Salaman, Raphael, 40, 74, 113–115, 151–154, 178, 179, 181, 298–299
Salaman, Redcliffe: childhood of, 17–20; choice of career of, 22; coat of arms of, 188–189; fight against antisemitism by, 210–215, 231–239; communal work of, 36–37, 44–45, 300; death of, 292; and demographic research, 206, 210–215; eagerness of to serve in World War I, 119–121; as English gentleman, 4, 5, 59–64, 297; and Esther Polianowsky, 178–183; eugenics views of, 199–200; family background of, 9–17; genetic research by,

316 | *Index*

67–69; health of, 58–59, 77n2, 254–255; and Hebrew University, 130, 223–225; history of the potato by, 187, 254–267; honors and recognition of, 3, 187, 253–254; and Israel Zangwill, 1, 184–185; and Jewish Committee for Relief Abroad, 229; Jewish environment of childhood home of, 19–20; and Jewish Health Organization of Great Britain, 195–200, 202, 205, 206–214, 215–216; and Jews' College, 166–175; Lucien Wolf Lecture by, 281–288, 297; and marriage to Nina, 38–40; medical training of, 31–35, 54; and Nina's death, 178; opposition to racial views of, 90–92; origins of family name of, 9–10; political allegiances of, 35–36; potato research by, 68–69, 82, 185–187, 251–253; at preparatory school, 20; priggishness of, 120, 135, 182–183; racial thought and race science of, 7, 24–25, 37–38, 48, 52–53, 81–87, 90–97, 176, 195–196, 226–227, 269–273, 296–297; refugee work, 227–229, 230; report on Jewish students at Oxford and Cambridge, 160–162; and search for a second wife, 178–179, 183–184; on self-discipline, 244–245; self-doubt and depression of, 26, 119–121, 127; and service in the Jewish Legion, 126–133, 137; and *shehitah* controversies, 275–281, 283, 287–289, 291; at St. Paul's, 20–26; on the transformation of Anglo-Jewry, 1–2, 4, 6, 236, 238–239, 269, 281–285, 301; at Trinity College, Cambridge, 26–28; views of on Arabs, 141–142; views of on Jewish achievement, 269–272; views of on Judaism, 24, 37–38, 165–166, 239–246, 274–275; views of on Mizrahi and Sephardi Jews, 135, 145n62; visit of to the United States and Canada, 87–89; work by to endow readership in rabbinics at Cambridge, 246–247; and Zionism, 223–225

Salaman, Ruth. *See* Collet, Ruth Salaman
Salaman, Sarah, 13–16, 17, 18, 27, 154
Salomon, Sidney, 213, 215, 233
Sampter, Jesse, 105
Samuel, Beatrice, 286

Samuel, Dorothy Salaman, 128, 137–138, 180, 301
Samuel, Edgar, 286
Samuel, Frank, 246, 274
Samuel, Frederick, 128, 137–138, 180
Samuel, Herbert, 6–7, 176, 276, 286
Samuel, Phillip, 161
Samuel, Walter, second Viscount Bearsted, 231
Samuel, Wilfred, 286, 287–288
Samuel family, 54
Sassoon, Solomon D., 278
Schechter, Solomon, 40, 41, 247
Schiller-Szinessy, Solomon Marcus, 246
Schnurmann, Nestor, 20
Schryver, Rosalind, 200
Schryver, Samuel, 36
Schwartzman, Mikhail, 195
Scott, C. P., 124
Sebag-Montefiore, Robert, 168
Seligman, Brenda Salaman, 228, 301
Seligman, Charles, 20, 36, 67, 87, 96, 121, 166, 224, 227, 228, 231, 301
shehitah, 88, 275–280, 287, 288–289, 292
Shrubsall, F. C., 197
Silbergleit, Heinrich, 215
Silverman, Sydney, 237
Simmons, Abraham, 13
Simon, Leon, 108, 288
Simon, Oswald, 41
Singer, Charles, 9, 29n20, 36, 161, 162, 170, 213, 231, 279, 287, 294n51
Singer, Dorothea, 161, 162
Snowman, Jacob, 200–202
Society for the Protection of Jewish Health (OZE), 193–195
Society for Protection of Science and Learning, 227–228
Solomon, Aaron (Solomon of Leghorn), 10
Solomon, Henry Naphtali, 32
Solomon, Simeon, 32
Solomon, Solomon J., 41, 44, 75, 151, 153
Solomons, Israel, 82
Spielman, W., 197
Stein, Leonard, 237
Steinberg, Aaron, 228

Stern, Frederick C., 174
Stone, Dan, 273
St. Paul's School, London, 20–26
Strauss, Leo, 228
suffrage movement, 105–108
Sylvester, Henry, 11

Talmud Torah for Girls, 108
Talmud Torahs, 108, 197–198
Taylor, Derek, 283
Tello, Julio C., 187
Tennant, Ernest, 231
Theilhaber, Felix, 206, 207
Trager, Hannah, 105
Tuck, Adolph, 167
Tucker, Denys W., 290

United Synagogue, 41, 105, 173
Universal Races Congress, 86–87

Van der Zyl, Werner, 244

Waley Cohen, Robert, 7, 168–175, 231–232,
    242, 243, 246, 274, 279–280, 300
Waley family, 153
Walston (Waldstein), Charles, 70, 79n29, 90
Wanderers, 40–41, 53
Wassilevsky, Saul, 161
Weissenberg, Samuel, 82
Weizmann, Chaim, 4, 123, 140, 180, 223, 228

Westall, L. M., 120, 148
Western Synagogue, London, 11
West London Synagogue, 173
Wilensky, Mordecai, 228
Wolf, Lucien, 36, 40, 87
Wolfe, Humbert, 122
Wolfenstein, Martha, 105
Woolf, Leonard, 21, 30n34
Woolfson, Isaac, 274
World War I: British campaign in Egypt
    and Palestine, 118–119, 124; conscription
    of Jewish aliens, 124–125. *See also* Jewish
    Legion

Yehudah Ha-Levi, 111–112

Zaidman, Lazar, 234–236
Zangwill, Ayrton, 151, 152
Zangwill, Edith Ayrton, 43, 92–93, 105, 151,
    152
Zangwill, Israel, 1, 7, 36, 40, 41, 43, 46, 54, 72,
    87, 89, 92–93, 105, 125, 151, 152, 154, 157–158,
    176
Zarchi, Liba, 197
Zeitlin, Elsley, 278, 289
Zionism, 105, 112–113, 136–137, 138, 140, 223
Zionist Commission, 140
Zionist paramilitary attacks in
    Britain, 278
Zollschan, Ignaz, 82, 86, 206

TODD M. ENDELMAN (PhD, Harvard) is Professor Emeritus of History and Judaic Studies at the University of Michigan. His many books include *Radical Assimilation in English Jewish History, 1656–1945* (IUP, 1990), *The Jews of Britain, 1656–2000, Broadening Jewish History: Toward a Social History of Ordinary Jews,* and *Leaving the Jewish Fold: Conversion and Radical Assimilation in Modern Jewish History.*